In accordance with the latest syllabus prescribed by the
Central Board of Secondary Education, New Delhi.

AF483168

CBSE
PHYSICAL EDUCATION

(Including Practicals)

Class XII

Dr. Sanjib Kumar Bhowmik
Ph.D. [LNIPE, Gwalior]
Assistant Professor
Deptt. of Physical Education
Tripura Central University

M. K. Gulia
M.Phil., M.P.Ed
Head of Faculty [Sports and Activities]
The Lawrence School, Sanawar
Kasauli.

Dr. Raji Philip
M.Phil., Ph.D. [LNIPE, Gwalior]
HOD Physical Education
The Lawrence School, Lovedale, Ooty

OSWAL PUBLISHERS

1/12, Sahitya Kunj, M. G. Road, Agra-282 002

No part of this book can be reproduced in any form or by any means without the prior written permission of the publisher.

Edition : 2020

ISBN : 978-93-88623-93-3

OSWAL PUBLISHERS

Head office	:	1/12, Sahitya Kunj, M.G. Road, Agra-282 002
Phone	:	(0562) 2527771– 4, +91 75340 77222
E-mail	:	contact@oswalpublishers.com, sales@oswalpublishers.com
Website	:	www.oswalpublishers.com
Facebook link	:	https://www.facebook.com/oswalpublishersindia
Available at	:	amazon.in, Flipkart, snapdeal, paytm

Preface

In this rapidly changing and conflicting cultural and social environment, the subject of physical education is facing unprecedented as well as intricate problems and challenges. Therefore, it has become adire requirement and extremely important for the professionals operating in the field of physical education to keep themselves aware and abreast of the latest developments, alterations and modifications in this subject. In the past few years, there has been tremendous increase in the number of books on the subject, yet, somehow there is a lack of qualitative reference so far. Hence this book is an attempt towards the aspect, of maintaining the quality and meeting the exact demands and requirements of class XII CBSE students and faculty. The book is written in an easy language and uses clear figures so that students find it easy to conceptualize various topics of health and physical education. Deliberate and prudent attempts have been made to update the information from the latest literature available in the area of health and physical education.

The entire syllabus consists of ten chapters which explain the dynamics of physical fitness in the life of an individual over the span of their lifetime. It intends to put across the psychological benefits of sports in terms of cognitive and coordinative abilities and the ways of improving them.

Dr. Sanjib Kumar Bhowmik born in Agartala, had acquired the degree of B.P.E., M.P.E., M.Phil., Ph.D. and Certificate Course of Sports Jounalism from Lakshmibai National Institute of Physical Education, Gwalior. He completed his D.Y.Ed. from Kaivalyadhama, Lonavala and also qualified UGC-NET with JRF. As far as professional experience is concerned, he has worked at LNIPE as Lecturer (Contractual basis) for two years, then as Assistant Professor in Physical Education at Mugberia Gangadhar Mahavidyalaya, Purba Medinipur, West Bengal. Presently he is working as Assistant Professor at the Department of Physical Education at Tripura University (A Central University), Tripura.

I am privileged and grateful to the publisher for showing keen interest in bringing this book to completion. I also would like to express my sincere thanks to Mr. Sorokhaibam Premananda Singh (Ph.D. Scholar, Department of Physical Education, Tripura University, Tripura) and Dr. Saon Sanyal (Assistant Professor, LNIPE, NERC, Guwahati, Assam) for redering academic guidance and their rich expertise during the course of writing this text

I hope that this book will guide the students and teachers in numerous ways. Valuable suggestion for further enhancing this title are always welcome.

Authors

Physical Education (Code 048)
Class XII (2019-20)

Theory	Times 3 Hours	Max. Marks : 70

Unit I   **Planning in Sports**
- Meaning and Objectives of Planning
- Various Committees and its Reponsibilities (Pre, During and Post)
- Tournament : Knock-Out, League or Round Robin and Combination
- Procedure to Draw Fixtures : Knock-Out (Bye and Seeding) and League (Staircase and Cyclic)
- Intramural and Extramural : Meaning, Objectives and its Significance
- Specific Sports Programme (Sports Day, Health Run, Run for Fun, Run for Specific Cause and Run for Unity)

Unit II   **Sports and Nutrition**
- Balanced Diet and Nutrition : Macro and Micro Nutrients
- Nutritive and Non-nutritive Components of Diet
- Eating for Weight Control : A Healthy Weight, The Pitfalls of Dieting, Food Intolerane and Food Myths

Unit III   **Yoga and Lifestyle**
- Asanas as Preventive Measures
- Obesity : Procedure, Benefits and Contraindications for Vajrasana, Hastasana, Trikonasana, Ardh-matsyendrasana
- Diabetes : Procedure, Benefits and Contraindications for Bhujangasana, Paschimottasana, Pavan Muktasana, Ardh-matsyendrasana.
- Asthema : Procedure, Benefits and Contraindications for Sukhasana, Chakrasana, Gomukhasana, Parvatasana, Bhujangasana, Paschimottasana, Matsyasana
- Hypertension : Tadasana, Vajrasana, Pavan Muktasana, Ardha Chakrasana, Bhujangasana, Shavasana
- Back Pain : Tadasana, Ardh-matsyendrasana, Vakrasana, Shalabhasana, Bhujangasana

Unit IV   **Physical Education and Sports for CWSN (Children with Special Needs–Divyang)**
- Concept of Disability and Disorder
- Types of Disability, its causes and nature (Cognitive Disability, Intellectual Disability, Physical Disability)
- Types of Disorder, its Cause and Nature (ADHD, SPD, ASD, ODD, OCD)
- Disability Etiquettes
- Advantages of Physical Activities for Children with Special Needs
- Strategies to make Physical Activities Assessable for Children with Special Need

Unit V   **Children and Women in Sports**
- Motor Development and Factors Affecting it
- Exercise Guidelines at different stages of Growth and Development
- Common Postural Deformities : Knock Knee; Flat Foot, Round Shoulders; Lordosis, Kyphosis, Bow Legs and Scoliosis and their corrective measures
- Sports participation of women in India
- Special consideration (Menarch and Menstural Disfunction)
- Female Athletes Triad (Oestoperosis, Amenoria, Eating Disorders)

Unit VI   **Test and Measurement in Sports**
- Motor Fitness Test : 50 m Standing Start, 600 m Run/Walk, Sit and Reach, Partial Curl Up, Push Ups (Boys), Modified Push Ups (Girls), Standing Broad Jump, Agility–4 × 10 m Shuttle Run
- General Motor Fitness : Barrow three item general motor ability (Standing Broad Jump, Zig Zag Run, Medicine Ball Put – For Boys : 03 kg and For Girls : 01 kg)
- Measurement of Cardio Vascular Fitness : Harvard Step Test/Rockport Test–

- Computation of Fitness Index :

$$\text{Fitness Index} = \frac{\text{Duration of the Exercise in Seconds} \times 100}{5 \cdot 5 \times \text{Pulse Count of } 1\text{-}1\cdot5 \text{ min. after Exercise}}$$

- Rikli and Jones : Senior Citizen Fitness Test–
  1. Chair Stand Test for Lower Body Strength
  2. Arm Curl Test for Upper Body Strength
  3. Chair Sit and Reach Test for Lower Body Flexibility
  4. Back Scratch Test for Upper Body Flexibility
  5. Eight Foot Up and Go Test for Agility
  6. Six Minute Walk Test for Aerobic Endurance

Unit VII Physiology and Injuries in Sports
- Physiological Factor Determining Component of Physical Fitness
- Effect of Exercise on Cardio Respiratory System
- Effect of Exercise on Muscular System
- Physiological Changes due to Ageing
- Sports Injuries : Classification (Soft Tissue Injuries : (Abrasion, Contusion, Laceration, Incision, Sprain and Strain) Bone and Joint Injuries : (Dislocation, Fractures, Stress Fracture, Green Stick, Communated, Transverse Oblique and Impacted) Causes, Prevention and Treatment
- First Aid – Aims and Objectives

Unit VIII Biomechanics and Sports
- Meaning and Importance of Biomechanics in Sports
- Types of movements (Flexion, Extension, Abduction and Adduction)
- Newton's Law of Motion and its Application in Sports
- Friction and Sports

Unit IX Psychology and Sports
- Personality; its definition and types : Trait and Types (Sheldon and Jung Classification) and Big Five Theory
- Motivation, its type and techniques
- Exercise Adherence; Reasons to Exercise, Benefits of Exercise
- Strategies for Enhancing Adherence to Exercise
- Meaning, Concept and Types of Aggressions in Sports

Unit X Training in Sports
- Strength : Definition, types and methods of improving Strength–Isometric, Isotonic and Isokinetic
- Endurance : Definition, types and methods to develop Endurance–Continuous Training, Interval Training and Fartlek Training
- Speed : Definition, types and methods to develop speed–Acceleration Run and Pace Run
- Flexibility : Definition, types and methods to Improve Flexibility
- Coordinative Abilities : Definition and Types
- Circuit Training : Introduction and Importance

Practical   **Max. Marks : 30**

01.	Physical Fitness Test	6 marks
02.	Proficiency in Games and Sports (Skill of any one Game of choice from the given list*)	7 marks
03.	Yogic Practices	7 marks
04.	Record File**	5 marks
05	Viva Voce (Health / Games and Sports / Yoga)	5 marks

*Basketball, Football, Kabaddi, Kho-Kho, Volleyball, Handball, Hockey, Cricket, Bocce and Unified Basketball [CWSN (Children with Special Needs–Divyang)]

****Record File shall include :**

Practical-1 : Fitness Tests administration for all items.

Practical-2 : Procedure for Asanas, Benefits and Contraindication for any two Asanas for each lifestyle disease.

Practical-3 : Procedure for administering Senior Citizen Fitness Test for 5 elderly family members.

Practical-4 : Any one game of your choice out of the list above. Labelled diagram of Field and Equipment Rules, Terminologies and Skills).

Suggested Question Paper Design
Physical Education (Code No. 048)
Class XII (2019-20)

Marks : 70   **Duration : 3 hours**

S. No.	Typology of Questions	Objective Type/MCQ 1 mark	Short Answer I 3 marks	Short Answer II 5 marks	Marks
1.	**Remembering :** Exhibit memory of previously learned material by recalling facts, terms, basic concepts, and answers.	5	3	2	24
2.	**Understanding :** Demonstrate understanding of facts and ideas by organising, comparing, translating, interpreting, giving descriptions, and stating main ideas.	5	3	1	19
3.	**Applying :** Solve problems to new situations by applying acquired knowledge, facts, techniques and rules in a different way.	5	2	1	16
4.	**Analysing and Evaluating :** Examine and break information into parts by identifying motives or causes. Make inferences and find evidence to support generalizations. Present and defend opinions by making judgments about information, validity of ideas, or quality of work based on a set of criteria. **Creating :** Compile information together in a different way by combining elements in a new pattern or proposing alternative solutions.	5	2	–	11
	Total	**20 × 1 = 20**	**10 × 3 = 30**	**4 × 5 = 20**	**70 (34)**

There will be **Internal Choice** in questions of 1 mark (4 choices), 3 marks (3 choices) and 5 marks (2 choices). In all, total 9 internal choices.

CONTENTS

PLANNING IN SPORTS

1.1. MEANING AND OBJECTIVES OF PLANNING IN SPORTS

Planning is a process of setting goals, developing strategies, and outlining tasks and schedules to accomplish the goals.

Planning aims to ensure positive preparation for the sport, enabling the right facilities in the right places, based on the robust and up-to-date assessments of needs for all levels of sport and all sectors of the community. To achieve these planning objectives, one must seek to protect sports facilities from loss as a result of development, to enhance existing facilities through improving their quality, accessibility and management, and to provide new facilities that are fit for the purpose to meet demands for participation, now and in the future. The purpose of planning is to identify the work to be carried out to achieve objectives. Plans should be drawn up for meeting the long term (4 years) objectives as well as short term objectives for the forthcoming season.

Meaning and Concept of Planning

In simple words, planning is to decide in advance, what is to be done, when, where, how and by whom it is to be done. Planning bridges the gap between where we are and where we want to go. It includes the selection of objectives, policies, procedures and programmes among alternatives. A plan is a predetermined course of action to achieve a specified goal. It is an intellectual process characterized by thinking before doing. It is an attempt on the part of management to anticipate the future in order to achieve better performance.

Definitions of Planning

Different authors have given different definitions of planning from time to time. The main definitions of planning are as ahead :

According to **Alford and Beatt**, *"Planning is the thinking process, the organized foresight, the vision based on fact and experience that is required for intelligent action."*

According to **Theo Haimann**, *"Planning is deciding in advance what is to be done. When a manager plans, he projects a course of action for further attempting to achieve a consistent co-ordinate structure of operations aimed at the desired results."*

According to **Billy E. Goetz**, *"Planning is fundamentally choosing and a planning problem arises when an alternative course of action is discovered."*

According to **Koontz and O' Donnell**, *"Planning is an intellectual process, conscious determination of course of action, the basing of decision on purpose, facts and considered estimates."*

According to **Allen**, *"A plan is a trap laid to capture the future."*

Objectives of Planning in Sports

1. **Protect existing facilities :** Planning in sports seeks to help protect them and recreational places and land, including playing fields, and expects these to be retained or enhanced as a part of redevelopment unless an assessment has demonstrated that there is an excess of provision and they are surplus to requirements or clear evidence supports their relocation. Sport is a statutory consulted on all planning applications affecting playing field land and will object to such an application unless one of five exceptions applies.

2. **Enhance the quality, accessibility and management of existing facilities :** Planning in sport desires the best use of existing sports facilities through improving their quality, access and management. Planning has developed a wide range of supporting advice on understanding and planning for facility provision, including efficient facility management such as community access to school sites.

3. **Provide new facilities to meet demand :** Planning in sports seeks to ensure that communities have access to sufficient, high quality sports facilities that are fit for purpose. Using evidence

and advocacy, we help to guide investment into new facilities and the expansion of existing ones to meet new demands that cannot be met by existing provision.

4. **To reduce unnecessary pressure or immediacy :** For conducting any event there should be a proper planning to avoid any rush or immediacy. To organize an event efficiently and smoothly, an organizer needs to prepare a good plan beforehand. Perfect planning will naturally avoid unnecessary pressure.

5. **To keep good control over all the activities :** In any planning and management, controlling is the basic principle and objective of planning. In any tournament and competition, an organizer needs to have a good control over all the activities and events related to that particular competition and tournament. Planning helps in keeping a good control in organizing a tournament successfully.

6. **To facilitate proper co-ordination :** This objective of planning is related to facilitate proper co-ordination among the various members of committees, formed for organizing the competition smoothly. Without proper coordination among the officials of the tournament, it will not be easy to conduct or organize the sports tournament. A proper planning helps in proper coordination.

7. **To reduce the chance of mistake :** To minimize the chance of mistake is also significant objective of planning in sports. A proper plan helps to minimize the chances of mistakes in any field. Mistakes in organizing an event leads to a bad impression on the participants.

8. **To increase the efficiency :** To enhance the efficiency of sports officials in conducting sports event and competition is one of the main objectives of planning. Through proper planning, members of the committee perform their duties efficiently and effectively.

9. **To increase the creativity :** It leads to increase in creativity among officials, coaches and physical education teachers. In fact, planning helps innovative and creative thinking among sports officials because many new ideas emerge when they are planning.

10. **To enhance the sports performance :** It is one of the significant objectives to enhance the sports performance of athletes or players. With proper planning it is possible to improve the performance of sportspersons.

1.2. VARIOUS COMMITTEES AND THEIR RESPONSIBILITIES (PRE, DURING AND POST)

Sports competitions are the formal way of presenting sports programmes. To conduct any tournament or championships properly, there are many imperative requirements that should be planned beforehand and must be fulfilled before initiation of the event. For conducting a tournament, various aspects are to be seriously considered as there are numerous duties which are to be performed and accomplished for successful completion of the event. In order to fulfill and perform every duty meticulously, several individuals collectively work under the heading of different committees in which the manpower and the duties are evenly distributed. The aspects taken care of by different committees and personnel follows the phases of management *i.e.*, planning, organizing, staffing, directing, controlling, coordination and supervision. To put up a grand show requires a prolonged period of turmoil in three phases of the event that is the duties and responsibilities performed before, during and after the tournaments. No matter in what level the tournament is to be organized it always require precise planning of different bases of management involving the tasks to be carried out to conduct the event. There are various committees which are usually formed according to the need of the tournament to be conducted smoothly. Here are the mentions of those major committees which are broadly structured in almost all the events irrespective of any level of the tournaments to be conducted. Let us now know the committees working as the pillars for smooth conduct of the tournaments.

1. Organizing committee : This committee comprises of significant heads who work as the backbone of the conducting the event. This includes the key person behind the event, *viz.*, chairman or chief patron of the competition, organizing secretary, etc. The chief patron or the chairperson is usually the head of the institution or any organization whereas organizing secretary is the head of the department or any individual particularly related to the sports going to be conducted.

(a) **Pre-work :** (i) To plan accordingly by forming the other committees and dignified personnel for the smooth conduct and successful completion of the competition. (ii) The Committee may arrange the funds and the financial assistance to be required to conduct the event. (iii) To get prior approvals related to the venue to be selected from the concerned authority to conduct the event. (iv) To arrange the equipments and other major necessities for the smooth conduct of the event. (v) To make use of the available resources. (vi) To inform other institutions or organizations about the dates of the tournament and receive consent for participation.

(b) During work : (i) During work, the prime responsibility is to supervise the smooth conduct of the competition. (ii) To have a check on every duty distributed to different committees and individuals on the day of initiation of the event. (iii) The Committee looks after the overall arrangements on the big day and also welcomes dignified and distinguished guests invited for the tournament. (iv) To handle the immediate problems arisen in the event.

(c) Post-work : (i) To summarize the task done by the work force and congratulate the team members for smooth conduct of the tournament. (ii) This committee makes the final report of the tournament after its completion, reviews the budget and expense details of each and every committee.

2. Technical committee : This committee is responsible for the technical conduct of the tournament. It comprises of individuals who is responsible of making draws and officiating in the event. The officials are informed in advance so that they make their prominence on the day of the event. This committee consists of the Chief technical advisor who is usually a very well qualified, experienced expert from the sports or game to be conducted. It also consists of other experts and officials who work under the supervision and direction of the advisor. These individuals work collaboratively to smoothly conduct the tournament.

(a) Pre-work : (i) The prime task of this committee is to reach the venue of the event well in advance and take care of the technical aspects of the event like preparation of the playing arena, cross-checking whether markings are as per the rules of the particular sports to be conducted. (ii) To ensure standard equipments as per the sports are available. (iii) To prepare the fixtures and also takes care of the things like score-sheets, stopwatches, whistles, etc., required on and off the ground for smooth conduct of the event.

(b) During work : (i) This committee comes into focus on the day and initiation of the event. (ii) It keeps a check on the tournament following the rules and regulations of the sport conducted. (iii) It manages and controls the conduct of the sports as per the schedule. (iv) It checks the eligibility and other details of the players, the members of this committee during the event works as the referee, umpires, scorer, time keeper, etc. (v) It handles the situations on and off the field by keeping track of the scores of the matches and the teams or players. (vi) It updates the spectators, coaches, managers and other players with the scores of the game during the match.

(c) Post-work : (i) To maintain the record of the matches played in the tournaments. (ii) To keep the coaches, managers and other players about the upcoming matches if any. (iii) To prepare a day to day report of the tournament and submit to the organizing committee. (iv) To inform the sports organization or federation about the smooth conduct and success of the tournament.

3. Finance committee : This committee is responsible for the making of the budget for the event. The financial functioning of the game is done by this committee. It works for getting and managing the sponsorship of this event and makes all the payments.

(a) Pre-work : (i) It attempts and functions to get the expenses from various other committees. (ii) It plans for collecting the funds and getting sponsorship for providing financial assistance to conduct the tournament smoothly. (iii) To get the approvals and other major financial sanctions from the higher concerned authority.

(b) During work : (i) To provide funds to various other committees for different kind of activities on the day of the event. (ii) To keep record of the officiating fees paid by the teams prior to playing the match. (iii) To provide travelling and diet allowances to the teams or players participating in the tournaments.

(c) Post-work : (i) To fetch the expenditure from the various committees after completion of the event. (ii) It plays the lead role in settling the bills of the expenses made throughout the event. (iii) It prepares the exact financial report covering the total expenditures of the tournament.

4. Ground arrangement committee : This committee takes care of preparing the ground or the venue up-to-the mark for the conduct of the event. This usually comprises of the grounds-men working under the supervision of the sports related experts. It prepares the ground by marking it as per the specifications given in the rules of the sport to be conducted. It also takes care of the area in and around the main playing field.

(a) **Pre-work :** (i) This committee usually works by doing all the ground arrangements as per the rules of the sports by marking it properly. (ii) It also prepares the venue for other ceremonial functions like the opening and closing of the tournament.

(b) **During work :** (i) The individuals working under this committee ensure the availability of the necessary equipments during the matches. (ii) It keeps the equipments related to the sports in proper shape and supplies it to the officials and players whenever asked for. (iii) It also manages the other facilities in and around the main playing area.

(c) **Post work :** (i) To collect all the equipments used in the event and ensure whether the equipments are in proper shape and size. (ii) If borrowed items were used in the event, to collect them and return it after the event comes under the responsibilities of this committee.

5. Reception committee : This committee takes care of receiving, greeting and acknowledging the distinguished and dignified guests and players of the event. It makes a check list of the guests to be invited and also keeps a track of the teams or players responded towards attending the event. This committee works very closely with the accommodation and ceremonial committee.

(a) **Pre-work :** (i) To make checklist of the invited guests, coaches, managers and players or teams going to attend the event. (ii) To provide details of guests and other individuals' arrival and departure date and time to the accommodation committee. (iii) To check every details of their transportation, boarding and lodging at the time of the event accordingly with other committees.

(b) **During work :** (i) This committee is the first one to interact with the guests and teams on the day of the event. It receives and extend greeting on behalf of the organizing committee to the guests and the teams. (ii) This committee informs the teams or players about the tournament schedule, boarding and lodging arrangements and other important information as well. (iii) It checks the eligibility proformas and collects it from the team. The committee collects the security deposit from each and every team participating from the teams. (iv) It informs other committees about the day-to-day arrival of teams for the event.

(c) **Post work :** (i) It prepares the report of the total teams reported for the event to the organizing committee. (ii) To keep a track and work collaboratively with the accommodation committee so as to refund the security deposit of the teams at the time of their departure.

6. Accommodation committee : This committee takes care of arranging the stay for the duration of the event for guests, officials, coaches, managers and teams or players. This committee makes the booking for arranging the stay beforehand as according to the number of the individuals expected at the event.

(a) **Pre-work :** (i) This committee attempts to get the details of the out-stationed participants and guests well in advance and plan the boarding and lodging arrangements accordingly. (ii) It also makes the staying arrangements for the guests, officials, coaches, managers and teams or players properly.

(b) **During work :** It allots the rooms and issues other required items to the teams after their arrival for their event or during the stay.

(c) **Post work :** (i) It ensures that rooms allotted to the teams are not damaged. It collects the issued items from the teams. (ii) It also returns the borrowed and rented items immediately after the event.

7. Refreshment committee : This committee ensures providing refreshment to the guests, officials and players throughout the event. This committee is responsible for providing meals to the individuals during the event including the opening and closing ceremony as well.

(a) **Pre-work :** This committee selects the food items to be provided during the event considering the budget. It plans for proving food to the teams at reasonable charges.

(b) **During work :** It makes sure that the food or meals are provided to the teams on time without creating much of a disturbance to the match schedules. It provides light refreshment time-to-time to the guests, officials and players during the event.

(c) **Post work :** It prepares a report on the consolidated amount of the total amount spent on the food items and the amount earned by the food coupons sold to the participants of the events. The total expenditure report is submitted to the organizing committee after that.

8. Transportation committee : This committee deals with providing transportation to the guests, officials and players before initiation, during and after completion of the tournaments.

(a) Pre-work : This committee plans the means and modes of transport to be provided to the team well in advance. This committee keeps track of the dates and time of arrival and departure of the guests, officials and players. According to the details collected about the arrival and departure of the total number of guests, officials and players, it arranges transport.

(b) During work : This committee provides the transportation means to the guests, officials and teams as per the closing and opening ceremony of the tournament. It also provides transport to the teams and officials as per the match schedule to reach from their place of stay to the venue of the tournament.

(c) Post work : To return the modes of transport hired for providing hassle free transportation facilities for the guests, officials and players of the event.

9. Ceremonial committee : This committee is majorly responsible for smooth conduct of the opening and closing ceremony of the event. It welcomes and felicitates the guests and other recognized individuals in the event. The prime function of this committee is prize distribution.

(a) Pre-work : (i) This committee plans the opening and closing ceremony of the event. It processes with the formal welcoming and felicitation by keeping the names or list of the guests beforehand. (ii) It also assists in decoration of the stage area in the opening and closing ceremony. (iii) It arranges for every necessary items and prizes required for the ceremony as per the events conducted.

(b) During work : The committee welcomes and felicitates the guests invited for the event. It keeps track of the result of the event and prepares for prize distribution as accordingly and conducts the same smoothly.

(c) Post work : This committee submits the report of the total number of the prizes and certificates presented to the teams to the organizing committee. It returns the left over prizes to the organizing committee.

10. Publicity committee : The most important role of this committee is to provide a wide publicity of the event. It organizes the press releases and press conferences of the tournament in the process of publicity. The results of the matches or the tournaments are sent to this committee for publicity.

(a) Pre-work : (i) This committee informs the press and media about the event in advance so that society comes to know about the tournament level and its nature. (ii) It also informs about the sports events, dates and venues, expected invited guests and players at the event.

(b) During work : (i) This committee keeps a day-to-day track of the tournament information making press notes and inform about the matches of the event to the press and media. (ii) It works collectively with individuals of press and media.

(c) Post work : This committee summarizes the major features of the tournament and presents the concrete report of the entire event in an impressive attractive way to the press and media for publicity.

11. Medical committee : For organizing a sports meet, this committee plays a significant role because as experts say 'if there is sports then there will be chances of injury'. This committee provides medical assistance to the participants in the event. It comprises of doctors, nurses and physiotherapists. It offers first-aid and treats any emergency situation requiring medical assistance.

(a) Pre-work : (i) This committee arranges for the medical personnel during the event. (ii) It arranges the medicines, bandages, sprays, etc., and other items required for providing medical help.

(b) During work : (i) The individuals of this committee keep track of the medicines and other medical items used in the event. (ii) It also provides treatment to those in need and gives medicine after collecting brief information about the medical history of the players. (iii) It handles and treats any emergency situation if arisen in the event.

(c) Post work : To remove the medical assistance counters and restore or return the left over medicine to the concerned individuals.

All the committees are formed well in advance for conduct of the tournament. The duties and responsibilities of the individuals working under various committees are distributed beforehand so that they can function properly. These committees perform their duties before, during and after the event to make it a grand success.

1.3. TOURNAMENT

Meaning and Definition

Tournament is a series of games or matches that are used to decide the winner of a competition. In sports, a tournament is often organised to crown the league's champion. Tournaments are usually conducted over a short time period. In addition to sporting events, tournaments are often staged for card games like poker, rummy and bridge. The tournament format indicates the matchups and the criteria for advancement and elimination.

Tournaments are a popular way to allow people or teams to compete against each other. Since the outcome is based strictly on the results, an indisputable winner can thus be crowned. Competition can take place using one of several tournament format types. The dictionary meaning of tournament is a large contest of many rounds among various teams. A tournament is a competition held among various teams in a particular activity according to affixed schedule where a winner is decided.

According to **Dr. Ajmer Singh et al.,** *"a tournament vs competition held among various teams in a particular activity is according to a fixed schedule where winner is decided"*.

Tournaments are events that take place over a short period, often just a single day, weekend or week. They involve a relatively large number of teams or players playing lots of matches at the venue. Often the competition features an abbreviated form of the sport (for example, a tennis match comprising just two/three sets, a team game involving short periods, or a small sided game, such as 7-a-side rugby).

Importance of Tournament

In the field of sports, tournament plays a major role to expose the ability of an athlete and sports person. Players participate in tournaments with a great zeal and zest. Tournaments also play a significant role for the players, coaches and physical education teachers. The importance of tournaments is described below.

1. **Development of sports skills :** Through participating in tournaments, various skills of sports are developed. The maximum number of participations in tournaments helps to develop technical skills of the sports as well as tactical skills. They acquire efficiency in skills and help to overcome the competition fear and finally improve the game.

2. **Propaganda of sports :** A tournament helps in promoting and publishing about the sports in society. Society comes to know about the value of sports through the medium of TV, newspapers and media.

3. **Selection of players :** A tournament is the way by which good players are selected based on their performance. A good performer can be selected for upper level tournament.

4. **Development of national and international integration :** Sports tournaments are helpful in developing national integration as well as international unity and brotherhood. A tournament is one of the best means of enhancing international peace.

5. **Development of social qualities :** Social traits such as tolerance, sympathy, cooperation, group cohesion, brotherhood and discipline, and team spirit are developed among participants through sports tournaments.

6. **Source of recreation :** Sports tournaments provide ample recreation to the spectators. Sports and games provide the recreational activity through tournaments and competition. So, tournaments are a good source of recreation.

Types of Tournament

There are mainly four types of tournaments, which are mentioned below.

1. Knock-out Tournament.

2. League or Round Robin Tournament.

3. Combination Tournament.

4. Challenge Tournament.

Knock-out Tournament

In Knock-out or Elimination tournament, a team which is once defeated, automatically gets eliminated from the tournament. Only the teams which win continue in the tournament. It means that no second chance is given to the defeated team. Chances are given only to the winning teams or players. For example, if four teams are participating in a knock-out tournament, the winning team is declared in the following way.

Teams   I Round   II Round

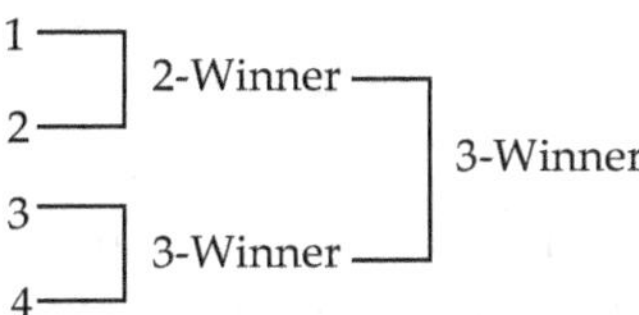

In the 1st round, team 1 and 2 as well as team 3 and 4 play their matches. If team 2 and team 3 become winners of 1st round, these teams, *i.e.*, team 2 and team 3 get chance to play in the 2nd round and team 1 and team 4 will be eliminated from the tournament.

Types of Knock-out Tournament

There are four types of knock-out tournament, which are listed below.

1. Single Knock-out or Single Elimination Tournament
2. Double Knock-out or Double Elimination Tournament
3. Triple Knock-out or Triple Elimination Tournament
4. Bagnall Wild Elimination Tournament

Advantages of Knock-out Tournament

1. **Simplicity :** Knock-out is simple to understand. Win and you keep playing; lose and you do not. If a team fears of losing to some other team, then they are gone. Just win one game at a time and you win the tournament.

2. **Fewer games :** Because each team is eliminated upon one loss, it takes fewer games to complete a tournament. This is both an advantage and a disadvantage. It makes the tournament shorter and means each game has a greater importance. It also means fewer games for fans and spectators. Each team must play their best in every game and there is no saving players or energy for another game.

3. **More teams :** knock out tournaments allow for more teams to compete in a tournament, which is beneficial to the athletes and fans.

Disadvantages of Knock-out Tournament

1. **Fairness :** The fact that one loss puts a team out of a tournament can be unfair. The better team does not always win one single game which is a disadvantage of single elimination.

2. **Interest of good players :** Due to loss in the earlier rounds, players may lose their interest and motives.

League or Round Robin Tournament

League or round robin tournament is one in which the each competitor faces every other competitor a set number of times. At the end of all matches, the competitor with the best win-loss record is declared the champion. **Mr. Burger** was the first person who imagined about the league tournament and owing to that, it is also called **Burger system.** It is a competition "in which each contestant meets all other contestants in turn". It contrasts with an elimination tournament. It can be called as the best type of tournament because it provide the maximum number of opportunities to show the best performance. In fact, there is no element of chance and the real winner is picked up easily at the end.

There are two types of league or round robin tournaments.

1. Single league tournament
2. Double league tournament

Single League Tournament

In a single round-robin schedule, each team plays with every other team once and the number of matches is determined with the help of following formula.

$$\frac{N(N-1)}{2}$$

Here 'N' means the number of teams participating in the tournament. For example, if 9 teams are taking part in a tournament, the number of total matches will be 36 as given below :

$$\frac{9(9-1)}{2} = \frac{9(8)}{2}$$
$$= \frac{72}{2}$$
$$= 36 \text{ matchs}$$

9 Team Round Robin

Team	Wins	Losses
1.		
2.		
3.		
4.		
5.		
6.		
7.		
8.		
9.		

Round 1	Round 2	Round 3	Round 4	Round 5	Round 6	Round 7	Round 8	Round 9
1 vs 8	5 vs 3	2 vs 9	6 vs 4	3 vs 1	7 vs 5	4 vs 2	8 vs 6	9 vs 7
2 vs 7	6 vs 2	3 vs 8	7 vs 3	4 vs 9	8 vs 4	5 vs 1	9 vs 5	1 vs 6
3 vs 6	7 vs 1	4 vs 7	8 vs 2	5 vs 8	9 vs 3	6 vs 9	1 vs 4	2 vs 5
4 vs 5	8 vs 9	5 vs 6	9 vs 1	6 vs 7	1 vs 2	7 vs 8	2 vs 3	3 vs 4
9-Bye	4-Bye	1-Bye	5-Bye	2-Bye	6-Bye	3-Bye	7-Bye	8-Bye

Double League Tournament

If each team plays with all other teams twice, this is frequently called a *double round robin*. The term is rarely used when all participants play with one another more than twice, and is never used when one participant plays with others in unequal number of times. The number of total matches is determined with the help of following formula :

$$N (N - 1)$$

If nine teams are participating in a double league tournament, the total number of matches will be 72 according to the formula.

$$9 (9 - 1) = 72 \text{ matches}$$

Advantages of League or Round Robin Tournament

1. Round robin allows a guaranteed number of games and luck does not play a big role as it does in case of an elimination tournament.
2. Only strong team becomes victorious in the tournament.
3. Every team gets full opportunity to show its efficiency or performance.
4. The spectators also get good opportunity to watch the game for many days.
5. Appropriate opportunities are available to the players to improve their performance.

Disadvantages of League or Round Robin Tournament

1. The round robin tournament is not as exciting, for the most part there is no championship final match.
2. The matches in the latter half of the tournament could have no impact on the final outcome of the tournament.
3. One team may not be in the running for the championship, therefore, may not give as much effort.
4. It consumes more time to decide the winner.
5. Costly (it involves lot of money and facilities).

Combination Tournaments

These types of tournaments are usually conducted whenever matches shall be played among the teams belonging to faraway places and the number of teams is larger or when larger numbers of teams compete for a particular game. Then the teams may be divided into a few groups. The teams belonging to the con-cerned group play among themselves either on knock-out or league basis and decide the winner of the group. This type of tournaments is highly recommended for conducting, the inter-school, inter-colleges, district and university levels to save time and money.

It involves following tournaments :

1. Knock-out cum knock-out
2. League cum league
3. Knock-out cum league
4. League cum knock-out

Knock-out cum Knock-out

In this type of tournament the total numbers of teams are divided in four equal zones. At first, the teams of each zone play on knock-out basis. In this way, a team becomes the winner from each zone. All the four winner teams again play their matches on knock-out basis. The team that wins in the final becomes the winner of inter zone tournament.

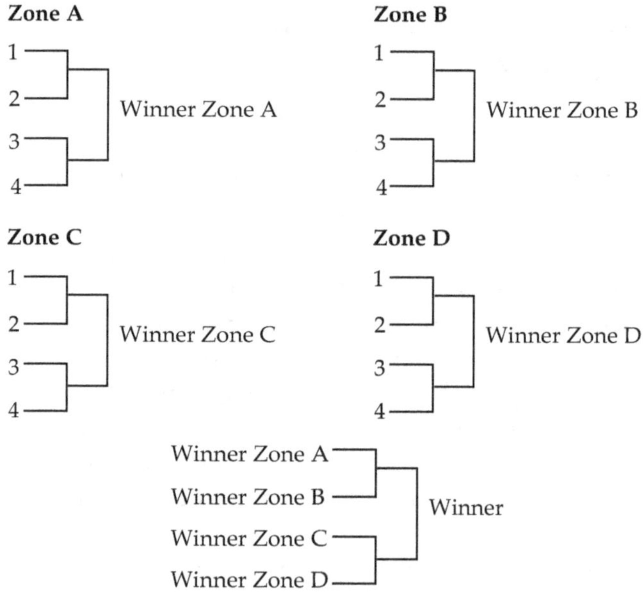

League cum League

In this type of tournament all the teams play their matches in their respective zones on league basis. Total number of teams are divided in four zones. One team from each separate zone becomes the zonal winner. This tournament is also considered to be a zonal or group tournament. All the zonal winner teams again play the matches on the league basis and one team becomes the winner of inter zonal or group tournament.

Example : Group or zonal tournament-on league basis.

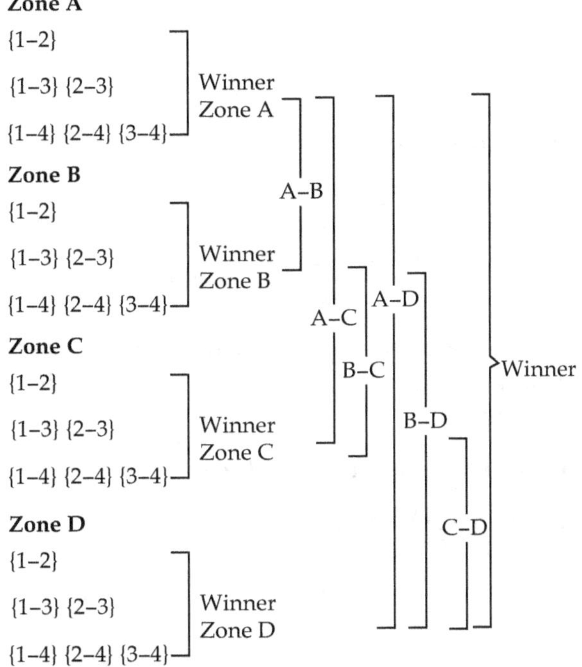

Knock-out cum League

First of all the teams play their matches in their respective zones on knock-out basis and one team becomes the winner from each zone. All the teams are divided in four zones. After that the four winner teams again play their matches on league basis and one team becomes the winner of inter group or zone tournament.

Example : Zonal tournament on knock out basis

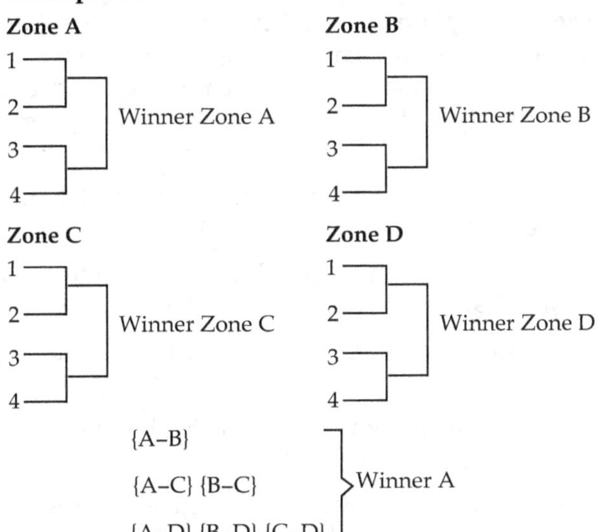

League cum Knock-out Tournament

All the teams play their matches in their own zone on the league basis. One team from each zone or group becomes the winner. All the teams are divided into four zones. After that, the four winner teams play their matches on knock-out basis and one team becomes the winner of intergroup or zonal tournament.

Example : Zonal tournament on league basis.

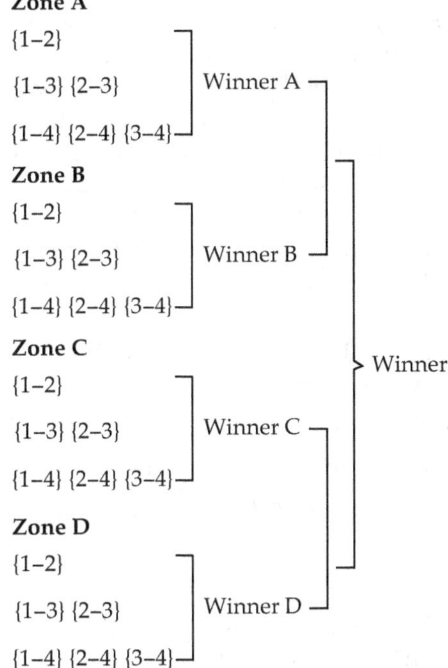

1.4. PROCEDURE TO DRAW FIXTURES

Knock-out Tournament

To plan the fixtures for knock-out tournament is actually very important part. The following points must be taken into consideration while preparing fixtures :

1. The total numbers of teams participating in the tournament.
2. The total number of byes.
3. The number of teams in each half or quarter.
4. The number of byes to be given in each half or quarter.
5. The total number of rounds.
6. The total number of matches.

Method of Preparing Fixtures in Knock-out Tournament

In knock-out tournament, the overall number of matches can be calculated by subtracting one from the total number of teams. For instance, if 8 teams are participating in the tournament, then the number of total matches will be, 8 – 1=7. It means that there will be only 7 matches in the tournament. These 8 teams should be divided into two halves. It is probably simple, if the total number of teams is the power of 2, such as 2, 4, 8, 16, 32 & 64 etc. It is very effortless to draw the fixtures in these cases. The total number of teams is divided into equal halves and then matches are determined by drawing of lots. If the total number of teams is not the power of 2 such as 3, 5, 7, 9, 10, 11,13, 15, 17, 19, 20, 21, 22, 23 and 24 etc., in these cases, byes are given. The teams, which are given byes, do not play in the 1st rounds. In the first round byes are given by which the number of teams playing in the later on rounds is reduced to a power of 2. Actually, a bye refers to a team that participates in the 2nd round and does not play in the first round. The number of byes in a fixture is the real distinction between the number of teams participating in the tournament and the next maximum number, which is the power of 2.

Example 1 : How many byes will be given if 13 teams are participating in a tournament?

Solution : Total number of teams = 13

Next highest number of power of two = 16

Difference between total number of teams and next highest number of power of two =16 – 13= 3

Hence, 3 byes will be given.

Example 2 : How many byes will be given if 21 teams are participating in a tournament?

Solution : Total number of teams = 21

Next highest number of power of two = 32

Difference between total number of teams and next highest number of power of two = 32 – 21 = 11

Hence, 11 byes will be given.

Method of Calculating Teams in Each Half

If the number of teams is in the power of two, it becomes easy to divide the teams in two halves. But if the number of   teams is not the power of two, the following procedure is applied :

$$\text{Upper Half} = \frac{\text{Total number of teams} + 1}{2}$$

It means $\dfrac{N + 1}{2}$, where 'N' is the total number of teams.

$$\text{Lower Half} = \frac{\text{Total number of teams} - 1}{2}$$

It means $\dfrac{N - 1}{2}$, where 'N' is the total number of teams.

Example 1 : How many teams will be kept in upper half and lower half if 15 teams are participating in a tournament?

Solution : Total number of teams in upper half

$$= \frac{N + 1}{2}$$

$$= \frac{15 + 1}{2} = \frac{16}{2} = 8 \text{ teams.}$$

Teams in lower half

$$= \frac{N - 1}{2}$$

$$= \frac{15 - 1}{2} = \frac{14}{2} = 7 \text{ teams.}$$

Example 2 : How many teams will be kept in upper half and lower half if 9 teams are participating in a tournament?

Solution : Total number of teams = 9

Teams in upper half

$$= \frac{N + 1}{2}$$

$$= \frac{9 + 1}{2} = \frac{10}{2} = 5 \text{ teams.}$$

Teams in lower half

$$= \frac{N - 1}{2}$$

$$= \frac{9 - 1}{2} = \frac{8}{2} = 4 \text{ teams.}$$

Method of Fixing Byes

In case of 11 teams, the numbers 1 to 11 are written on a plain paper. After that, lots are drawn and the names of teams are written against their numbers. The total numbers of teams are divided into two halves. After that the byes are fixed in upper and lower halves in the following order :

1. The first bye will be given to the last team of lower half.

2. The second bye will be given to the first team of upper half.

3. The third bye will be given to the first team of lower half.

4. The fourth bye will be given to the last team of upper half.

5. The next bye or byes will be given in the same order as described above.

Example : 11 teams

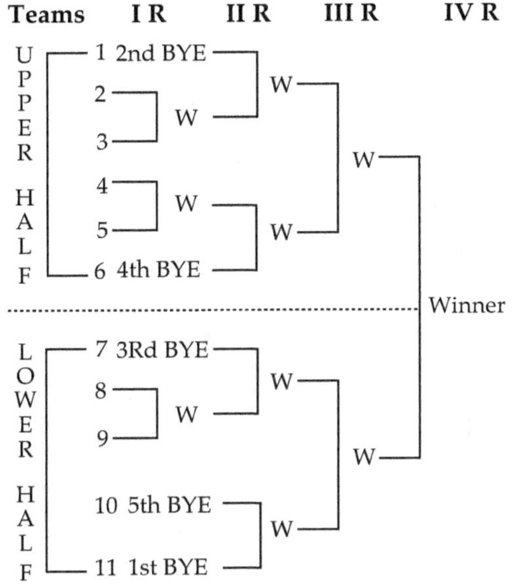

N : B.

$$\text{Total number of teams} = 11$$

$$\text{Next highest power of two} = 16$$

$$\text{Number of byes} = 16 - 11 = 5 \text{ byes}$$

$$\text{Teams in upper half} = \frac{NB - 1}{2} = \frac{5 - 1}{2} = \frac{4}{2}$$

$$= 2 \text{ byes}$$

$$\text{Teams in lower half} = \frac{NB + 1}{2} = \frac{5 + 1}{2} = \frac{6}{2}$$

$$= 3 \text{ byes}$$

Number of Matches in Knock-out Tournament

The numbers of matches in knock-out tournament is (N – 1), where 'N' denotes number of teams participating in a tournament.

Example : 11 Teams
Number of matches = N – 1 = 11 – 1 = 10 matches

Number of Rounds in Knock-out Tournament

If the number of participating teams is the power of two. *i.e.,*

In case of 16 teams = 2 × 2 × 2 × 2 = 4 rounds.

If the number of participating teams is not the power of two, the number of rounds will be based on the next highest power of two, *i.e.* In case of 15 teams = 2 × 2 × 2 × 2 = 4 rounds. (N : B next power of highest of 15 is 16).

In case of 17 teams = 2 × 2 × 2 × 2 × 2 = 5 rounds. (N : B next power of highest of 17 is 32).

Number of Teams in Each Quarter

If the number of teams is less the teams are divided into upper half and lower half only. On the other hand, if number of teams is more, teams are divided into upper and lower halves and these halves are further divided into two parts. It means that the upper half has two quarters, *i.e.,*

UPPER HALF	LOWER HALF
1st quarter	3rd quarter
2nd quarter	4th quarter

For determining the number of teams in each quarter, the total number of teams is divided by 4. If the remainder remains zero, there will be 4 quarters with equal number of teams. If the remainder remains 1, the first quarter will comprise of 1 extra team, whereas, the remaining quarters will have equal number of teams. If the remainder remains 2, each quarter (1st and 3rd) will have one extra team and the 2nd and 4th quarters will comprise of same number of teams. If the remainder remains 3, each quarter (1st, 2nd and 3rd) will have one extra team. This procedure can be easily understood with the help of following example :

Number of Teams	1st Quarter	2nd Quarter	3rd Quarter	4th Quarter
28	7	7	7	7
29	7+1	7	7	7
30	7+1	7	7+1	7
31	7+1	7+1	7+1	7
32	8	8	8	8
33	8+1	8	8	8
34	8+1	8	8+1	8

Fixtures on Knock-Out Basis

Example 1 : 11 teams fixure on knock-out basis

Solution : Total number of teams = 11

$$\text{Teams in upper half} = \frac{N + 1}{2} = \frac{11 + 1}{2} = \frac{12}{2}$$

$$= 6 \text{ teams.}$$

$$\text{Teams in lower half} = \frac{N - 1}{2} = \frac{11 - 1}{2} = \frac{10}{2}$$

$$= 5 \text{ teams.}$$

$$\text{Next highest power of two} = 16$$

$$\text{Number of byes} = 16 - 11 = 5 \text{ byes}$$

$$\text{Teams in upper half} = \frac{NB - 1}{2} = \frac{5 - 1}{2} = \frac{4}{2} = 2 \text{ byes}$$

$$\text{Teams in lower half} = \frac{NB + 1}{2} = \frac{5 + 1}{2} = \frac{6}{2} = 3 \text{ byes}$$

$$\text{Number of rounds} = 4 \text{ rounds}$$

$$(\because 2 \times 2 \times 2 \times 2 = 16)$$

Number of matches = N – 1 = 11 – 1 = 10 matches

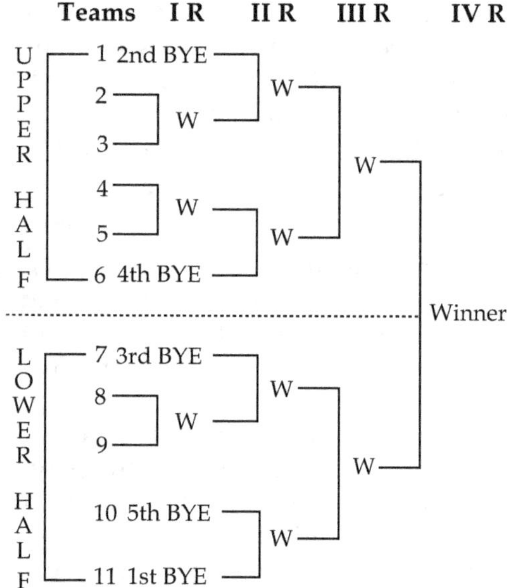

Example 2 : 19 teams fixure on knock-out basis

Solution : Total number of teams = 19

$$\text{Teams in upper half} = \frac{N+1}{2} = \frac{19+1}{2} = \frac{20}{2}$$

$$= 10 \text{ teams.}$$

$$\text{Teams in lower half} = \frac{N-1}{2}$$

$$= \frac{19-1}{2}$$

$$= \frac{18}{2}$$

$$= 9 \text{ teams.}$$

Next highest power of two = 16

$$\text{Number of byes} = 32 - 19 = 13 \text{ byes}$$

$$\text{Teams in upper half} = \frac{NB-1}{2}$$

$$= \frac{13-1}{2}$$

$$= \frac{12}{2}$$

$$= 6 \text{ byes}$$

$$\text{Teams in lower half} = \frac{NB+1}{2}$$

$$= \frac{13+1}{2}$$

$$= \frac{14}{2}$$

$$= 7 \text{ byes}$$

Number of Round = 5 rounds ($2 \times 2 \times 2 \times 2 \times 2$ = 32)

Number of matches = N – 1

$$= 19 - 1 = 18 \text{ matches}$$

Teams in each quarter

1st quarter = Q+1 = 4+1 = 5 Teams

2nd quarter = Q+1 = 4+1 = 5 Teams

3rd quarter = Q+1 = 4+1 = 5 Teams

4th quarter = Q = 4 = 4 Teams

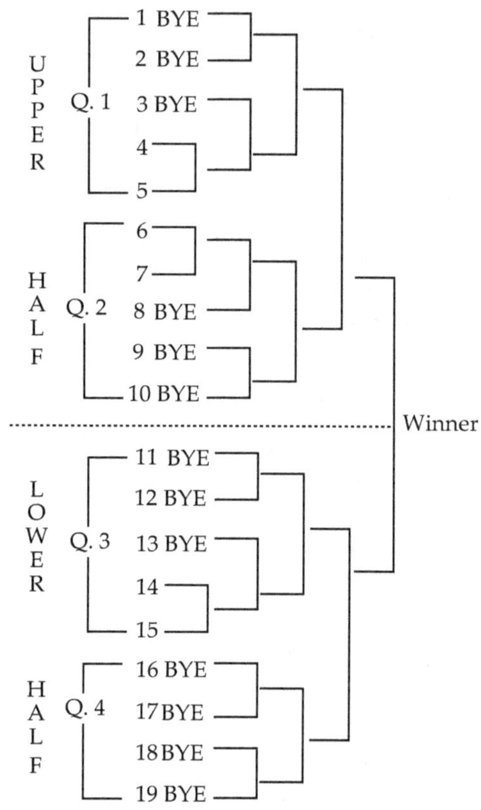

Consolation Tournament

Consolation tournament is organized but it depends solely on the organizers, whether they organize it or not. In consolation tournament, one additional chance is given to the defeated teams. In this tournament, the winner is declared from the defeated teams. The consolation tournament is of two types which are discussed below.

First Type : Here, each team will get two opportunities to play the matches. The teams, which are defeated in first round, get the opportunity to play in this type of tournament. Byes are given to those teams which did not get byes in the regular knock-out tournament.

Example : 9 teams' fixture

Solution : Total number of teams = 9

Numbers of total byes = 16 – 9 = 7

Regular Rounds

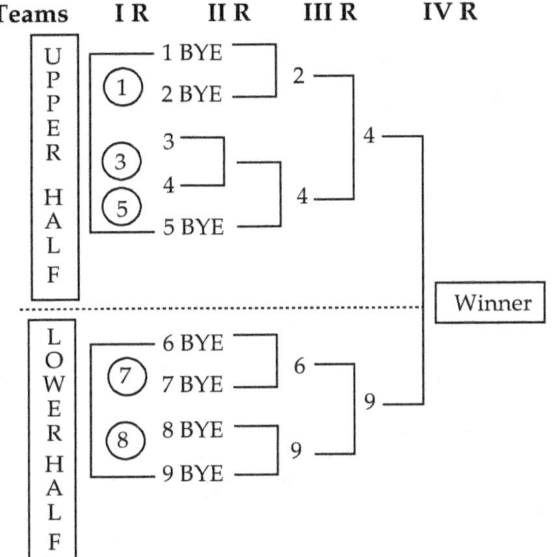

Consolation : Encircled teams are defeated in the first round.

Total number of defeated teams = 5

Number of byes = 8 – 5 = 3 byes.

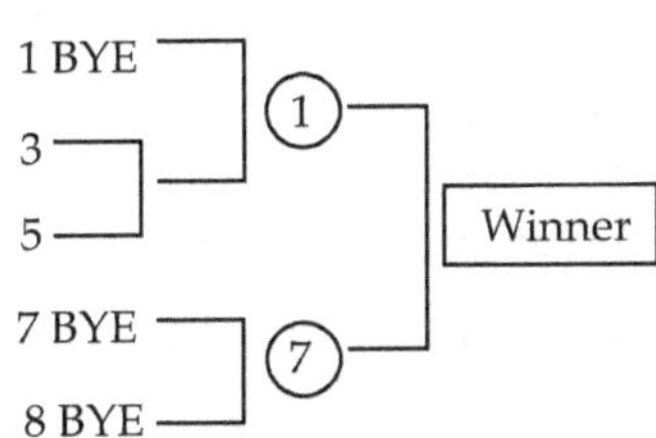

Second Type : The teams defeated in all the rounds are given an opportunity to take part in competition.

Example : 8 team's fixture

Solution : Total number of teams = 8

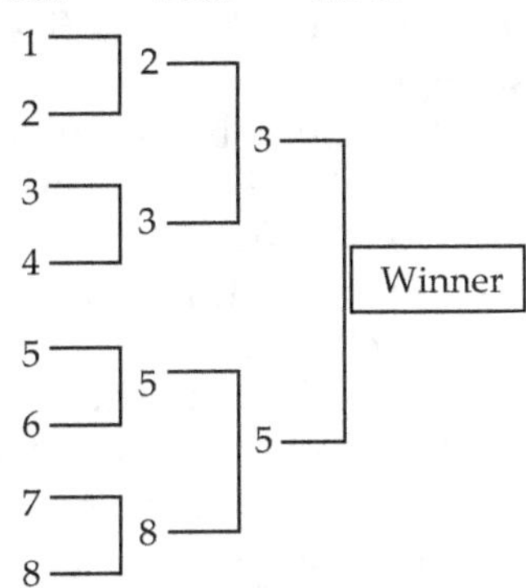

Here, the teams 1, 4, 6 and above 7 are the losers of 1st round, 2 and 8 are losers of 2nd round and team number 5 is the loser of 3rd round.

Consolation Round

Seeding Method

A seed is a competitor or team in a sports or other tournament who is given a preliminary ranking for the purposes of the draw. Players/teams are "planted" into the bracket in a manner that is typically intended so that the best do not meet until later in the competition. In knock-out tournament there is always a possibility that strong teams may be paired with weak teams or all strong teams might have been grouped in upper half or lower half. There is a possibility for strong teams that have the possibility to be eliminated in the preliminary round. So this may be a setback to the strong teams. To avoid such a situation, seeding method is used. By using this method the strong teams are selected to keep them at appropriate places in the fixture. For a systematic seeding the organizers must be well aware regarding the previous performance of the teams.

For two teams (one team will be kept on the top of the upper half and one team will be kept at the last of the lower half).

For four teams (the first two teams will be kept on the top of the upper half and third seeded teams will be kept at the top of the lower half and the fourth seeded teams will be kept at the lowest of the upper half). All the teams except seeded teams are to be kept in the fixture by lots. Generally, the number of seeded teams shall be the power of two like 2, 4, 8, 16 etc.

Example : 11 teams' fixture

Total number of teams = 11

Number of seeded teams = 4

Number of byes = 16 – 11 = 5

$$\text{No. of Teams in upper half} = \frac{N+1}{2}$$

$$= \frac{11+1}{2}$$

$$= \frac{12}{2}$$

$$= 6 \text{ teams.}$$

$$\text{No. of Teams in lower half} = \frac{N-1}{2}$$

$$= \frac{11-1}{2}$$

$$= \frac{10}{2}$$

$$= 5 \text{ teams}$$

No. of byes in upper half $= \dfrac{NB - 1}{2}$

$$= \frac{5 - 1}{2}$$

$$= \frac{4}{2}$$

$$= 2 \text{ byes}$$

No. of byes in lower half $= \dfrac{NB + 1}{2}$

$$= \frac{5 + 1}{2}$$

$$= \frac{6}{2}$$

$$= 3 \text{ byes}$$

Number of Round = 2 × 2 × 2 × 2 = 4 rounds

Number of matches = N – 1 = 11 – 1 = 10 matches

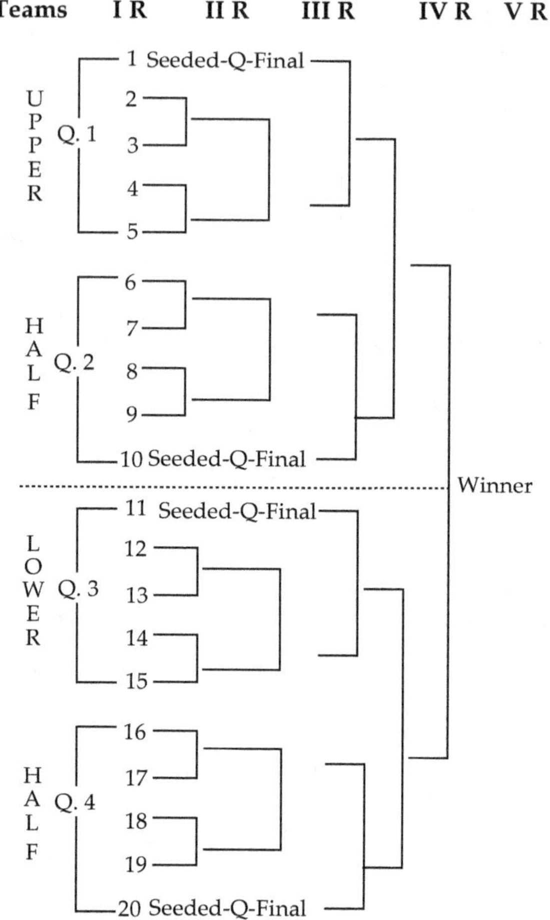

League Tournament

The following methods are used for fixtures in league tournament :

1. Cyclic method
2. Staircase method
3. Tabular method

Cyclic Method

In cyclic method, if the number of teams is in even number, the team number 1 is fixed on the top of right hand side and then other team numbers in ascending order consecutively downward and then upward on the left side. If the number of teams is in odd number, the bye is fixed on the top of the right side. The rest of the procedure remains the same. Teams are rotated in clockwise direction. If number of teams is in even number, the number of rounds will be (N – 1). On the other hand, if the number of teams is in odd number, the number of rounds will remain the same. It means equal to the number of teams.

Example 1 : Fixture of 5 teams on league basis according to the cyclic method.

Special seeding : This is the special case and advantage is given to the good performer of the last tournament. In special seeding, the seeded players participate directly in quarter-final or semi-final.

Example : Knock-out squash tournament.

20 players are participating in a Tournament.

Special seeding = 4 players

Total number of teams = 5

$$\text{Total number of matches} = \frac{N\,(N-1)}{2} = \frac{5\,(5-1)}{2}$$

$$= \frac{5 \times 4}{2} = \frac{20}{2}$$

$$= 10 \text{ matches}$$

Total number of rounds = N = 5

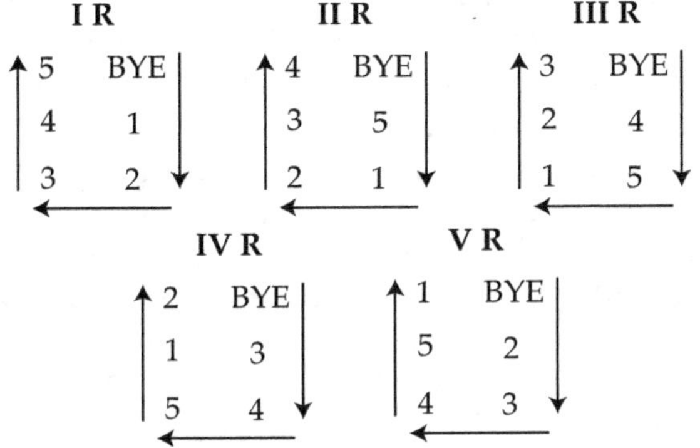

Example 2 : Fixture of 6 teams on league basis according to the cyclic method.

Total number of teams = 6

$$\text{Total number of matches} = \frac{N\,(N-1)}{2} = \frac{6\,(6-1)}{2}$$

$$= \frac{6 \times 5}{2} = \frac{30}{2}$$

$$= 15 \text{ matches}$$

Total number of rounds = N = 5

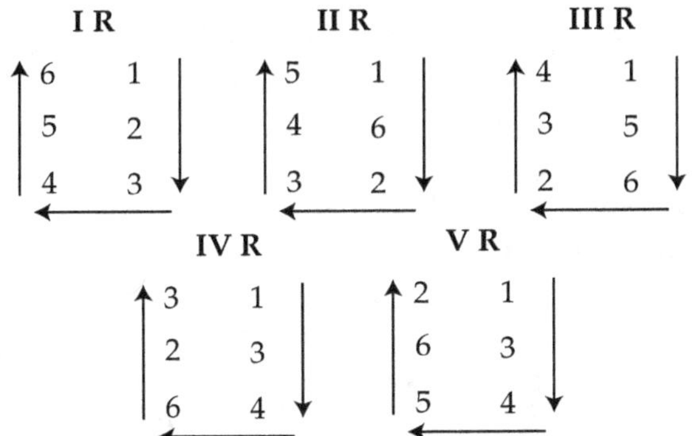

Staircase Method

In staircase method fixtures are made just like a ladder or a staircase. This method is the easiest method because no bye is given to any team and there is no problem of odd and even number of teams.

Example : Draw a fixture of 9 teams on league basis according to staircase method.

```
1 – 2
1 – 3   2 – 3
1 – 4   2 – 4   3 – 4
1 – 5   2 – 5   3 – 5   4 – 5
1 – 6   2 – 6   3 – 6   4 – 6   5 – 6
1 – 7   2 – 7   3 – 7   4 – 7   5 – 7   6 – 7
1 – 8   2 – 8   3 – 8   4 – 8   5 – 8   6 – 8   7 – 8
1 – 9   2 – 9   3 – 9   4 – 9   5 – 9   6 – 9   7 – 9   8 – 9
```

Method of Deciding the Winner in League Tournament

The winner of the tournament is decided when a team gets maximum points in a tournament. To give the points the following method is used :

Winner of the match = 2 points

Each team in a Draw = 1 point

Loser of the match = 0 point

In case the points of two teams are equal, their match is conducted all over again. But, it remains a draw, the team which wins the maximum number of matches is stated as the champion. If the tie still remains, the team who scored highest number of goals is confirmed as the champion. If the tie still remains, a match is held all over again among these teams. If there is a draw again, the winner is confirmed by a toss. In addition to this, further methods are also used to announce the winner.

1.   British method : The total points obtained are divided by the total possible points.

Example :

Number of matches played by a team = 8 matches

Number of matches won = 6 matches

Number of draw = 2 matches

Total points = 12 + 2 = 14

Possible points = 16

$$\text{Percentage points} = \frac{\text{Total Points}}{\text{Possible Points}} \times 100$$

$$= \frac{14}{16} \times 100 = 87{\cdot}5$$

2. American method : Divide the number of games won by the total number of games played.

Example :

Number of matches played by a team = 8 matches

Number of matches won = 5 matches

$$\text{Percentage points} = \frac{\text{Matches won}}{\text{Matches played}} \times 100$$

$$= \frac{5}{8} \times 100$$

$$= 62{\cdot}5$$

1.5. INTRAMURAL AND EXTRAMURAL

Intramural

An intramural competition is an athletic competition within the four walls of the school premises. The word **"intramural"** came from Latin words *intra* meaning **"within"** and *'muralis'* which means **"wall"**. The activities are conducted within the school for the students to participate. It means that the activities which are performed within the walls of an institution are called 'intramurals'. Intramural competition gives the positive exposure towards the students to develop the social values, sportsman spirit, teams work, team spirit etc. Student's experience in playing and officiating will contribute to the successful management of school, sports intramural. The intramural sports program provides to participate in organized sports events, take part in various leisure activities. This participation is governed only by the students' time and interest. In fact, intramural competition is one of the best means to motivate all the students of an institution for taking part in the games and sports. **"A game for each and each for a game"** is considered the motto of intramurals. These activities are the most pleasurable as well as enjoyable for the students. They get maximum educational benefit from such competitions. So, a large number of students must be involved in a wide range of intramural activities.

Objectives of Intramurals

The purpose of the intramural sports program is to provide opportunities for students, faculty, and staff to actively engage in activities involving sport, recreation, and play while providing structure for an experiential education. The objectives of the intramural sports program are as follows :

1. To provide opportunities to actively engage in programs and activities promoting an enhanced quality of life.
2. To provide opportunities for personal development through leadership, diversity, and teamwork.
3. To provide a forum for an experiential education for students, faculty, and staff.
4. To provide equipment, facilities and encourage wholesome participation in a large number of sports activities by students, faculty, and staff members.
5. To stimulate an interest in athletics and recreation through a high quality program.
6. To provide an opportunity to develop sportsmanship of the highest order.
7. To provide the opportunity to belong to a group.
8. To provide an opportunity to make social contacts and friendships which could not readily be developed in the classroom.
9. To provide the opportunity for every student, regardless of his/her ability, to realize the joy and fun of participation in their favourite sport.
10. To provide an opportunity to learn the important values developed through team spirit and cooperation.
11. To teach them the value of teamwork. In real work environment teamwork is one of the most valuable attributes an employee should have. Ability to work well with other people with efficiency and efficacy, can lead you to promotion and security with your job tenure.

Significance of Intramural

Intramural or sports competition is essential to the well-being of the students. Sports instills how to win, how to accept defeat, how to interact with other people and how to mould them to have desirable character traits that are vital in achieving success in the future. The following points can express the significance of intramurals for students.

1. Intramural helps in developing the psycho-motor of the students; this way they will able to channel their energy and time the right way.
2. To instill and inculcate discipline among the students. Engaging in sports will help students refrain from various forms of vices such as drugs, smoking, drinking and even gambling.
3. To develop healthy competition among the participants.
4. To develop fair play among the athletes. Cheating is null and void; same can be said about dirty tactics.
5. These programmes also lay stress on moral and ethical values of students.
6. Intramurals provide maximum recreation to the students.
7. The personality of the students.
8. Intramurals are also essential for developing the leadership qualities among the students

Extramural

Extramural sports are an opportunity for intramural participants to compete in a setting where they compete against teams from other schools or institutions. The word **"extramural"** came from *external* meaning **"outside"** and *muralis* which means **"wall"**. For developing and promoting the positive sports environment, the extramural competition is an essential element. It means that the activities, which are organized by an institution/school and the students of two or more schools also participate in sports related activities. Extramural competitions are also called inter-school competitions. Extramurals are fixed well in advanced so that the students of other schools may prepare well for such competitions.

Major Games	Minor Games	Rhythmic	Creative Activities	Combative Activities
Volleyball, Hockey, Cricket, Basketball, Kabaddi , Swimming, Athletics, Cycling, Wrestling, Lawn Tennis, Football, Softball, Badminton etc.	Runs, Kho-Kho, Circle Games, Tag Game, Roller Skating, Potato Race, Snack Race, Three-Legged Race etc.	Lazium, Dumbell, Marching, Folk Dance, Solo Dance, Mass P.T, Rhythmic Gymnastics etc.	Painting, Drawing, Sculpturing, making Models etc.	Boxing, Judo, Taekwondo, Karate, Wushu, Wrestling, Arm Wrestling etc.

Activities for Intramural Competition

Objectives of Extramural

1. **To improve the standard of sports :** For promoting the sports in the society extramural competitions take a major role by participating, the students become technically and tactically efficient in respective to sports. Students able to overcome the competition fear and help to enhance the performance at the time of main competitions. In this way, extramural improve the standard of sports.

2. **To provide experience to students :** Experience has its own value in any field. Extramural provide to gain experience to all the students who are actively and passively involved in such competitions. By actively participating in extramural competition they help to enhanced the performance in the competition.

3. **To develop sportsmanship and fraternity :** For every sportsperson developing a sportsmanship and fraternity is considered as one of the prime factors. By active participation in extramural competitions, it tends to develop the traits of sportsmanship and fraternity in students.

4. **To exposed the performance :** By actively participating in extramural, it helps the best performer to broaden the scope and level of competition to a higher competitive levels. And it also helps to motivate the players and sportsperson.

5. **To provide the knowledge of new rules and advanced techniques :** Participating in extramural competitions helps the sportsperson or students to upgrade the new rules and regulation or techniques of the games. Students learn new techniques as well as tactics which enable them efficient in improving their performance.

Significance of Extramural

The following points show the significance of extramural competition.

1. The standard of performance of the participants will be improved.

2. Loyalty of the institution is developed.

3. There is ample scope for the development of leadership, followership and sportsmanship qualities.

4. The participants derive pleasure, fun and enjoyment through healthy competitions.

5. Provides opportunities to schools to show their sports capabilities.

6. For enhancing the standard of sports performance.

7. Provides appropriate knowledge of sports technique.

8. For making and implementing the programmes of physical education more effective.

9. Improving the opportunities to participate in sports.

1.6. SPECIFIC SPORTS PROGRAMME

Specific sports programmes are not usually related to competitions.

Sports Days

Nowadays, as the sports have been developed as an important area to provide the movement education to children through physical activity, stress is laid down on the harmonious development of children in schools. The sports day is organized in schools so that the all round development and multidisciplinary development of children could be done. On sports days, ample opportunities are provided to every child to take part in any activity. On this day young children take specific interest in such activities.

On the sports day, various sports activities in which physical and recreational activities are included are conducted. On this day children are very must interested to take part in specific activities according to their own specific interest. They are usually seen more enthusiastic to take part in various sports activities.

Active participation in the sports activities helps the children to develop the leadership qualities and team spirit. The activities conducted on sports day provide ample opportunities for recreation of children and owing to that they do not fall in the trap of stress, tension and depression. It also helps to develop physical, mental and emotional health among the children. Apart from that, sports day helps to develop social qualities and discipline such as honesty, brotherhood, friendship, cooperation, tolerance, unity, feeling of respect and group cohesion through participation in various kinds of sports activities.

Health Runs

Health runs are organized by health department, sports department or social organizations. Usually their purpose is to restructure the standard of health in a country along with the raising of funds for charity. Health run is such a great physical activity that offers a significant health benefits among youths and adolescents. Health run does not require any specific preparation. For health runs the requirement is only a pair of shoes and light clothes. There is no competition in it but registration of participants is performed in advanced. The date and time is also fixed well in advance. There is no age limitation in health runs and the distance is also fixed up. Before going to health runs, everyone should take a role of the following suggestions to make the running experiences safe and effective :

1. Avoid tension. Make sure that the arms, shoulders, neck and fingers are relaxed, hands should be unclenched.
2. Don't bend the body from hip level.
3. Run softly and the strides should be normal.
4. Both arms should swing equally.
5. Always consume adequate amount of fluid before and after the run, especially in heat.
6. Consult the doctor as a precautionary measure if one is above 60 year old and not exercising regularly.

Run for Fun

Generally, the main motives of organizing this event are to publicize and spread the message to remain healthy and fit. To motivate the people to exercise regularly and stay healthy, this event may be same equally effective as the health runs. The main purpose of run for fun is more related to have ample amount of fun and frolic during running. In fact, run for fun is a friendly race that involves either road running or own enjoyment and recreation rather than competition.

Run for Specific Causes

It is the run which is generally related to a good and noble cause. It can be organized for various categories of those who are really interested. According to the categories of participants the distance might be different. The main aim of this run is to stay fit and healthy in life. Another objective of this run is to raise the funds for specific cause but the cause should be noble. Prize can be given to the position holders. This event is generally organized by the non-profit organizations for helping the patients of cancer, mentally handicapped, arthritis and orphanage children etc. Each and every category of participants including children, adults and old can take part in these events and can help in raising funds for the needy persons.

Example : Mumbai Marathon, Delhi Marathon etc.

Run for Unity

Generally run for unity is organized with a specific purpose *i.e.,* to show unity and peace among the people of different religions. The main purpose may be national and international integration and brotherhood. Basically in some countries, run for unity is organized to celebrate their independence. It may be in the form of relay race of long distance. Interested participants can run for some short distance. In the form of relay they feel united. Generally, to promote the events in the country, stars like film celebrities, sports icons of the countries also take part. The prize is given to the first three position holders. In fact, such runs promote harmony, peace and solidarity among people of different religion. It brings a sense of togetherness among people.

EXERCISES

Multiple Choice Questions

1. Administration and organisation of Physical Education should be based on the principles of :
   (a) Activity   (b) Biomechanics
   (c) Humanity   (d) Teaching

2. A tournament where every team plays with every other team once and the number of matches is determine with the help of N(N-1) is called as :
   (a) Single league tournament
   (b) Double league tournament
   (c) Knock-out tournament
   (d) None of the above

3. A league tournament is otherwise known as :
   (a) Round Robin tournament
   (b) Knock-out tournament
   (c) Combination tournament
   (d) None of the above

4. Seeding method refers to :
   (a) Pairing of all weak teams together
   (b) Pairing of all strong teams together
   (c) Strong teams paired with weak or all strong teams grouped in upper half or lower half
   (d) None of the above

5. In special seeding, the seeded players participate directly in the :
   (a) Finals
   (b) Semi-finals
   (c) Quarter-final or semi-final
   (d) None of the above

6. Which of the following are rhythmic activities ?
   (a) Lazium, Dumb bell, Marching, Folk dance, Group dance, Solo dance.
   (b) Shuttle run, Kho-Kho, Circle game, Tag game, Roller skating.
   (c) Painting, drawing, sculpturing, making models.
   (d) Boxing, Judo, Taekwondo, Karate.

7. A team which is defeated automatically gets eliminated from the tournament, it is known as :
   (a) League tournament
   (b) Knockout tournament
   (c) Combination tournament
   (d) None of the above

8. The activities which are performed within the walls are called :
   (a) Extramural   (b) Intramural
   (c) Both (a) and (b)   (d) None of these

9. A system in which responsibility for planning lies with the highest level is called :
   (a) Centralised planning
   (b) Decentralised planning
   (c) Strategic planning
   (d) Flexible planning

10. Which of the following is not a benefit of planning ?
    (a) Coordination of effort
    (b) Preparation for change
    (c) Development of standards
    (d) None of the above

Very Short Answer Type Questions (Carrying 1 mark)

1. What is planning ?
2. What is tournament ?
3. What is knock-out tournament ?
4. What is league tournament ?
5. What is single league tournament ?
6. What is double league tournament ?
7. What is combination tournament ?
8. What do you mean by term 'Bye' ?
9. What is seeding ?
10. What is special seeding ?
11. What do you mean by term 'intramural' ?
12. What do you mean by term 'extramural' ?
13. What do you mean by specific sports programme ?
14. Define planning.
15. List the steps to form committees for tournaments.
16. Enlist the various types of tournaments.
17. Enlist various types of knock-out or elimination tournament.
18. Briefly explain the advantages of knock-out tournament.
19. Briefly explain the disadvantages of knock-out tournament.
20. Briefly explain the advantages of league tournament.
21. Briefly explain the disadvantages of league tournament.
22. Briefly explain about types of league tournament.
23. Mention any two objectives of intramurals.
24. Enlist the activities which are included in intramurals.

25. Distinguish between intramural and extramural programmes.
26. What do you mean by 'health run' ?

Short Answer Type Questions (Carrying 3 marks)

1. Write down the objectives of planning in sports.
2. Draw a fixture of 9 teams on knock-out basis.
3. Draw a fixture of 16 teams on knock-out basis.
4. Explain the procedure of placement of teams in each quarter on knock-out basis.
5. Discuss the cyclic method of league tournament.
6. Discuss the staircase method of league tournament.
7. Write down the methods of deciding the winner in league tournament.
8. Briefly discuss the combination tournament.
9. Write down the significance of intramurals.
10. Write down the significance of extramural.
11. Discuss any three specific sports programmes.
12. Discuss in detail about sports day.
13. Discuss in detail about run for unity.
14. Discuss in detail about run for specific causes.

Long Answer Type Questions (Carrying 5 marks)

1. What is Planning ? Explain the objectives of planning in sports in detail.
2. Enlist the committees for organizing sports events and explain them in detail.
3. What is tournament? Explain the importance of tournament in detail.
4. Define and classify 'Fixture'. Draw a league fixture for 16 teams.
5. Write down the method of preparing fixture in knock-out tournament in detail.
6. What do you mean by knock-out tournament? Draw a fixture of 21 teams on knock-out.
7. What do you mean by single knock-out tournament ? Discuss its merits and demerits. And also, briefly explain the method of removing its drawbacks.
8. Enlist various types of knock-out/elimination Tournament. Draw a knock-out fixture of 12 teams.
9. What do you understand by league/round robin tournaments ? Enlist their types, advantages and disadvantages.
10. What are intramurals ? Discuss the significance of intramurals for school children write down the objectives of intramurals.
11. Write down the objectives of extramural.
12. What do you mean by specific sports programmes ? Explain about any two of them in detail.

❑ ❑

2.1. BALANCED DIET AND NUTRITION

Nutrition may be defined as the science of food and its relationship to health. Human beings, like all other living things, need food to live, food supplies the energy for every action we undertake from eating banana to running a race. Food also provides material that our body needs to build up and repair its tissues and to regulate the functions of its organs and systems.

Nutrition also focuses on how diseases, conditions and problems related to health can be prevented or lessened with a healthy diet.

Balanced Diet

A diet may be defined as the sum of food consumed by a person or the other. We can say that :

"A diet that contains adequate amounts of all the necessary nutrients i.e., carbohydrates, proteins, fats, minerals, vitamins and water required for healthy growth and activity".

We should take a Balanced Diet

In other words, "balanced diet is defined as a diet which contains a variety of nutrients in such quantities and proportions that the need for energy, amino acids, vitamins, minerals, fats, carbohydrates and other nutrients is adequately met for maintaining health, vitality and general well-being and also make a small provision for extra nutrients to withstand short duration of leanness." Diet varies from individual to individual.

Why is it Important to Have a Balanced Diet ?

1. **It promotes growth and development of healthy body :** A well-balanced diet helps the body to grow and maintain proper functions. It also provides energy for the various activities of the body. It also replaces worn out tissues. Therefore, it is very important especially for growing children and adolescents.

2. **It prevents diseases and infections :** Balanced diet helps our body to fight many diseases and infections. When the body receives enough nutrients, the immune system functions well, which prevents infections, reduces the risk of chronic diseases and also promotes good mental function, boosts energy, with enhancement of memory.

3. **It helps control weight :** Eating a balanced diet helps people to maintain proper weight, which includes reducing the risk for either obesity or under nutrition. This is very important for the athlete.

Nutrition

Nutrients are organic and inorganic compound contained in food. There are about 50 different nutrients, which are normally supplied through the foods we eat. Each nutrient has specific function in the body. Most natural foods contain more than one nutrient.

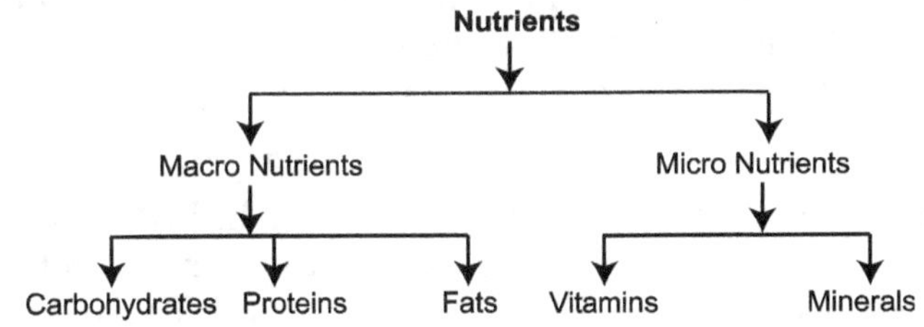

Types of Nutrients

There are two types of nutrients :

1. Macro nutrients   2. Micro nutrients

Macro Nutrients

The nutrients that are needed in large amounts are called **macro nutrients**. They provide energy and are required for growth, metabolism, and for other body functions. They are of three types :

1. Carbohydrates   2. Proteins   3. Fats

Carbohydrates

Carbohydrates are the main source of energy for all activities. They provide quick energy to the body and are not stored in the body for long. The ratio of carbohydrates is increased in endurance events or activities. In carbohydrates the ratio of hydrogen and oxygen is 2 : 1.

There are two main types of carbohydrates, *i.e.,* **simple carbohydrates** and **complex carbohydrates**. Simple carbohydrates are sweet, crystalline and soluble in water. These are called sugars. Glucose, fructose, galactose, and sucrose are simple carbohydrates. Complex carbohydrates are not sweet, not crystalline and insoluble in water. Their energy content is higher than sugar but it is released slowly. Starch, dextrin, glycogen, cellulose are the complex carbohydrates or polysaccharides.

Functions of Carbohydrates :

1. Carbohydrates provide the body with a source of fuel and energy that is required to carry out daily activities and exercise.
2. Our body needs a constant supply of energy to function properly and lack of carbohydrates in the diet can cause tiredness or fatigue, poor mental function and lack of endurance and stamina.
3. Carbohydrates are also important for the proper functioning of our brain, heart, muscles, kidneys, nervous system and digestive system.
4. Carbohydrates can be stored in the muscles and liver and later used for getting energy.
5. Fiber, which is also a form of carbohydrate, is essential for the elimination of waste materials and toxins from the body and helps to keep the intestines disease free and clean.

Proteins

The word Protein is derived from the Greek word "proteios", which means "of prime importance". Proteins are essential nutrients for the human body. They are the building blocks of body. These are complex organic compounds. The basic structure of proteins is a chain of amino acids that contain carbon, oxygen, hydro-gen, nitrogen and sulphur also. The presence of nitrogen differentiates proteins from carbohydrates and fats. Proteins are composed of 23 amino acids, 9 of them cannot be synthesized by the body and therefore must be provided in foods, rest others can be synthesized by the body. If proteins are not taken in proper amount, it can cause their deficiency disease named *marasmus* and *kwashiorkor* in children.

Functions of proteins :

1. Proteins are required for growth (especially important for children, teens, and pregnant women) and repairing of body tissues (including muscles).
2. Essential body processes such as water balancing, nutrient transport, and muscle contractions require protein to function.
3. Enzymes, used for digestion, protection, and immunity, are made of protein.
4. Protein is a source of energy, when carbohydrates are not available.
5. Protein helps keep the skin, hair, and nails healthy.
6. Protein, like most other essential nutrients, is absolutely crucial for overall good health.

Fats

Fats are organic compounds that are made up of carbon, hydrogen, and oxygen. Fats in food are found in several forms, including saturated, monounsaturated, and polyunsaturated. Fats belong to a group of substances called lipids, and come in liquid or solid form. Fats also has many other important functions in the body, and a moderate amount is needed in the diet for good health. Too much fat or too much of the wrong type of fat can be unhealthy. The body uses fat as a fuel source, and fat is the major storage form of energy in the body.

Functions of fats :

1. Fats are the most concentrated source of energy.
2. Fats are essential for the proper functioning of the body. Fats provide essential fatty acids, which are not prepared inside the body and must be obtained from food. These are important for controlling inflammation, blood clotting, and brain development.
3. Fat serves as the storage substance for the body's extra calories. It fills the fat cells (adipose tissue) that help insulate the body.
4. Fats help the body to absorb the vitamins A, D, E, and K through the bloodstream and in the production of hormones.
5. Fats also provide taste, consistency, and stability to foods.
6. Fats also help in normal growth and development as also in maintaining cell membranes and providing cushioning for the organs.

Micro Nutrients

The nutrients that are needed in very less amounts are called **micro nutrients**. Its amount may vary from a fraction of a milligram to several grams. These are vitamins and minerals.

Vitamins

Vitamins are organic compounds, which are an essential part of our diet. Without an adequate amount of vitamins, a deficiency will occur. Vitamins are naturally found in the foods that we consume except for Vitamin D and Vitamin K, which the body can produce. A well-balanced diet is often enough to meet the vitamin needs of healthy individuals.

The thirteen different kinds of vitamins required for effective functioning of the human body may be classified into two categories namely,

1. Fat soluble vitamins : The fat soluble vitamins are those vitamins that are soluble in fat. These include vitamin A, D, E and K stored in the liver and in body fat.

2. Water soluble vitamins : The water soluble vitamins are those vitamins that are soluble in water. Vitamin C and members of the Vitamin B complex are water soluble vitamins.

Fat soluble vitamins

Vitamin 'A'

Vitamin A (retinol) is a fat soluble vitamin that acts as an antioxidant, which may help in reducing the risk of cancer. Vitamin A, like many other nutrients, is found in different forms. The Vitamin A that we obtain from animal products is called retinoids and can be used by our body without any modification. The form of Vitamin A found in fruits and vegetables is known as carotenoids. The most common type of carotenoid is β-carotene (beta carotene). These carotenoids are used to build the type of Vitamin A used by our body.

Since Vitamin A is fat soluble, it is not needed daily, in large quantities. Fat soluble vitamins are stored in the body in organs such as the liver. Most of the Vitamin A that we consume goes to the liver to be stored until it is needed by another part of the body. Therefore, our intake of Vitamin A should be enough to replenish our liver stores.

Sources : Carrots, collard greens, spinach, broccoli, eggs, whole milk, cream, cod liver oil, cereals, oranges/juice, dried apricots, etc.

Deficiency : Deficiency of this vitamin can cause night blindness (inability to see in dim light), keratomalacia (eye disorder that results in a dry cornea) and also irregular growth of teeth.

Vitamin 'D'

Vitamin D is different from other essential vitamins because our own bodies can manufacture it with sunlight exposure. It is also known as the "Sunshine Vitamin". The main function of Vitamin D is to regulate the absorption of calcium and phosphorus in our bones and aid in cell-to-cell communication throughout the body. Five forms of vitamin D has been discovered, vitamin D1, D2, D3, D4, D5. The two forms that seem to matter to humans the most are Vitamins D2 (ergocalciferol) and D3 (cholecalciferol).

Sources : Sunlight (Vitamin D is synthesized by the body by the action of UV rays of sunlight on 7-dehydrocholesterol, which is stored in large abundance in the skin. Exposure to UV rays is critical: these can be filtered off by air pollution. Dark-skinned races such as Negros, also suffer from these disadvantages because black skin can filter off up to 95 per cent of UV rays).

Foods (Vitamin D occurs only in foods of animal origin. Liver, egg yolk, butter and cheese, and some species of fish contain useful amounts. Fish liver oils, although not considered to be a food, are the richest source of Vitamin D).

Deficiency : Its deficiency may cause *rickets* in which bones of children get softened and become prone to fractures and deformity and *osteomalacia* which occurs mainly in women, especially during pregnancy and lactation when requirements of Vitamin D are increased.

Vitamin 'E'

Vitamin E (tocopherol) is a powerful, fat-soluble antioxidant that helps to protect cell membranes against the damage caused by free radicals, prevents the oxidation of LDL cholesterol and is also important in the formation of red blood cells (RBC), thus essential for blood coagulation. It also helps in curing cancer and prevent from heart attacks.

Source : Vegetable oils (such as wheat, gram, sunflower, corn and soyabean oils), Nuts (such as almonds, peanuts, and hazelnuts/filberts), seeds (such as sunflower seeds), etc.

Deficiency : Deficiency is uncommon; may cause degeneration of muscles, paralysis and slow growth. It might cause mild hemolytic anemia in newborns.

Vitamin 'K'

The name Vitamin K is derived from the German word "Koagulations vitamin." Vitamin K occurs in atleast two major forms- Vitamin K_1 and Vitamin K_2.

Vitamin K is known as the clotting vitamin, because without it, blood would not clot. It also helps in prevention of haemorrhage. Some studies suggest that it helps to maintain strong bones in the elderly.

Sources : Green leafy vegetables, such as kale, spinach, turnip greens, mustard greens, green leaf lettuce. Vegetables such as broccoli, cauliflower and cabbage, fish, liver, meat, eggs etc.

Deficiency : Its deficiency causes excessive bleeding from wounds and anemia.

Water Soluble Vitamins

Vitamins, which dissolve in water are called water soluble vitamins. They are carried to the body's tissues but are not stored in the body. They are found in plant and animal foods or dietary supplements and must be taken in daily. Vitamin C and members of the Vitamin B complex are water-soluble.

'B'-complex

Eight of the water-soluble vitamins are known as the vitamin B-complex group : thiamin (vitamin B_1), riboflavin (vitamin B_2), niacin (vitamin B_3), pantothenic acid (vitamin B_5), vitamin B_6 (biotin), folic acid (vitamin B_9) and Cobalamin (vitamin B_{12}). The B vitamins are widely distributed in foods, and their influence is felt in many parts of the body. They function as coenzymes that help the body obtain energy from food. The B vitamins are also important for normal appetite, good vision, healthy skin, nervous system, and red blood cell formation.

Vitamin 'B_1' (Thiamin)

Vitamin B_1 or Thiamin, helps to release energy from foods, promotes normal appetite, and is important in maintaining proper nervous system function.

Sources : Thiamin is found in :
1. Enriched and fortified whole grain products such as bread, cereals, rice, pasta, and flour.
2. Beef liver and pork.
3. Dried milk.
4. Egg.
5. Legumes and peas.
6. Nuts and seeds.

Dairy products, fruits, and vegetables are not very high in thiamin, but when eaten in large amounts, they become a significant source

Deficiency : Symptoms of deficiency include mental confusion, muscle weakness, wasting, water retention (edema), impaired growth, and the disease known as beri-beri.

Vitamin 'B_2' (Riboflavin)

Riboflavin, or Vitamin B_2, helps to release energy from foods, promotes good vision, and healthy skin. It also helps to convert the amino acid tryptophan (which makes up protein) into niacin.

Sources : Dairy products, Eggs, Green leafy vegetables, Lean meats, Legumes Milk, Nut Breads, Cereals, etc.

Breads and cereals are often fortified with riboflavin. Fortified means the vitamin has been added to the food.

Because riboflavin is destroyed by exposure to light, foods with riboflavin should not be stored in glass containers that are exposed to light.

Deficiency : Symptoms of deficiency include cracks at the corners of the mouth, dermatitis on nose and lips, light sensitivity, cataract, and a sore, red tongue.

Vitamin 'B_3' (Niacin)

Vitamin B_3, or niacin, works with other b-complex vitamins to metabolize food and provide energy for the body. Niacin was first discovered by researchers looking for a link between diet and the disease pellagra. They determined that pellagra was common among people with a corn-based diet, and they were able to treat the disease with nicotinic acid, a form of niacin. Vitamin B_3 or Niacin, is involved in energy production, normal enzyme function, digestion, promoting normal appetite, healthy skin, and nerves. Niacin is used for high cholesterol. It is also used along with other treatments for circulation problems, migraine headache, dizziness, and to reduce the diarrhea associated with cholera. Niacin is also used for preventing positive urine drug screens in people who take illegal drugs.

Sources : Sources include liver, fish, poultry, meat, peanuts, enriched grain products, etc.

Deficiency : A deficiency of niacin causes Pellagra. The symptoms include digestive problems, inflamed skin and mental impairment. Large doses of niacin can cause increased blood sugar (glucose) level, Liver damage, Peptic ulcers, Skin rashes, etc.

Vitamin 'B_6' (Pyridoxine)

Vitamin B_6, also known as Pyridoxine is a water-soluble vitamin as it dissolves in water. It is a key factor in protein and glucose metabolism, as well as in the formation of hemoglobin. Hemoglobin is a component of red blood cells - it carries oxygen. Vitamin B_6 is also involved in keeping the lymph nodes, thymus and spleen, healthy.

Sources : Sources include pork, meats, whole grains and cereals, legumes, and green leafy vegetables.

Deficiency : Deficiency symptoms include skin disorders, dermatitis, and cracks at the corners of the mouth, anemia, kidney stones, and nausea. Vitamin B_6 deficiency in infants can cause mental confusion.

Folate (Folic Acid, Folacin)

Folate, also known as folic acid or folcin, aids in protein metabolism promoting red blood cell formation, and for women who may get pregnant, it is really important. Getting enough folic acid before and during pregnancy can prevent major birth defects of our body. It helps the body make healthy new cells. Folate may also play a role in controlling homocysteine levels, thus reducing the risk for coronary heart disease.

Sources : Sources include dark green leafy vegetables, meats, fish, whole grains, fortified grains and cereals legumes and citrus fruits.

Folate deficiency may cause :

1. Folate deficiency affects cell growth and protein production, which can lead to overall impaired growth.
2. Deficiency symptoms also include anemia and diarrhea.
3. A folate deficiency in women who are pregnant or of child bearing age may result in the delivery of a baby with neural tube defects such as spina bifida.
4. Gray hair
5. Mouth ulcers
6. Peptic ulcer
7. Swollen tongue (glossitis)

Vitamin 'B₁₂' (Cobalamin)

Vitamin B_{12} is also known as Cobalamin, aids in the building of genetic material, production of normal red blood cells, and maintenance of the nervous system.

Sources : Vitamin B_{12} can only be found in foods of animal origin such as meats, liver, kidney, fish, eggs, milk and milk products, oysters, and shellfish. Some fortified foods may contain vitamin B_{12}.

Deficiency : Vitamin B_{12} deficiency can be slow to develop, causing symptoms to appear gradually and intensify over time.

It can also come on relatively quickly. Given the array of symptoms it can cause, the condition can be overlooked or confused with something else. Symptoms may include :

1. Strange sensations, numbness, or tingling in the hands, legs, or feet
2. Difficulty in walking (staggering, balance problems)
3. Anemia
4. A swollen, inflamed tongue
5. Yellowed skin (jaundice)
6. Difficulty in thinking and reasoning (cognitive difficulties), or memory loss
7. Paranoia or hallucinations
8. Weakness
9. Fatigue

Biotin

Biotin is a coenzyme and a B vitamin and is also known as Vitamin H. As a supplement, biotin is sometimes used for diabetes, brittle nails, and other conditions. Biotin plays a key role in the body. Biotin helps release energy from carbohydrates and aids in the metabolism of fats, proteins and carbohydrates from food. It supports the health of the skin, nerves, digestive tract, metabolism, and cells. Biotin may also help to treat some types of nerve pathology, such as the peripheral neuropathy that can result from kidney failure or diabetes.

Sources : Sources of Biotin include liver, kidney, egg yolk, milk, most fresh vegetables, yeast breads and cereals. Intestinal bacteria also make biotin.

Deficiency : Biotin deficiency is uncommon under normal circumstances, but symptoms include fatigue, loss of appetite, nausea, vomiting, depression, muscle pains, heart abnormalities and anemia.

Pantothenic Acid

Pantothenic acid, also called Vitamin B_5, is one of eight B vitamins. All B vitamins help the body convert food (carbohydrates) into fuel (glucose), which is used to produce energy. B_5 is critical to the manufacture of red blood cells, as well as sex and stress-related hormones produced in the adrenal glands, small glands that sit atop the kidneys. Vitamin B_5 is also important in maintaining a healthy digestive tract, and it helps the body use other vitamins, particularly B_2 or riboflavin. It is sometimes called the "anti-stress" vitamin, but there is no real evidence whether it helps the body withstand stress.

Sources : Sources include liver, kidney, meats, egg yolk, whole grains, and legumes. Pantothenic Acid is also made by intestinal bacteria.

Deficiency : Pantothenic Acid deficiency is uncommon due to its wide availability in most foods.

Vitamin 'C'

Vitamin C is also called Ascorbic acid, which is a water soluble vitamin and cannot be stored in the body. Most plants and animals can produce their own vitamin C, but humans cannot. Vitamin C is needed for proper growth, development, and to heal wounds. It is used to make the collagen tissue for healthy teeth, gums, blood vessels and bones. Since vitamin C is a powerful antioxidant, it is also used to prevent damage to our bodies from toxicities and pollutants, such as cigarette smoke.

Sources : Good sources of vitamin C include oranges, grapefruits, lemons, limes, tomatoes, green and red peppers, strawberries, spinach, mangoes, winter squash, cantaloupe, broccoli and potatoes (sweet and white), etc.

Deficiency : Vitamin C deficiency is called scurvy. This was once a common and fatal disease among sailors who were unable to eat fresh fruits and vegetables for long periods of time. Scurvy usually starts with skin rashes and bleeding gums. The skin also becomes rough, scaly and dry.

Minerals

Minerals are important for your body to stay healthy. Our body uses minerals for many different purposes, including building bones, producing hormones and regulating our heartbeat.

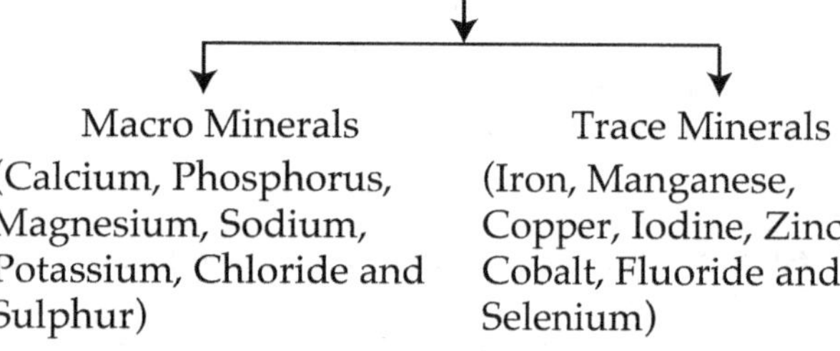

Types of Minerals

There are two kinds of minerals : macro minerals and trace minerals. Macro minerals are minerals that our body needs in large amounts. They include calcium, phosphorus, magnesium, sodium, potassium, chloride and sulphur. Our body needs just small amounts of trace minerals. These include iron, manganese, copper, iodine, zinc, cobalt, fluoride and selenium.

Macro Minerals

Calcium

Calcium is a necessary element which requires building and maintaining strong bones, teeth and healthy communication between the brain and various parts of the body and also for clotting of blood. Proper levels of calcium over a lifetime can help prevent osteoporosis. Calcium is found in milk and milk products and green leafy vegetables.

Phosphorus

Next to calcium, phosphorus is the most abundant mineral in the body. These two important nutrients work closely together to build strong bones and teeth. About 85% of phosphorus in the body can be found in bones and teeth, but it is also present in cells and tissues throughout the body. Phosphorus helps filter out waste in the kidneys and plays an essential role in how the body stores and uses energy. It also helps reduce muscle pain after a hard workout. Phosphorus is available in meat, eggs, fish and whole grains.

Magnesium

Magnesium is an essential mineral for human nutrition. Every organ in the body especially the heart, muscles, and kidneys need the mineral magnesium. It also contributes to the makeup of teeth and bones. Most important, it activates enzymes, contributes to energy production, and helps regulate calcium levels as well as copper, zinc, potassium, vitamin D, and other important nutrients in the body. Magnesium is available in meat, brown rice, beans and whole grains, etc.

Sodium

Sodium is an important mineral and electrolyte necessary for many functions in the body. It has an important role in maintaining water balance within cells, and is involved in proper functioning of both nerve impulses and muscles within the body. Along with potassium, sodium also plays a crucial role in blood pressure regulation. Sodium is only needed in small quantities, and the kidneys are responsible for excreting extra sodium from the body. It is found in common salt and also in meat and milk products.

Potassium

Potassium is an essential mineral and a major electrolyte found in the human body. It plays an important role in electrolyte regulation, nerve function, muscle control, and blood pressure. Potassium is found within all cells of the body, and the kidneys control its level. Primarily, potassium functions to regulate water and mineral balance throughout the body. Potassium works with sodium to maintain the body's normal blood pressure. Research suggests that increasing dietary potassium may provide a protective effect against high blood pressure by increasing the amount of sodium excreted from the body. A high potassium intake has also been linked to a reduced risk of death due to cardiovascular disease. Potassium is found in many foods, especially those of plant origin such as oranges, avocados, bananas, and tomatoes. Potassium can also be found in fish, meat, and dairy products.

Chloride

Chloride is a type of electrolyte. It works with other electrolytes such as potassium, sodium, and carbon dioxide (CO_2). These substances keep the proper balance of body fluids and maintain the body's acid-base balance. Chloride is needed to keep the proper balance of body fluids, muscle and nerve function. It is an essential part of digestive (stomach) juices. Chloride is found in table salt or sea salt as sodium chloride. It is also found in many vegetables. Foods with higher amounts of chloride include seaweed, rye, tomatoes, lettuce, celery, and olives. Chloride, together with potassium, is also found in most foods and is usually the main ingredient of salt substitutes.

Sulphur

Sulphur is a mineral that is present in every cell of the body. It plays a key role in liver metabolism and the function of the joint cartilage and keratin of the skin & hair. It is also critical for metabolism and anti-oxidant defense systems that protect the aging patterns of the brain. Sulphur is readily available in protein foods-meats, fish, poultry, eggs, milk, and legumes are all good sources. Egg yolks are one of the better sources of sulphur. Other foods that contain this somewhat smelly mineral are onions, garlic, cabbage, brussels sprouts, and turnips. Nuts have some, as do kale, lettuce, kelp and other seaweed, and raspberries.

Trace Minerals

Iron

Iron is a mineral that our bodies need for many functions. For example, iron is part of hemoglobin, a protein which carries oxygen from our lungs throughout our bodies. It helps our muscles store and use oxygen. Iron is also a part of many other proteins and enzymes. Iron is found in meat, fish, liver, eggs, green vegetables, turnip, germinating wheat grains and yeast.

Manganese

Manganese is a mineral that is found in several foods including nuts, legumes, seeds, tea, whole grains, and leafy green vegetables. It is considered as an essential nutrient, because the body requires it to function properly. Manganese is used for prevention and treatment of manganese deficiency, a condition in which the body doesn't have enough manganese. It is also used for weak bones (osteoporosis), a type of "tired blood" (anemia) and symptoms of premenstrual syndrome (PMS).

Copper

Copper is an essential trace mineral present in all body tissues. It is helpful in red blood cells, connective tissues and nerve fibers formation and functioning. It is found in grains, nuts and chocolate.

Iodine

Iodine is a trace mineral, required by the body for the synthesis of the thyroid hormones, thyroxine (T_4) and triiodothyronine (T_3). T_4 contains 4 iodine atoms. When one of the iodine atoms is stripped off of T_4, it becomes T_3, with 3 iodine atoms remaining. Under normal circumstances, our body contains approximately 20 to 30 mg of iodine, most of which is stored in our thyroid gland, located in the front of your neck, just under our vocal chords. Smaller amounts of iodine are also found in lactating mammary glands, the stomach lining, salivary glands, and in the blood. Lack of enough iodine (deficiency) may occur in places that have iodine-poor soil. Many months of iodine deficiency in a person's diet may cause goiter or hypothyroidism. Without enough iodine, the thyroid cells and the thyroid gland become enlarged. Iodine is found in iodized salt, seafood and water.

Zinc

Zinc is an essential trace element for all forms of life. It is required for insulin production and also for functioning of male prostate, digestion and metabolism. It is available in meat, eggs and fish.

Cobalt

Cobalt is another essential mineral needed in very small amounts in the diet. It is an integral part of vitamin B_{12} (cobalamin), which supports red blood cell production and the formation of myelin nerve coverings. Some authorities do not consider cobalt to be essential as a separate nutrient, since it is needed primarily as a part of B_{12}, which is itself essential. Cobalt is available in meat, liver, kidney, clams, oysters, and milk all contain some cobalt. Ocean fish and sea vegetables have cobalt, but land vegetables have very little cobalt. Some cobalt is also available in legumes, spinach, cabbage, lettuce and pigs.

Fluoride

Fluoride is important to make the enamel of the teeth hard and prevents dental cavities. It is available in coffee, spinach, onion and tea.

Selenium

Selenium is a mineral found in the soil. Selenium naturally appears in water and some foods. While people only need a very small amount, selenium plays a key role in the metabolism. Selenium content of food is largely dependent on location and soil conditions, which vary widely. Good natural food sources of selenium include :

1. Nuts, like brazil nuts and walnuts

2. Many fresh and saltwater fish, like tuna, cod, red snapper, and herring

3. Beef and poultry

4. Grains

2.2. NUTRITIVE AND NON-NUTRITIVE COMPONENTS OF DIET

Nutritive Components of Diet

Food contains a variety of nutritional components that can be categorized by macronutrients and micronutrients. Macronutrients are nutrients needed in large amounts that provide calories or energy for growth, metabolism and other functions in our body. The macronutrients include carbohydrates, fats and proteins. Micronutrients, such as vitamins, minerals and antioxidants, are involved with cellular and chemical processes in our body. Nutritive components are discussed earlier in this chapter.

Non-nutritive Components of Diet

Foods contain some compounds that are not classified within the basic nutrient groups. All sorts of substances can be found in food-natural, intentional, and unintentional. Non-nutritive components of diet means, components, which do not add or supply energy or calories. Non-nutritive components of diet are discussed below :

1. Colour compounds : Food is made more appetizing and interesting to be hold by the wide spectrum of colours made possible through pigments. Most natural pigments are found in fruits and vegetables, the colours of foods from animal products and grains are less varied and bright. The dominant pigments found in plants are carotenoids (orange-yellow), chlorophyll (green), and flavonoids (blue, cream and red).

Although foods of animal origin are less colorful, even meat varies in color depending on its stage of maturity. When first sliced with a knife, a cut of beef is purplish red from the presence of a pigment called myoglobin. As it is exposed to air, the myoglobin combines with oxygen to turn the meat a bright color. The meat then turns grayish brown during cooking when the protein holding the pigment becomes denatured. Cured meats present and altogether different scenario as added nitrites, compounds which are used as a preservative, react with the myoglobin to cause the meat to be a red color, which converts to pink (denatured protein) when cooked. Milk appears white as light reflects off the colloidal dispersion of milk protein. The yellowish hue of cream comes from carotene and riboflavin (vitamin B_2). Carotene, a fat soluble pigment, is also the substance that gives butter its yellow color.

2. Flavor compounds : The flavors in foods are derived from nutrient and non-nutrient compounds. These are sometimes too numerous to track as the source of a specific flavor. Among the non-nutrient compounds in foods are the organic acids that determine whether foods are acidic or basic. An acidic pH in foods not only contributes to a sour taste, but the color of fruit juices, the hue of chocolate in baked products, and the release of carbon dioxide in a flour mixture. An alkaline pH contributes a bitter taste and soapy mouth feel to foods.

3. Plant compounds : In addition to colour and flavor compounds, some plants contain other non-nutritive substances that, when ingested, may have either beneficial or harmful effects. Many of the possible anti-carcinogens, or compounds that inhibit cancer, come from plants. In particular, phyto-chemicals, a special group of substances found in plants, appear to have a protective effect against cancer. One class of these phytochemicals, called indoles, is found in vegetables such as cabbage, cauliflower, kale, kohlrabi, mustard greens, swiss chard, and collards. Laboratory animals given indoles and then exposed to carcinogens developed fewer tumors than animals exposed to the same carcinogens, but not given indoles.

2.3. EATING FOR WEIGHT CONTROL – A HEALTHY WEIGHT, THE PITFALLS OF DIETING, FOOD INTOLERANCE AND FOOD MYTHS

Meaning of Healthy Weight

Reaching and maintaining a healthy weight is important for overall health and can help us prevent and control many diseases and conditions. If we are overweight or obese, we are at higher risk of developing serious health problems, including heart disease, high blood pressure, type 2 diabetes, gallstones, breathing problems, and certain cancers. That is why, maintaining a healthy weight is so important. It helps us lower our risk for developing these problems, helps us feel good about ourselves, and gives us more energy to enjoy life. Now the question is, What is healthy body weight? It may be defined, as *"A healthy body weight is a weight at which the body functions most efficiently and effectively, affording maximum protection against illness and disease"*.

A healthy body weight is more about function and well being than socially defined beauty standards. There are usually two popular methods to find out or calculate the healthy weight *i.e.,* Height and weight chart and BMI (Body mass index).

Height (Feet/Metres)	Men Weight (kgs)	Women Weight (kgs)
5'-0" or 1.523 m	50.8 - 54.4	50.8 - 54.4
5'-1" or 1.548 m	51.7 - 55.3	51.7 - 55.3
5'-2" or 1.574 m	56.3 - 60.3	53.1 - 56.7
5'-3" or 1.599 m	57.6 - 61.7	54.4 - 58.1
5'-4" or 1.624 m	58.9 - 63.5	56.3 - 59.9
5'-5" or 1.650 m	60.8 - 65.3	57.6 - 61.2
5'-6" or 1.675 m	61.6 - 66.7	58.9 - 63.5
5'-7" or 1.700 m	64.0 - 68.5	60.8 - 65.3
5'-8" or 1.726 m	65.8 - 70.8	62.2 - 66.7
5'-9" or 1.751 m	67.6 - 72.6	64.0 - 68.5
5'-10" or 1.777 m	69.4 - 74.4	65.8 - 70.3
5'-11" or 1.802 m	71.2 - 76.2	67.1 - 71.7
6'-0" or 1.827 m	73.0 - 78.5	68.5 - 73.9
6'-1" or 1.853 m	73.3 - 80.7	73.3 - 80.7
6'-2" or 1.878 m	77.6 - 83.5	77.6 - 83.5
6'-3" or 1.904 m	79.8 - 85.9	79.8 - 85.9

Standard Height and Weight for Indian Men and Women

Method to calculate BMI : Body Mass Index (BMI) is a simple index of weight for height that is commonly used to classify underweight, overweight and obesity in adults.

This is calculated in the following way :

BMI = Weight in kilograms / (Height in meters)

The BMI can be compared with the following ranges :

BMI	Category
16—18.5	Underweight
18.5—24.9	Normal
25—29.9	Overweight
30—34.9	Obesity Class I
35—39.9	Obesity Class II
Above 40	Obesity Class III

Methods To Control Healthy Body Weight

In today's world of healthcare, everybody wants to be healthy. But, many people don't know how to be healthy. We need to follow a combination of strategies like a perfect diet, quit all our bad habits, do proper exercise and so on to control our weight and thus to be healthy.

1. Know about own weight : The first step in controlling weight is to know about own body weight. A scientific method to check whether we are overweight, underweight or normal weight is by calculating Body Mass Index (BMI). So, before choosing the methods for controlling our weight, we should calculate our BMI. By calculation of BMI we can know that are we under weight, right-weight and overweight or obese.

2. Make a weight control plan : We should have a clear weight control plan before starting the actual control. It should be attainable and reasonable. If we just plan something that we can never attain and if we try to do it, then we will completely fail and even quit the program. So, if we really want to control our weight, just start with a realistic plan. Then for many people, weight control means avoiding food. This is utter blunder. We control our weight to maintain our health. But, avoiding food will really have an opposite effect. If our body does not get the nutrition required at proper level, then we can become ill. So, what is actually required to control body weight is following a proper diet (it should be nutritionally balanced, with reduced calorie), active life style and exercises.

3. Drink water : Soda, juice and other beverages have an excess of sugar, and calories. Water helps re-hydrate our body and is calorie-free. Our bodies can fight off illness and stay energized when well hydrated.

4. Eat at least five servings of fruits and vege-tables a day : Fruits and vegetables are low in calories and filled with many vitamins, minerals and fiber to prevent illness and disease. Fiber is essential because it fills up and helps keep us satisfied longer.

5. Have breakfast : Breakfast will jumpstart our metabolism for the day, helping our body burn calories and giving us energy throughout the day. Individuals who skip breakfast tend to eat up to 500 calories more per day than those who plan a satisfying morning meal. As a result, people who skip breakfast usually have a high body mass index (BMI) than those who eat breakfast.

6. Eat until you are no longer hungry : Many people eat out of boredom, loneliness, stress, or eat until they are uncomfortably full. Avoid these eating pitfalls by eating slowly and paying attention to when our body is no longer hungry.

7. Exercise and physical activity : Another important aspect in weight control is proper exercise. Proper exercise is a must for maintaining good health. We need to choose the exercise, which is suitable for our current physical condition. There are many different exercise methods like walking, cycling, swimming, skipping and weight lifting and so on. Regular physical activity burns calories and builds muscle — both of which help us look and feel good and keep weight off. Walking the family dog, cycling to school, and doing other things that increase our daily level of activity can all make a difference. If we want to burn more calories, increase the intensity of workout and add some strength exercises to build muscle.

8. Reduce screen time : One reason people get less exercise these days is because of an increase in "screen time" — the amount of time spent watching TV, working at the computer, using mobile devices, or playing video games. If we are with friends at the mall, we are getting more exercise than if we are chatting with them from our room.

9. Avoid alcohol, smoking and drugs : Always, it should be kept in the mind that alcohol, smoking and drugs always tend to increase weight. Alcohol is directly absorbed from the stomach into the blood stream and with no trouble stored as fat; it is also applicable in case of smoking and drugs. Thus, it is advisable never to use such things, if one wants to lose weight.

10. Behavior modification : Behavior modification is an important component of a weight management program. Behavior modification consists of three components : self-monitoring, stimulus control and self-reward.

Self-monitoring involves a daily record of place and time of food intake, as well as accompanying thoughts and feelings. It helps to identify the physical and emotional conditions under which the person craves food. Once these conditions have been identified, they must be modified and controlled. This is called Stimulus Control. Successful stimulus control should be rewarded. Self-reward includes techniques of rewarding self for eating control.

The Pitfalls of Dieting

In today's scenario, everyone desires to remain slim and trim. Those overweight or obese individuals also crave to reduce or drop weight. For reducing weight, they use various methods of weight loss. Majority of them stick on to dieting to drop weight. Dieting produces good results or success in the beginning, but later on, after early success it adds on more weight. Studies pointed out that 90% of the dieters increase all of their weight back and sometimes more than that. We all are conscious that shedding or losing weight is not as easy as it sounds. Eating less and exercising more to burn calories is much more advisable. We are aware of this logical fact but it is hard to put into practice. There are some pitfalls/ dangers of dieting that keep us away from losing or reducing weight which are discussed below :

1. Extreme reduction of calories : The intakes of calories are reduced tremendously for dieting. Studies indicated that to meet all the nutritional requirements of an individual, 1800 calories a day is not sufficient. If more intake of calories is reduced, it produces a havoc weight loss, which can be harmful for an individual. It certainly lowers the metabolism and as result of it, the body weight is not reduced appropriately.

2. Restriction on some nutrients : Some nutrients like carbohydrates and fats are normally restricted in dieting. Practically our body wants all types of nutrients. If intake of all the nutrients in desired amounts is not done then proper functioning of the body will be impaired.

3. Skipping meals : If one has good metabolic rate, it is a reality that, one can maintain or lose weight. If metabolic rate is low, weight is gained very easily. Therefore, if meals are skipped, it lowers the metabolism to preserve energy. Hence, skipping meals work against the weight loss plans. Studies revealed if one meal is skipped, there is more calories intake at the next meal.

4. Intake of calories through drinking : To lose weight, most probably more stress is on not to eat more and not on what to drink. As a fact, beverages, coffee with cream and sugar, sweetened juices and sodas really add to weight gain.

5. Underestimating the calories : Most of the individuals who go on dieting regularly underestimate the number of calories they consume. Hence, it is necessary to be more conscious about the number of calories one takes in the diet.

6. Intake of labeled foods : The majority of the individuals who go on dieting generally go for such food products that bear the label 'lean', 'sugar free', 'low calories' or 'no fat or fat free'. This type of labeled food is not always the finest for losing the weight; it does not meet all the necessities of the body. The differences are insignificant in case of three chocolate biscuits containing 140 calories whereas three non-fat cookies containing 120 calories. Therefore, when one eats such a product he/she thinks that these products have few calories leading one to eat more as result of it one intakes more calories.

7. Not performing exercise : If an individual does not perform exercise and goes on dieting, it will not work properly. In place of losing weight, possibility will be likely to gain weight. As a fact, exercise has a constructive effect on metabolism and also helps to burn some additional calories. Exercise increases metabolic rate which in due course reduces body weight. Hence, dieting is helpful if one performs exercise along with it.

Food Intolerance

Food intolerance is more widespread than food allergy. Food intolerance is a term used broadly for wide-ranging physiological responses related with a particular food. In easy words, food intolerance means the individual elements of particular foods that cannot be correctly processed and absorbed by the digestive system. Various individuals can bear a reasonable amount of the food but if eaten in a large amount or too often, they get symptoms of food intolerance because the body cannot tolerate unlimited amounts. Food intolerance comes on slowly not regularly, it is not life threatening.

Causes of Food Intolerance

Partial or complete absence of activity of the enzymes accountable for breaking down or absorbing the food elements, causes food intolerance. These deficiencies are generally by birth. Occasionally, food intolerance can be diet associated or can be due to illness.

Symptoms of Food Intolerance

Food intolerance can be prominent by nausea, stomach pain, diarrhea, vomiting, flatulence, gas, cramps, heartburn, headaches, irritability or nervousness etc.

Management of Food Intolerance

Minor changes in diet by individuals can be tried to keep out food causing apparent reactions. At times it can be managed effectively in such a way with no requirement for specialized aid. If an individual is not able to find out which food is causing trouble, then one should seek experts or medical guidance. Direction and supervision can also be provided by the general practitioner to help in diagnosis and management. Fructose intolerance therapy, lactose intolerance therapy and histamine intolerance therapy can be applied for managing food intolerance.

Food Myths

Numerous food myths exist not only in India but also all over the world as they sound like they could be true. Individuals usually get confused with questions like what to eat, when to eat and how often to eat. These days, we have logical information and on the basis of that information we should not consider or believe in food myths. The most common food myths, which are still widespread in our modern society, are discussed below :

1. Potatoes make you fat : Previously, people used to believe that carbohydrate loaded foods such as rice and potato etc., increases body weight. Thus for losing or reducing weight, carbohydrate rich foods were eliminated from diet. At present we know that carbohydrates are the body's ideal energy source, potatoes do not automatically make one fat. As a result, there is no problem to consume potatoes in moderate quantity.

2. Fat-free products will help you in losing weight : Consumption of fat-free labeled products can lead to weight loss. In fact these foods have more calories. In comparison to other regular food approximately, these products have same number of calories or may be slightly less. In addition, most of the individuals eat more quantity of labeled food under the misconception that it consists of fewer calories. Nevertheless intake of these foods gives a total of more calories, which can cause weight gain.

3. Eggs increase cholesterol levels so avoid them : There is no distrust that eggs are excellent source of health. Various nutrients such as protein, vitamin A, B, D, zinc, iron, calcium and phosphorus, etc. are provided by eggs. It is as per on a daily basis requirement of cholesterol by the bodies. Thus, if one egg is taken daily there will be no trouble in cholesterol level.

4. Drinking while eating makes you fat : The genuine fact following this misconception is that enzymes and their digestive juices will be diluted by drinking water while eating. It slows down the digestion which might lead to excess body fat. In contrast, there is a logical fact that drinking water while eating improves digestion.

5. Do not take milk immediately after eating fish : The majority of the individuals believe that one should not drink milk instantly after intake of fish as it might make one sick. Several individuals think that spots can become visible on the skin. As a fact, there is no logical reason in drinking milk instantaneously after eating fish. Practically, these products may be taken together; there is no problem at all.

6. Starve yourself if you want to lose weight : Ingestion of a good diet is more vital than not to eat when one is on a weight loss program. Such food items are included in the diet which suppresses appetite and increases metabolism so that one does not eat too much. Thus, starving is not required for the one who wants to lose weight.

7. There are some magical foods that cause weight loss : Some foods, such as grapefruit or kelp, are said to burn off body fat. This is not true. Dietary fibre comes closest to fulfilling this wish, because it provides a feeling of 'fullness' with minimal kilo joules. High-fibre foods such as fruits, vegetables, whole grain breads and cereals, and legumes also tend to be low in fat.

8. Exercise makes you to eat more : Hunger might increase due to exercise as it burns calories. Studies conducted in this area have not revealed that the individuals doing exercise consume more calories, than those who do not exercise. Thus, there is no certainty in this declaration.

EXERCISES

Multiple Choice Questions

1. When should athletes hydrate ?
   (a) 2 hour before the exercise
   (b) 15 min. before the exercise
   (c) During the exercise
   (d) After the exercise

2. What is the primary nutrient that contributes to bone health ?
   (a) Iron   (b) Potassium
   (c) Calcium   (d) Phosphorus

3. Which of the following food helps in sustaining prolonged routine of exercise ?
   (a) Fats   (b) Proteins
   (c) Vitamins   (d) Carbohydrates

4. Before running a marathon, the trainer asked the athlete to monitor her vitamins and mineral levels to fight against free radicals which ?
   (a) Damages cell
   (b) Limit conversion of proteins in ATP
   (c) Reduce effectiveness of electrolytes
   (d) Destroy stored glucose

5. Rahul is a top tri-athlete, getting ready to race. In order to avoid digestive issues during the event and remain a front runner, he should limit his intake of which nutrient(s) in his pre-competition meal ?
   (a) Proteins   (b) Fluids
   (c) Carbohydrates   (d) Vitamins and mineral

6. A weightlifter whould include .... in his/her diet.
   (a) Carbohydrate   (b) Protein
   (c) Fat   (d) Vitamins and minerals

7. Heavy dose of vitamin A causes :
   (a) Swelling of feet   (b) Digestive problems
   (c) Liver damage   (d) None of these

8. Fats contain :
   (a) Carbon, hydrogen and oxygen
   (b) Carbon, hydrogen and nitrogen
   (c) Carbon and oxygen
   (d) Hydrogen and oxygen

9. Vitamin E deficiency causes :
   (a) Anaemia
   (b) Weakness in heart and muscle
   (c) Both (a) and (b)
   (d) None of the above

10. Name the scale that measures the rise in blood glucose due to a particular type of food.
   (a) BMI   (b) Glycemic Index
   (c) Both (a) and (b)   (d) None of these

Very Short Answer Type Questions (Carrying 1 mark)

1. What is nutrition ?
2. What are carbohydrates ?
3. What is protein ?
4. What is vitamin ?
5. What do you mean by healthy weight ?
6. What do you mean by food intolerance ?
7. What do you mean by food myths ?
8. What are nutrients ?
9. Define balanced diet in brief.
10. What do you mean by macro and micro-nutrients?
11. Briefly explain about vitamins.
12. Enlist the forms of vitamin B.
13. What are nutritive and non-nutritive components of diet ?
14. What do you mean by purging and non-purging bulimia ?

Short Answer Type Questions (Carrying 3 marks)

1. What are macro nutrients ? Explain about any two macro nutrients.

2. What are micro nutrients ? Discuss about macro and micro minerals.

3. What is a vitamin ? Explain about fat soluble and water soluble vitamins.

4. What do you mean by water soluble vitamins ? Explain about them in brief.

5. Discuss minerals.

6. Enlist the non-nutritive components of diet. Explain about any two components of diet.

7. Discuss pitfalls of dieting.

8. Write down the causes and management of food intolerance.

9. What do you mean by food myths ? List four food myths.

Long Answer Type Questions (Carrying 5 marks)

1. What are the nutrients ? Describe in brief.

2. What is Protein ? Discuss its functions and source.

3. "Vitamins are essential for our metabolic process". What happens if our diet is devoid of vitamins ?

4. What do you mean by nutritive components of diet ? Explain about any three of them in detail.

5. "Diet can enhance the performance of a sportsperson". Discuss.

6. What is healthy body weight ? Write down the methods to control healthy body weight.

❑❑

3.1. ASANAS AS PREVENTIVE MEASURES

In this present time, the demand and requirement of the medicine as preventive means are prominently recognized. Sophisticated diagnostic tools, drugs and high level of specialization are making medical treatment more expensive. There are numerous public health measures which are initiated to prevent severe diseases among which eradication of plague and small pox have proved most successful. Even with providing mass education on health by demonstrating clean surroundings, childhood immunizations and family planning, prevention from infectious diseases, early and regular screening for diseases like tuberculosis and cancer were not enough. Yet taking serious health measures the illnesses are on the rise.

Considering and treating these severe problems related to health of human being this is where yoga sets in. Patanjali's sutras put down the foundation for a healthy life. It gives the guidelines for healthy living as it is known that the mind is the root of the majority of physical problems.

The Yoga Vasishta states that the path of events is as according to our thought, as for instance, it is known that smoking is injurious to health even though the consumption and manufacturing of cigarettes continues proving that the body is not in need of nicotine it is only the mind which needs.

To preserve health, great emphasis is made on practicing yoga as it prevents illness and offers healthy mind and body. Generally, asana means a 'sitting condition' or 'position' of the body, which contributes to the steadiness of the body and mind and a sense of well-being. The word 'Asana' has been derived from the Sanskrit root 'as' meaning 'to sit'. Maharishi Patanjali defines asana as "Sthiram-sukhamasanam" (PYS II : 46). It means, a state of being in which one can remain steady, calm, quiet, and comfortable, physically and mentally.

A habitual practice of physical exercises has been shown preventive values in preventing any medical disorders to occur like coronary, respiratory and orthopedic problems. Any kinds of practice of exercises are good, but asanas are considered to be the idyllic as they are completely non-invasive, gentle and soothing. It is indeed true that practicing yoga has provided chances to experience better body alignment and posture, stronger muscular strength, increased self-awareness, greater flexibility, lower blood pressure, and more pliant to mental and physical capacities.

Apart from the physical benefits, asanas assist in establishing the holistic well-being providing mental and even spiritual benefits. Practicing asanas regularly helps to manage stress and develops coping skills, leading to reach a more positive outlook on life in an individual. Regular practice of asanas creates mental clarity and calmness, increases body awareness, relieves chronic stress patterns, relaxes the mind, centers attention and sharpens concentration. For majority of people regular practice of asanas are the best procedures to keep the body fit and healthy, it makes us ready for facing any critical conditions and have several kinds of positive effects.

The effectiveness of practicing asanas is usually on the tissues and muscles of the human body. As the tissues collectively make the organs to function, the health of the tissues is most vital to keep up healthy. The supply of proper nourishment of the body mostly depends on the quality of food intake, power of digestion and absorption of the digestive systems. Practicing asanas gives a gentle massage to the digestive systems making the abdomen muscles strong and elastic helping to preserve health.

The supply of oxygen to the body is totally reliant on the respiratory system. Practicing asanas increases the flow of oxygen throughout the body as well. The efficiency of the respiratory system increases with continuous deep and rhythmic breathe. Additionally, the body turns to be healthy and remain fresh when oxygen-rich blood is supplied to every tissue of the body.

The muscular system gets strengthened with the practice of asanas. The asana gives proper attention to each and every body part to ensure giving a good stretch aiming in achieving strength and thus promoting health. It is technically established that the practice of asanas brings about maximum contractibility of the complete muscular system and as a result raise tones and increases efficiency of the muscles.

Habitual practice of asana offers many benefits to the practitioners. It helps to control the mind, exercise the spine, maintaining the efficiency of nervous system and even improving the functioning of the endocrine glands. It is a known fact that asanas have a vital impact on the Endocrine systems which gets rejuvenated by the regular practice of asanas. The endocrine glands secrete hormones and these secretions are powerful enough to control the functioning of nervous system and maintaining the physiological balance of the human body. Asanas are the most probable natural ways to regulate activities of these glands. Yogic practices aims at maintaining and restoring the internal secretions to their normality and providing good health to the practitioners.

In context to the endocrine system, yogic practices attempts to avoid any diseases to occur and make sure establishing physiological harmony in the human body. The pituitary gland controlled by the brain directly, is said to be the master gland as it regulates secretion in all the other endocrine glands. The most beneficial asana for this gland is **Sirshasana.** The control unit of the basal metabolic rate, growth and cell processes is the thyroid and parathyoid glands, are benefitted with the asana named **Sarvangasana.** The pancreatic and adrenal glands secrete affecting the emotional and physical state strongly and are greatly helped by the practice of **Mayurasana.**

The systematic study of the yogic science initiates with the practice of asanas, in way can be referred as the postural training along with the rhythmic breathing and the process of nerve purification provides ample of preventive measures including rejuvenation of various systems, elimination of unwanted wastes from the body and providing absolute rest to all vital organs as well.

Currently, the awareness about asana and other yogic practices as the preventive measures has spread significantly among people. Yoga has become the need of the hour as huge number of people has started opting fitness and wholesome healthcare. As the schools, colleges, universities and corporate offices in both government and private sectors have initiated and introduced wellness programmes to promote yogic practices that unifies the body, mind and soul. Thus, the habitual practice of yoga helps in dealing with a numerous diseases or health problems consequential from hormonal disharmony or dysfunction into complete state of healthy body and mind.

3.2. OBESITY : PROCEDURE, BENEFITS AND CONTRAINDICATIONS FOR VAJRASANA, HASTASANA, TRIKONASANA AND ARDH-MATSYENDRASANA

Obesity is common in all ages and also in both sexes. It is caused due to metabolic disorders which results in excessive accumulation of fat. It creates lots of stress on the circulatory, respiratory and excretory system due to the extra surface area of the body leading to severe health problems like coronary heart diseases, diabetes mellitus and hypertension etc. The physical work capacity reduces due to obesity.

Causes of Obesity

Main causes of obesity are as follows :

1. Overeating/eating without having appetite,
2. Calorie intake is more than calorie expenditure,
3. Sedentary lifestyle,
4. Lack of exercises.

Symptoms of Obesity

The following are the most common symptoms that indicate obesity.

1. Weight is excessively high,
2. Inertia,
3. Lethargy,
4. No willingness for work,
5. Flabby abdomen,
6. Accumulated fat around abdomen, neck, hips and thighs,
7. Anxiety, depression,
8. Other psychosomatic diseases may be associated such as hypertension, diabetes.

Some useful asanas for obesity are mentioned below :

Procedure, Benefits and Contraindications for Vajrasana, Hastasana, Trikonasana, Ardh-matsyendrasana

Vajrasana

Vajrasana is one of the best yoga poses for beginners as it is a simple 'sitting asana'. The term Vajrasana is a combination of two Sanskrit words

'Vajra' meaning thunderbolt and 'asana' meaning 'posture'.

Procedure of vajrasana :

1. Sit erect in long sitting position.
2. Fold the legs back one by one along the same thighs.
3. Bring the knees close to each other.
4. Bring the big toes together and separate the heels.
5. Lower the buttocks onto the inside surface of the feet with the heels touching the sides of the hips.
6. Keep the right palm on right knee and left palm on left knee.
7. Sit erect and look straight.
8. Breathe normally and fix the attention on the flow of air passing in and out of nostrils.

Benefits of vajrasana :

1. Vajrasana loosens the stiff joints and ligaments of the legs and strengthens the hips, thighs, knees, calves, ankles and toes.
2. It calms the mind and brings stability in mind.
3. Improved digestion is one of the main benefits of Vajrasana. Sitting in this pose helps with digestion and gets rid of constipation and other stomach disorders.
4. Those suffering from gas problems can practice immediately after lunch or dinner.
5. It helps in combating acidity.
6. It helps to reduce obesity.
7. It improves blood circulation throughout the body.
8. Vajrasana acts as a pain killer for individuals suffering from arthritis.
9. It cures urinary problems.

10. It is also preferred for meditation and concentration.

Contraindications of vajrasana :

1. Individual suffering from joint pain should avoid this asana.
2. Individual who have any spinal column ailments, especially on the lower vertebrae should not attempt this pose.
3. Individual with hernia, intestinal ulcers and other diseases of the small and large intestine should practice this pose under expert guidance and advice.

Trikonasana

As the name suggests, 'Trikona' means 'triangle' in Sanskrit, where 'Tri' signifies 'three' and 'Kona' denoting 'angle'. It is a position where the straight leg and the floor between the feet look a lot like the three sides of a triangle in this asana.

Procedure of trikonasana :

1. Stand erect. Now, keep distance between your legs about 3 to 4 feet.
2. Extend arms at the shoulder level.
3. Inhale and raise the right arm by the side of the head.
4. Now, bend the right arms with exhaling towards the left side by keeping the body weight equally on both the feet. The right arm should become parallel to the ground.
5. Maintain the position as per the comfort with normal breathing and come to the original position by inhaling.
6. Do the same procedure with the left arm.

Benefits of trikonasana :

1. Trikonasana gives a powerful lateral stretch and rotary twist to the whole vertebral column and keeps it flexible. All the lateral ligaments and muscles supporting the vertebrae are brought into play while executing the movements.
2. It helps to correct the shoulder alignment.
3. It helps to reduce neck, knees and shoulders stiffness.
4. This asana relieves gastritis, backache, indigestion, flatulence and acidity.
5. It helps to relieve constipation by invigorating the peristaltic movement of the bowels.
6. This asana relieves lower back pain.
7. This asana reduces excess fat in the abdomen, waist and hips.
8. It helps to reduce obesity.
9. It stimulates the nervous system and alleviates nervous depression.
10. This asana stimulates thymus and the adrenal glands.
11. It massages the abdominal and pelvic organs.

Contraindications of trikonasana :

1. Avoid performing this asana if suffering from severe back pain.
2. Those suffering from migraine should avoid performing this asana.
3. This asana should be avoided if suffering from diarrhea, high blood pressure, neck and back injuries.
4. Individuals with Cervical spondylosis should perform it with proper safety measures.
5. One should avoid looking at floor in the final stage if experiencing dizziness.
6. Pregnant women should avoid practice of this asana.

Ardh-matsyendrasana

This asana known as Ardh-matsyendrasana as it does not require the entire technique of the full matsyendrasana. The full matsyendrasana was invented by Matsyendra, one of the pioneer of Yoga. Ardh-matsyendrasana (Half Spinal Twist) is an important series of asanas for spinal health.

Procedure of Ardh-matsyendrasana :

1. Sit erect in a long sitting position.
2. Bend the right leg placing it flat on the floor on the outer side of the left knee.
3. Place the toes of the right foot facing in forward direction.

4. Bring the foot around the right buttock by bending the left leg making sure that the outer edge of the foot remains in contact with the floor.
5. Through the gap between the chest and the right knee pass the left arm by placing it beside the outer side of the right leg.
6. Grip the ankle with the left hand and make sure the right knee is kept close to the left armpit.
7. Make sure to sit up straight and erect as possible.
8. Raising the right arm in front of the body and keep gazing at the fingertips.
9. Slowly twist to the right, simultaneously moving the arm, trunk and head.
10. Make use of the left arm as a lever aligned with the right leg so as to twist the trunk as far as possible with no using the back muscles.
11. Look over the right shoulder by following the tips of the right hand fingers with a gaze.
12. Avoid straining the back too much.
13. The right elbow should be bent by placing the arm around the back of the waist.
14. The back of the right hand should warp around the left side of the waist.
15. On the other hand, it can be placed as high as probable between the shoulder blades with the fingers pointing up as the arm position enforces the straightness of the spine.
16. Reverse the movements to come out of the asana.
17. Do the same procedure with other side.

Benefits of ardh-matsyendrasana :

1. Ardh-matsyendrasana helps to loosen the joints at the hips, shoulder, neck and also releases stiffness.

2. This asana stimulate heart, kidneys, liver, spleen and lungs.

3. It helps to relieve fatigue, sciatica, backache and menstrual discomfort. It also helps to cure a slipped disc.

4. It helps to releases excess toxins and heat from tissues and organs.

5. This asana increases the elasticity of the spine.

6. It helps to open the chest and increases the oxygen supply to the lungs.

7. It helps to relieve stiffness and back pain between the vertebrae.

8. This asana twisting the abdominal organs, therefore increasing the digestive juices and increasing the functioning of the digestive system.

9. This asana helps to massage and stimulate the pancreas, and thus, helps those suffering from diabetes.

10. It helps to regulate the secretion of both adrenalin and bile.

11. This asana also helps to cure urinary tract infections.

Contraindications of ardh-matsyendrasana :

1. Individuals, who have recently undergone abdominal, heart or brain surgeries, should not practice Ardh-matsyendrasana.

2. Individual with a hernia or peptic ulcers must do this asana carefully and under the supervision of yoga teacher.

3. Individual with severe spinal problems should avoid and those with mild slipped disc can benefit but in severe cases it should be avoided.

4. During the pregnancy and menstruation, women should avoid practice of this asana.

3.3. DIABETES : PROCEDURE, BENEFITS AND CONTRAINDICATION FOR BHUJANGASANA, PASCHIMOTTA-NASANA, PAVAN MUKTASANA AND ARDH-MATSYENDRASANA

The word diabetes is derived from the Greek word 'diabaineine', which means a tubular organ that takes-in or expels water, in other way known as excessive urine discharge disease. Diabetes is known to be as a metabolism disorder. As metabolism is the way our bodies use digested food for production of energy and growth. The majority of the food we eat is broken down into glucose which is a form of sugar and the main source of fuel in our body. A diabetic person has a condition in which the quantity of glucose in the blood gets elevated known as hyperglycemia. This is caused because the body is not able to produce enough insulin, produces no insulin or has cells that do not act properly in response to the insulin produced by the pancreas. This results in too much glucose building in the blood which ultimately passes out of the body in urine. Accordingly, even though the glucose level is high in blood the cells do not get essential energy and growth requirements.

Types of Diabetes

There are three main types of diabetes. These are as follows :

1. Type 1 diabetes : Type 1 diabetes is sometimes called insulin-dependent, immune-mediated or juvenile-onset diabetes. It is caused by an auto-immune reaction where the body's defence system attacks the insulin-producing cells. The reason why this occurs is not fully understood. People with type 1 diabetes produce very little or no insulin. The disease can affect people of any age, but usually occurs in children or young adults. People with this form of diabetes need injections of insulin every day in order to control the levels of glucose in their blood. If people with type 1 diabetes do not have access to insulin, they will die.

2. Type 2 diabetes : Type 2 diabetes is sometimes called non-insulin dependent diabetes or adult-onset diabetes, and accounts for at least 90% of all cases of diabetes. It is characterized by insulin resistance and relative insulin deficiency, either of which may be present at the time that diabetes becomes clinically manifest. The diagnosis of type 2 diabetes usually occurs after the age of 40 but can occur earlier, especially in populations with high diabetes prevalence. Type 2 diabetes can remain undetected for many years and the diagnosis is often made from associated complications or incidentally through an abnormal blood or urine glucose test. It is often, but not always, associated with obesity, which itself can cause insulin resistance and lead to elevated blood glucose levels.

3. Gestational diabetes mellitus (GDM) : Gestational diabetes mellitus (GDM) is a form of diabetes consisting of high blood glucose levels during pregnancy. It develops in one in 25 pregnancies worldwide and is associated with complications in the period immediately before and after birth. GDM usually disappears after pregnancy but women with GDM and their offspring are at an increased risk of developing type 2 diabetes later in life. Approximately half of women with a history of GDM go on to develop type 2 diabetes within five to ten years after delivery.

Causes of Diabetes

Most commonly understood causes are:

1. Heredity.
2. Obesity.
3. Mental and emotional stress and strain.
4. Prolonged anxiety and conflict.
5. Sedentary lifestyle.
6. Lack of physical activity and wrong food habits.

Symptoms of Diabetes

Common warning symptoms of diabetes are as follows :

1. Elevated blood sugar level (hyperglycemia).
2. Appearance of sugar in urine (glycosuria).
3. Excessive thirst and excessive fluid intake (medically termed as Polydipsia).
4. Increased hunger/appetite (Polyphagia) and craving for sugar.
5. Excessive urination and frequent trips to toilet - (Polyuria) - especially at night.
6. Loss of weight.
7. Sweating.
8. Sleeplessness or disturbed sleep.
9. Headache.
10. Vomiting.
11. Lack of concentration, confused mind, memory loss and irritability.
12. Numbness and tingling sensation in extremities or in any parts.
13. Dryness of skin (with or without itch) and mucous membrane (example - dryness of mouth).
14. Development of recurrent boils.
15. Delay in wound healing/gangrene formation.
16. Blurred vision.
17. Recurrent urinary tract infection.
18. Itching especially of the genitals.
19. Development of vascular problems - BP, Stroke, Vasculitis, etc.
20. Development of foot complaints due to numbness/prone to infection.
21. Weakness and debility.

Procedure, Benefits and Contradiction for Bhujangasana, Paschimottanasana, Pavan Muktasana, Ardh-matsyendrasana

Bhujangasana

Bhujanga means a cobra in Sanskrit. This asana known as Bhujangasana because the final position of it gives the appearance of a hooded snake under irritation with its neck dilated like a hood.

Procedure of bhujangasana :

1. Lie down on stomach with the legs straight, feet together and the soles of the feet uppermost.
2. Place the palms on the floor with the hands flat, by the side of the shoulders keeping the fingers together and pointing forward.
3. The arms should be placed close to the sides of the body in such a position so that the elbows point backward.
4. Place the forehead on the floor and keep the eyes closed.
5. The whole body should be relaxed particularly the lower back.
6. Gradually raise the head.
7. Smoothly lean the head backward in a way that the chin points forward compressing the back of the neck and subsequently raise the neck followed by the shoulders.
8. With the help of the back muscle straighten the elbows first and progressively the arm muscles to raise the trunk further to create an arch in the back.
9. The pubic bone remains in contact with the floor in the final position and the navel gets raised to a maximum of 3 cm.
10. In case the navel is raised too high the curve is created in the knees and not in the back.
11. Depending on the flexibility of the back, the arms may or may not be kept straight.
12. Maintain the final position.
13. In order to return to the straight position gradually release the upper back by bending the arms, lowering the navel, chest, shoulders and as a final point touch the forehead to the floor.

Benefits of bhujangasana :

1. In bhujangasana, the spine receives a good backward stretch. Each vertebra is pulled back and provided with rich blood supply. The nerves and muscles or the spine are rejuvenated.

2. It helps to relieves hunchback, back pain and lumbago. It also activates, strengthens and shapes the back muscles, particularly in the lumbar region.

3. This asana also gives a stretch to upper back (thoracic vertebrae), opens the chest and increases the lung capacity. It is also helpful to relieve chronic asthma problems.

4. This asana decreases stiffness of the lower back and increases flexibility.

5. It strengthens the arms and shoulders. It tones the buttock muscles.

6. It promotes a more smooth flow of prana (life energy) within the body.

7. This asana tones the ovaries and uterus, and helps in menstrual and some other gynaecological disorders.

8. Bhujangasana stimulates the appetite, alleviates constipation and is beneficial for all the abdominal organs, especially the liver and kidneys.

9. It helps to relieve stress and fatigue.

Contraindication of bhujangasana :

1. People should not practice Bhujangasana with severe problems of the spine, stomach ulcers and hernias.

2. This asana should be practiced with care for those with stiff backs and for those who are menstruating.

3. It is also not recommended for people with heart diseases. Should not be practiced by those who have undergone surgeries of spine, brain, abdomen, heart and lungs.

4. During the pregnancy and menstruation, women should avoid practice of this asana.

Paschimottanasana

This asana is known as Paschimottanasana because it stretches the posterior muscles of almost the whole body. In Sanskrit Paschima means the posterior and the root, Tan means to stretch; so it means stretching the posterior.

Procedure of paschimottanasana :

1. Sit erect in long sitting position, feet together; raise the arms over the head and stretch.

2. Gradually bend forward from the hips, descending the hands down the legs and trying to take hold of the big toes with the fingers and thumbs.

3. Move slowly without forcing or jerking and try to attain the final position.

4. Maintain the position for few seconds. Then subsequently relax the back and leg muscles, allowing them to stretch gently.

5. Keep the legs straight and utilize the arm muscles bending the elbows and lightly bringing the trunk towards the legs downward so as to maintain a firm grip on the toes, feet or legs.

6. Without straining try to touch the knees with the forehead.

7. Maintain the position for as long as comfortable and relax.

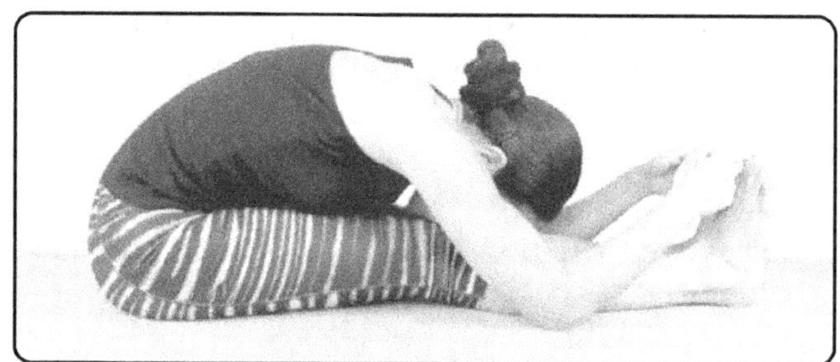

Benefits of paschimottanasana :

1. Paschimottanasana reduces fat of the abdomen.

2. This asana is a specific exercise for corpulence or obesity and for the enlargement of spleen and liver.

3. Paschimottanasana for the stimulation of abdominal viscera, such as kidneys, liver, pancreas, etc. It increases the peristalsis of the bowels. Peristalsis is the vermicular movement of the bowels or intestines by which food and faecal matter are pushed from one portion of the bowels to another.

4. This asana relieves constipation, removes sluggishness of liver, dyspepsia, belching and gastritis.

5. Lumbago or stiff back and all sorts of myalgia and other diseases of the back muscles are cured. This asana cures piles and diabetes also.

6. The muscles remained toned up and are kept in a healthy and sound condition.

Contraindication of paschimottanasana :

1. Person suffering from slip disc or sciatica problem, asthma should avoid paschimottanasana.

2. Ulcer patient should not practice.

3. During the pregnancy women should avoid paschimottanasana.

Pawanmuktasana

Pawanamuktasana the name is derived from the Sanskrit word where 'pawana', means 'wind,' mukta, means 'to release' and asana denotes 'pose'. It is a curative pose which is effective in helping to release gas from the abdomen whilst massaging the complete back and spine.

Procedure of pawanmuktasana :

1. Lie on the back with the feet joined together and arms by the side of the body.

2. Inhale and while exhaling bring the right knee towards the chest and press the thigh on the abdomen with clasped hands.

3. Inhale again and while exhaling, lift the head and chest from the floor and touch the chin to the right knees.

4. Maintain the position and keep taking long and deep breaths in and out.

5. Next while exhaling come back to the ground and relax.

6. Perform this pose with the left leg and afterwards with both the legs together.

> **Note :** During exhalation increase the pressure on the chest by tightening the grip of the hands on the knee and during inhalation loosen the grip.

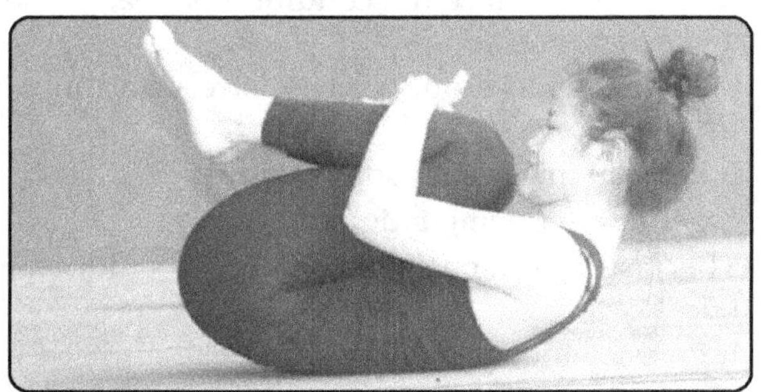

Benefits of pawanmuktasana :

1. Pawanmuktasana helps to improve the efficiency of the digestive system. It cures acidity problems, indigestion and constipation. Pawanamuktasana is very good for the abdominal organs.

2. Regular practice of pawanmuktasana cures gastric problems.

3. This asana provides a gentle massage to the organs of the digestive system. It helps to improve the efficiency of the internal organs, stimulates the nerves, and increases the circulation of blood to the internal organs of the body.

4. It is very helpful for people suffering from arthritis pain, heart problems, waist pain and acidity.

5. Pawanmukatasana strengthens the digestive system, purifies impure air, helps to control diabetes and high blood pressure.

6. It also loosens the spinal vertebrae and strengthens the muscles of the lower back.

7. The pawanamuktasana is also an excellent abdominal workout and helps tone and strengthen your core muscles.

8. It helps massage the reproductive organs and pelvic muscles and is considered to be good for menstrual disorders.

Contraindication of pawanmuktasana :

1. Pawanmukasana must be avoided if you have had an abdominal surgery recently. Also, people suffering from hernia or piles must avoid this asana.

2. People suffering from heart problems, hyper-acidity, high blood pressure, slip disc, hernia, back and neck problems, or a testicle disorder must avoid this asana.

3. During the pregnancy, women should avoid this asana.

Ardh-matsyendrasana

Mentioned earlier in this chapter.

3.4. ASTHMA : PROCEDURE, BENEFITS AND CONTRAINDICATIONS FOR SUKHASANA, CHAKRASANA, GOMUKHASANA, PARVATASANA, BHUJANGASANA, PASCHIMOTTASANA AND MATSYASANA

Asthma is a condition in which the airways become narrow and get swollen and producing extra mucus. Asthma makes breathing difficult and produces coughing and breathlessness. It can be a major problem interfering with daily activities which may be life-threatening as well.

Though asthma cannot be cured but its symptoms can be controlled. As asthma frequently changes with time, it is advisable that one remains in continuous consultation with the doctor to keep a track of the signs and symptoms so that proper timely adjustment with the treatment is done.

Causes of Asthma

1. Airborne substances namely pollen, mold spores, dust mites, pet dander or particles of cockroach waste causes asthma.
2. Respiratory infections, such as the common cold.
3. Physical activity (exercise-induced asthma).
4. Cold air.
5. Air pollutants and irritants, such as smoke.
6. Certain medications, including beta blockers, aspirin, ibuprofen (Advil, Motrin IB, others) and naproxen (Aleve).
7. Strong emotions and stress.
8. Sulfites and preservatives added to some types of foods and beverages, including shrimp, dried fruit, processed potatoes.
9. Gastroesophageal reflux disease (GERD), a condition in which stomach acids back up into the throat.

Symptoms of Asthma

1. Mucus is accumulated in the chest, bronchi are constricted and therefore the respiration is obstructed. It gives rise to dyspnoea or breathing trouble.
2. There is a spasm in chest.
3. There is sudden onset of cold symptoms like nasal congestion, nasal irritation, sneezing, and swollen nasal mucus membrane.
4. Person gasps for air.
5. Distress and anxiety increases due to laborious breathing.
6. Eosinophil count in blood increases.
7. Mucus secretion becomes thick and sticky.
8. The chest becomes hyper-expended and the lungs hyper-inflated. So the person has to do expiration with efforts. This becomes very short.
9. Inspiration is also shallow and short.
10. Bluish colour of mucus membranes indicates less oxygen supply.

Procedure, Benefits and Contraindications for Sukhasana, Chakrasana, Gomukhasana, Parvatasana, Bhujangasana, Paschimottasana and Matsyasana

Sukhasana

Sukhasana is derived from the Sanskrit word 'Sukham' which means 'comfort', 'pleasure', etc. This asana is also referred to be as the easy sitting pose and one of the simplest pose for meditation, suitable for all beginners and can be performed by all age groups.

Procedure of sukhasana :

1. Stretch out the legs while sitting on the floor.
2. Firstly, fold the left leg and tug it inside the right thigh.
3. Then fold the right leg and pull it inside the left thigh.
4. Place the hands on the knees.
5. Jnana or Chin mudra is used for meditation.
6. Keep the spine erect by sitting straight.
7. Breathe normally and relax the whole body.

Benefits of sukhasana :

1. Sukhasana stretches and lengthens the spine.
2. It helps to broaden the collarbones and chest.
3. This asana calms the mind.
4. It helps to enhance the condition of peacefulness and serenity.
5. Sukhasana kicks out anxiety, stress and mental tiredness.
6. It helps in improving body posture.
7. It helps in reducing fatigue.
8. This asana strengthens the back, ankles and knees.
9. It gives gentle massage to knees, calf muscles and thighs also.

Contraindication of sukhasana :

Though, the Sukhasana is very easy to perform for majority people irrespective of the ages and levels of physical fitness. Nevertheless, it is imperative that an individual avoid this asana in case of :

1. Recent or chronic knee injuries.
2. Hip injuries.
3. Inflammation in the knee or hip.
4. Spinal disc problems.

Chakrasana

Chakrasana, the name is derived from the Sanskrit words 'Chakra' signifying 'wheel' and 'asana' meaning 'pose' or 'seat'. Chakrasana is also known as the wheel pose which is performed by bending the body backward. The final position in this asana looks like a wheel.

Procedure of chakrasana :

1. Lie down on the back keeping the feet apart, bending the knees and placing the feet on the ground closer to the body.
2. Next bring the palms below the shoulders in a way that the fingers point towards the shoulders keeping the elbows shoulder width apart.
3. Press the palms steadily on the floor and inhale.
4. Lift the shoulders and elbow from the floor.
5. The feet should be remaining firm in contact with the floor.
6. Breathe in and lift the hips up.
7. The spine roll in should create a semi circular arch resembling a wheel.
8. Set straight the arms and legs out as much as possible in a way that the hips and chest are pushed up.
9. Maintain the position for at least 15-30 seconds.
10. For going back to initial position bend the elbows and lower the head and shoulders to the floor.
11. Gradually bend the knees and bring the spine and hips back to the floor and relax.

Benefits of chakrasana :

By performing this asana, we can get many benefits especially in the abdominal areas.

1. The lungs get more oxygen as the chest cavity increases.
2. It decreases the stress and tension of the body.
3. Eye sight becomes sharp.
4. Helps in increasing the elasticity of the spine.
5. It reduces the fat and tones up the muscles in abdominal area.
6. Improves the digestive process and functioning of reproductive organs.
7. Increases the strength of hands and the legs muscles.
8. It helps to maintain the metabolism normally.
9. It refreshes the brain by inducing the brain cells.
10. It helps in treating the uterine and menstrual problems in women.
11. It enhances the functioning of the liver, spleen and kidneys.
12. It helps in purifying the blood.
13. It cures the hernia.

Contraindication of chakrasana :

1. Avoid performing the asana if suffering from severe spinal column ailments like cervical and lumbar spondylitis.
2. Avoid doing the asana if the spine is stiff or rigid.
3. Women should avoid this asana during pregnancy.

Gomukhasana

The name gomukhasana is derived from the Sanskrit words 'Go' which means 'cow', and mukha means 'head' or 'mouth' and the 'asana' means 'pose'.

Procedure of gomukhasana :

1. Sit on the floor with legs extended forward.
2. Fold the left leg and rest it beneath the right buttocks.
3. Fold up the right leg and put it on top of the left thigh.
4. Both the knees should be placed one above the other.
5. Bend the left arm and take it behind the back.
6. Subsequently, bend the right arm and take it over the right shoulders and put it on the back. as far as it can go.
7. Then try to touch the both hands behind the back.
8. Expand the chest and keeping the trunk erect and pulling the head a little to the back.
9. Hold this position for as long as comfortable and keep breathing normally and deeply.

Benefits of gomukhasana :
1. This asana helps to make the back flexible.
2. Remove stiffness of the shoulders and back pain.
3. It helps in the treating back pain.
4. It stimulates the functioning of kidneys helping those suffering from diabetes.
5. It assists in developing the chest.
6. It helps treating sexual ailments.

Contraindication of gomukhasana:
1. Avoid performing this asana in case of neck, shoulders, knee and hip injury.
2. Avoid straining beyond the capabilities.
3. Do not tie up the hands behind the back.

Parvatasana-I

Parvatasana usually called as the mountain pose derived from the Sanskrit word 'Parvata' which means mountain and is a part of the surya namaskar. It looks like the body posture attained as in the 4th pose and the 9th pose in the Surya Namaskara. From the sides the posture looks like mountain which resulted in naming the asana as Parvatasana.

Procedure of parvatasana-I :
1. Ashwa Sanchalanasana or the equestrian pose is the initial position for Parvatasana.
2. From Ashwa Sanchalanasana, place the right and left foot together and straighten the bend leg by taking it backwards. Keep exhaling during this process.
3. Lift up the buttocks upwards.
4. Place both the arms be on the floor for supporting the body weight.
5. Lower the head in between the two arms the body making the shape of a triangle or like a mountain.

Benefits of parvatasana-I :
1. It helps to increase the strength of arms and legs muscles.
2. It tones the spinal nerves sending a good flow of blood to the spinal region.

Contraindication of parvatasana-I :
Cautions for inverted postures are applicable.

Parvatasana-II

Parvatasana is also called the mountain pose and one of the important seated yogic asana. It has vast benefits and is one important asana for weight loss.

Procedure of parvatasana-II :
1. Take position as in padmasana.
2. Stretch the arms sideward and gradually bring them over the head.
3. Place the palms touching each other.
4. Keep the elbows straight without bending by stretching the hands well.
5. Make sure that the spine is erect.

Benefits of parvatasana-II :
1. It helps in stretching the spine.
2. For those who are below 18 years, it helps to gain some height.
3. Helps in reducing extra fat in the back and waist areas.
4. It tones and stimulates the abdominal muscles and organs.
5. It treats the respiratory disorders including asthma.
6. It helps in reducing back pain.
7. It improves the concentration level.

Contraindication of parvatasana-II :
1. Avoid performing this asana if suffering from knee problems and reeling sensation.
2. If not able to do Padmasana then in that case can practice Parvatasana sitting in Sukhasana.

Bhujangasana

Bhujangasana mentioned earlier in this chapter.

Paschimottasana

Paschimottasana mentioned earlier in this chapter.

Matsyasana

Matsyasana is one of the beginners yoga pose inbuilt with lot of health benefits. In Sanskrit, Matsya means the fish. What that means Fish in a pond eats every dirt and clean the water. Likewise, Matsyasana purifies our blood and keeps us healthy. So it is called as Fish Pose.

Procedure of matsyasana :
1. Lie flat on the back keeping the legs together and placing the hands comfortably by the side of the body.
2. Place the palms underneath the hips in a way that the palms face the ground.
3. Then place the elbows close to the waist.
4. Cross the legs in such a manner that the feet cross each other in the middle keeping the thighs and knees flat on the floor.
5. Inhale and lift the chest and head making the crown touching the floor.
6. Ensure the weight of the body is on the elbows and not on the head.
7. Maintain the position as long as comfortable and keep breathing normally.
8. Breathe out and release the position by lifting the head initially and then resting the chest on the floor.
9. Straighten out the legs and relax.

Benefits of matsyasana :

Performing matsyasana helps in getting few amazing benefits mentioned as under :
1. As it stretches the chest and neck areas which help in releasing tension from those areas.
2. It helps it stimulating nutrient absorption.
3. It removes the respiratory problems.
4. It tones the pituitary, parathyroid and pineal glands.
5. It strengthens the muscles of the upper back and the back of the neck.
6. It stretches the hip flexors and the muscles between the ribs.
7. It helps in activating and toning the abdominal muscles.
8. It stretches the throat and the digestive organs as well.
9. It helps in improving posture.
10. It cures problems like constipation, respiratory ailments, mild backache, fatigue, anxiety and menstrual pain.

Contraindication of matsyasana :
1. Avoid performing the asana if suffering from high or low blood pressure.
2. Those suffering from insomnia and migraine should also avoid doing the asana.
3. It is strongly recommended to avoid doing the asana if having back injury.

3.5. HYPERTENSION : TADASANA, VAJRASANA, PAWANMUKTASANA, ARDHA CHAKRASANA, BHUJANGASANA AND SHAVASANA

High blood pressure (HBP) or hypertension signifies high tension or pressure in the arteries. Excessive emotional tension does not mean high blood pressure even though emotional tension and stress can provisionally increase blood pressure. Normal blood pressure is usually below 120/80; a blood pressure of 140/90 or above is considered high blood pressure and between 120/80 and 139/89 is called 'pre-hypertension'.

The rise of the systolic and/or diastolic blood pressure increases the danger of developing cardiac diseases, kidney diseases, hardening of the arteries, eye damage and stroke (brain damage). These complications of hypertension are frequently referred to as 'end-organ damage' as damage to these organs is the end product of suffering from long duration high blood pressure. As for this reason, the diagnosis of high blood pressure is vital so that efforts can be made to control blood pressure and put a stop to the complications.

Causes of Hypertension

1. Hectic and stress filled life style.
2. Unhealthy food habits.
3. Obesity.
4. Excessive consumption of liquors.
5. Smoking.
6. Over consumption of tea/coffee.
7. Insufficient rest and sleep.
8. Metabolic disorders.
9. Hardening of the arteries.
10. Excessive use of pain killers and other strong medicines.
11. Genetic disorders.
12. Over consumption of oily food and fast food.
13. High salt intake.
14. Lack of physical exercise.
15. Emotional and Physical stress.
16. Family history of hypertension.

Symptoms of Hypertension

1. Headache may be experienced due to elevation in blood pressure. Sometimes morning headaches can also be due to hypertension.
2. Dizziness is often experienced by people with high blood pressure. However, dizziness cannot always be treated as a symptom of hypertension. If dizziness is experienced, it is always wise to consult a medical practitioner.
3. Heart pain.
4. Palpitations.
5. Nosebleeds without particular reason might be a symptom of high blood pressure. It is better to check the blood pressure in such cases.
6. Difficulty in breathing.
7. Tinnitus (ringing or buzzing in the ears)
8. Blurred vision.
9. Frequent urination.

Procedure, Benefits and Contraindication for Tadasana, Ardh-matsyendrasana, Vakrasana, Shalabhasana and Bhujangasana

Tadasana

The word 'tadasana', comes from the two Sanskrit word 'tada' meaning 'mountain' and 'palm tree' and 'asana' means 'posture'. This asana is also known as mountain posture or palm tree posture. Tadasana provides physical and mental benefits to the practitioner along with propter stretch to the arms, chest, abdominal muscles, spine, knee, ankles, foot, etc. Regular practice of tadasana improves balance and strength.

Procedure of tadasana :

1. Stand erect, and place the legs slightly apart, with hands side by the body.
2. One should raise the hands straight in front up to arms and the palms should face each other.
3. Then bring the hands up straight forwards towards the sky, fingers pointing upward.
4. Slowly stand on the toes, and raise heels as much as possible. The body should stretch up as much as possible. Look slightly upward.
5. Feel the stretch in the body right from the feet to head. Hold the position for a few seconds.
6. While returning to the starting position, bring the heels on the ground first, and then bring down the hands also.

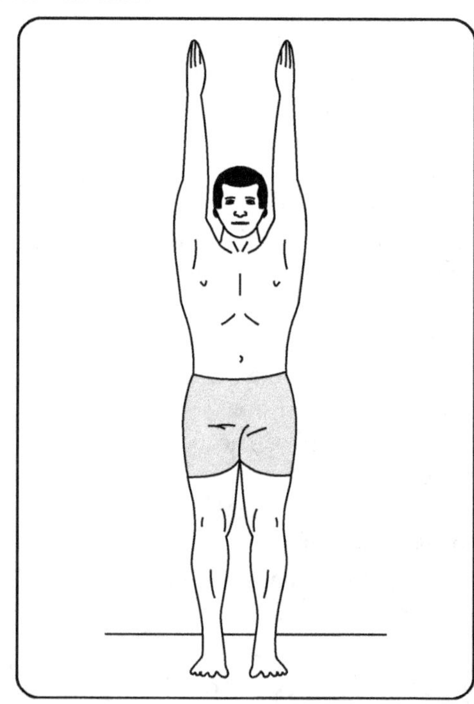

Benefits of tadasana :

The benefits of the tadasana are mentioned below:

1. Tadasana improves balance and concentration as well as increases alertness.
2. It helps to increase height of the growing children. Since it gives maximum stretch to the body from toes to fingers thus helpful for those who desire to increase his/her height.
3. It strengthens the nervous system and regulates respiratory and digestive functions.
4. Tadasana strengthenes the vertebral column and heart. It is helpfull in regulating the menstrual.
5. By practicing tadasana regularly, one can develop correct way of standing.
6. Tadasana helps to strengthen legs, knees, ankles, buttocks, lower abdomen, shoulders and neck. It also helps to reduce flat feet.
7. This asana helps in increasing the flexibility of the ankles, thighs and joints. It is effective in treating backache. It also alleviates symptoms of sciatica.
8. Tadasana is helpful in shedding extra fat from the different parts of the body.

Contraindications of tadasana :

1. People prone to low blood pressure, headache, insomnia, lightheaded and dizziness should avoid this asana.
2. Avoid this asana during pregnancy.

Vajrasana

Vajrasana is mentioned earlier in this chapter.

Pawanmuktasana

Pawanmuktasana is mentioned earlier in this chapter.

Ardhachakrasana

The name of the asana is derived from the Sanskrit word, where 'Ardha' means 'half', 'chakra' means 'wheel' and 'asana' denotes 'pose'. The pose is attained by standing and bending the body from trunk backward. This asana is also known as half moon or half wheel. It is effectual to strengthen the hands, chest, back and stomach so as to perform this asana.

Procedure of ardhachakrasana :

1. Keep distance between the feet and stand erect.
2. Keep arms by the side of the body.
3. Raise the arms over the head by keeping it straight and keep inhaling.

4. Next bend backward by keeping the hands, knees and elbows straight while breathing out.
5. Maintain the position for few seconds and keep breathing normal.
6. While breathing out release the pose to come back to the initial position.

Benefits of ardhachakrasana :

1. Increases flexibility.
2. Improves digestion process.
3. Helps in stretching the back, chest and hands.
4. Strengthens the back and reproductive system.

Contraindication of ardhachakrasana :

Individuals suffering from the following problems should avoid performing this asana :

1. High blood pressure.
2. Spine problems.
3. Hernia patient.
4. Most importantly pregnant women should not practice this asana.

Bhujangasana

This asana is already mentioned earlier in the chapter.

Shavasana

Shavasana is a yogic relaxation pose also known as the corpse pose. It is the simplest and the most important relaxation pose used in yoga. The name is derived from the Sanskrit words 'Shava' which means 'corpse' and 'Asana' signifying 'posture'. This asana is usually performed at the beginning and at the end of yoga practices. It is used as a resting pose in between other yogic asanas as well.

Procedure of shavasana :

1. Lie down in a sleeping pose keeping the back flat and legs separated.
2. Relax keeping the arms at the side and the palms facing up.
3. Breathe deeply and slowly through the nostrils and keep the eyes closed.
4. Consciously relax each part of the body starting from the head to feet.
5. In the process of inhalation and exhalation assume the body to be totally relaxed.
6. Practice the asana for 3-5 minutes. Those having good concentration level can practice for a longer duration of time.

Benefits of shavasana :

1. It helps in relaxing the whole body.
2. It helps in releasing stress, fatigue, depression and tension.
3. Concentration is improved.
4. Treats and cures insomnia.
5. Muscles get relaxed.
6. It helps in improving the mental health and calms the mind.
7. It stimulates blood circulation.
8. Extremely advantageous for those suffering from neurological problem, constipation, indigestion, diabetes and asthma.

Contraindications of shavasana :

The deep relaxation as well as decrease in nerve impulses will not be possible if fallen asleep while doing this asana, therefore avoid going to sleep while performing the asana.

3.6. BACK PAIN : TADASANA, ARDHA-MATSYENDRASANA, VAKRASANA, SHALABHASANA AND BHUJANGASANA

In case there is a dull, constant pain and tenderness in the back muscles, particularly in the lumber, lumbo-sacral or sacroiliac regions are commonly understood to be back pain. It is said to be back or 'low back pain' if any pain is experienced in the region.

Causes of Back Pain

Causes of back pain are varied such as :

1. Spondylosis.
2. Spondylitis.
3. Spondylisthesis.
4. Slipped disc.
5. Strain.
6. Sprain.
7. Spasm.
8. Weak abdominal or back muscles.
9. Lumbago.

The major cause of back pain is attaining faculty posture while sitting, standing, walking, sleeping and lifting weight. Back pain may also be caused due to structural changes due to accidental (spinal) injury and spinal fracture at various levels of spine. Backache can be caused because of the psychological problems *viz.,* anxiety, depression, mental tension, emotional stress, phobia, etc. Physical stress like heavy muscular work and exertion gives rise to backache as well. The other causes of back ache may be obesity, overweight, constipation and gas troubles.

Symptoms of Back Pain

1. Dull.
2. Continuous/Acute/unbearable pain.
3. Chronic/bearable/long lasting pain in the back.
4. Heaviness.
5. Numbness.
6. Tingling sensation in hand/leg.
7. Pain along the sciatic nerve.
8. Patient is unable to sit, stand walk and sleep comfortably.

Procedure, Benefits and Contraindications for Tadasana, Ardha-Matsyendrasana, Vakrasana, Shalabhasana and Bhujangasana

Tadasana

This asana is mentioned earlier in this chapter.

Ardha Matsyendrasana

This asana is mentioned earlier in this chapter.

Vakrasana

In Sanskrit, 'Vakra' means 'twisted'. As the spine is twisted in practicing this asana it is known to be as the Vakrasana or Twisted Pose. In this asana, the spine, muscles of hands, the legs and the back are stretched as the upper part of the body is fully turned and twisted.

Procedure of vakrasana :

1. Sit down on the ground stretching the legs forward.

2. Keep the hands alongside the thighs or buttocks.

3. Bend the right leg in a straight line and keep it stretched.

4. Keep the left foot raised upward after keeping it by the side of the right knee.

5. Keep inhaling and simultaneously raise the arms keeping the elbows straight at shoulder height.

6. Twist to the left, while exhaling and placing the right arm outside of the left knee holding the left ankle with the right hand.

7. Keep the palms on the floor by taking the left hand behind the back.

8. Try to look backward towards the left side.

9. Maintain the final position as long as comfortable.

10. At each stage the final position should be maintained while keeping the breathing natural.

11. Subsequently inhale and raise the right arm keeping the elbows straight at shoulder height.

12. Release the left twist while exhaling and place the right hand beside right buttock and left hand next to left buttock.

13. Take a deep breath and keep the body relaxed.

14. Perform the same from the other side again.

15. Practice should be done on both sides.

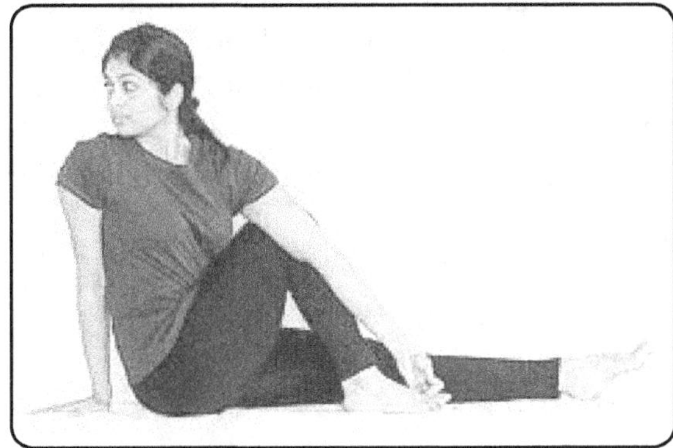

Benefits of vakrasana :

Vakrasana contributes in making the spine flexible. It is extremely useful in treating distended and congested liver and inactive kidneys. Vakrasana brings relief to patients suffering from hypertension, constipation and diabetes as well. Below given are the benefits of vakrasana :

1. It helps in curing constipation, liver and nervous weaknesses.

2. It helps in reducing the stiffness of the spine.

3. It is extremely helpful for treating kidneys and other stomach diseases.

4. Kundalini shakthi gets sublimated.

5. It helps in reducing back aches.

6. The elasticity of the spine is attained.

7. Fat on the either sides of the abdomen gets reduced as well.

8. Increases the elasticity of the spine and tones the spinal nerves.

9. Stretches the muscles.

10. Helps to get relief in stiffness of vertebrae.

11. Massages the abdominal organs.

12. Reduces belly fat.

13. Regulates the secretion of digestive juices useful for different digestive disorders.

14. Loosens the hip joints, relieving stiffness.

15. Flab on the lateral side of the abdomen gets reduced.

Contraindications of vakrasana :

1. Even though practicing this asana is easy, however Individuals with big belly may feel uncomfortable and may find difficult to place the hand to the other side of the knee; in that case they are recommended to place the hand on the knee or if it is not doable he/she can place it on the ground.

2. Patients suffering from hernia and ulcer should avoid this asana.

3. This asana should be avoided if having severe back pain.

4. Avoid this asana, if recently have undergone abdominal surgery.

Salabhasana

The word 'Salabha' signifies 'locust' or 'moth'. After attaining the final position of this asana it resembles like a locust hence it is known as Salabhasana.

Procedure of salabhasana :

1. Lie down on the ground by keeping the face downwards.

2. Place the hands by the side of the body with the palms turned up or the hands can be placed underneath the belly as well.

3. Slightly inhale and after that retain the breath until finishing the asana and then slowly exhale.

4. Keep the body tight and raise both the legs high in air simultaneously raise the head as done in Bhujangasana.

5. The soles of the feet should be turned up.

6. Lift up the legs, thighs and lower portion of the abdomen.

7. Maintain the final position for 5 to 30 seconds.

8. Then gradually bring the legs down.

9. Exhalation will be slow.

10. Repeat the asana for 6 to 7 times.

11. The asana can also be performed by keeping the hands near the chest with palms facing and touching the ground.

Benefits of salabhasana :

This asana serves as a counter-pose to Paschimottanasana, Halasana and Sarvangasana in which the spine is bending forward (anteriorly). This asana gives a posterior curving to the spine as the spine bends backwards. Salabhasana develops the lower half of the body and the lower extremities as well and increases the intra-abdominal pressure like Mayurasana. the benefits of this asana are as follows :

1. It tones up the muscles of the abdomen, thighs and legs.

2. It brings down the accumulated faecal matter of the stomach through the intestines very easily out of the body.

3. This asana is good for the abdomen.

4. It helps in relieving constipation.

5. It tones the abdominal visceral organs like liver, pancreas, kidneys, etc.

6. It helps in removing several diseases of the stomach and bowels.

7. It cures sluggishness of liver and rectifies hunchback.

8. It helps the lumbo-sacral bones to get toned up as the lumbago gets removed.

9. It helps to remove all forms of myalgia of the lumbar region (hips).

10. It improves the digestive process helping in having a very good appetite and removing indigestion.

Contraindications of salabhasana :

1. Avoid this asana if experiencing a headache or a migraine.

2. Avoid this asana if suffering from a neck or spinal injury.

3. This asana should be strictly avoided for pregnant women.

4. If having neck injury, while performing the asana it must be ensured one looks down at the floor and keeps the head in a neutral position.

Bhujangasana

This asana is mentioned earlier in this chapter.

EXERCISES

Multiple Choice Questions

1. Which one of the following is not the proved effect of Meditation ?
   (a) Decreases Stress
   (b) Normalies Blood Pressure
   (c) Normalises Blood Sugar
   (d) Increases Cortisol

2. Which of the following is one of the Five Principles of Yoga by Sivanandi ?
   (a) Tantra   (b) Jnana
   (c) Bhakti   (d) Savasana

3. The appropriate amount of time to wait after a meal before beginning a yoga practice is :
   (a) 30 min.   (b) 60 min.
   (c) 90 min.   (d) 2 hours

4. The purpose of Yoga as taught by the ancients is to attain :
   (a) Perfect health
   (b) Peace of mind
   (c) Stress relief
   (d) Enlightenment or Self-realisation

5. The half spinal twist pose is otherwise known as:
   (a) Ardha Matsendrasana
   (b) Pranayama
   (c) Paschimottasana
   (d) None of the above

6. Which of the following yogic asanas can help benefit people with diabetes ?
   (a) Bhujangasana   (b) Pawan Muktasana
   (c) Paschimottanasana (d) All of these

7. Name the disease that affects the airways.
   (a) Cardiac arrest   (b) Asthma
   (c) Wheezing   (d) None of these

8. Which of the following asana can help manage back pain ?
   (a) Tadasana   (b) Bhujangasana
   (c) Vakrasana   (d) All of these
9. Yoga asana recommended for obesity :
   (a) Vajrasana   (b) Hastasana
   (c) Both (a) and (b)   (d) None of these
10. Thunderbolt pose refers to which asana ?
   (a) Vajrasana
   (b) Hastasana
   (c) Trikonasana
   (d) Ardh Matsyendrasana

Very Short Answer Type Questions (Carrying 1 mark)

1. Mention any two causes of obesity.
2. From which word the name 'vajrasana' was derived ?
3. How does 'trikonasana' look like ?
4. State the benefits of doing the 'ardh-matsyendrasana'.
5. How many types of diabetes are there ?
6. State any three causes of diabetes.
7. What does the word 'bhujangasana' mean in Sanskrit ?
8. What is the meaning of 'pawanamuktasana' in Sanskrit ?
9. What is asthma ?
10. What is 'parvatasana' ?
11. State any two benefits of performing vakrasana.
12. List any two symptoms of obesity.
13. State any two contraindication of performing trikonasana.
14. What is the meaning of the word ardhmatsyendrasana and how does the asana look like ?
15. What is type 1 diabetes ?
16. What is gestational diabetes mellitus (GDM) ?
17. What is known to be as 'paschimottanasana' ?
18. Mention any two causes of asthma.
19. What is tadasana ?
20. How can shavasana help in regulating hypertension ?

Short Answer Type Questions (Carrying 3 marks)

1. Explain the causes and types of diabetes.
2. Explain the three symptoms and three causes of back pain.
3. Define the benefits and contraindications of shalabhasana.
4. Explain the benefits of gomukhasana.
5. What is the procedure doing of chakrasana ?
6. Define hypertension with its causes.
7. Explain the procedure of doing paschimottanasana ?
8. Mention three benefits of performing the vajrasana.
9. Write down any three symptoms of asthma.

Long Answer Type Questions (Carrying 5 marks)

1. 'Asana is a preventive measure'. Discuss in detail.
2. Discuss in detail about the procedure and contraindications of performing Hastasana, Trikonasana and Ardha matsyendrasana.
3. Elaborately discuss the procedure, benefits and contraindications of performing Bhujangasana, Paschimottanasana and Pawanmuktasana.
4. Discuss the procedure, benefits and contraindications for Sukhasana, Chakrasana, Gomukhasana and Matsyasana.
5. Discuss the hypertension its causes and symptoms and asanas useful for treating hypertension.
6. Write down detailed information about causes and symptoms of back pain along with the asanas useful in treating the back pain.

❑❑

PHYSICAL EDUCATION AND SPORTS FOR CWSN (Children with Special Needs - Divyang)

4.1. CONCEPT OF DISABILITY AND DISORDER

Historically, the disabled had to endure oppression at the hands of the elites and were marginalised and stigmatized in almost all societies throughout centuries. Constituting the most backward and neglected section of the population, people with disability are disadvantaged in all spheres of life—socially, educationally and economically. Thus, they have been historically deprived of their right to self-assertion, identity and development. Their victimisation is most prominent in the domains of education, employment and physical access to resources. Sometimes the terms like 'impairment' and 'handicap' are used interchangeably or synonymously along with 'disability', but these terms have different meanings. In 1980, the World Health Organization came up with the international classification of impairment, disability and handicap, to differentiate among them for proper usage of the terms. The WHO defined these concepts as follows :

Impairment explains *the loss or abnormality of psychological, physiological, or anatomical structure or function of the bodily systems or organ that may or may not be enduring, thus may or may not resulting in disability.*

Disability is a state in which an individual has limitation or restriction of an activity resulting from impairment.

Handicap is the disadvantage resulting from an impairment or disability creating a blockade in fulfilling a role or reaching a goal.

Conceptions of disability are culturally construed and are therefore highly contextual and subjective. According to 2001 census, 21.9 million people are disabled in India, constituting 2.13 per cent of the total population. Out of the 21,906,769 people with disabilities, 12,605,635 are males and 9,301,134 are females. The number includes persons with different types of disability including visual, hearing, speech, locomotor and mental disabilities. It has been observed that seventy five per cent of persons with disabilities are found to be living in rural areas, only 49 per cent of disabled population is literate and only 34 per cent among them have employment. Social rehabilitation has come to replace the initial emphasis on medical rehabilitation. The earlier medical model of rehabilitation did not adequately address the phenomena of disability as seen from the experiences of rural India. The disabled persons in villages are isolated and oppressed, denying them access to school, participating in family celebrations or working in fields. It is not the result of an individual's impairment, but the result of society's reaction to it. The individual's medical condition is not so much of a concern compared to the hostile reaction of the society which pushes them towards abject misery, poverty and extreme marginalization. It debars the disabled people from collective social activities and deprives them of their basic rights. Their presence is often considered unlucky in any kind of auspicious event, thus they are excluded from taking part in social celebrations, political decision making apparatus or in religious ceremonies. These people are less challenged by their individual medical impairments, and more disabled by the insensitivity of the society.

Disability

Disability poses as a significant public health problem in developing country like India. Its threat is most likely to increase in the coming years since the rate of non-communicable diseases has gone up along with changes in age structure, increase in life expectancy and lower mortality rate. A disability may be inherited since birth, or occurred / acquired during a person's lifetime.

'Disabilities are an umbrella term, covering impairments, activity limitations, and participation restrictions. Impairment is a problem in body function or structure; an activity limitation is a difficulty encountered by an

individual in executing a task or action; while a participation restriction is a problem experienced by an individual in involvement in life situations. Disability is thus not just a health problem. It is a complex phenomenon, reflecting the interaction between features of a person's body and features of the society in which he or she lives'.

—World Health Organisation

Impairment results from any kind of restriction or lack that limits the ability to perform an activity within the range or normal capacity of human beings. In other words, it could be identified as any kind of restriction in the normal or basic functions of human beings resulting from impairment. For instance, difficulties in performing basic activities like seeing, hearing, walking, writing or speaking. Thus, the term disability often serves as an umbrella term denoting impairments, activity limitation and participation restrictions.

There are people with disabilities in every community. Some people with disabilities lead their lives like any other person in the community. There are also those persons with disabilities who face severe problems in performing even the basic activities of life on their own. Experts say that 7 out of every 100 people suffer from a disability. They fail to lead a normal life without external assistance like other members of their family.

People with disabilities may experience a narrower margin of health, due to both poverty and social exclusion, and also as they are more vulnerable to secondary conditions, such as pressure sores or urinary tract infections. They are no different from non-disabled people when it comes to health needs – like immunization, cancer screening, etc. Unfortunately in most cases people with disabilities face obstacles and non-cooperation in accessing the health and rehabilitation services they need owing to their social and economic marginalization.

In sum, disability can be referred as the condition of an impairment that may be physical, cognitive, mental, sensory, emotional, developmental, or a combination of some or all of these.

Disorder

A disorder is referred to as a problem or illness affecting someone's mind or body. Disorder can be defined as a state of confusion resulting from mental or physical crisis that could be limiting, affecting or even interrupting normal function of a person. Any kind of derangement or abnormality of function in the body or mind can be termed as a disorder; causing an imbalance in the physical or mental state.

For certain type of disorders such as psychiatric, anxiety and personality disorders, it is a disruption in functions, structures, movements, senses or a combination of these. It could result from any internal factor such as genetic problem or embryonic failure in development or from exogenous factors such as exposure to poison, trauma, or any chronic disease.

4.2. TYPES OF DISABILITY, ITS CAUSES AND NATURE (COGNITIVE DISABILITY, INTELLECTUAL DISABILITY, PHYSICAL DISABILITY)

Numerous authors have discussed disability and its types in a varied way. Let us understand by discussing the different types of disability *i.e.,* the cognitive, intellectual and physical disability in a detailed manner.

Cognitive Disabilities

The term cognitive disability is used when someone has definite limitations in mental functioning and in skills such as communication, taking care of him or herself and other social skills. This issue leads the child to learn and develop more slowly than other normal child. Children having this disability take longer time learning to speak, walk and take care of their personal needs as well. The children with cognitive disabilities take longer time and there may be few things they cannot learn hence have trouble in learning in school.

Signs and Symptoms of Cognitive Disabilities

There are many signs and symptoms of cognitive disabilities. Children with cognitive disabilities may have below mentioned signs and symptoms :

1. Late in performing basic movements like sit up, crawl or walk than other children;

2. Difficulty in speaking and learning to talk lately.

3. Tendency to forget things.

4. Inability in paying for things.

5. Difficulty in understanding social rules.

6. Difficulty in solving problems.

7. Difficulty in thinking rationally.

Causes of Cognitive Disabilities

The most common causes of cognitive disabilities are discussed below :

1. **Genetic factors :** This disability may occur because of abnormality in genes which are inherited from parents, errors when genes

combine or may be due to other factors as well. For instance, Down syndrome, fragile X syndrome and phenylketonuria (PKU) are examples of genetic factors causing cognitive disability.

2. **Problems during pregnancy :** This disability can occur if inside womb the fetus does not develop properly as there may be complications with the manner the baby's cells divide as it grows. If during pregnancy a woman consumes alcohol or gets an infection like rubella, the baby may develop the cognitive disabilities.

3. **Problems at time of birth :** If the child does not get sufficient amount of oxygen at the time of labor and birth he or she may have a cognitive disability.

4. **Health issues :** Cognitive disabilities can occur because of diseases like whooping cough, the measles or meningitis. This disability can also be caused due to extreme malnutrition, inadequate medical care or getting exposed to poisons like lead or mercury.

Intellectual Disabilities

Intellectual disability was earlier known as mental retardation. It is the disability in which the individuals have below-average intelligence, low mental ability and a lack of skills needed for daily life. Individuals suffering from intellectual disabilities learn to perform new skills but they learn them slowly varying from mild to profound degrees of intellectual disability.

Intellectual disability involves difficulty in functioning in two areas such as :

1. Intellectual functioning like learning, problem solving, judgment.

2. Adaptive functioning like activities of everyday life namely communication and independent living.

Intellectual functioning known as IQ (intelligence quotient) as well referring to individual's ability to learn, reason, decision making and problem solving ability. IQ can be measured by an IQ test which reveals that the average IQ is 100 and majority of people scores between 85 and 115. The individual who scores less than 70 to 75 in an IQ test is considered to be as the intellectually disabled.

This disability is considered to be affecting about 1% of the population out of those 85% are affected with mild intellectual disability which means slow learning of new information or skills. If these individuals are given proper guidance, most of them are able to live independently as adults. Males are more probable than females to be diagnosed with intellectual disability. As per the American Psychiatric Association (APA), intellectual disability is diagnosed based on these three domains, *viz.,* conceptual, social and practical.

According to **American Association of Intellectual and Development Disability,** *"Intellectual disability is a disability characterized by significant limitations in both intellectual functioning and in adaptive behavior, which covers many everyday social and practical skills. This disability originates before the age of 18."*

Signs and Symptoms of Intellectual Disabilities

Some of the most common signs and symptoms of intellectual disability include :

1. Slow learning and developing process.
2. Late initiation of the movements like rolling over, sitting up, crawling or walking.
3. Problem in communicating and socializing.
4. Problems in speech.
5. Low memory power.
6. Inability to solve problem and think logically.
7. Difficulty in school learning.
8. Difficulty in doing daily necessary tasks.

In case of severe intellectual disabilities additional health problems may exist and appear such as seizures, vision and hearing problems and mental disorders. The following categories are used to explain intellectual disability from mild to profound.

Common Causes of Intellectual Disabilities

The most common causes of intellectual disabilities are discussed as under :

1. **Genetic factors :** It may be caused due to abnormal genes inherited from parents, errors when genes combine or there may be other reasons for intellectual disabilities to occur. Down syndrome, Fragile X syndrome and phenylketonuria (PKU) are some examples of genetic factors responsible for the cause of intellectual disabilities.

2. **Complications during pregnancy :** A woman consuming alcohol or if she gets an infection like rubella during pregnancy may give birth to baby with this disabilities.

3. **Problems during birth :** A child may have intellectual disability if at the time of birth the baby does not get enough oxygen resulting into complications during labor and birth.

4. Diseases or toxic exposure : Intellectual disabilities can occur if the child suffers from diseases like whooping cough, measles or meningitis. Extreme malnutrition and improper medical care or exposure to poisons like lead or mercury can lead to intellectual disabilities.

Physical Disabilities

A physical disability is the long-term loss or impairment of a part of the body and its physical function. It can involve difficulties with walking and mobility, sitting and standing, use of the hands and arms, sight, hearing, speech, breathing, bladder control, muscle control, sleeping, fits and seizures or chronic tiredness. It can also come about through something that happened before or during birth or later in life through an illness or injury. A physical disability may be obvious, such as loss of a limb.

In other words, a person with a physical disability is constrained by his ability to perform an activity independently such as walking, bathing, toileting, etc. A person can be physically disabled due to two reasons: Congenital/Hereditary— the person has physical disability since birth or the disability developed at a later stage due to genetic problem, problems with muscle cells or injury during birth. Acquired– the person acquired the physical disability through road or industrial accidents, infections such as polio or diseases and disorders such as stroke or cancer.

Types of Physical Disabilities

There are two major categories under the physical disability group, they are :

1. **Musculo-skeletal disability :** The inability to perform typical activities related with movements of the body parts because of the muscular or bony deformities, diseases or degeneration. The following disabilities are clustered under musculo-skeletal disabilities :

   (a) Loss or deformity of limbs.

   (b) Osteogensis imperfect.

   (c) Muscular dystrophy.

2. **Neuro-musculo disability :** The inability to carry out controlled movements because the body parts are affected due to diseases, denegation or disorder of the nervous system. The under mentioned are the categories of this disability :

   (a) Cerebral palsy

   (b) Spina bifida

   (c) Poliomyelitis

   (d) Stroke

   (e) Head injury

   (f) Spinal cord injury.

Signs or Symptoms of Physical Disabilities

1. Child's neck is twisted so that their head is tilted one way and they strain to look in the opposite direction.

2. Children with Spina Bifida usually have lower muscle strength because the nerves that supply the muscles in their body are damaged.

3. Cerebral Palsy is a motor condition that causes difficulty in controlling movement, posture and balance.

4. Low muscle tone (baby feels 'floppy' when picked up).

5. Unable to hold up his/her own head while lying on their stomach or in a supported sitting position.

6. Muscle spasms or feeling stiff.

7. Poor muscle control, reflexes and posture.

8. Feeding or swallowing difficulties.

9. Prefer to use one side of their body.

10. Do not reach their developmental milestones at expected times. Delay can occur in one or many areas such as gross or fine motor movement, language, social, or thinking skills.

11. Loss or deformity of limbs.

12. Skeletal limb abnormalities.

13. Inability to carry out controlled movements.

14. Impairment of vision, speech, hearing or intellectual functioning.

Causes of Physical Disabilities

There are many reasons which may cause disability. These are discussed below :

1. **Diseases :** Some diseases affect the mental and emotional health of an individual and can strike nearly in any part of the body. Cardiac diseases reduce the endurance ability of the individual and strokes result in paralysis and loss of speech. The disease of arthritis and other bone diseases lead to deformity. Nerve diseases are responsible for blindness, deafness and lack of coordination. Damage of brain occurs before, during, or after birth and is known as cerebral palsy and depending on the part damaged it can cause problems like mental retardation, muscular weakness, speech impairment and involuntary movement of the arms and legs.

2. **Malnutrition :** It is an unhealthy condition resulting because of poor intake, absorption, or use of nutrients by the body. Children with malnutrition have learning disabilities, blind, partially sighted or may have hearing loss. In young children, malnutrition may be the reason for impair brain development. In developing and poor countries, malnutrition is the root cause of numerous disease and impairments which lead to disability.

3. **Poor prenatal care :** The general acute childhood illness not only causes disability but also causes death. There are numerous childhood disability caused due to several childhood illnesses such as Poliomyelitis affecting limbs, causing difficulties in walking and moving; Measles/vitamin-A deficiency causes xerophthalmia and blindness; Rubella (German measles) causes deafness, in the unborn baby; Iodine deficiency causes cretinism and learning difficulties and many more.

4. **Accidents :** Disability also results from the violence, conflict, traffic and occupational accidents causing injuries. Accidents causes severe disability including spinal damage and loss of limbs, etc.

4.3. TYPES OF DISORDER, ITS CAUSE AND NATURE (ADHD, SPD, ASD, ODD, OCD)

ADHD (Attention Deficit Hyperactivity Disorder)

The Attention Deficit Hyperactivity Disorder (ADHD) is a medical or neurobiological state which leads the brain's neurotransmitter chemicals, such as noradrenaline and dopamine not to function appropriately. If not identified properly and provided with proper treatment and management, this disorder has severe and enduring effects and complications for an individual. This is a genetic and long duration disorder affecting the learning and behavior since schooling years and goes beyond adulthood in numerous cases. This disorder results in poor school performance in children. In modern society, children with ADHD are given proper attention particularly in the tasks, the children with disorder find interesting. The co- existence of the disorder of ADHD can be in a greater or lesser degree along with other disorders like dyslexia, autism, learning disorder, conduct disorder, dyspraxia, etc.

Types of ADHD

The term ADHD is used synonymously with the other words such as "hyperactive" or "out of control". Diagnosis of ADHD becomes difficult if the symptoms are not apparent in a child. Kids who do not look agitated constantly are not diagnosed early. Though there are three types of ADHD but one of the types do not include symptoms of impulsive and hyperactive behaviour.

1. **Predominantly hyperactive-impulsive presentation, ADHD :** Children with this type of disorder struggle with impulse control. The children show symptoms of hyperactivity and sense the requirement of moving constantly in this disorder.

2. **Predominantly inattentive presentation, ADHD :** This disorder is also known as the attention-deficit disorder (ADD). The children with this disorder have difficulty in paying attention and get distracted easily without having issues with impulsivity or hyperactivity.

3. **Combined presentation, ADHD :** This disorder is the most general type of ADHD in which the children shows all kind of symptoms of the above described types.

Symptoms of ADHD

Symptoms of ADHD are listed as under and it falls into three categories, *viz.*, inattention, impulsivity and distractibility.

Inattention :

1. Appears to be "day-dreamy" type, confused, tends to forget things and looks like not to be paying attention and listening.

2. Lack of concentration and quickly switching over one activity to another.

3. Tendency to get bored if the activity is not interesting.

4. Works really hard to get organized and complete the given tasks.

5. Difficulty in learning new things and understanding directions.

6. Though smart but is known to be as the slow learners as understands things slowly in comparison to that of his peer groups.

Impulsivity :

1. Lack of patience and struggles to wait for his/her turn.

2. Says (something) unexpectedly without careful consideration and interrupts others.

3. Emotionally unstable and over-reacts to emotional situations.

4. Lack of understanding regarding the result of his/ her own actions.

Hyperactivity :

1. Extremely talkative.

2. Keeps moving constantly even if in sitting position.

3. Very fast in moving from one place to another.

4. Keeps fidgeting picking up almost everything and playing with it.

5. Faces difficulty in sitting still even for meals and other sedentary activities.

> **Note :**
>
> The symptoms of ADHD keep changing the age but it can't be outgrown. For instance, few of the symptoms such as hyperactivity may get reduced with age whereas the troubles with the organization and time management become apparent with middle school or high school children.

Causes of ADHD

The exact causes of ADHD are still unknown to researchers. But the researchers have established and identified the factors revealing that it is a brain-based biological condition explaining the clinical reasons of this disorder, therefore the probable causes are discussed as under :

1. **Genes and heredity :** It is revealed by several researches that ADHD is genetic as it is thought to be inherited from the parents in majority of the cases. Studies have shown that a child with ADHD has higher probability of having this disorder if both parents have ADHD themselves.

2. **Brain differences :** If the child is having the disorder of ADHD, certain areas of the brain develops at a slower pace or the child may be less active. The medical report of Johns Hopkins states that the children with ADHD have lower levels of a brain chemical known as dopamine which is responsible for regulating mood, movement and attention.

3. **Environmental factors :** Consumption of alcohol and smoking at the time of pregnancy causes fetal alcohol spectrum and problems with central nervous system development thus resulting into disorders including the ADHD that come under heading of environmental factors. The exposure of children to toxic substances like lead or polychlorinated biphenyls develops the disorder of ADHD.

4. **Brain injury :** Though traumatic brain injury (TBI) is a lot less common than ADHD however ADHD are sometimes present in children who suffers from TBI. Researchers have revealed higher rates of attention problems resulting due to acquired brain injuries like concussion and brain tumors.

5. **Other possible causes :** Numerous other reasons responsible for development of ADHD are children prematurely born before the 37th week of pregnancy, less weight at time of birth of a baby and damage of brain in the womb, etc.

SPD (Sensory Processing Disorder)

This disorder is also referred to as the sensory integration dysfunction, as in this disorder the brain has difficulty in receiving and responding to information which comes in through the senses. Individuals suffering from this disorder are over-sensitive to things in their surroundings such as a common sound may be overwhelming or may be painful. It also includes other sensory processing disorders such as :

1. Being uncoordinated and awkward.

2. Getting banged or bumped into things.

3. Inability to get engaged in conversation or play.

Sensory processing problems are generally identified in children however it can affect adults as well and are usually seen in developmental conditions like autism spectrum disorder.

Types of SPD

Sensory processing disorders are divided into three broad categories, *viz.*

1. Sensory modulation disorder.

2. Sensory-based motor disorders.

3. Sensory discrimination disorders.

1. **Sensory modulation disorder (SMD) :** Sensory modulation means a difficult central nervous system process that transmits information with reference to the intensity, frequency, duration, complexity and novelty of sensory stimuli with the help of a neural messages are adjusted. In this disorder, the children face difficulties in processing the degree of intensity, duration, frequency, etc., of information and show signs of a fearful or anxious behaviours, negative or stubborn behaviors, self-absorbed behaviors which are hard to engage or inventive or keenly looking for sensation. SMD are of three types which are stated as below :

(a) Sensory over-responsivity.

(b) Sensory under-responsivity.

(c) Sensory craving or seeking.

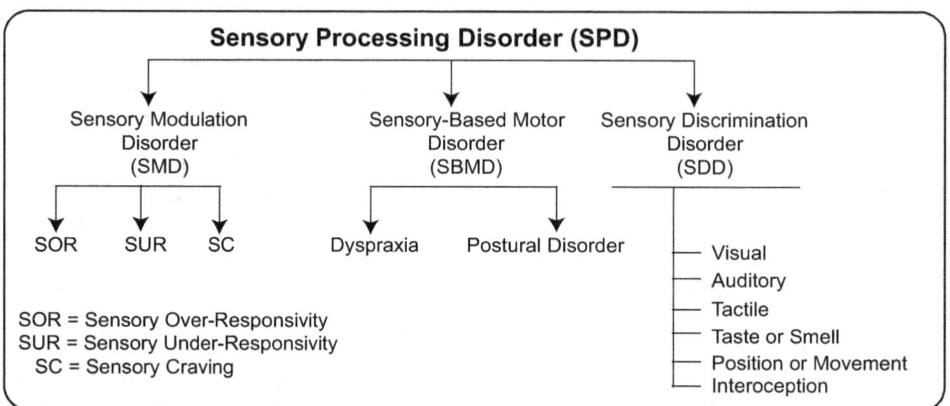

(a) Sensory over-responsivity : Children with the sensory over-responsivity are more sensitive as their bodies feel the sensation too easily or intensely than the majority of people. They keep feeling as being continuously bombarded with information. They often experience the "sensory defensiveness" as they try to evade or diminish sensations like pull out from being touched or covering ears so as to avoid loud sounds. Symptoms of sensory over-responsivity are as follows :

(i) Have an aversion to textures in fabrics, foods, grooming products or other materials used in day to day life which other people may not even notice.

(ii) To avoid crowds and noisy places.

(iii) Motion sickness with no medical reason.

(iv) Severe discomfort, sickness or threat may be experienced because of some normal sounds, lights or movements, etc.

(v) Selective in eating.

(vi) Disturbance in sleep as waking up by any sounds or problems in falling asleep because of sensory overload.

(vii) Being in state of complete restlessness and feeling a constant stress.

(b) Sensory under-responsivity : Children with this disorder are a lot quiet and passive and are under-responsive to the usual intensity of the sensory environment. As the children do not sense the sensory input of their environment they are more withdrawn, difficult to engage and or self-absorbed leading to poor body awareness, clumsiness or movements. The children with this disorder have poor perception about objects being extremely hot or cold and they do not notice pain with regard to bumps, falls, or cuts. Symptoms of sensory under -responsivity are as follows :

(i) Lethargic and lack of receptiveness.

(ii) Complexity in waking up.

(iii) Lack of consciousness of pain or other people.

(iv) Noticeable deafness.

(v) Trouble with toilet training.

(c) Sensory craving or seeking : In this disorder, the children actively seek sensory stimulation and seem to have more or less unquenchable craving for sensory input making them to move, crash, bump and/or jump continuously. This disorder makes the child become disorganized with additional stimulation as he/she receives more input and knows nothing about regulating them. The children with this disorder have the tendency to touch everything and are very friendly without understanding the concept of 'their space' versus 'other's space'. This kind of disorder is often thought to similar as that of the Attention Deficit Hyperactivity Disorder (ADHD) or Attention Deficit Disorder (ADD). Symptoms of sensory craving or seeking are as follows :

(i) Making loud and disturbing noises.

(ii) Fidgeting.

(iii) Climbing, jumping and crashing constantly.

(iv) Looking for "extreme" sensations.

(v) Sucking or biting fingers, clothing, pencils, etc.

(vi) Recklessness.

2. Sensory-based motor disorder (SBMD) : In this disorder, the motor output is disorganized which results because of inaccurate processing of sensory information thus affecting postural control challenges, postural disorder, or developmental coordination disorder.

The SBMD are classified into two types as stated under :

(a) Dyspraxia.

(b) Postural disorder.

(a) Dyspraxia : In this disorder, the children have difficulty in processing sensory information appropriately thus facing problems in planning and carrying out new-fangled motor actions. The children with this disorder have problems in structuring a goal or idea, scheduling a chain of actions or performing new motor tasks making the children clumsy, awkward and accident prone. The children suffering from this disorder prefers sedentary activities or tries to conceal their motor planning problem with articulation.

(b) Postural disorder : This disorder results in problem of stabilizing the body in movement or at rest so as to fulfill the demands of a motor task. The child can perform various movements if the posture control is good and has good resistance against force whereas the child with poor postural control does not have body control to maintain the body in standing or sitting position.

Symptoms of Sensory-based motor disorder are :

(a) Extremely slow and awkward movements.

(b) Poor handwriting and posture.

(c) Late in performing movements like crawling, standing, walking or running.

(d) Using more words than needed so as to avoid motor tasks.

3. **Sensory discrimination disorder (SDD) :** Children with this disorder do not process the information received from their senses correctly, even they are unable to differentiate or remember small tasks. For example, if you place a pencil in front of the child and ask to pick the pencil from a desk that contains a pencil, box and eraser, the child would not able to discriminate from the objects or would have forgotten the object or activity that we had mentioned. Working memory span of the child would be less so that the child would have difficulty to retain any information.

There are six SDD sub-types which are as follows:

(a) Visual

(b) Auditory

(c) Tactile

(d) Taste or Smell

(e) Position or Movement

(f) Interoception.

Symptoms of SDD are as follows :

(a) Dropping things constantly.

(b) Struggling in dressing and eating.

(c) Improper vigour used to handle objects.

Causes of Sensory Processing Disorder

The specific cause of this disorder is not identified unlike the most neurological disorders. Though it is believed by several researchers that the onset of SPD is the consequence of a mixture of numerous factors which may include :

1. **Genetic :** Though genetic markers have not yet been identified however it is revealed from numerous researches that sensory processing disorder can be inherited.

2. **Physical :** Studies have shown that this disorder has abnormal brain activity at the time of responding to certain stimuli. Researchers also found that children with SPD have differences in their structure of brain which gives a biological basis for the inception of this disorder.

3. **Environmental :** Researchers believe that there are numerous environmental factors which are responsible for an individual to develop the disorder or not. Not being exposed to proper amounts of stimulation at some point in crucial developmental stages is one of the most major environmental factors.

ASD (Autism Spectrum Disorder)

ASD (Autism Spectrum Disorder) is a developmental disorder affecting behavior, communication skills (verbal and nonverbal) and social skills. Children with ASD have their own unique way of interpreting and understanding the world and their surroundings which is generally different from the other children. Every case of ASD is different for every child affecting individual kids differently. The word 'spectrum' is used to accommodate a wide range of differences that ASD affected children can have. The differences vary with age and can also change over a period of time in a child. The range of severity also varies in ASD as mild, moderate or severe.

Research suggests that one in every 100 children is afflicted by ASD. Boys are about 4 times more prone to ASD than girls. ASD can also occur in adults. ASD is usually diagnosed in childhood, but in some instances a proper diagnosis is not made until the child has grown up or reached adulthood.

Characteristics of Children with ASD

1. They deviate from the normal ongoing process of socialization and have difficulty in expressing, communicating and interacting with others.

2. They show certain repetitive behaviours as well as a lack or limited interest in certain activities.

3. There are certain symptoms that could be typically recognized as ASD in the first two years of a child's life.

4. There are certain symptomatic behaviours that affect the individual's ability to perform socially, at school, at work, or in other spheres of life.

Symptoms of ASD

The following patterns of behavior or activities are identified as the symptoms of ASD :

1. **Social behavior and social understanding:** Sociality or elementary social interactions can be difficult for children with ASD. Symptoms may include :

   (a) Abnormality in the form of unusual or inappropriate body language, gestures, and facial expressions (*e.g.,* avoiding eye contact or facial expressions contradictory to what he or she is saying).

   (b) Lack of interest in other people or any interaction with other people, no effort in sharing a common interest or achievements indicating a kind of introversion (*e.g.,* showing you a painting or sharing a personal thought, pointing to a bird and the like).

   (c) They hardly are the first ones to approach others and shy away from social interaction; they seem aloof and detached from a very early age and prefer to spend time alone.

   (d) They often lack cognition skills like difficulty in understanding other people's feelings, reactions and picking up non-verbal cues.

   (e) They tend to resist any kind of physical touch.

   (f) They often face difficulty in making friends with children of the same age.

2. **Speech and language skills:** Many children with Autism Spectrum Disorder have problems with speech and language comprehension and communicative skills. Symptoms may include:

   (a) They are late-learners of speaking skills implying either there is delay in learning how to speak (even after the age of two) or they don't talk at all.

   (b) They either speak in an unusual tone of voice, or in an atypical rhythm or pitch.

   (c) In some cases they may be found to be repeating words or phrases as a behavioural pattern but without any intention to communicate.

   (d) They are hardly ever seen to be initiating a conversation and generally have trouble in starting a conversation or any kind of interaction.

   (e) They lack the clarity or comprehensive skills to communicate or express their needs, feelings or desires.

   (f) They often face difficulty in understanding simple statements, phrases, directions or even questions.

   (g) They have a tendency to take things at face value implying they tend to interpret things literally and often cannot recognize humour, irony, and sarcasm.

3. **Restricted behavior and play:** Children with ASD often display rigid and even obsessive tendencies in their behaviours, activities and interests. Symptoms may include:

   (a) Restless behaviour leading to constant movements, sometimes paired with repetitive body movements (hand flapping, rocking and spinning).

   (b) They are often obsessively attached to unusual objects (like rubber bands, keys, light switches).

   (c) There is often a keen preoccupation with a narrow topic of interest. It might be something regarding numbers or symbols (maps, license plates, and sports statistics).

   (d) A compulsive need for order and routines (*e.g.,* lines up toys, follows a rigid schedule, things should be kept in the exact place, etc). Any change in their routine or environment unsettles them and are not welcome.

   (e) They often show an abnormal posture, clumsy movements or an unusual way of moving.

   (f) They have a fascination towards spinning objects, moving pieces, or parts of toys in isolation (*e.g.,* spinning the wheels on a race car, instead of playing with the whole car).

   (g) They are hyper-reactive or hypo-reactive to certain sensory inputs (*e.g.,* reacts badly to certain sounds or textures, nonchalant towards temperature or pain).

Causes of ASD

ASD cannot be assigned to any single known cause. The symptoms and severity vary according to the complexity of the disorder and may have multiple causes. Both genetics and environment are consi-dered as causal factors.

1. **Genetics:** Several genes seem to be involved in Autism Spectrum Disorder. In some children, ASD can be linked to a genetic disorder, such as Rett syndrome or fragile X syndrome. While in other cases, genetic changes (mutations) may increase the risk of ASD making the child more vulnerable to it. Some genes may affect brain development in cases where genetic mutations seem to be inherited, although they can also occur spontaneously. All these factors determine the severity of symptoms.

2. **Environmental factors:** Factors such as viral infections, incorrect medications or complications during pregnancy, or air pollutants are still being explored and researches are being conducted to identify if they also play a role in triggering autism spectrum disorder.

ODD (Oppositional Defiant Disorder)

Oppositional behavior is a typical component of development for child of two to three year old and those in early adolescents. Children become oppositional from time to time predominantly when tired, hungry, stressed or upset making them to argue, disobey and confront parents, teachers and other adults. Though, being overtly uncooperative and hostile in behavior may be considered seriously if these behaviors are frequently and consistently seen in the child of these ages as it deeply affects the child's social, family and academic life. There is a constant pattern of disobliging, disobedient and hostile behavior toward authority figures in the children with ODD that critically interferes with the day to day functioning of the child.

In other way, Oppositional defiant disorder (ODD) is a continual behavioral pattern of being angry or in irritable mood, unkindness, quarrelsome, disobedient behavior towards authority figures. The already mentioned behavioral disturbances are sometimes evident in only one setting like generally at home and in more severe cases the symptoms and the disorder may occur in multiple settings.

Symptoms of ODD

There are numerous symptoms of ODD which keeps varying from individual to individual as well as on the basis of the gender as well. The below stated are the signs and symptoms giving indication that a child is suffering from oppositional defiance disorder:

1. **Behavioural symptoms :**
   (a) Short tempered.
   (b) Quarrelsome and fighting.
   (c) Undisciplined.
   (d) Irritating others on purpose.
   (e) Blaming others.
   (f) Hostile.
   (g) Inability to adjust.
   (h) Destroying friendships keenly.
   (i) Hurtful and revengeful.
   (j) Disobedience.

2. **Cognitive symptoms:**
   (a) Frustrated.
   (b) Inability to concentrate.
   (c) Inability to think prior to speaking.

3. **Psycho-social symptoms:**
   (a) Trouble in socializing.
   (b) Loss of self-esteem.
   (c) Continual pessimism.
   (d) Constant irritation.

Causes of ODD

The actual cause of ODD is not yet established and it is apparently believed that there are several combinations of factors working together leading an individual to develop the oppositional defiant disorder. The below discussed are few factors responsible for the development of ODD:

1. **Genetic :** It is obvious for the children diagnosed with ODD that their family members also have suffered from other various mental illnesses like mood, personality and anxiety disorders. It is an established fact that the genetic component leads a child to be more prone in developing oppositional defiant disorder in comparison to an individual who is not exposed to the similar kind of genetics.

2. **Physical :** It is found that the disorder of ODD occurs because of the presence of certain brain chemicals known as neurotransmitters in abnormal amounts. These brain chemicals are responsible for working towards helping to keep the brain balanced properly. Symptoms of ODD become apparently visible when an imbalance exists and there is inability to communicate properly with other aspects of the brain.

3. **Environmental :** Every individual is raised in a particular environment which significantly effects on whether or not the individual will fall in to the symptoms of oppositional defiant disorder. If a child is experiencing chaotic home life it would contribute towards developing ODD in the child as similarly, if children are exposed to violence it correlates with the onset of ODD as well.

OCD (Obsessive Compulsive Disorder)

Obsessive Compulsive Disorder (OCD) is a common and chronic disorder. It refers to a kind of an anxiety disorder where people have unwanted thoughts, ideas or sensations in the form of obsessions on a recurrent basis that drives them to do something compulsively. There are certain repetitive behaviors, such as washing one's hands frequently, double-checking on things continuously or obsessive cleaning which interfere with a person's everyday activities and social interactions.

It is a different thing to have focused thoughts or particular habits to stay organized. Such behaviors do not have negative impact on daily life rather they increase efficiency in regular activities. But in case of OCD, persons get unwanted thoughts persistently and they are highly obsessed with their routines and behaviors so much, that failing to do them causes huge distress. Many people with OCD suspect their obsessions themselves to not be true; while others may accept them as real (known as poor insight). But in both cases, people with OCD can hardly keep their focus off their obsessions or control their compulsive actions.

Obsessions

Obsessions are recurrent thoughts, desires, sensations, impulses, or mental imagery that leads to distressing emotions such as anxiety, restlessness or even disgust. Many people with OCD recognize that the irrational and extreme thoughts, impulses, or images are a product of their mind. Yet they fail to overcome such intrusive thoughts by rationalizing their thought process. Most people with OCD try to suppress such obsessions by distracting themselves with some other thoughts or actions. Examples of a few typical obsessions include excessive concern about contamination or harm, the need for symmetry and order, or forbidden sexual and queer fetishes or religious thoughts.

Compulsions

Compulsions are repetitive behaviors or actions that compel an individual to act in response to an obsession. Apparently such actions are believed to prevent or reduce stress or calm the nerves. In severe cases of OCD, an entire day might be preoccupied with a constant repetition of rituals, interrupting and often impeding a normal routine. Although giving into such irrational compulsions may provide temporary relief and a sense of calm, but the obsession returns in a cyclic way leading to a state of perpetual anguish.

Symptoms of OCD

People with OCD may show symptoms of obsessions or compulsions, or both. Such behaviors can affect all aspects of life, such as educational life, professional sphere or career, social and personal relationships.

1. **Obsessive thought :** Some common obsessive thoughts in OCD can be identified as follows :

   (a) A perpetual phobia of contamination by germs or dirt or even the fear of contaminating others.

   (b) Fear of losing control and causing self-harm or being harmful to others.

   (c) Sexually explicit or violent thoughts, fantasies and images in the mind.

   (d) Excessive obsession with religious or moral ideas.

   (e) Fear of losing things or not having things one might need at one's disposal.

   (f) Obsession with order and symmetry. A mental idea of perfection and that everything must turn out "just right" according to their plan.

   (g) Excessive attention to superstitions or prejudices (designating something as lucky or unlucky).

2. **Compulsive behaviours :** Common compulsive behaviours in OCD include:

   (a) Persistent double-checking of things, such as locks, appliances and switches.

   (b) Excessive worrying about security and checking in on loved ones to ensure they're safe.

   (c) Compulsive counting, tapping of hands or feet, recurrent use of certain words in their vocabulary and engaging in other pointless activities to reduce anxiety.

   (d) Persons with OCD often engage in obsessive washing or cleaning.

   (e) Ordering or arranging things just for the sake of it.

   (f) Excessive praying or engaging in ritualistic activities out of some unexplained religious fear.

   (g) Some persons start accumulating "junk" such as old newspapers or empty food containers as a hobby.

Causes of OCD

1. **Genetics :** OCD often seems to be a "family trait". In fact, most cases show a familiar pattern inherited from the family. Various research reports indicate that parents, siblings and children of a person with OCD run a greater risk of developing OCD than someone who has no family history of the disorder.

2. **Brain structure and functioning :** Modern brain imaging techniques have been employed to study the activity of specific areas of the brain. Such studies have revealed that people with OCD have increased activity in three areas of the brain. These are :

   The caudate nucleus, specific brain cells in the basal ganglia, are located deep in the centre of the brain. This area of the brain mainly functions as a filter for thoughts coming in from other areas. The caudate nucleus is also concerned with controlling habitual and repetitive behaviors.

3. **Environmental factors :** There are environmental stressors that act as external triggers of OCD in persons who are prone to developing the condition. Certain environmental factors may also aggravate the symptoms. These factors include:

   (a) Abuse (both physical and mental leading to trauma).

   (b) Abrupt and unprecedented changes in living situation or life style.

   (c) Chronic illness.

   (d) Loss of a loved one through death or otherwise.

   (e) Work or school-related changes or problems leading to professional stress.

   (f) Relationship concerns affecting interpersonal experiences.

4. **Behavioral factors :** The Behavioral theory suggests that people with OCD tend to relate certain objects or situations with fear, so they develop and improvise ways to either evade such situations to avoid the things they are afraid of or they perform rituals that help reduce the fear and anguish.

People resort to such ritual practice and avoidance of situation or objects when they are under high emotional stress, such as any drastic change in life like starting a new job or ending a relationship.

Emotional stress increases one's vulnerability to fear and anxiety. Even objects regarded as "neutral" begin to elicit feelings of fear. For example, a person who has always been able to swim, when under stress, may feel scared of water with a sudden fear of drowning and harming one's life, making a connection between water and a fear of losing control.

The connection between an object and the associated feeling of fear can take the form of a phobia, and people with OCD tend to avoid the things they fear, instead of confronting or overcoming the fear. For instance, the person who fears getting contaminated by germs from public toilets will avoid using them. If forced to use a public toilet at any helpless situation, he or she will perform elaborate cleaning exercises, such as thorough cleaning of the toilet seat, even cleaning the door knobs, taps, followed by a detailed self-cleansing procedure. These actions provide temporary relief from fear, but the anxiety crisis is never addressed. Since the fear is never dealt with but is reinforced through rituals, it develops into a compulsive behavior. There is a high risk of such fears or obsessions spreading to other objects and situations if not properly dealt with through therapy.

4.4. DISABILITY ETIQUETTES

Disability etiquette specifically refers to a set of guidelines concerned with how to approach people with disabilities. On a broader note, the rules of etiquette and good manners for dealing with people with disabilities are similar to the rules of good etiquette in society. These guidelines cover specific issues which are related to disability or issues faced by the people with disabilities to outline basic etiquettes for working with people with different kinds of disabilities.

Disability etiquette at the basic level begins with treating people with disabilities with respect. For example, instead of addressing the person accompanying them, one should speak to the person with disability directly. Since the nature, degree and the impact of a specific disability can vary widely from person to person, assumptions about what they can or cannot do must not be made in haste. Assistance should be offered only if it is asked for or it seems necessary. The individual's ability to make decisions and judgments on their own behalf must be acknowledged and respected. They should be addressed in "people first" language.

For example, the term "people with disabilities" must be used. Terms such as "the disabled" or "the handicapped" are to be avoided. By all means any person must not be referred by his/her disability. For example, instead of saying, "She is an epileptic", she should be referred as, "She has epilepsy." Terms like "wheelchair-bound" or "confined to a wheelchair" are considered to be rude since most wheelchair confined persons perceive their wheelchair as a liberating tool or support, and not as any appendage. Instead one must say, "She uses a wheelchair". Any negative, offensive, or outdated term such as "cripple", "deaf and dumb," or "retarded" which might injure the dignity and the sentiments of such persons must never be used. Often people with disabilities do not wish to be referred to euphemistically. One must be sensitive to their wish by avoiding terms such as "physically challenged" or "differently abled". Furthermore, referring to an individual with a disability as someone who is "suffering from cerebral palsy or Parkinson's" must be avoided.

General Rules of Etiquette

1. One must always be mindful that while having a conversation with a person with a disability, that person should be addressed directly, and not through their companion. While this may need some practice, remember making eye contact can make positive difference.

2. If, at any point of time, it seems like someone with a disability requires assistance, they should be asked first. They could be reluctant to take help and at the most can say, "No, thank you."

3. Any assistance should be offered in a dignified manner, with sensitivity and respect. Remember that persons with disabilities deserve sensitivity and respect and if your offer is declined, do not proceed to give assistance forcibly. If the offer is accepted, listen carefully and adhere to the instructions.

4. Be patient with an individual who uses a communication device.

5. Adults should be treated as adults. People with disabilities must not be undermined or looked down upon.

6. The following words must be avoided while conversing with or in reference to a person with a disability: Cripple, victim, defect, invalid, sick, diseased, wheelchair bound, handicapped, retard, mentally retarded, deformed, dumb, moron, imbecile, or idiot. These words have a derogatory implication.

7. The following terms are appropriate to refer to someone with a disability: blind, visually impaired, hard of hearing, intellectually disabled, non-disabled, physically disabled.

8. Avoid terms that might unnecessarily imply that people with disabilities are too bold, brave, special, or super human.

9. People with disabilities ask for equal treatment, not special treatment.

10. It must always be remembered that ultimately people with disabilities are people first and disabled later.

11. One must be sensitive and respectful while asking about their disability. If the person is reluctant to discuss it, do not pry.

Now we will discuss about **some disability etiquettes** in accordance with the needs of disability:

1. **Speech disability etiquette :**

    (a) One must never assume these individuals to be mentally retarded or mentally ill. Be patient in finding out the communication method that works best for them.

    (b) Be very attentive while conversing with an individual who has difficulty in speaking. They need our full attention to be understood properly.

    (c) Do not panic if you are in a noisy or a crowded environment. Try to move to a quieter location to talk.

    (d) Be patient till they complete their own sentences. Do not try to speak for them. One must never pretend to understand either. Tell them what you have understood and allow them to respond.

    (e) Do not try to criticize or correct them, rather, be encouraging.

    (f) If the situation so demands, it's alright to ask short questions that require short answers.

2. **Wheelchair etiquette :**

    (a) **Points to remember :**

    (i) Individuals using wheelchairs do not have similar disabilities and may require different degrees of assistance.

    (ii) Some wheelchair users might be capable of using canes or other assistive devices and may not need his/her wheelchair round the clock.

    (b) It is okay to offer assistance but one must not start assisting the individual without his/her prior permission. If your offer is not accepted, respect his/her decision.

    (c) In case you are speaking to an individual in a wheelchair for more than two minutes, try to find a place to sit down for the conversation. This will prevent the individual from straining his neck for a prolonged period of time and will give the individual a more comfortable and better viewing angle.

(d) A person's wheelchair is considered as an integral part of his/her own personal space and is linked to their privacy. One must never move, push, lean on, rock, or touch his/her wheelchair without prior permission of the owner. Not only is it rude, it can also prove to be dangerous.

(e) Wheelchair users must never be demeaned or shown unnecessary pity as if it is a tragedy. Wheelchairs can be a means to engage in everyday activities and a means to attempt to lead a normal life.

3. **Hearing disability etiquette :**

(a) Never shout at a hearing impaired person unless they request you to speak loudly. Speak in a normal tone where your lips are visible.

(b) A quiet location with minimum background noise should be chosen to communicate and conversations must be kept simple and clear.

(c) Never answer with phrases like "nothing, it's not important" when asked to repeat yourself. It is insulting and might hurt the sentiments of the person; Be patient enough to comply.

(d) Be mindful to face the light source and not keeping any stuff that might obstruct or cover your mouth while speaking (such as cigarettes or your hands).

(e) Try to make eye contact and speak directly to the person rather than addressing the interpreter or the companion of the individual.

(f) Facial expressions, body language and natural gestures enhance communication and one must be conscious of them while conversing with a person with hearing disability.

(g) It is best to clarify and mutually establish which method of communication and language is preferred and is to be used.

4. **Visual disability etiquette :**

(a) When meeting a person with a visual disability, always identify yourself and others accompanying you (*e.g.,* "Sanjeev is on my left and Nisha is on my right.").

(b) If you go out to dinner with an acquaintance with a visual disability, ask if he/she would like you to give a description of the surrounding, what is on the menu or may be what is on his/her plate.

(c) When assisting a person with a visual impairment in walking, offer them your arm for guidance. Walk at their pace and do not rush. Most likely they are to walk half-step behind to anticipate curbs and steps.

(d) When you are in a room with someone with a visual disability, let the person know before leaving the room.

4.5. ADVANTAGES OF PHYSICAL ACTIVITIES FOR CHILDREN WITH SPECIAL NEEDS

Children need more engages in the physical activities, exercises rather than being a spectator or counting score in the name of taking part of physical education. Physical activities not only provide health but also provide social benefits to all the children and along with the children with disabilities. Even though, people with disabilities know that they need physical activities to promote their health and reduce the chances of getting ill/diseases, only few are engaged in physical activities as compared to the normal people or people without disabilities. This may be due to the effect of the social support they are getting from their family members, society and their friends. The activities like gymnastics which provide the basic fundamental movement along with the movement education gives positive effect to such children.

People with special needs can improve their lifestyle through physical education, such program involved connection with the society and friends. From the research findings from many sources proved that the enhancement in the academic performance and cognitive process can be done through physical education. For the children with special needs, physical education program gives benefits to many ways like providing opportunities to build collaboration and social skills, to teach how to set the goal and how to focus on it by overcoming the problem.

To take part in physical education by the children with special needs means that it is not only the responsible for the children itself but also the parent and the teachers to provide a safety and creative program for them. Research has also proved that by doing physical education programs, the children with special needs can enhance their lifestyles; they can improve the gross motor skills, also enhance the engagement with the social activities which help them to improve self-esteem as well as positive thinking and self-motivated. The important aspect of physical education classes is to promote positive advancements for the children with special needs.

The most beautiful thing about participating in the physical activities or sports events is that they can perform many tasks easily which they were not able to performed before. There are some advantages for taking part in regular physical activities:

1. **Physical improvements :** A finding of scientific research especially for special children shows that the physical health and well-being were improved through participation in games and sports. Participating in physical activities and sports regularly can improve the specific skill they need, like cardiovascular efficiency, endurance, eye-hand coordination, strength and flexibility. Not only improving in the motor fitness component, participating in physical activities and various sports gives benefits according to their needs and requirement like maintaining their weight, enhancing required muscles, increase their movement around the joints, and keep away from obesity, diabetes and other health complications.

2. **Mental improvements in confidence and well-being :** Participating in physical education classes regularly not only give benefits physically but also helps their mental health. Peoples with some mentally disorder, anxiety and depression get relax through participating physical activities and sports. As the normal individuals need to improve their self-esteem, self confidence and social engagement, individuals with special needs also require the same, and can enhance through participating regularly in such program. It also shows the level of confidence of children who undergo such programme and those who do not take part. They gradually feel free from being neglected, isolated and remain out of the group as they improve their self-esteem through physical education classes.

3. **Behavioral improvements in attention, relationships and academics :** The limitations of traditional classroom setting give some restriction that do not allow them to access their skills, but such restrictions are free in the nature of physical education classes and enhance the improvement in the thought process of children with special needs. Every sports comes with its own rules and regulations along with its organizations, through this they lead to exercise self-regulation and lead to improve their decision making efficiency. They also learn to set their goals and practice to achieve their specific goal.

Physical education is a wide area, not simply learning how to engage in a particular sport — it educates the children of different categories in different area of skill, starting from taking part in the games, following the rules and regulations, solving the task, motivating themselves and many more. Such skill can also help in the traditional classroom setting so as to improve the learning abilities and naturally lead to sharing their ideas.

4.6. STRATEGIES TO MAKE PHYSICAL ACTIVITIES ASSESSIBLE FOR CHILDREN WITH SPECIAL NEED

Every individual has their own uniqueness; likewise each child is unique and has different needs and requirement. The activities should be made according to the needs and requirement of the children with special need. To plan such program which makes physical activities accessible for them, need various kinds of strategies. These are discussed below:

1. **The environment :** To make the safe and creative environment which help the children to motivate themselves in taking part to the physical activities, is one of the basic strategies. The environment has a direct impact on the children which influences their learning process. Not only in physical activities classes but also in traditional class room, a child may get interest to read, write or listening to the lecture of the teacher if he feels comfortable with the environment and can learn in better way. So, to provide a suitable environment according to the need and requirement of the child with or without disabilities is one of the key strategies which give a direct impact on the learning. If such kind of learning environment is given to the children with disabilities, they can do their work without much depending upon others and it will make them feel independent.

2. **Identify unique needs :** To create such environment, the initial step is to find out the needs of the students. Only after this step, one can move toward the content of the programme and the objectives can be set. Every child have unique needs, so to find out their unique needs is the primary task for the physical activity classes

which should to incorporate with the safety environment.

3. **Determine appropriate instructional settings and support services :** After indentifying the unique needs, the next step is to find out the settings for instruction and supplementary or support services. The instructional setting depends on the supplementary requirement as it includes ways to promote individualized attention with the help of team teaching, peer tutoring, teaching assistants or volunteers.

4. **Individualize instruction :** The teacher engaging in such program should have a good quality to give instruction separately for each child according to their needs and requirement. When the teacher makes some modification in their objectives, way of assessment, content, the tools used, the methods applied and the way of teaching according to the child uniqueness, individualization takes place. There may be several strategies applied for individualization which may be differred from one another according to the needs and requirement.

5. **Class size and type :** The size of the class is an essential aspect to consider while placing the students in instructional class. A class should have not more than 30 students if a quality instruction is expected in regular setting. The number of the students should be arranged in such a way which can give most comfortable to the children with disabilities and also fulfill their needs and requirement. Their helping tools, gadgets, equipments should be easily available with safely. In some special classes the number of students should not cross 12 students, even in some case it can decrease up to 6 or less than that, when some special needs are required. In some cases, individualized instruction is warranted. It is also important to keep in mind about the availabilities of the teachers, gadgets while setting down the size of the class. Until and unless the ages of the students are 16 or older, the difference in their age in one class should not exceed three years.

6. **Scheduling :** The next strategy is to provide activities and programs which the children with special needs enjoy to do. This will helps them to do further activities and to enhance their weak area as well as maintaining their body. There may be long term goal and short term goal also which should be achieved through the physical activities provided and the short term goal should act as the motivational tool that can help the children to achieve their long term goal. While planning out the activities and program one much take care of their capabilities and their weakness too, it should not affect any kind of small muscle group which may lead to injury or over used. The activities and program should be in continuous process.

7. **Facilities :** The next important strategy is the kind of facilities provided for organizing physical activities program for children with special needs. The facilities give a direct impact on the teaching learning environment. The more facilities provided, the more positive impact will come. Each and every facility should be easily available to the children when needed. There must be separate attention for indoor and outdoor facilities, changing room and restrooms, lockers etc. Indoor facilities should have proper lighting, ventilation, acoustics, sufficient space for activities without any disturbance and obstacles. The height of the hall should not affect in any kind of play. The floors should be free from any kind of injury and should have enough space for wheelchairs; the walls should have protective padding if necessary.

Like indoor areas, outdoor areas should be injury free and well leveled. Each area should be marked clearly with the right specification regarding the particular sports. The facilities of water fountain for both the hand and the leg should be kept in such area where every child with the special needs can easily use. The total facilities, colorful signs, and tactual orientation map should be posted to guide visually impaired child. The restrooms, toilets, changing rooms etc., should have proper space and disabled friendly which meet all kind of needs and requirements of the children.

The facility of swimming pool is mandatory because swimming enhances the individual body endurance in many ways. The safety measure for the children should be kept in mind while constructing the swimming pool. The depth and temperature of the water inside the swimming pool should be adjusted according to the needs of the children with special needs. The swimming pool can also be used for other activities rather than learning like, recreational activity, therapeutic activity, and competitive needs also. Routine maintenance of the pool is essential. The other essential facilities attached with the swimming pool *i.e.*, dressing room, showering, and toilet should be kept close to the swimming pool and made comfortable for the children with special needs.

EXERCISES

Multiple Choice Questions

1. What terminology is used in place of "disabled"?
   (a) Differently abled
   (b) God's messenger
   (c) With varied abilities
   (d) None of the above

2. Which of the following is a cognitive disability ?
   (a) Speech disorders
   (b) Dyslexia
   (c) Short attention span
   (d) All of the above

3. What does SEN stand for ?
   (a) Spatial Emotional Negotiation
   (b) Social Education Needs
   (c) Special and Education Needs
   (d) Special and Exceptional Needs

4. A disability may be present in which of the following ?
   (a) Speech, hearing or eyesight
   (b) Mobility, perception or memory
   (c) Continence, dexterity or physical coordination
   (d) All of the above

5. Which of the following points is consistent with the social model of disability ?
   (a) Impairments or difference should be fixed or changed by medical or other treatments.
   (b) Society must focus on what is wrong with the person and how they can adapt.
   (c) It is impossible to cater for all requirements and disadvantage is ievitable.
   (d) Disability is caused by the way society is organised, not by a person's impairment. We need to remove barriers to enable independence and equality.

6. How many stages of support are available to children with special educational needs ?
   (a) 3   (b) 2
   (c) 5   (d) 4

7. On averagte, how long does the statutory assessment process take ?
   (a) Up to 26 weeks   (b) Up to 12 weeks
   (c) Up to 8 weeks   (d) Up to 52 weeks

8. Which of the following treatments can be used to improve the processes underpinning motor skills?
   (a) Sensory integration therapy
   (b) Mathematic remediation programming
   (c) Exposure and operant conditioning
   (d) None of these

9. Applied Behaviour Analysis is used to support children with which of the following conditions ?
   (a) Attentional deficit disorder
   (b) Dyslexia
   (c) Autism
   (d) Dyspraxia

10. Which of the following statements is inconsistent with the medical model ?
   (a) Intervention is defined by diagnosis.
   (b) The child is valued in their own right.
   (c) Society remains unchanged.
   (d) Impairment is the focus of attention.

Very Short Answer Type Questions (Carrying 1 mark)

1. What is disability ?
2. What is impairment ?
3. What is handicap ?
4. What is disorder ?
5. Enlist the types of disabilities.
6. State two causes of cognitive disabilities.
7. Define intellectual disabilities.
8. What are the types of physical disabilities ?
9. Name the types of the Attention Deficit Hyperactivity Disorder (ADHD).
10. What do you understand by sensory under responsivity ?
11. State two characteristics of Autism Spectrum Disorder.
12. Enlist five symptoms of Oppositional defiant disorder (ODD).
13. What is Obsessive Compulsive Disorder (OCD) ?
14. What is disability etiquette?
15. What are the strategies of making physical activities assessible for children with special help?
16. What is cognitive disability ?
17. What is intellectual disability ?
18. What is physical disability ?
19. What is Attention Deficit Hyperactivity Disorder (ADHD) ?
20. What is SPD (Sensory Processing Disorder) ?
21. What are the types of Sensory Processing Disorder ?

22. What is Dyspraxia ?
23. What is Oppositional defiant disorder (ODD) ?
24. What are the causes of Sensory Processing Disorder ?
25. State the symptoms of the Autism Spectrum Disorder in terms of speech and language skills.
26. What is Oppositional defiant disorder (ODD) ?
27. What are Obsessive thoughts ?
28. What do you understand by Wheelchair Etiquette ?
29. What is Visual Disability Etiquette ?
30. State the advantage of physical activities for special children.

Short Answers Type Questions (Carrying 3 marks)

1. Explain the three common causes of intellectual disability.
2. Mention the types of physical disability.
3. Explain the three types of Attention Deficit Hyperactivity Disorder (ADHD).
4. What are the causes of Attention Deficit Hyperactivity Disorder (ADHD) ?
5. Briefly describe the symptoms of Sensory Processing Disorder.
6. Explain Autism Spectrum Disorder.
7. Explain the characteristics of children with Autism Spectrum Disorder (ASD).

8. Describe the causes of Oppositional defiant disorder (ODD).
9. Explain any four symptoms of Obsessive Compulsive Disorder (OCD).
10. Briefly explain the general rules of disability etiquette.
11. Describe the three advantages of physical activity for children with special needs.

Long Answers Type Questions (Carrying 5 marks)

1. Discuss in details any two disabilities along with its causes and types.
2. Elaborately discuss the types, symptoms and causes of Attention Deficit Hyperactivity Disorder (ADHD).
3. Discuss in details about SPD (Sensory Processing Disorder).
4. What is ASD ? Discuss in details about its types, symptoms and causes.
5. Discuss ODD and OCD in details.
6. Discuss in details about the disability etiquettes.
7. Explain the advantage of physical activities along with the strategies of making the physical activities assessible for the children with special need.

❏ ❏

CHILDREN AND WOMEN IN SPORTS

Children have to be active every day. Sports help children to develop the physical skills, get exercise, make friends, have fun, learn to play as a member of a team, learn to play fair and improve their self-esteem. Research shows that the importance of sports in children is stronger than ever. Sport, not just only exercise, but gives a child more than physical well-being; it contributes to a child's development both psychologically and socially. Many sports psychologists have emphasized that sport is an important learning environment for children. Because sport is essential to children, being good at sports is a strong social asset. Young boys in particular, use sports and games to assess themselves against their friends. Children who are competent at sports are easily accepted by other children of their own age, and are more likely to be team captains and group leaders. Such children usually have better social skills. Physical education and sport have an educational impact on shaping the overall development of children. Changes can be seen in (i) motor skills development and performance and (ii) educational potential. This shows the positive relationship between being involved in physical activities and psychosocial development.

Sport and physical education are fundamental to the early development of children and youth and the skills learned during games. Physical education and sport contribute to the holistic development of children. They learn the values of honesty, teamwork, fair play and respect for themselves and others through participation in sport and physical education. These learning aspects highlight the impact of physical education and sport on a child's social and moral development in addition to physical skills and abilities. In terms of physical and health aspects of child, there is an overwhelming amount of evidence that focuses on the (mostly positive) effects of sport and exercise on physical health, growth and development.

5.1. MOTOR DEVELOPMENT AND FACTORS AFFECTING IT

The growth and development of child's bones, muscles and capability to move around and operate in his or her surroundings is referred to as motor development. In simple words, the development of movements and various motor abilities starting from birth till death is motor development, it is a progressive change of movement all the way through the life cycle. Different motor movements or motor skills are necessary to carry out day-to-day life activities as the ability to move is vital for human development. Activities involved in day to day life are sitting, walking, running, climbing, catching or holding, jumping, skipping, throwing, etc. Motor development furthermore, involves how finely children's muscles work as muscle tone. A balanced muscle tone is needed by children in order to build up their muscles and make use of them with ease while standing, sitting, rolling, walking, running, and swimming and all other postures and actions. Motor development can be divided into two sections : gross motor development and fine motor development.

Motor Development

Gross Motor Development	Fine Motor Development
(*e.g.,* Walking, Running, Climbing, etc.)	(*e.g.,* Holding of Racket, Pole, Smashing Volleyball, Performing Asana, etc.)

Gross Motor Development

Gross motor development involves the development of the large muscles in the child's body. These muscles allow us to sit, stand, walk and run, among other activities.

Fine Motor Development

Fine motor development involves the fine muscles of the body, mainly in the hand. For instance, holding of hammer, gripping discuss and pole, catching cricket ball, smashing volleyball and performing gymnastic exercises, etc.

Motor Development in Children

Under the following three stages of childhood, motor development in children can be studied effectively :

1. Early childhood (2 to 6 years)
2. Middle childhood (7 to 10 years)
3. Late childhood (11 to 12 years)

1. **Early childhood :** This phase of early childhood begins as of 2nd year and prolongs till 6th year. The motor development in this phase takes place rapidly and well known as the preschool years. Within this period a child becomes perfect in a variety of fundamental movements such as running, jumping, throwing and acquires the skill to combine these movements. Children's stride length increases and in addition to that they develop an additional mature running pattern in this period along with the ability to climb on ladders, become efficient and they can hop and gallop skillfully. The motor development at the last phase of early childhood achieves a satisfactory level as they can bring together these movements efficiently under varying and complex conditions so as the systematic training in different sports such as gymnastics and swimming can be in progress for the reason that their fundamental movements like rolling, hanging, pushing and pulling, etc., develop efficiently. Though the children grow to be capable in performing various movement combinations such as running and jumping, catching and throwing and running and throwing, etc., still, competitions at this stage should be avoided.

2. **Middle childhood :** The middle childhood stage begins from 7th year and continues up to the 10th year. Children in this period happen to be agile and energetic aspiring to get engaged in a variety of physical movements and activities competing with children of their own age having an urge to progress upon their earlier performance. The majority of the children acquire mature patterns of fundamental motor skills through this period advancing the posture and balance. They try to gain mastery in the variety of movements, which they had previously learnt. In reality, the similar movements are performed in a different way aiming at jumping for distance or height and throwing for distance, height, etc. They become competent in movement coupling, movement accuracy and movement flow. The speed abilities increase at a rapid rate. Coordinative abilities as well develop in this age group at higher level but flexibility develops very slowly. In this phase, stress must be given on movement rectification and there should be minimum competition.

3. **Late childhood :** This stage of late childhood initiates from 11th year and continues up to 12th year or else till the starting of sexual maturation development. In this phase, girls are for the time being taller and heavier in comparison to boys as a reason of the earlier initiation of puberty. Strength begins to vary but the differences are negligible. Both boys and girls are capable to compete equally. The majority of children have mastery of nearly all complicated motor skills. They are prepared to become skilled at strategies and additional difficult play situations such as running and jumping movements both qualitatively as well as quantitatively which is developed at much more faster rate than in the middle childhood phase. Teachers of physical education and coaches must carry on encouraging skill development by means of increasing pressure on strategies and tactics.

Factors Affecting Motor Development

There are numerous factors, which affect motor development of children. These factors are :

1. **Biological factors :** The genes are related to biological factors which are also known as heredity or genetic factors. Various types of development, including motor development, depend on the genes we inherit from our parents such as the proportion of fast twitch fibers and slow twitch fibers depend on biological factors. In actuality, these factors are probable to have an effect on the rate and ability of motor development, as the factors are associated to body weight, size as well as strength. Research studies have evidence that the non-obese children with proportionately longer legs generally walk earlier than those with shorter legs.

2. **Nutrition :** Nutritious food promotes good motor development. Sensory motor development is dependent upon nutrition that a child gets to a great extent. Children get stronger and development is good if they get nutritious food.

3. **Immunization :** If mother and child both are immunized at a proper time, it leads to good sensory motor development.

4. **Environmental factors :** Physical and social environmental factors are expected to influence the motor development of children. Children who are encouraged to explore the surroundings, their motor development takes place at a much faster rate as per several research studies. In the majority of society, it is generally observed that boys are encouraged and more likely to be involved in sports in comparison to girls. Boys are given extra opportunities to take part in sports activities. As a matter of fact, encouragement, affection along with security facilitates the child to take risk in order to explore without any fear further leading to better motor development.

5. **Physical activities :** The motor development enhances more rapidly with regular physical activities; yet, the activities have to be according to the capability of children. Lack of regular practice of physical activities makes the motor development process slow in children and motor development takes longer duration of time to develop.

6. **Opportunities :** Children who get more opportunities to do more activities, motor development is better in them. Opportunities to play to gain knowledge give a better chance of developing sensory motor activities.

7. **Sensory impairments :** Children are liable to get affected in their motor development due to sensory impairments such as visual impairments and hearing impairments, etc. Hearing impairment leads to difficulty in following the instructions in relation to any type of motor activity. Similarly, visual impairments slow down the development of motor activity. Children with no sensory impairments will definitely have better motor development.

8. **Postural deformities :** The motor development in children definitely gets affected by postural deformities. In the pathway of motor development of children, hindrances or obstacles are created by any of postural deformities viz. spinal curvature deformities, flat foot, knock knees and bow legs, etc. The motor development takes place more rapidly in children when there is absence of postural deformities.

9. **Obesity :** Being overweight or obesity negatively affects the motor development of children, thus resulting into lack of enthusiasm for participating in any motor activity and the children might even feel uncomfortable to perform the activity. These kind of children take more time to perform motor movement as the development takes place very gradually.

5.2. COMMON POSTURAL DEFORMITIES

There are a number of postural deformities which may either be acquired or may be congenital. Each type of postural deviation has its own peculiar causes and effects. Each postural deformity, therefore, demands and requires proper attention and specific treatment for correcting the same. The common postural deformities are mentioned below :

1. Kyphosis
2. Round shoulders
3. Lordosis
4. Scoliosis
5. Flat foot
6. Knock knees
7. Bow legs

Kyphosis

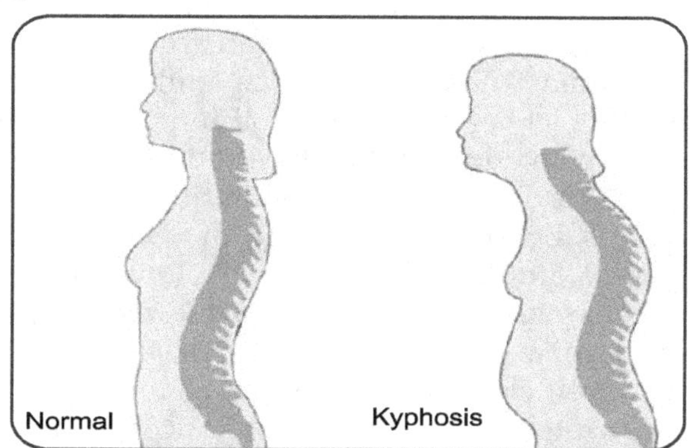

The increased posterior curvature of the spine is called kyphosis. This occurs in the thoracic spine where the normal posterior curve becomes excessive and it may be regarded as thoracic kyphosis. In cervical and lumber region, normally, an anterior curvature exists. However, if that curvature is reversed, it will result in cervical and lumber kyphosis respectively.

This deformity is often termed as "round back" when it takes the form of long and rounded curve. If there is an acute and localized sharp posterior bending, it is regarded as "hump back".

In this deformity, the head is usually carried forward, chest is flattened, shoulders are round, both the scapulas are apart and are more forwarded.

Kyphosis can occur at any age but it is common in the endomorphic type girls.

Causes of Kyphosis

A number of causes; can lead to the kyphosis.

1. Habitual bad posture, mental and physical fatigue.

2. Weakness or paralysing of long extension muscles of the back.
3. Rickets, arthritis and lung diseases.
4. Injury and diseases of the spine and compression fracture of vertebral body in thoracic region.
5. Heredity is also one of the causes of kyphosis.
6. Degeneration of inter-vertebral discs or senile osteoporosis is one of the causes of kyphosis among elderly women.
7. Excessive treatment of lordosis may lead to kyphosis.

Precautions

The teachers and parents should pay specific attention from the very beginning, should teach appropriate posture of sitting, standing and walking to children so that their postures may remain balanced.`

Remedies

1. The family physician or the medical doctor should give attention if the deformity is due to poor health or malnutrition. Any defect of vision or hearing should be treated by the respective specialist doctor.
2. If fatigue is the cause, rest is a vital factor in such children. For lifelong result, habitual faulty posture of a child must also be corrected. Any psychological factor must be paid due attention.
3. Relaxation of the body, mainly the upper back.
4. Stretching of shortened anterior chest structures.
5. Strengthening of the back muscles, in particular those which are stretched and weakened.
6. Develop and improve in breathing or respiration.
7. Mobilization of the spinal column.
8. Postural re-education.

Round Shoulders

Round shoulders is a term frequently linked and described with kyphosis. Appropriate terminology of round shoulders, is a deformity of forward deviation of shoulder girdle in which the scapulae are separated beyond normal and the acromion points of the shoulders come forward, falling anterior to the line of gravity. The sternoclavicular joint (support for the shoulders) is depressed. The vertebral borders of scapulae protrude backward and prominiently develop presenting the picture of winged scapulae.

Simply, in this postural deformity, the shoulders become round and sometimes they seem to be bowed forward. This state of deformity very frequently accompanies kyphosis. Round shoulders and kypho-sis should not be confused with each other as both occur separately. Round shoulders is an abnormality of shoulder girdle with no spinal deviation and completely different muscle-groups are responsible for this abnormality.

Causes

1. If you're sitting in front of the computer all day, your posture is that of someone with round shoulders. You are forced to do activities in front of you all day. It used to be that this type of problem was reserved for hairstylists and mechanics, people whose occupation forced them to have their arms up in front of them all day. Now it's all about being on the computer.
2. Round shoulders may also result when sitting, standing and walking are performed in bowed position.
3. This condition can also occur when the muscles and the ligaments have the least resistance to the mechanical strains due to inaccurate position in bed due to a severe illness.
4. The other factors causing this deformity can be psychological aspect and shyness in the adolescent girls with heavy developing breasts or any injury or disease in the upper dorsal region.
5. By wearing very tight clothes.
6. Lack of proper exercise especially of shoulders may also lead to round shoulders.

Precautions

1. Don't sit, walk or stand in bowed position.
2. Avoid tight-fitting clothes.
3. Avoid sitting on improper furniture.

Remedies

1. Rest, right amount of nutrition and the remedial exercises are applicable to most of the postural defects.
2. The stress should also be made on the right breathing process and on the normal correct body positions in lying, sitting, standing, walk-ing, etc.

Lordosis

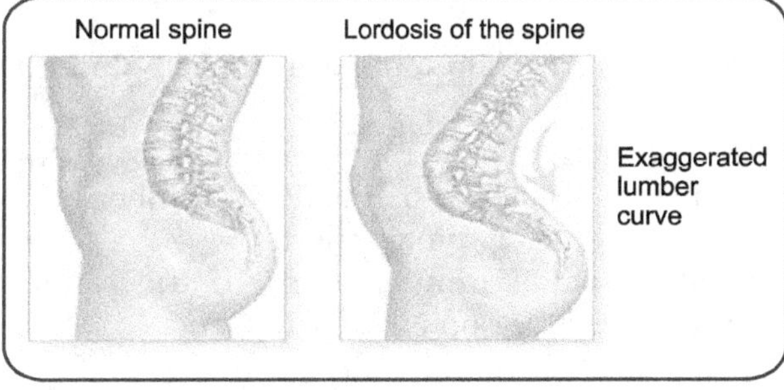

Lordosis denotes or indicates increased anterior curvature of spine. It is an exaggeration or increase in the amount of the normal concavity of the lumber region of the spine, *i.e.,* an increase in the extension curve of the lumber region beyond normal region. It is inward curvature of the spine with protruding abdomen resulting in hollow back. This deformity is opposite of kyphosis.

This state may occur as a compensatory adjustment to the deviations in the spine above the lumber region. Relaxation and poor tonus of the abdominal muscles may also allow the curve to collapse. In some cases, when the hips are thrust forward, the curve increases in order to throw the upper trunk back into balance. The muscles of the lower back are shortened and the abdominal muscles are elongated. When this position becomes habitual, too much weight is thrown on the posterior edge of the bodies of the lumber vertebrae.

Causes of Lordosis

1. Habitual, bad or faulty posture or habits.
2. The weakness and paralysis of abdominal muscles.
3. Careless treatment of kyphosis.
4. Obesity with big belly.
5. Injury or disease of lumber spine.

Precautions

1. Balanced diet should be taken.
2. Obesity should be kept away especially in early age.
3. The body should be kept straight while carrying weight.
4. Excessive intake of food should be avoided.

Remedies

1. The family physician or the medical doctor should give attention if the deformity is due to poor health or malnutrition. Any defect of vision or hearing should be treated by the respective specialist doctor.
2. If fatigue is the cause; rest is a vital factor in such children. For lifelong result, habitual faulty posture of a child must also be corrected. Any psychological factor must be paid due attention to.
3. Strengthening of abdominal muscles, glutei and hamstrings.
4. Stretching of posterior structures of lumber region, *e.g.,* Posterior ligaments of lumber region, and lower erector spinal muscles.
5. Mobilization of lumber spine, if the range of motion in this region is restricted, and
6. Correction of habitual faulty posture.

Scoliosis

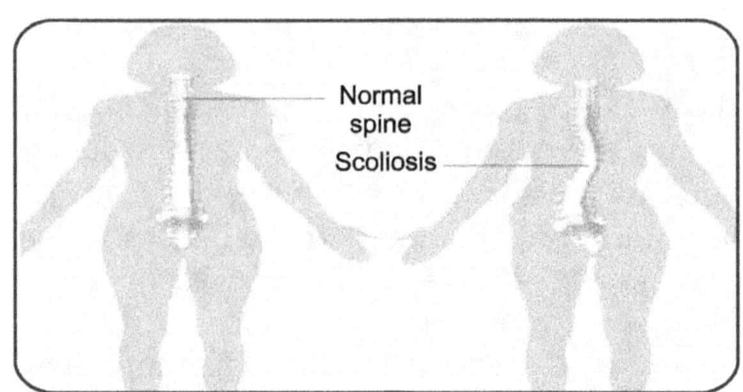

The term scoliosis is derived from a Greek word, which actually means twisting or bending. Scoliosis means a lateral bending of spine to one or more sides from midline. It is an exaggerated lateral curvature *i.e.,* sideward curvature or deviation of the spine, with the shoulder lower and hip higher on one side. It may be present in a very small part of spine or it can involve the whole or major part of spine. Usually there is a single curve in one direction only and called 'C' curve scoliosis. When two or more than two lateral curves are present in the spine, that is called 'S' curve scoliosis or compound and double scoliosis.

The shoulder on one side will be lower than the other. The hip of the opposite side will be higher, the arms hang loosely at the sides, the angle between arm and body is greater on one side than the other. Most of the people are having stronger muscles on the right side of the body as they are right handed; the scoliosis tends to develop with the convexity to the left. It is more common among girls than boys.

Causes of Scoliosis

1. Faulty habitual posture.
2. Weakness or paralysis of the muscles particularly trunk back extension, abdominal.
3. Injuries and disease of the spine (ligament, bones fracture of transverse process).
4. T.B. and Rickets of the spine.
5. Congenital deformity (defect since birth), like hemivertebra, congenital short limb, club foot, polio, etc.
6. Deformity of some other body part can cause secondary scoliosis, *e.g.,* knock knee, shortening of one leg, deformity of the neck, etc.

Precautions

1. Balanced diet should be taken.
2. The study should be avoided in sideways bending position.
3. Avoid walking for long time while carrying weight in one hand.

Remedies

1. Fatigue and under-nourishment are usually the root causes of scoliosis; proper diet and rest are of great significance.
2. The nourishing food, plenty of fresh air, good hygienic condition and generalized exercises are all very vital part of the common healing as relevant to other postural defects.
3. If the faulty seating is the cause of abnormality, then specific steps must be taken to correct the seating. Where it is not likely to get rid of the cause, every attempt must be made to prevent the deformity.
4. Strengthening of the muscles concerned in postural control, so that they can keep up the corrected position.
5. Stretching of the tightened structures, and to get better flexibility and mobility of the spine if preferred.
6. Improving ventilation (breathing), mainly if the scoliosis is in the thoracic region.
7. Relaxation of the tensed soft structures.
8. Correction of faulty habitual posture and re-education of accurate postural sense.

Flat Foot

Flat foot is a deformity in which the medial longitudinal and transverse arches of foot are depressed

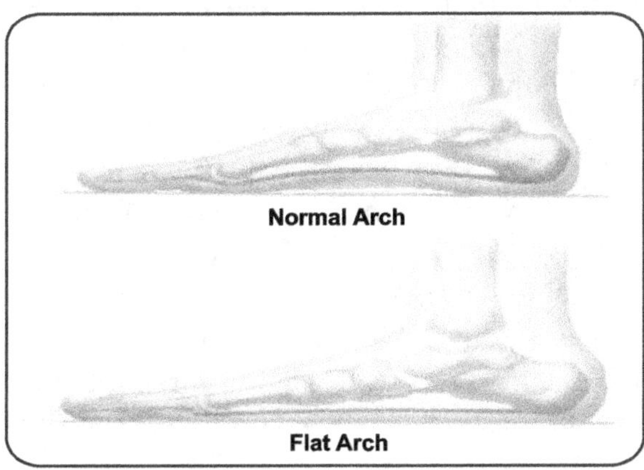

and medial border of foot comes in contact with ground. This is usually associated with some degrees for eversion. True flat foot or **"Pes-Planus"** is a structural deformity, which may not necessarily be accompanied by discomfort or impaired foot function in all the individuals having it. Flat foot can be diagnosed with a very simple test called as **wet foot test.** The other recognized method of assessing the flat foot is '**Pedograph test'**, in which a foot print of the under surface or planter aspect of the foot is taken.

Causes of Flat Foot

1. The faulty posture (habitual standing on one leg or walking for long periods with the feet in extreme eversion position).
2. Long or continuous weight bearing and being over-weight may lead to flat foot.
3. Improper shoes or footwear.
4. Weakness or paralysis of the tibialis anterior or posterior muscle.
5. Secondary reasons like Knock-knee and scoliosis may lead to this deformity.
6. Injuries particularly to the lower leg ankle or foot may lead to flat foot.

Precautions

1. The shoes should be of proper shape and size; high heeled shoes should be avoided.
2. Avoid bare foot walking for a long duration.
3. Obesity should be avoided.
4. Don't force babies to walk at very early stage.
5. Carrying heavy weight in early childhood should be avoided.

Remedies

1. If the children are malnourished, corrections relating to diet are to be made.
2. Weight-reduction is extremely essential, in case of obesity.
3. If suffering from rickets, the essential medical treatment is necessary.
4. Attention should be paid to the children having postural flat feet by preventing too much standing and by wearing of proper footwear.
5. The general exercises and re-education of correct posture are the vital parts of the remedial treatment, apart from the specific exercises for muscle-strengthening and restorations of mobility.
6. The remedial treatment should be aimed at the maintenance or restoration of the joint-mobility to the level possible, strengthening of the muscles that support the foot arches and directions in appropriate posture.
7. Obese individual is not likely to get much better with corrective treatment unless he loses weight. He should therefore be given advice on diet, suitable footwear probably with an arch support. When the individual regains sufficient muscle-power and postural sense, then the support can be discarded.
8. Mobilize the joints of the foot, if required.

9. Strengthen the weak muscles.

10. Re-educate the correct postural sense.

11. Restore the arches of the foot as far as possible.

Knock knees or Genu Valgum

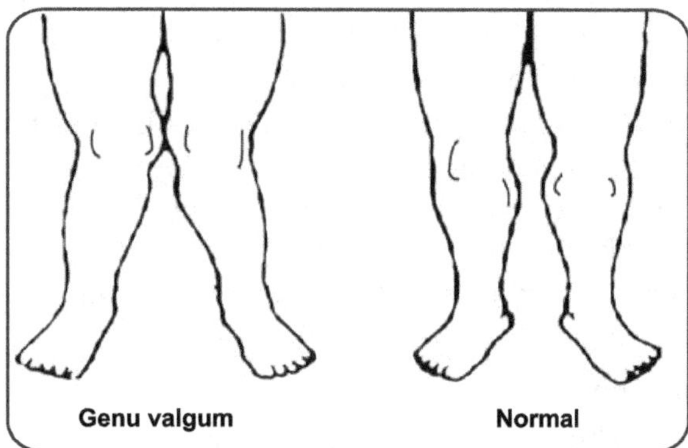

The Knock knee or Genu valgum is one of the major postural deformities. It is a defect in which there is an inward rejection of the leg at the knee so that the tibia remains abducted in relation to the femur and that is why both the knees knock or touch each other in normal standing position. The gap between ankles goes on increasing. It is a position that tends to shift the body weight towards the medial border of the foot and bring about a foot position of pronation. The individual faces difficulty in walking and running.

Causes

1. The lack of balanced diet especially vitamin 'D', calcium and phosphorus.

2. It may also be due to rickets.

3. Due to growth imbalance and weakness of leg muscles and joint ligaments.

4. Chronic illness, obesity, flat foot, scoliosis and carrying heavy weight in early age.

Precautions

1. Balanced diet should be taken.

2. Babies should not be forced to walk at very early age.

Remedies

1. Knock knees occurring in the children often get corrected and in general no treatment is required.

2. If occurred due to any other cause or due to defect during childhood or adolescence whether it is rickets or otherwise, proper medical treatment is required.

3. The weak and malnourished children would require rest and proper nutrition.

4. The obese children below the age of one year should be allowed protected and supported weight bearing and walking.

5. If condition of knock-knee is the result of a disease process (*e.g.,* Rheumatoid arthritis), then the treatment would be essential.

6. When the deformity is due to the soft tissue structures such as lengthening of medical ligament and weakness of muscles, the rectification may be advised with proper splinting.

Bow Legs

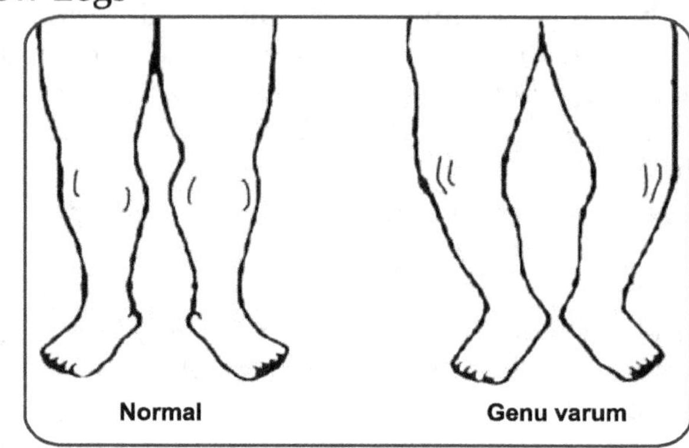

'Bow legs' is also a postural deformity. It is opposite to knock knees position. In this postural defect there is lateral bowing or angulation of the leg in relation to the knee. A wide gap between the knees can be observed when an individual stands with feet together. In fact, bow legs is a deformity of the lower leg having maximum bowing only at the middle of the leg, whereas **genu-varum** is a deformity of the whole lower limb with maximum curvature and bowing at the knee. This deformity can be observed easily, when an individual walks or runs. Bow legs are quite common during infancy and childhood.

Causes

1. Deficiency of vitamin 'D', calcium and phosphorus in bones.

2. Long bones of legs become soft.

3. Increases when the children become overweight.

4. Improper way of walking and forcing the babies to walk or carrying heavy weight at very early age.

5. Rickets, injuries such as fracture around the medial side of the knee joint, osteoarthritis, limb length discrepancy, high arches of foot, tightness of leg muscles, etc.

Precautions

1. Don't let the children become overweight.

2. Don't force the babies to walk at a very early age.

3. Balanced diet should be given to children. There should not be any deficiency of calcium, phosphorus and vitamin-D in the diet.

Remedies

1. The mild deformity in young children may not necessitate any specific treatment unless the deformity is making progress.

2. In the higher level causing functional impairment, instantaneous attention needs to be paid.

3. Underlying cause of the deformity should be removed whatever the degree of abnormality is.

4. Rest and proper nutrition should be given due care in younger children.

5. If the child suffers from rickets, it should be correctly treated.

6. The weak and malnourished children would require rest and proper nutrition.

5.3. CORRECTIVE MEASURES FOR POSTURAL DEFORMITIES

We often get victimized by postural deformities as our surroundings include many forces that operate upon our bodies. Most likely, the postural deformities may owe to pull of gravity, congenital factor, mal nutrition and long-drawn-out illness. Postural deformities are of two types, namely functional and structural.

In functional deformity, just the soft tissues, *i.e.*, the muscles and the ligaments are affected. Through various types of physical activities, the corrections of postural deformities are possible. On the other hand, structural deformities crop up when the bony structure is affected. Physical activi-ties in cases of structural deformities cannot play any important role. In fact, in these cases, the surgery can be useful for securing the preferred improvement.

In particular, during elementary school years the role of physical activities in functional deformities is very effective. Certainly physical activities or exercise in various forms can counteract the effect of gravitational force. The rectification of postural deformities should be a part of school education.

For increasing general strength, endurance, balance and flexibility, students should also be encouraged to engage themselves in exercises. Relaxation procedures should also be performed. Along with the exercises, such students who have postural deformities should be made aware about proper postures.

There are a variety of physical activities or exercises which can be used as remedial measures for correction of postural deformities. The remedial exercises related to particular postural deformities are stated as under :

Exercises for Kyphosis

1. Swimming, Bench Press and Push-ups are beneficial as remedial measures.

2. In corner exercises, the patient stands facing a corner with one hand on each wall, arms at the shoulder level and elbow at 90°. From this position, the body moves forward mainly from the ankle joint. This is a very good exercise for stretching the pectoral muscles.

3. Lying on the back on a narrow bench with ring weight hanging from elbows the arms may flex to avoid any stress to elbows.

4. Holding a towel or stick in a wide hand grips with arm extended above the hand and shoulder gives a good stretch to pectoral muscle and also strengthens the posterior neck and upper back muscle.

5. Yogic asanas can help reverse the abnormal hunchback curve of the spine that occurs in postural kyphosis. Upper back bending poses will help reverse the hunchback curve as well as stretch the muscles on the front of the torso which often have become chronically tight in this condition. Spine lengthening poses promote good posture and proper alignment of the vertebrae. Weight bearing back bends will strengthen the back muscles to assist the holding of a corrected posture. Matsyasana, Bhujangasana, Ardha Salabhasana, Salabhasana, Setu Bandhasana, Dhanurasana, etc., are useful for kyphosis.

6. Breathing exercises are also to be given. These exercises help in improving vital capacity of lungs and also help in expanding the lungs and improve thoraces flexibility.

Exercises for Round Shoulders

1. In corner exercises, the individual stands facing a corner with one hand on each wall arms at the shoulder level and elbow 90° from this position the body moves forward mainly from the ankle joint. This is an extremely good exercise for stretching the pectoral muscles.

2. Active hanging can be an excellent exercise for young and strong individuals, as it raises the chest and places the head in a better position.

3. Back stroke – swimming, volleyball, medicine ball throwing from overhead positions, etc., are excellent for correcting the deformity.

4. Yogic asanas such as Bhujangasana, Setu bandhasana, Gomukhasana, Dhanurasana, Ushtrasana and Chakrasana are very useful asanas to correct the round shoulders.

5. Emphasis should be laid on correct breathing since the forceful respiratory movements prevent round shoulders. The deep inhalation in correcting position is very essential and should be repetitively practiced.

Exercises for Lordosis

1. Lying down in prone position, with hands under abdomen. Then keeping hips and shoulders down, pressing hands up on abdomen and raising lower back.

2. Bending knees forward while allowing hips to bend behind, keeping back straight and knees pointed in same direction as feet. Descending until thighs are just parallel to floor. Extending knees and hip until legs are straight. Coming back in starting position and then repeating the same.

3. Lung forward with knees on a mat. Taking position of one foot beyond the knee, place both hands on knee. Straighten the hip of rear leg by pushing hips forward and holding the stretch. Hold for 30 secs. Repeat with opposite side.

4. Sitting on a chair with feet wide apart. Bending and positioning the shoulders between knees. Then reaching to the floor under back of the chair. Hold the position for some duration.

5. Lying in prone position on the floor. Keep the palms of the hands on the floor according to shoulders' width. Push the torso up keeping pelvis on floor. Hold the position for some time.

6. Sitting down with knees extended, feet together and hands at sides. After that bend forward and touch the fingers toes. Hold the position for some time. Then coming back and repeat the same.

7. Yoga can help reverse the swayback curve that occurs in postural lordosis. To correct this swayback curve, one must learn to "tuck your tailbone under" to help flatten the low back through the engagement of the abdominal and core muscles of the body. Using rounding poses of the low back, engage the tailbone tuck to reverse the swayback curve and to stretch the muscles of the low back. Building strength through poses that engage the core muscles of the abdominals and low back will be most helpful. Spine lengthening poses promote good posture and proper alignment of the vertebrae. Halasana, Balasana, Marjariasana, Sasangasana, Tadasana, Trikonasana, Setu bandhasana, etc., are useful.

Exercises for Scoliosis

Exercise is the best way to strengthen and straighten the physical posture and will avoid curvature on one side. Even though yoga has been known in the past to cure a lot of physical ailments, it may not create magic in case of Scoliosis, but can definitely make the posture strong and give the muscles some balance. During the course of exercise – in the initial period pain will be felt but with the continuous practice this can be altered. Breathing exercises like strong chest movements with deep breaths are known to cause temporary rotation of the thoracic vertebrae in a ritualistic direction. This occurs in some people with scoliosis and helps them to attain the perfect formation. Some exercises are mentioned below for scoliosis.

1. Bending exercise should be performed in opposite side of 'C' shaped curve.

2. Holding the horizontal bar with your hands and swing your body to the left and right side.

3. Stand in erect position with feet several inches apart. Keeping left hand's finger tips on left shoulder and bending the upper body in right side if there is an opposite 'C' curve in the spine. But if there is no opposite 'C' curve means if there is 'C' curve, bend the upper body to left side. The tips of the fingers of right hand should be on right shoulder. Repeating the exercise for some time as per the 'C' curve.

(a) Hip Roll and Bridge as an exercise incline one's pelvis area – raise one's vertebrae to form a full circle; and give movements to the hip which is a must during Scoliosis. As the circular position is maintained in the opposite direction, the problem gets good outcome after a full fledged warm up session.

(b) To swim by using breast stroke technique.

(c) Hanging from the horizontal bar.

(d) A consistent, regular practice of yoga can offer relief from scoliosis and its side effects, including back pain, sciatica, intervertebral disc prolapse, sacroiliac issues, and tingling in the hands. The amount and intensity of practice required varies according to the degree of misalignment, overall muscle tone, and age. Scoliosis is a very individual condition; no two cases are exactly the same. Tadasana, Vrikshasana, Trikonasana, Matsyasana Sarvangasana, Halasana, Naukasana etc., are helpful.

Exercises for Flat Foot

For correcting functional flat foot one should exercise :

1. By rising on the toes, by climbing stairs on the toes, by rope skipping and by cycling.

2. The emphasis should be upon the exercises involving toe flexion, foot and ankle flexion and supination.

3. Exercise like sitting on a chair : grasp a pencil under the toes of one foot and try to write the alphabets with large strokes.

4. Sitting on a chair, with a soft rubber ball placed between the feet, grasp the ball between soles of the feet and raise it from the floor off and place it back.

5. One should wear special shoes properly fitted with arch support, made by an orthopedic centre.

Exercises for Knock Knees

The best way to correct knock knees is to strengthen the knee by doing a series of exercises :

1. Horse riding is the best exercise for this deformity.

2. Performing Padmasana and Gomukasana regularly for some time.

3. Keeping a pillow between the knees and standing erect for some time.

4. Use of walking calipers may also be beneficial.

5. Seated quadriceps contraction, leg strengthening exercises and hamstring curls.

6. Yoga can be beneficial for a variety of musculoskeletal conditions, including knock knees. Knock knees are musculoskeletal deformities resulting in poor knee alignment, affecting the upper leg area including the femur and tibia leg bones plus related tissues. If used consistently, yoga postures can help retrain muscles and improve overall functioning levels. Virbhadra asana, Pavanmuktasana, Trikonasana, Salabhasana, etc., are useful.

7. The modifications in the footwear are advised by the expert therapist, in which medial heel wedge is given in the heel of the shoes to shift the line of the weight bearing which further helps in increasing the gap between the knees.

Exercises for Bow Legs

The following exercises may be advantageous for rectification of bow legs :

1. Standing erect with feet together. Wrapping a soft piece of cloth on both legs at knee level. Tightening it with assistance of a partner. Trying to squat as far as possible. Holding that position of squat for some time. Coming up and repeating it for 4 to 6 times.

2. Walking for some distance on the inner edge for the feet.

3. Walking by bending the toes inward.

5.4. WOMEN AND SPORTS

In sports more often people do not acknowledge women's sports as much as men's sports. From the time of early Olympics the role of women in sports and games was neglected. The end of the 19th century and turn of the 20th century saw the rising interest of women in sports both as participants and spectators.

However compared to men's participation in sports, women's sports are newer and this is the reason for them not getting the recognition they deserve. But the world of sports has begun to see how women's sports can be just as interesting and exciting as men's sports can be.

An important role in encouraging women to participate is played by the educational society, be it at school or at college. The provision of sporting facilities on an even scale to both women and men shows the new trend. This has seen a rise in the number of women participating in sports. More people want to see women play sports now than in the past because of the better quality of players.

However a few discriminations still persist. For example, television time is something that both men and women teams have to compete over. In most areas men get most of this television time which is not fair at all. There should be equal television time for both the sexes. Women are just as important as men are. Also it is seen that when it comes to salaries, coaching positions, cash awards and television time men are again given preference.

So to an extent along with the concerned authorities even the media is responsible in promoting equality to women in recognizing their accomplishments. It is beginning to even out a lot more though, than what it used to be. Nowadays you can usually catch a girl's game on some odd channel. The main stations mainly have men's games on them.

Equality amongst men and women in sports should not merely be measured by their physical drive and prowess on the playing field but also by the percentage of athletes compared to the total number eligible. Great strides have been made to provide an equal opportunity for females in the sports world and even greater steps have to be taken.

Women have come a long way and yet have a long way to go. Increases in scholarships, salaries, airtime, operating and recruiting expenses will help encourage female athletes. Women should be treated as equals to men when it comes to sports and this seems very possible in the absolute near future.

About 53% of participants in India's only rural-sports programme, the Panchayat Yuva Krida Khel Abhiyan (PYKKA or Village-level Youth Sports Programme), are women. The scheme is now called the Rajiv Gandhi Khel Abhiyan (RGKA, or the Rajiv Gandhi Sports Movement). RGKA funds sports infrastructure in villages and promotes annual competitions at the block, district, state and national level.

There is no separate budget for female sportspersons. However, a minimum expenditure of 30% is allocated to women under neutral programmes by the government.

Over the last four years, ₹ 148 crore was spent under the PYKKA/RGKA competitions. Of this, 10%, or ₹ 14 crore went to sports for women. Only ₹ 357 crore was released for rural sports infrastructure.

The North-Eastern states of Arunachal Pradesh, Manipur, Meghalaya, Mizoram, Nagaland, Sikkim and Tripura received only ₹ 14.27 crore over the last four years (Assam got no money). These are states that are home to India's global sportswomen including M.C. Mary Kom, 2012 Olympics bronze medalist and a five time world amateur-boxing champion, boxer L. Sarita Devi, silver medalist at the 2014 Glasgow Commonwealth Games, and weightlifter K. Sanjita Chanu, who won gold at the 2014 Glasgow Commonwealth Games.

Recognizing the importance of sports infrastructure in what is now becoming India's sporting crucible, especially for women, the central government set aside ₹ 100 crore in the budget of 2014-15 to set up a sports university in Manipur.

5.5. SPORTS PARTICIPATION OF WOMEN IN INDIA

Sport in India is yet to reach its peak. The Mughals ruled India for centuries, the Britishers for another one and a half century. It was only after 1947, when we achieved independence that we started developing as a modern nation, with special rights to half of its citizens namely women. Indian women are still trying to establish their own identity. Women in India are still unable to take a stand for themselves.

Gender inequality is a deep-rooted issue and in order to change the situation, drastic steps/measures need to be taken. Gender inequality is one of the many issues because of which India is not being able to progress at a faster rate. Gender inequality and several other factors like sociological factors, economical factors, psychological factors, physiological factors, other factors (such as political, cultural and religious) were considered as the reason for poor participation of women in sports in India. The study by M. Singh et al., stated that Women participation in games and sports was mostly affected by sociological factors and economical factors.

In modern society, many female athletes participate in sports. Female athletes also undergo training just like the male athletes; however they are not given the same recognition or money that the male athletes make.

Other reasons why women don't participate in sports include :
1. Time constraints (women generally have less free time because of family commitments)
2. Social stereotyping
3. Access to safe and appropriate environments
4. Lack of childcare
5. Concerns for personal safety
6. Lack of skill

Presently the changing attitude towards women in the society that promoted the growth of sports, participation was greatly enhanced by passage of title IX of the Education Amendment Act of 1972, which prohibits discrimination on the basis of sex in any educational programmes or activity receiving federal financial assistance.

The school as well all other facts of the society such as agencies and clubs have opened wide doors to provide girls and women with the same opportunities as boys and men to meet their biological, psychological, sociological and emotional needs through play and competitions. In any event women are now responding to their newly found freedom in sports as well as in particularly all other facts of society where there has been over and covert discrimination with aggressiveness purpose and more clarified goals.

Integrating sports with education is a key reason for increasing participation of women in Indian sports. The Right to Education Act of 2009 requires sporting facilities in every school and the CBSE, a central government education system made sports mandatory.

Participations of women in villages, districts, states and national level sports competition have grown. Rural female participation in sports has increased from 2,49,190 in 2008-09 to 1.07 million in 2013-14, despite a drop in budgets.

Karnataka topped the list with 1,63,520 female participants in 2013-14 under the PYKKA/RGKA programme. Maharashtra with 1,58,836 female participants was second, followed by Tamil Nadu (1,34,790), Gujarat (1,01,497) and Madhya Pradesh (88,116).

Some of the examples of Indian female athletes are Sania Mirza (Tennis), Anju Bobby George (Track and Field), Seema Antil (Indian Discus Thrower), P.T. Usha (Track and Field), Bachendri Pal (Mountaineering), Soma Biswas (Track and Field), Saina Nehwal (Badminton), Jyotirmoyee Sikdar (Track and Field), Mary Kom (Boxing), Karnam Malleshwari (Weight Lifting), Shiny Wilson (Athletic), Ashwini Ponnappa (Badminton), Jwala Gutta (Badminton), Heena Sidhu (Pistol Shooter), Deepika Kumari (Archery) etc.

5.6. SPECIAL CONSIDERATION (MENARCHE AND MENSTRUAL DYSFUNCTION, PREGNANCY)

Menarche

Menarche is a young woman's first menstrual cycle and bleed. Throughout history, menarche has been an important social rite, marking a girl's passage to adulthood. However a young girl's first menstruation cycles are different to those of adults in that she usually does not ovulate. About 80 percent of menstrual cycles within a year of menarche are anovulatory (no egg is released). This reduces to 50 percent in the third year and 10 percent by the sixth year. However, some girls can ovulate on their first period.

A girl usually has her first period between the ages of 9 and 15. In 5 percent of cases menarche occurs between the ages of 16 and 18. Menstruation which starts before 9 is either precocious puberty or a symptom of endocrine disease. Generally a period starts about two years after the breasts first start to develop in puberty.

One may get delayed menarche, if body fat levels fall below 15 to 22 percent of total body weight, girls with type 1 diabetes and who have not gotten proper nutrition due to long-term illnesses. Also, some young girls who undergo intense physical training for a sport, such as running or gymnastics, start puberty later than normal.

In other cases, the delay in menarche is not just due to slow maturation but occurs if the child has a long-term medical condition known as hypogonadism, in which the sex glands (the testes in men and the ovaries in women) produce few or no hormones.

Menstrual bleeding itself is the first sign of menarche. The other signs include discomfort in the stomach region, bloating, fatigue and mood swings.

The symptoms one may experience are like light or heavy menstrual bleeding, headache, backache, and even leg pain. Stomach cramps are a common symptom of menarche. These abdominal cramps may last for a first few days of the menstrual cycle. The first period may cause a lot of discomfort. However, one should not feel scared or become worried. It is very normal to experience pain as the uterus contracts during periods. The symptoms are different for each and every individual. For example, one may expe-rience low intensity cramps, whereas the other may experience severe cramps.

Menstrual Dysfunction

Menstrual Dysfunction is defined as abnormal bleeding in the absence of intracavitary or uterine pathology. Menstrual dysfunction in athletes may include primary amenorrhea, secondary amenorrhea, oligomenorrhea, and luteal phase deficiency.

In adolescent it is considered to have delayed puberty when breast development has not begun by 13.3 years of age. Involvement in sports or poor nutrition may be associated with a delay in development; evaluation might be postponed until 14 years of age, as determined by clinical judgment.

The absence of menses by age 16 years is called Primary amenorrhea. If menses have not occurred within 4.5 years after the onset of breast development, evaluation should be considered. The absence of at least 3 to 6 consecutive menstrual cycles in a female who has begun menstruating is called as Secondary amenorrhea and the menstrual periods that occur at intervals longer than every 35 days refers to Oligomenorrhea. Although adolescents may have irregular periods or amenorrhea for 3 to 6 months in the first several years after menarche, the cessation of menses for longer than 3 months after regular cycles have begun or persistent oligomenorrhea is considered abnormal.

Menstrual dysfunction is more common in athletes than in the general population. Athletes and dancers who begin training before menarche occurs may experience a later menarche and have an increased incidence of menstrual dysfunction when compared with girls who begin training after menarche occurs. The prevalence of secondary amenorrhea in adult athletes ranges from 3.4% to 66% (depending on the sport studied and the criteria used to define amenorrhea), compared with 2% to 5% of women in the general population. The prevalence of secondary amenorrhea in the young athlete is unknown.

Menstrual dysfunction may lead to decreased BMD. Other long-term consequences of a chronically estrogen-depleted state in young women are unknown at this time.

Exercise-induced or athletic menstrual dysfunction is more common in active women and can significantly affect health and sport performance. Although athletic amenorrhoea represents the most extreme form of menstrual dysfunction, other forms can also result in suppressed estrogen levels and affect bone health and fertility. A number of factors, such as energy balance, exercise intensity and training practices, body weight and composition, disordered eating behaviors, and physical and emotional stress levels, may contribute to the development of athletic menstrual dysfunction.

Pregnancy

The state of carrying a developing embryo or fetus within the female body. It lasts for about nine months, measured from the date of the woman's last menstrual period (LMP). It is conventionally divided into three trimesters, each roughly three months long.

First Trimester (0 to 13 Weeks)

The first trimester is the most crucial to the baby's development. During this period, the baby's body structure and organ systems develop. Most miscarriages and birth defects occur during this period.

Second Trimester (14 to 26 Weeks)

The second trimester of pregnancy is often called the "golden period" because many of the unpleasant effects of early pregnancy disappear. During the second trimester, one is likely to experience decreased nausea, better sleep patterns and an increased energy level.

Third Trimester (27 to 40 Weeks)

Third trimester is a final stretch of pregnancy; the probable period of excitement and anxiousness for the birth of baby. Some physical symptoms may be experienced during this period including shortness of breath, hemorrhoids, urinary incontinence, varicose veins and sleeping problems.

Exercise during pregnancy can increase energy, relieve constipation, leg cramps, bloating and swelling, promote the spirit, relaxation, maintain your posture and sleep quality, build muscle mass, control diabetes, fighting back pain, increase stamina during labor, as well as help the body get back into shape faster.

Most exercises are safe to perform during pregnancy, as long as exercise with caution and do not overdo it. The safest and most productive activities are swimming, brisk walking, using an indoor exercise bike, step or elliptical machines and low-impact aerobics (taught by a qualified aerobics instructor). These activities carry little risk of injury, benefit entire body, and can be continued until birth.

Some racquet sports, such as tennis, are generally safe activities, but changes in balance during pregnancy may affect rapid movements; in general contact sports should be avoided. Other activities such as jogging can be done in moderation, especially if one has the habit of doing it before pregnancy.

Mind-body classes like tai chi, yoga and pilates are suitable for pregnant participants as well. These types of classes can do wonders for the management of stress and teach students new methods of relaxation.

There are certain exercises and activities that can be harmful if performed during pregnancy. They include :

1. Holding the breath during any activity.
2. Activities where falling is likely (such as skiing and horse riding).
3. Contact sports such as football and basketball.
4. Any exercise that may cause even mild abdominal trauma such as activities that include jerking motions or rapid changes in direction.
5. Activities that require extensive jumping, hopping, skipping, bouncing or running.
6. Deep knee bends, full sit-ups, double leg raises, and straight-leg toe touches.
7. Bouncing while stretching.
8. Waist-twisting movements while standing.
9. Exercise in hot, humid weather.
10. Exercises after 16 weeks of pregnancy that involve lying on the back.

This condition can be indicated by positive results on an over-the-counter urine test, and confirmed through a blood test, ultrasound, detection of fetal heartbeat, or an X-ray.

Menopause

Menopause is a normal condition that all women experience as they age. The term "menopause" can describe any of the changes a woman goes through either just before or after she stops menstruating, marking the end of her reproductive period.

Natural menopause is not brought on by any type of medical or surgical treatment. The process is gradual and has three stages :

Premature Menopause

The average age of women at the time of menopause is 51 years. The women experience menopause commonly at age range of 48-55 years. If menopause occurs in a woman younger than 40 years, it is considered to be premature. Menopause is considered late if it occurs in a woman older than 55 years. For most women, menopause is a normal occurrence. Menopause is more likely to occur at a slightly earlier age in women who smoke, have never been pregnant, or live at high altitudes. If premature menopause occurs, a health care professional will check for other medical problems. About 1% of women experience premature menopause.

Perimenopause

The hormonal changes associated with menopause actually begin prior to the last menstrual period, during a three to five year period called the Perimenopause. During this transition, women may begin to experience menopausal symptoms and may lose bone density, even though they are still menstruating.

Surgical Menopause

Surgical menopause is induced menopause by the removal of the ovaries. Women who have had surgical menopause often have a sudden and severe onset of the symptoms of menopause.

Menopause may be caused when the ovaries no longer release an egg every month and menstruation stops. Menopause is considered a normal part of aging when it happens after the age of 40. But some women can go through menopause early, either as a result of surgery, such as hysterectomy, or damage to the ovaries, such as from chemotherapy.

5.7. FEMALE ATHLETE TRIAD (ANEMIA, OSTEOPOROSIS AND AMENORRHEA)

Sports and exercise are healthy activities for girls and women of all ages. Occasionally, a female athlete who focuses on being thin or lightweight may eat too little or exercise too much. Doing this can cause long-term damage to health, or even death. It can also hurt athletic performance or make it necessary to limit or stop exercise.

Three interrelated illnesses may develop when a girl or young woman goes to extremes in dieting or exercise. Together, these conditions are known as the "Female Athlete Triad."

The three conditions are :

Triad Factor 1 : Disordered Eating (Anemia)

Most girls with female athlete triad try to lose weight as a way to improve their athletic performance. The disordered eating that accompanies female athlete triad can range from not eating enough calories to keep up with energy demands to avoiding certain types of food the athlete thinks are "bad" (such as foods containing fat) to serious eating disorders like anorexia nervosa or bulimia nervosa.

Anorexia Nervosa

Anorexia nervosa is characterized by the refusal to eat. It can affect anyone of any gender or age but disproportionately affects young women in their late teens and early twenties. It is a disorder (or illness), which stems from low self-esteem and an inability to cope safely with worries and problems. It involves lowering of food intake by skipping meals and cutting down the types and amounts of food; some people over-exercise as well. It may be believed that if the individual loses weight his/her life would be happier, people will like them more, they will be more successful.

Types of anorexia nervosa :

There are two different types of anorexia that people suffer from; the first is restricting anorexia and the second is binge eating/purging anorexia. The underlying characteristics for both types are basically the same; with both types of anorexia, the sufferer will have a total fear of weight gain.

1. Binge/purging anorexia : The person suffering from bingeing anorexia will have the tendency to induce vomiting once he/she has eaten. The sufferer will eat and once the food is digested, they will immediately be overcome with a sense of guilt for the actions and will force themselves to be sick to rid themselves of the food. This can lead to serious problems with the digestive system and in particular the oesophagus, which due to the acid could burst.

2. Restrictive anorexia : The sufferer will restrict the amount of food taken into the body, with this type of anorexia. The sufferer won't eat binge food and then vomit, they just don't eat.

Physical signs and **symptoms** of anorexia :

1. Extreme weight loss.
2. Thin appearance.
3. Abnormal blood counts.
4. Fatigue.
5. Insomnia.
6. Dizziness or fainting.
7. A bluish discolouration of the fingers.
8. Hair that thins, breaks or falls out.
9. Soft, downy hair covering the body.
10. Absence of menstruation.
11. Constipation.
12. Dry skin.
13. Low blood pressure.

14. Dehydration.
15. Osteoporosis.
16. Intolerance of cold.
17. Irregular heart rhythms.
18. Swelling of arms or legs.

Bulimia Nervosa

Bulimia nervosa, commonly called bulimia, is a serious, potentially life-threatening eating disorder. Bulimia nervosa is a severe mental illness that can go undetected for a long time. People with this condition need treatment so that they are able to begin the journey to recovery. People with bulimia nervosa will binge eat at least once a week and feel that they have no control over the amount of food consumed, or the ability to stop.

People with bulimia nervosa try to compensate or make up for the excess energy intake using a variety of techniques including vomiting, laxatives and diuretics, fasting, excessive exercise and even using medications inappropriately to control body weight. These activities are not a lifestyle choice but a sign of a complex mental health problem.

People with bulimia nervosa tend to have body weight closer to the healthy weight range. If their weight drops into a low range for their height and age and indulge in binging, using a compensatory behavior such as vomiting or laxatives, they would fit the diagnosis of anorexia nervosa subtype-binge eating/purging.

Types of bulimia nervosa : There are two types of bulimia which are stated below :

1. **Purging bulimia :** In this type of bulimia, the individuals regularly self-induce vomiting or misuse laxatives, diuretics or enemas after bingeing.

2. **Non-purging bulimia :** In this type of bulimia, the individuals use other methods to rid themselves of calories and prevent weight gain, such as fasting, strict dieting or excessive exercise.

Bulimia to display a combination of these **symptoms :**

1. Frequent changes in weight (loss or gain).
2. Signs of damage due to vomiting including swelling around the cheeks or jaw, calluses on knuckles, damage to teeth and bad breath.
3. Feeling bloated, constipated or developing intolerance to food.
4. Loss of or disturbance of menstrual periods in girls and women.
5. Fainting or dizziness.
6. Feeling tired and not sleeping well.
7. Preoccupation with eating, food, body-shape and weight.
8. Sensitivity to comments relating to food, weight, body-shape or exercise.
9. Low self-esteem and feelings of shame, self-loathing or guilt, particularly after eating.
10. Having a distorted body image (*e.g.,* seeing themselves as overweight even if they are in a healthy weight range for their age and height).
11. Obsession with food and need for control.
12. Depression, anxiety or irritability.
13. Extreme body dissatisfaction.
14. Evidence of binge-eating (*e.g.,* disappearance or hoarding of food).
15. Vomiting or using laxatives, enemas, appetite suppressants or diuretics.
16. Eating in private and avoiding meals with other people.
17. Anti-social behavior, spending more and more time alone.
18. Repetitive or obsessive behaviors relating to body shape and weight (*e.g.,* weighing themselves repeatedly, looking in the mirror obsessively and pinching waist or wrists).
19. Secretive behavior around food (*e.g.,* saying they have eaten when they haven't, hiding uneaten food in their rooms).
20. Compulsive or excessive exercising (*e.g.,* exercising in bad weather, continuing to exercise when sick or injured, and experiencing distress if exercise is not possible).
21. Dieting behavior (*e.g.,* fasting, counting calories/kilo joules, avoiding food groups such as fats and carbohydrates).
22. Frequent trips to the bathroom during or shortly after meals which could be evidence of vomiting or laxative use.
23. Erratic behavior (*e.g.,* spending large amounts of money on food).
24. Self-harm, substance abuse or suicide attempts.

Triad Factor 2 : Amenorrhea

Exercising intensely and not eating enough calories can lead to decrease in hormones that help regulate the menstrual cycle. As a result, a girl's periods may become irregular or stop altogether. Of course, it's normal for teens to occasionally miss periods, especially in the first year. A missed period does not automatically mean female athlete triad. It could mean something else is going on, like pregnancy or a medical condition.

Some girls who participate intensively in sports may never even get their first period because they've been training so hard. Others may have had periods, but once they increase their training and change their eating habits, their periods may stop.

Triad Factor 3 : Osteoporosis

Estrogen is lower in girls with female athlete triad. Low estrogen levels and poor nutrition, especially low calcium intake, can lead to osteoporosis, the third aspect of the triad. Osteoporosis is the weakening of bones due to loss of bone density and improper bone formation. This condition can ruin a female athlete's career because it may lead to stress fractures and other injuries.

Usually, the teen years are a time when girls should be building up their bone mass to their highest levels — called peak bone mass. Not getting enough calcium now can also have a lasting effect on how strong a woman's bones are later in life.

If a girl has risk factors for female athlete triad, she may already be experiencing some **symptoms** and **signs** of the disorder, such as:

1. Weight loss.
2. No periods or irregular periods.
3. Fatigue and decreased ability to concentrate.
4. Stress fractures (fractures that occur even if a person hasn't had a significant injury).
5. Continued dieting in spite of weight loss.
6. Preoccupation with food and weight.
7. Frequent trips to the bathroom during and after meals.
8. Using laxatives.
9. Brittle hair or nails.
10. Dental cavities because in girls with bulimia tooth enamel is worn away by frequent vomiting.
11. Sensitivity to cold.
12. Low heart rate and blood pressure.
13. Heart irregularities and chest pain.

EXERCISES

Multiple Choice Questions

1. Which of these are not gross motor skills ?
   (a) Throwing a ball
   (b) Jumping
   (c) Balancing on one foot
   (d) Standing

2. Development of a child's bone, muscles and ability to move around any manipulate their movement is referred to as :
   (a) Motor development
   (b) Physical activity
   (c) Both (a) and (b)
   (d) None of the above

3. Gorss motor development skills, head control, and sitting are the exercise guidelines for children belonging to the age group of :
   (a) 1-2 years   (b) 3-7 years
   (c) 8-12 years   (d) None of these

4. Which of the following is an example of food supplement ?
   (a) Vitamins   (b) Fatty acids
   (c) Both (a) and (b)   (d) None of these

5. Writing, Holding, Catching and Smashing are examples of :
   (a) Gross Motor Development
   (b) fine Motor Development
   (c) Both (a) and (b)
   (d) None of the above

6. There are how many stages of motor development in children ?
   (a) 3   (b) 2
   (c) 4   (d) 5

7. Absence of menses for 6 months or absence of menstrual cycle for the three cycles is referred to as :
   (a) Amenorrhhoea   (b) Menorrhagia
   (c) Metrorrhagia   (d) None of these

8. Menometrorrhagia refers to :
   (a) Irregular episodes of bleeding.
   (b) Longer duration of flow at unpredictable intervals.
   (c) Heavier and increased amount of flow.
   (d) Common disorder of blood.

9. Sania Nehwal belongs to which of the following games ?
   (a) Cricket   (b) Hockey
   (c) Boxing   (d) Badminton

10. What are the three components of the female athlete triad ?
    (a) Low energy availability, menstrual dysfunction and low bone density.

    (b) Low bone density, low energy availability and malnourishment.

    (c) Low energy availability, menstrual dysfunction and malnourishment.

    (d) None of the above

Very Short Answer Type Questions (Carrying 1 mark)

1. What is motor development ?
2. What is fine motor development ?
3. What is gross motor development ?
4. What is posture ?
5. What is correct posture ?
6. What are knock knees ?
7. What are bow legs ?
8. What is lordosis ?
9. What is kyphosis ?
10. What is scoliosis ?
11. What is flat foot ?
12. What are round shoulders ?
13. Define motor development.
14. What do you understand by gross motor development and fine motor development ?
15. What are the postural deformities ?
16. Write any two causes of kyphosis.
17. Write any two causes of lordosis.
18. Write any two corrective exercises of knock knees.
19. Write any two corrective exercises of bow legs.
20. Write any two corrective exercises of lordosis.
21. Write any two corrective exercises of kyphosis.
22. Write any two corrective exercises of scoliosis.
23. Write any two corrective exercises of flat foot.
24. What is meant by round shoulders ?
25. What is the full form of PYKKA ?
26. What is the new name given to the programme of PYKKA ?
27. State one reason why women do not participate in sports ?
28. What is the age of initiation of menarche period ?
29. State one factor of female athlete triad ?
30. What is gender inequality in sports ?
31. State two reasons why women do not participate in sports ?
32. List two names of female athletes in the field of boxing.
33. What is the full form of LMP ?
34. What is the period of second and third trimester?
35. What are the types of anorexia nervosa ?
36. What do you mean by purging and non-purging bulimia ?

Short Answer Type Questions (Carrying 3 marks)

1. Write in detail about the motor development in early childhood.
2. Write in detail about the motor development in middle childhood.
3. Elucidate any two factors affecting motor development.
4. Discuss the motor development in late childhood.
5. Detail any three physiological benefits of exercise on children.
6. How can physical activities be corrected by measures for common postural deformities ?
7. What are the main causes of lordosis ?
8. Discuss in brief the deformities of spinal curvature.
9. Discuss the corrective exercises related to knock knees.
10. Discuss the corrective exercises related to bow legs.
11. Discuss the corrective exercises related to lordosis.
12. Discuss the corrective exercises related to kyphosis.
13. Discuss the corrective exercises related to Scoliosis.
14. Discuss the corrective exercises related to Flat Foot.
15. Discuss the role of women in sports in the early ages.
16. Discuss two reasons why women do not participate in sports.
17. Discuss about the programmes government has initiated to promote sports.
18. Which are the states of India receiving financial aid for producing female athletes ?
19. What is menstrual dysfunction ?
20. Write the importance of first trimester of pregnancy period.
21. List down five exercises that are harmful if performed during pregnancy.
22. What is anorexia nervosa ?
23. What is bulimia ? Discuss its types and symptons in detail.

Long Answer Type Questions (Carrying 5 marks)

1. What is motor development ? Enlighten the motor development during childhood.

2. Explain the factors affecting motor development in detail.

3. Discus the physical and physiological benefits of exercise.

4. Mention the causes, precautions and remedies of bow legs.

5. Suggest physical activities as corrective measures for flat foot and lordosis.

6. Explain the causes, precautions and remedies of knock knees.

7. Explain scoliosis, its causes and suggest its preventive and remedial measures.

8. Explain knock knees, its causes, precautions and remedial exercises.

9. Discuss bow legs and its precautions.

10. Describe kyphosis and its causes.

11. Discuss any five common postural deformities.

12. Write a brief note on physical exercises as corrective measures for the deformities of spinal curvature.

13. Discus about the sports participation of women in India.

14. What is menopause ? Enlighten the three stages of menopause.

❐❐

6 TEST AND MEASUREMENT IN SPORTS

Test and Measurement is not a new concept to us. We measured our height and weight throughout our growing years. Even from the time of birth, the first question asked by the parents is, what is the weight of the baby born? Whether the baby is normal, underweight or above average ? The use of test and measurement is so vast that everyday, almost everybody is dependent on measurement. In the field of physical education and sports sciences, the initial performance of the athletes is assessed through tests like standing broad jump, 100 meter dash, discus throw distance etc. It is very significant for the individuals to set the objectives which they want to fulfill in physical education and sports programme. For example, if we want to improve our endurance, we will have to participate in endurance improving physical activities. After certain period, if we do not measure and evaluate our endurance we may remain in dark. Thus, test and measurement are very important in the field of Physical education and sports. Test and Measurement helps an individual to motivate, to classify in different categories, to evaluate instructions and programmes, to predict the performance potentials, to conduct research and so on.

6.1. MEANING AND DEFINITIONS OF TEST AND MEASUREMENT

Test

A test is a form of assessment used to measure the acquisition and retention of knowledge or ability.

According to **Philip & Hornak**, it is commonly defined as *"a tool for measurement that is used to obtain data for specific variable/characteristics of an individual or group"*.

According to **Johnson & Nelson**, *"It is an instrument required to check or record the performance of an individual"*.

According to **Jackson**, *"a test is something which describes among different ability, group throughout the range of ability"*.

According to **Barrow & McGee**, *"test is a set of questions or exercises for finding out the individuals' performance or ability/ knowledge & qualification"*.

Measurement

Various tools and techniques which are used to collect data along with a numeric value are called measurement.

According to **R. N. Patel**, *"it is an act or process that involves the assignment of a numerical index to whatever is being tested"*.

According to **Frank K. Venducci**, *"it is the means by which the quality aspect of characteristic attributes are determined with accuracy"*.

According to **Barrow & McGee**, *"measurement is a technique of evaluation that is used to give result to qualitative data"*.

According to **Jackson**, *"measurement is a score that has been assigned on the basis of test"*.

6.2. MOTOR FITNESS TEST

Meaning of Motor Fitness

Motor fitness can be defined as an athlete's capability to perform effectively during sports or other physical activity. An athlete's motor fitness is a combination of five different components, each of which is essential for high levels of performance. The components of motor fitness are: agility, balance, co-ordination, power which entails speed and strength and finally, reaction time.

1. **50 m standing start**

Purpose : Measure the acceleration speed of an athelete.

Equipments required:

Equipment Name	Image
Speed Measuring tape	
Stop watch	
Cone	
Flat and clear surface	

Administration and Direction :

1. The test involves running a single maximum sprint over 50 meters, with the time recorded. A thorough warm up should be given, including some practice starts and accelerations.

2. Start from a stationary standing position (hands cannot touch the ground), with one foot in front of the other.

3. The front foot must be behind the starting line.

4. Once, the subject is ready and motionless, the starter gives the instructions "set" then "go.". The tester should provide hints for maximising speed (such as keeping low, driving hard with the arms and legs) and the participant should be encouraged to not slow down before crossing the finish line.

Scoring: Two trials are allowed, and the best time is recorded to the nearest 2 decimal places. The timing starts from the first movement (if using a stopwatch) or when the timing system is triggered, and finishes when the chest crosses the finish line and/or the finishing timing gate is triggered.

2. 600 m Run/walk

Purpose : Measure the aerobic fitness of the athlete.

Equipments required:

Equipment Name	Image
Running track	
Marking cones	
Recording	
Sheets	
Stop watch	

Administration and Direction : Subject uses a standing start at the signal, the subject starts running 600 yard distance. The running may be interpreted with walking. It is possible to have a dozen pupils run at one time by having the pupils pair off before the start of the event. Each pupil listens for and remembers his partner's time as the pupil cross the finish.

Rule: Walking is permitted but the subject has to cover the distance in the shortest possible time.

Scoring: Record in minutes and seconds.

3. SIT and Reach

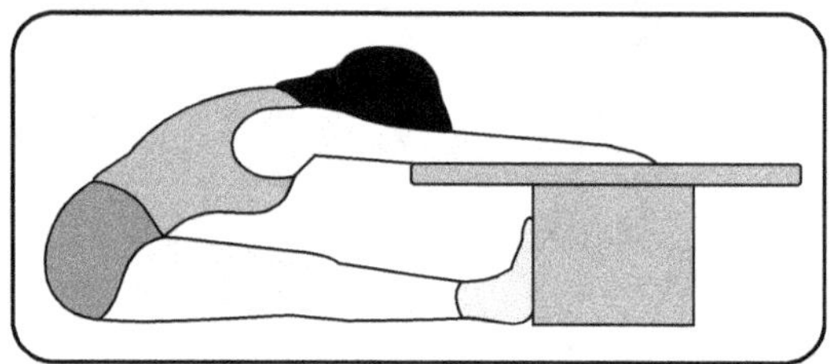

Purpose : Measure the flexibility of the athlete.

Equipments required:

Equipment Name	Image
Sit and Reach Box	
Measuring tape	

Procedure :

1. This test involves sitting on the floor with legs stretched out straight ahead. Shoes should be removed. The soles of the feet are placed flat against the box.
2. Both knees should be locked and pressed flat to the floor - the tester may assist by holding them down.
3. With the palms facing downwards, and the hands on top of each other or side by side, the subject reaches forward along the measuring line as far as possible. Ensure that the hands remain at the same level, not one reaching further forward than the other.

Scoring : The score is recorded to the nearest centimeter or half inch as the distance reached by the hand. Some test versions use the level of the feet as the zero mark, while others have the zero mark 9 inches before the feet. There is also the modified sit and reach test which adjusts the zero mark depending on the arm and leg length of the subject. There are some norms for the sit and reach test and also examples of some actual athlete results.

4. Partial Curl up

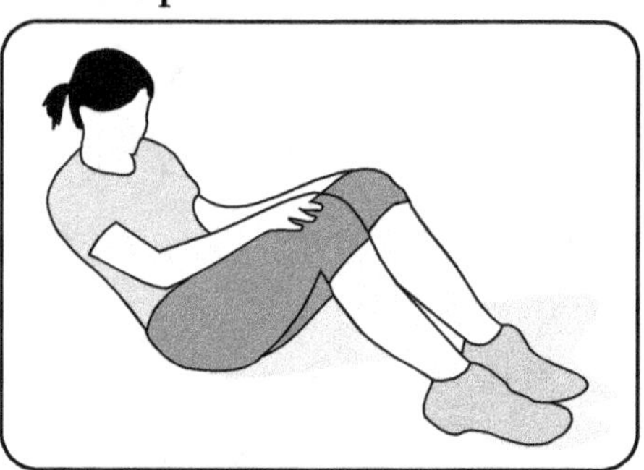

Purpose : Measure the abdominal strength of the athlete.

Equipment :

Equipment Name	Image
Stop watch	
Recording sheet	
Non-sliping surface	

Procedure :

1. The starting position is lying on the back with the knees flexed and feet 12 inches from the buttocks. The feet cannot be held or rest against an object.
2. The arms are extended and are rested on the thighs. The head is in a neutral position. The subject curls up with a slow controlled movement, until the student's shoulders come off the mat two inches, then back down again.
3. One complete curl-up is completed every three seconds (1.5 seconds up and 1.5 seconds down, with no hesitation) and are continued until

exhaustion (*e.g.,* the subject cannot maintain the rhythm). There is no pause in the up or down position, the curl-ups should be continuous with the abdominal muscles engaged throughout.

Scoring : Record the total number of curl ups. The completion of one complete curl up counts as one. Only correctly performed curl ups should be counted - the sit up is not counted if the shoulders are not raised up two inches; the head touches the mat; the heels come off the mat and or the student is off cadence. There are published norm tables for Connecticut students based on age.

5. Push ups (Boys)

Purpose : Measure the upper body muscles strength.

Equipment :

Equipment Name	Image
Stop watch	
Non-slipping surface	
Recording sheet	Recording Sheet

Procedure :

1. A standard push-up begins with the hands and toes touching the floor, the body and legs in a straight line, feet slightly apart, the arms at shoulder width apart, extended and at a right angle to the body.

2. Keeping the back and knees straight, the subject lowers the body to a predetermined point, to touch the ground or some other object, or until there is a 90-degree angle at the elbows, then returns back to the starting position with the arms extended.

3. This action is repeated without rest, and the test continues until exhaustion.

Scoring : Record the number of correctly completed push-ups.

6. Modified Push Ups (Girls)

Purpose : To measure shoulder strength.

Equipment

Equipment Name	Image
Stool	
Stop watch.	

Procedure : The push up test for girls is executed from a stool, 13 inches high by 20 inches long by 14 inches wide. It has placed on a floor about six inches from a wall. The subject grasp the outer edges at the nearest comers of stool and assume the front leaning rest position with the balls of the feet resting on the floor and with body and arms forming a right angle. The test is to lower the body so that the upper chest touches the near edge of the stool, then raise it to a straight arm position as many times as possible. In performing the test, the subject's body should be held straight throughout. If the body sways or arches or if the subject does not go completely up, half credit is given, up to 4 half credits.

Scoring : One point was given each time when the subject completed a modified push-ups only one trial was permitted.

7. Standing Broad Jump

Purpose : To measure explosive leg power in jumping horizontal distance.

Equipments :

Equipment Name	Image
Steel tape	
Measuring tape, floor mat	

Procedure :

1. The subject is asked to stand behind the starting line with the feet parallel to each other.
2. The subject is instructed to jump as farthest as possible by bending knees and swinging arms to take off for the broad jump in the forward direction.
3. The subject is given three trials.

Scoring : The score of the test is the distance between the starting line and the closest point of landing. The final score of the test considered is the best trial given.

> **Note :** A demonstration of the standing broad jump is given to a group of subjects to be tested.

8. Shuttle Run (4 × 10 mts.)

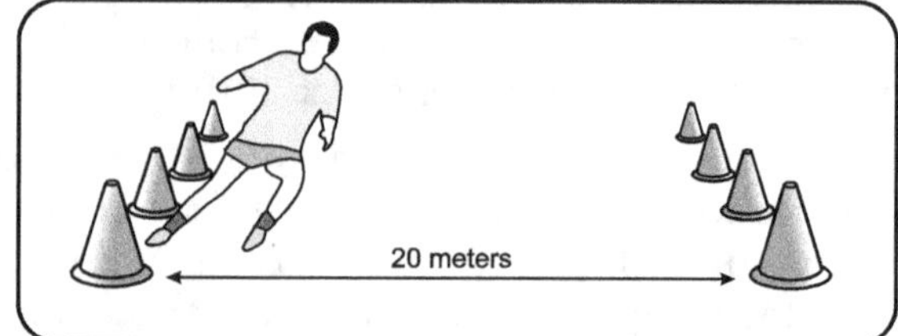

Purpose: To measure Agility.

Equipment:

Equipment Name	Image
Steel tape	
Two stop watches	
Marking powder	

Procedure : The subjects stood behind the line when command given 'go' the subject starts to run towards the opposite line (with distance of 10 mts. line) and touch the line with hand, soon taken turn towards the starting line then again touch that line soon, taken twin run towards the same lines. Time Keeper starts his watch along with command 'go' and stops when the subject touches the starting line.

Scoring : Time was considered to rear half second.

6.3. GENERAL MOTOR FITNESS-BARROW THREE ITEM MOTOR ABILITY TEST (STANDING BROAD JUMP, ZIG ZAG RUN AND MEDICINE BALL PUT)

Barrow general motor ability test was specially designed for school boys and college men students. For constructing general motor ability test battery, Barrow (1954) selected 29 test items measuring eight factors of motor ability which were identified by the experts. Once 29 items were tested Barrow studied multiple correlation coefficients of several combinations of test items with the total performance score of 29 test items. He found that the two batteries were highly correlated with 29 items. The first test battery having six items revealed a correlation coefficient of 0.95 and the three test item battery displayed a correlation coefficient of 0.92 with 29 item battery.

Standing Broad Jump

Topic discussed earlier.

Zig-Zag Run

Purpose of Test

To measure agility of high school boys and college men.

Equipments Required

Test Area (Floor area 30 feet by 50 feet), Equipment Stopwatch, Five cones, Floor tape and Score cards.

Administration and Directions

1. The course of zig-zag running is demonstrated to the subject.

2. The subject is instructed be in standing start position and on the signal ready 'go' they should start running three laps in the fast pace and should be continued until reaching the finish line. The subject slows down only after crossing the finish line.

3. The subject is specifically informed that the obstacles are neither to be grasped while going around them and nor to be misplaced in way.

4. If anybody fouls, then whole run is to be repeated.

5. After the signal ready? Go, the subject begins the zig zag run, the timer starts the stopwatch.

6. As soon as the runner crosses the finish point after the third round, the timer stops the watch.

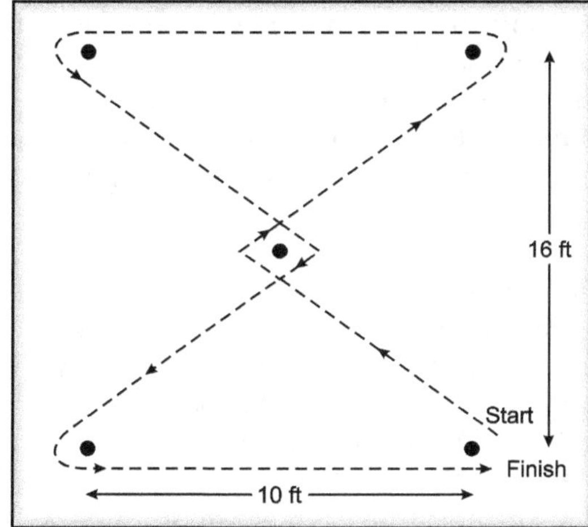

Arenas of Zig-Zag run

Scoring

The final score is considered as the time taken in running the three rounds of figure-of-eight which is evaluated according to the norms of local population. If in case the norms are not available, at that time the comparative ranking of the individuals tested should be assigned.

Medicine Ball Put

Purpose of Test

To measures arm and shoulder girdle strength.

Equipments Required

Floor (90 feet by 25 feet) and medicine ball for boys (3 kg) and girls (1 kg).

Administration and Directions

1. The following instructions are given to the subjects before initiating the test, "The Medicine ball is not to be thrown but to be put as will be demonstrated. The subjects are to stand between the two restraining lines and the ball is to put straight down the course. Each subject is to take three trials; fouls count a trial. However, in case of three continuous or more fouls the subjects will be asked to re-attempt until he makes a fair put".

2. The test is explained by giving demonstration after giving the above mentioned instructions about the test.

3. Then a subject is asked to take a position in the thrown areas and put the medicine ball as explained and demonstrated.

4. The subject is given three trails.

Medicine Ball Put

Scoring

The maximum distance out of three trials of putting the medicine ball is the final score which is evaluated with the help of norms if available on the local population or the comparative rankings are assigned to the subjects tested.

Norms of three items Barrow motor ability test for college men (17-20 years).

Standing Broad Jump (Inches)	Zig Zag Run (Sec)	Medicine ball put (Feet)	T-Score
Upto 68	29.5 and more	Upto 22	20
69-72	29.4-28.7	23-25	25
73-76	28.6-27.9	26-28	30
77-80	27.8-27.2	29-31	35
81-84	27.1-26.4	32-34	40
85-88	26.3-25.6	35-38	45
89-92	25.5-24.8	39-41	50
93-96	24.7-24.0	42-44	55
97-100	23.9-23.2	45-47	60
101-104	23.1-22.5	48-51	65
105-108	22.4-21.7	52-54	70
109-112	21.6-20.9	55-57	75
113 and above	20.8 or less	58 and more	80

6.4. MEASUREMENT OF CARDIOVAS-CULAR FITNESS : HARVARD STEP TEST/ROCK-PORT TEST

Cardiovascular fitness refers to the ability of our heart, lungs and organs to consume, transport and utilize oxygen. The maximum volume of oxygen our body can consume and use is our VO_2 Max. When we exercise regularly, we can increase our cardiovascular fitness as our heart becomes more efficient at pumping blood and oxygen to the body, and the body becomes more efficient at using that oxygen.

According to the many experts of this field, cardiovascular fitness is linked to :

1. Reduction in blood pressure.
2. Reduced risk of developing coronary heart disease.
3. Lowered incidence of diabetes.
4. Decreased risk of stroke and heart attack.
5. Lower resting heart rate.
6. Lower fat mass.
7. Increased bone mass.
8. Improved energy levels and greater resistance to illness and fatigue.

Harvard Step Test

In 1943, Brouhafor, measuring cardiovascular endurance, constructed a very simple and easy test by means of easily obtainable and economical equipment. This is possibly the most widespread test of cardiovascular endurance used in India as well as all-over the world. Since, this is a strenuous test, it should not be implemented on aged/older persons.

Purpose of the Test :

To estimate the capacity of the body to adjust to and recover from hard muscular work.

Equipments Required :

A stopwatch, 20-inch high bench, metronome or tape recorder (optional).

Harvard Step Test

Administration and Directions

1. The tester gives a demonstration of the stepping up style to be followed by the subjects during the test.
2. Permit the subjects to practice counting their pulse at the radial or carotid artery.
3. Pair up the subjects.
4. Subjects step up and down on a bench 30 times/minute for 5 minutes, unless they stop earlier because of fatigue.
5. The body should be erect each time the subject steps onto the bench and the lead foot may be changed during the test.
6. As soon as subjects stop the test, they sit down and remain sitting throughout the pulse count.

There are two forms of the test : Long form, Short form.

Long Form

In this, the pulse is counted for 30 seconds on three occasions : 1 minutes after exercise (1 to 1.5 minutes), 2 minutes after exercise (2 to 2.5 minutes), and 3 minutes after exercise (3 to 3.5).

Scoring : A physical efficiency index (PEI) is computed with the formula :

PEI = duration of exercise in seconds × 1002 × sum of pulse counts in recovery

The PEI standards for the long form are as follows :

Below 55 — poor
55 to 64 — low average
65 to 79 — high average
80 to 89 — good
Above 89 — excellent

For individuals who do not complete the 5-minute test, the following scoring standards may be used:

Less than 2 minutes	25
From 2 to 3 minutes	38
From 3 to 3.5 minutes	48
From 3.5 to 4 minutes	52
From 4 to 4.5 minutes	55
From 4.5 to 5 minutes	59

Short Form

In this, the pulse is counted for only 30 seconds *i.e.,* 1 minute after exercise (1 to 1.5 minutes).

Scoring : The scoring formula is :

PEI = duration of exercise in seconds × .005.5 × pulse count for 1 to 1.5 minute exercise.

PEI stands for Physical Exercise Index.

The PEI standards for the short form are as follows :

Below 50 — poor
50 to 80 — average
Above 80 — good

Advantages

1. For conducting this test, equipments required are bare minimum.
2. Test can be conducted in minimum cost.
3. It is easy to conduct and feasible to organize the set up.

Disadvantages

1. Differences exist amongst individuals in the bio-mechanical features.
2. Despite the difference in heights of the individuals, the box or bench's height remains same which is beneficial for taller individuals in comparison to those of shorter height.
3. The similar differences are apparent in case of body weight as it will be difficult for individuals with more weight.

Rockport One Mile Test

Rockport One mile Test is as well acknowledged as Rockport Fitness Walking Test. The Rockport Fitness Walking Test was developed by exercise physiologists and cardiologists at the Department of Exercise Science in the University of Massachusetts at Amherst. Researchers sought a low-impact, safe test that involved a well-liked exercise and appealed to the broadest spectrum of users. The Rockport Institute has been studying Walking and fitness since 1971 and has found this test to be the best in judging VO_2 max and fitness level. This test is suitable for both males and females of poor fitness who would not be able to complete a similar distance run test. The test is suitable for people of all ages, from the very young to the elderly. This test requires minimal equipment and costs, and the test can be self-administered.

Purpose of the Test

To check or observe the development of the individuals VO_2 max.

Equipments Required

Stopwatch, smooth and level marked 1 mile track or 400 m track, paper and pencil, heart rate monitor (optional), body weight scales.

Administration and Direction

This test requires the athlete to walk one mile as fast as possible.

1. The tester weighs and records the subject's weight.
2. The subjects warms up for 10 minutes.
3. The tester gives the command 'GO', starts the stopwatch and the subjects commence the test.
4. The subjects walk 1 mile as fast as possible.
5. The tester records the time taken by the subject to complete the test and the subject's heart rate immediately on finishing.

Calculation of VO_2 Max

The formula used to calculate VO_2 max is :

1. $132.853 - (0.0769 \times \text{Weight}) - (0.3877 \times \text{Age}) + (6.315 \times \text{Gender}) - (3.2649 \times \text{Time}) - (0.1565 \times \text{Heart Rate})$.
2. Where, Weight is in pounds (lbs)
3. Gender Male = 1 and Female = 0
4. Time is expressed in minutes and 100th of a minute.
5. Heart rate is in beats/minute
6. Age is in years

Note : This test is too easy for highly fit people. Also, since one must walk as fast as possible, the accuracy of this test depends on the pacing ability and level of motivation.

Advantages

1. Equipments required are bare minimum.
2. The set up of test is undemanding to conduct.
3. The test can be conducted by the athlete himself/herself.
4. More than one individual at a time can be involved for the test to be conducted on.

Disadvantage

1. For this test, specific facilities are required.

6.5. COMPUTATION OF FITNESS INDEX

The fitness Index score is determined by the following equations.

Fitness Index (short form) = (100 × test duration in seconds) divided by (5.5 × pulse count between 1 and 1.5 minutes).

Fitness Index (long form) = (100 × test duration in seconds) divided by (2 × sum of heart beats in the recovery periods).

Example:

If the total tests time was 300 seconds (if completed the whole 5 minutes)

The number of heart beats :

1. Between 1-1.5 minutes = 95
2. Between 2-2.5 = 85
3. Between 3-3.5 = 75

Long form Fitness Index score would be:

(100 × 300)/2 (95 + 85 + 75) = 58.8

Short form Fitness Index score would be:

(100 × 300)/(5.5 × 95) = 57.4

Rating	Fitness index (long form)
Excellent	> 96
Good	83 - 96
Average	68 - 82
Low Average	54 - 67
Poor	< 54

*(Norms from: Fox et al. 1973)

6.6. RIKLI AND JONES : SENIOR CITIZEN FITNESS TEST

Fitness is a very vital factor for those in their older existence. To complete everyday jobs, grown-up adults must have enough strength, endurance and flexibility. Before causing serious functional limitations, assessment of these components of fitness can be treated. At Fullerton University, Dr. Roberta Rikliand Dr. Jessie Jones developed the Senior Fitness Test as a component of the Life Span Wellness Program, the test is at times acknowledged as the Fullerton Functional Test. It is a user-friendly test battery that evaluates the functional fitness of older persons to measure aerobic fitness, strength and flexibility. The fitness test items include activities like getting up from a chair, lifting, walking, stretching and bending. Given below is the list of the test items and details for each item.

1. Chair stand test for lower body strength
2. Arm curl test for upper body strength
3. Chair sit and reach test for lower body flexibility
4. Back scratch test for upper body flexibility
5. Eight foot up and go test for agility
6. Six minute walk test for aerobic endurance.

Chair Stand Test for Lower Body Strength

Purpose of the Test :

To measure the lower body strength and endurance.

Equipments Required :

A straight back chair without arm rests (seat 17 inches/44 cm high) and Stop-watch.

Administration and Directions

1. Place the chair against a wall, or otherwise stabilize it for safety.
2. The subject sits in the middle of the seat, with his feet shoulder width apart, flat on the floor.
3. The arms are to be crossed at the wrists and held close to the chest.
4. From the sitting position, the subject stands completely up, then completely back down.
5. This is repeated for 30 seconds.
6. The total number of complete chair stands is counted (up and down equals to one stand).
7. If the subject has completed a full stand from the sitting position when the time is elapsed, the final stand is counted in the total.

> **Note :**
> 1. Each time subject stands during the test, make sure he/she comes to a full stand.
> 2. When the subject sits, make sure he/she sits all the way down. Do not just touch his/her backside to the chair. The subject must fully sit between each stand.
> 3. Subject must keep his/her arms against the chest crossed and must not allow the arms to swing up as he/she rises.

Scoring

The total number of completed chair stands during 30 seconds is the score. Given below is a table depicting the ranges for this test based on age groups (Jones & Rikli, 2002).

Age	Below Average	Average	Above Average
60-64	< 14	14 to 19	> 19
65-69	< 12	12 to 18	> 18
70-74	< 12	12 to 17	> 17
75-79	< 11	11 to 17	> 17
80-84	< 10	10 to 15	> 15
85-89	< 8	8 to 14	> 14
90-94	< 7	7 to 12	> 12

Norms for Men

Age	Below Average	Average	Above Average
60-64	< 12	12 to 17	> 17
65-69	< 11	11 to 16	> 16
70-74	< 10	10 to 15	> 15
75-79	< 10	10 to 15	> 15
80-84	< 9	9 to 14	> 14
85-89	< 8	8 to 13	> 13
90-94	< 4	4 to 11	> 11

Norms for Women

Arm Curl Test for Upper Body Strength

Purpose of the Test

To measure the upper body strength and endurance.

Equipments Required

A chair without armrests, Stopwatch, 5 lb. weight for women and 8 lb. weight for men.

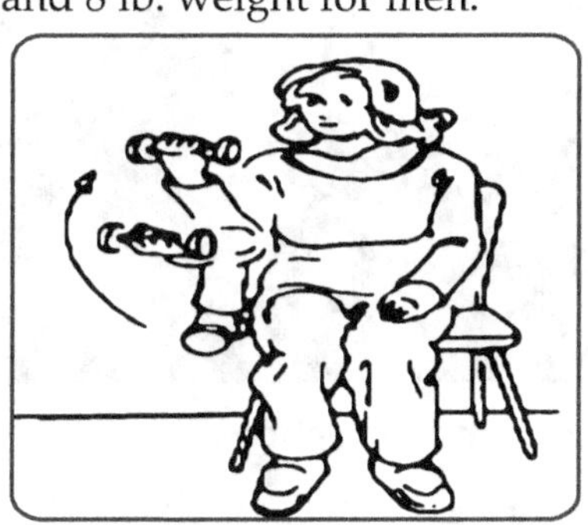

Administration and Directions

1. The aim of this test is to do as many arm curls as possible in 30 seconds.
2. This test is conducted on the dominant arm side (stronger side).
3. The subject sits on the chair, holding the weight in the hand using a suitcase grip (palm facing towards the body) with the arm in a vertically down position beside the chair.
4. Brace the upper arm against the body so that only the lower arm is moving (tester may assist to hold the upper arm steady).
5. Curl the arm up through a full range of motion, gradually turning the palm up (flexion with supination).
6. As the arm is lowered through the full range of motion, gradually return to the starting position. The arm must be fully bent and then fully straightened at the elbow.
7. The subject repeats this action as many times as possible within 30 seconds.

> **Note :**
> 1. Do not swing the weight.
> 2. It's important that the upper arm is kept stable throughout the test, and doesn't swing.

Scoring

The total number of controlled arm curls performed in 30 seconds is the score. The table below is depicting the suggested ranges for this test based on age groups (Jones & Rikli, 2002).

Age	Below Average	Average	Above Average
60-64	< 16	16 to 22	> 22
65-69	< 15	15 to 21	> 21
70-74	< 14	14 to 21	> 21
75-79	< 13	13 to 19	> 19
80-84	< 13	13 to 19	> 19
85-89	< 11	11 to 17	> 17
90-94	< 10	10 to 14	> 14

Norms for Men

Age	Below Average	Average	Above Average
60-64	< 13	13 to 19	> 19
65-69	< 12	12 to 18	> 18
70-74	< 12	12 to 17	> 17
75-79	< 11	11 to 17	> 17
80-84	< 10	10 to 16	> 16
85-89	< 10	10 to 15	> 15
90-94	< 8	8 to 13	> 13

Norms for Women

Chair Sit and Reach Test for lower body flexibility

Purpose of the Test :

To measure the lower body flexibility.

Equipments Required :

Ruler and straight back chair (about 17 inches/44 cm high).

Administration and Directions

1. On the chair placed against a wall for safety the subject sits at the edge of it.
2. One foot should stay flat on the floor; the other leg is extended forward with the straight knee, heel on the floor and ankle bent at 90°.
3. Position one hand on top of the other with tips of the middle fingers at same level.
4. The subject is asked to inhale first and as he exhales, keeping the back straight and head up, the subject is asked to reach forward towards the toes by bending at the hip.
5. Bouncing movements and stretching to the point of pain should be avoided. Keeping the knee straight, and the reach is to be maintained for 2 seconds.
6. The distance between the tip of the fingertips and the toes is measured. The score is zero if the fingertips touch the toes. If they do not touch, the distance between the fingers and the toes (a negative score) is measured, if they overlap, it is measured by the distance with a positive score.
7. Two trials are performed.

Scoring

The score is either a negative or positive score recorded to the nearest 1/2 inch or 1 cm as the distance reached; leg which was used for measurement is recorded. Table below is giving the ranges (in inches) for this test based on age groups (Jones & Rikli, 2002).

Age	Below Average	Average	Above Average
60-64	< – 2.5	– 2.5 to 4.0	> 4.0
65-69	< – 3.0	– 3.0 to 3.0	> 3.0
70-74	< – 3.5	– 3.5 to 2.5	> 2.5
75-79	< – 4.0	– 4.0 to 2.0	> 2.0
80-84	< – 5.5	– 5.5 to 1.5	> 1.5
85-89	< – 5.5	– 5.5 to 0.5	> 0.5
90-94	< – 6.5	– 6.5 to – 0.5	> 0.5

Norms for Men

Age	Below Average	Average	Above Average
60-64	< – 0.5	– 0.5 to 5.0	> 5.0
65-69	< – 0.5	– 0.5 to 4.5	> 4.5
70-74	< – 1.0	– 1.0 to 4.0	> 4.0
75-79	< – 1.5	– 1.5 to 3.5	> 3.5
80-84	< – 2.0	– 2.0 to 3.0	> 3.0
85-89	< – 2.5	– 2.5 to 2.5	> 2.5
90-94	< – 4.5	– 4.5 to 1.0	> 1.0

Norms for Women

Back Scratch Test for Upper Body Flexibility

The Back Scratch Test, or simply the Scratch Test, measures how close the hands can be brought together behind the back.

Purpose of the Test

To measure the upper body (general shoulder range of motion) flexibility.

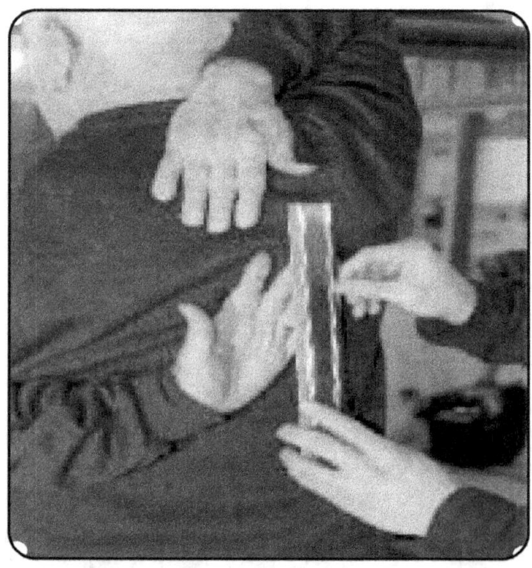

Administration and Directions

1. The test is performed in standing position.

2. The subject is instructed to place one hand at the back of head and back over the shoulder, then reach as far as possible down the middle of his/her back, the palm touching his/her body and the fingers directed downwards.

3. The subject keeps the other arm behind his/her back, palm facing outward and fingers upward and reaches up as far as possible attempting to contact or overlap the middle fingers of both hands.

4. To direct the subject, an assistant is required so that the fingers are aligned, and the distance between the tips of the middle fingers is to be measured.

5. The score is zero if the fingertips touch.

6. The distance between the fingertips (a positive score) is measured, if they overlap measure by how much (a negative score) if the fingertips do not touch.

> **Note :** Practice two times, and then test two times. Stop the test if the subject experiences pain.

Scoring

The best score to the nearest centimeter or 1/2 inch is recorded. Table below shows the ranges (in inches) for this test based on age groups (Jones & Rikli, 2002).

Age	Below Average	Average	Above Average
60-64	> 6.5	6.5 to 0	< 0
65-69	> 7.5	7.5 to – 1.0	< – 1.0
70-74	> 8.0	8.0 to – 1.0	< – 1.0
75-79	> 9.0	9.0 to – 2.0	< – 2.0
80-84	> 9.5	9.5 to – 2.0	< – 2.0
85-89	> 10.0	10.0 to – 3.0	< – 3.0
90-94	> 10.5	10.5 to – 4.0	< – 4.0

Norms for Men

Age	Below Average	Average	Above Average
60-64	> 3.0	3.0 to 1.5	< 1.5
65-69	> 3.5	3.5 to 1.5	< 1.5
70-74	> 4.0	4.0 to 1.0	< 1.0
75-79	> 5.0	5.0 to 0.5	< 0.5
80-84	> 5.5	5.5 to 0	< 0
85-89	> 7.0	7.0 to – 1.0	< – 1.0
90-94	> 8.5	8.0 to – 1.0	< – 1.0

Norms for Women

Eight Feet up and Go Test for Agility

The '8 Foot Up and Go' is a coordination and agility test for the senior citizens.

Purpose of the Test

To measure the speed, agility and dynamic balance.

Equipments Required

A chair (about 17 inches/44 cm high), cone marker, measuring tape, area clear of obstacles and stopwatch.

Administration and Directions

1. Place the marker 8 feet in front of the chair next to a wall.

2. The path between the chair and the marker should be cleared.

3. The subject starts completely seated with hands resting on the knees and feet flat on the ground.

4. Timing starts on the command, 'Go', and the subject stands and walks as quickly as possible (no running) to and around the cone and finally returning to the chair to sit down.

5. As he sits down the timing stops.

6. Two trials are performed.

Scoring

The best time of the two trials to the nearest 1/10th of a second is taken. Table below shows the suggested ranges in seconds for this test based on age groups (Jones & Rikli, 2002).

Age	Below Average	Average	Above Average
60-64	> 5.6	5.6 to 3.8	< 3.8
65-69	> 5.7	5.7 to 4.3	< 4.3
70-74	> 6.0	6.0 to 4.2	< 4.2
75-79	> 7.2	7.2 to 4.6	< 4.6
80-84	> 7.6	7.6 to 5.2	< 5.2
85-89	> 8.9	8.9 to – 5.3	< 5.3
90-94	> 10.0	10.0 to – 6.2	< 6.2

Norms for Men

Age	Below Average	Average	Above Average
60-64	> 6.0	6.0 to 4.4	< 4.4
65-69	> 6.4	6.4 to 4.8	< 4.8
70-74	> 7.1	7.1 to 4.9	< 4.9
75-79	> 7.4	7.4 to 5.2	< 5.2
80-84	> 8.7	8.7 to 5.7	< 5.7
85-89	> 9.6	9.6 to 6.2	< 6.2
90-94	> 11.5	11.5 to 7.3	< 7.3

Norms for Women

Six Minute Walk Test for Aerobic Endurance

The six minute walk test is planned to assess the functional fitness of senior citizens.

Purpose of the Test

To measure the aerobic fitness/aerobic endurance.

Equipments Required

Measuring tape and stopwatch.

Administration and Directions

1. The walking path is marked in a 50 yard (45.72 m) rectangular area (dimensions 45 × 5 yards); to indicate the distance walked, cones are placed at regular intervals.

2. The target of this test is to walk for six minutes as quickly as possible in order to cover as much as area as possible.

3. Subjects set their own pace and if they desire, are allowed to stop for a rest.

Scoring

The distance walked in 6 minutes to the nearest meter is measured. Jenkins et al. (2009) determined the regression equations which are given below:

In males : Walk Distance (meters)

= 867 – (5.71 age, yrs) + (1.03 height, cm)

In females : Walk Distance (meters) = 525 – (2.86 age, yrs) + (2.71 height, cm) – (6.22 BMI)

Note :

The test should be stopped if the subjects inform nausea, dizziness, excessive fatigue and pain. The examiners should be adequately trained in finding and recognizing any symptoms of concern and the required action should be placed in case of medical emergencies.

EXERCISES

Multiple Choice Questions

1. The ability to effectively integrate the moments of the body parts is :
   - (a) Agility
   - (b) Balance
   - (c) Coordination
   - (d) Speed

2. Which of the following tests cannot measure coordination ?
   - (a) Ball catches
   - (b) Jump ropes
   - (c) Vertical jumps
   - (d) Jumping jack

3. Which of the following is not measured using film analysis and EMG analysis ?
   - (a) Agility
   - (b) Balance
   - (c) Coordination
   - (d) Speed

4. The ability to make successive movements in different directions efficiently and rapidly refers to :
   - (a) Agility
   - (b) Balance
   - (c) Coordination
   - (d) Power

5. Which of the following test is a test for measuring speed, agility and dynamic balance ?
   - (a) Six minute walk
   - (b) Back Scratch
   - (c) Eight feet up
   - (d) Chair sit

6. Chair sit and reach test is :
   - (a) Lower body flexibility
   - (b) Upper body flexibility
   - (c) Anxiety
   - (d) Balance

7. The assignment of a number to express in quantitative terms the degree to which a pupil possesses a given characteristic is called :
   - (a) Test
   - (b) Measurement
   - (c) Evaluation
   - (d) None of these

8. From which of these test shoulder gets strengthens ?
   - (a) Sit up
   - (b) 600 m/Run/Walk
   - (c) Modified push/up
   - (d) None of these

9. According to whom measurement involves assignment of a numerical index ?
   - (a) Frank K. Venducis
   - (b) R.N. Patel
   - (c) Jackson
   - (d) Barrow and Mc Gee

10. 600 m run/walk test purpose is to measure :
    - (a) Flexibility
    - (b) Aerobic fitness
    - (c) Balance
    - (d) Strength

Very Short Answer Type Questions (Carrying 1 mark)

1. What is test ?
2. What is measurement ?
3. What is motor fitness ?
4. How many test items are there in Barrow motor ability test ?
5. What is cardiovascular fitness ?
6. What is Harvard Step Test ?
7. What do you mean by rockport one mile test ?
8. What is senior citizen fitness test ?
9. What do you understand by test and measurement ?
10. Briefly discuss cardiovascular fitness.
11. Write the method of calculating of VO_2 Max.
12. Write the fitness index score of short and long form of Barrow motor ability test.

Short Answer Type Questions (Carrying 3 marks)

1. Discuss the Rockport one mile test.
2. Briefly discuss the Harvard step test.
3. Explain the back scratch test for upper body flexibility.

Long Answer Type Questions (Carrying 5 marks)

1. Explain in detail the Harvard step test.
2. Discuss elaborately about the Barrow Three Item Motor Ability Test.
3. Describe the Rockport one mile test in detail.
4. Give details of the chair stand test for lower body strength.
5. Discuss the arm curl test for measuring upper body strength.
6. Explain the chair sit and reach test for lower body flexibility.
7. Elucidate the eight foot up and go test for measuring agility.
8. Discuss the six minute walk test for aerobic endurance.

❏ ❏

PHYSIOLOGY AND INJURIES IN SPORTS

7.1. PHYSIOLOGICAL FACTORS DETERMINING THE COMPONENTS OF PHYSICAL FITNESS

The components of physical fitness like strength, speed, endurance and flexibility etc., can be determined with the help of various physiological factors. Described below are the different physiological factors which determine the different components of physical fitness.

Physiological Factors Determining Strength

The strength of an individual is determined by the various physiological factors as discussed below.

1. Muscle size : The size of the muscle is largely responsible to the strength of the muscle. It is an acknowledged fact that more force can be produced by bigger and larger muscles. In males and females, the similar size of muscle produces the similar force even though males are found to be stronger in comparison to females for the reason that they have larger and bigger muscles. Strength can be improved with different methods of strength training such as weight training as the size of the muscle gets increased.

2. Body weight : Body weight determines the strength of an individual as well. It is known that the heavier individuals are stronger in comparison to the lighter individuals. Among international weight-lifters, there is a positive correlation involving body weight and strength as because of this, the heavier weight lifters lift heavier weight.

3. Muscle composition : It can be said that the proportion of the fibers determines the strength. Fundamentally each muscle consists of two types of muscle fibers *viz.,* white fibers (fast twitch fibers) and red fibers (slow twitch fibers). The fast twitch fibers produce more force as they can contract faster. On the other hand, the slow twitch fibers are capable to contract for a longer duration as they do not contract faster. The muscles which can produce more strength have more percentage of fast twitch fibers. The proportion of fast twitch and slow twitch fiber is determined genetically and thus cannot be altered by the help of training.

4. Intensity of the nerve impulse : The amount of strength can be determined by the intensity of the nerve impulse. A muscle consists of number of motor units. The entire force generated of the muscle depends on the number of contracting motor units. The muscle will contract more strongly whenever, from central nervous system, a stronger nerve impulse is there which in turn excites more number of motor units. Hence, it can be said that the muscle will generate more force or strength.

Physiological Factors Determining Speed

The subsequent component of physical fitness, Speed can be determined by the following physiological factors :

1. Mobility of the nervous system : In sprinting events, the muscles contract and relax at highest possible speed. This fast excitation and inhibition of the concerned motor centers of muscle is responsible for rapid contraction and relaxation of the involved muscles which is known as the mobility of the nervous system. This fast excitation and inhibition can be maintained only for a few seconds by the nervous system subsequent to which the excitation spreads to the neighboring centers causing strain in the whole body which results in decrease of speed. To a great extent, speed is determined by genetic factors even though the mobility of the nervous system can be trained to an extremely limited extent.

2. Muscle composition : Different parts of body have different speed performances as different muscles of the body contain different proportion of fast twitch fibers. The muscles with more proportion of fast twitch fibers contract with more speed in contrast to the muscles which have lesser proportion of fast twitch fibers. Actually, the composition of muscles is hereditarily determined and cannot be altered by training.

3. Explosive strength : Explosive strength is essential for all rapid and explosive movements. Explosive strength depends on muscle composition, size, and co-ordination and on the metabolic process as well. Apart from muscle composition, the left behind factors can be developed in the course of training which eventually improves the speed up to limited extent. The relative percentage of fast twitch and slow twitch fibers determines the highest possible speed in which a muscle can contract. This percentage of fibers is genetically determined. Due to that, sprinters possess more proportion of fast twitch fibers, while, endurance athletes possess more proportion of slow twitch fibers.

4. Flexibility : Flexibility enables complete utilization of explosive strength as well. To some point, flexibility determines the speed as well. Actually, flexibility allows utmost range of movement with not much of internal resistance.

5. Bio-chemical reserves and metabolic power : The bio-chemical reserves and metabolic power determine the speed as well. The muscles need more quantity of energy at an extremely high rate of utilization for maximum speed performance. And for this reason the phosphogen ATP and CP stores in the muscles should be sufficient. The muscle contraction due to inadequate energy supply turns out to be slow after a short time, if ATP and CP store is less in contracting muscles. The energy supply depends on definite enzymes which incise the metabolic power. Training can enhance the amount of ATP, CP and rate of energy supply.

Physiological Factors Determining Endurance

Another significant component of physical fitness is endurance which can be determined by following physiological factors :

1. Aerobic capacity : The muscles require energy to perform an activity continuously which can be supplied in the presence of oxygen. Therefore, for endurance performance, the ability to uphold the sufficient supply of oxygen to the working muscles for energy liberation is vital. The aerobic capacity depends on the following factors :

(a) Oxygen intake : It is quantity of oxygen which the lungs take from atmospheres. For achieving higher VO_2 max, this amount should be more. The intake of oxygen depends on the size of the lungs and chest cavity, number of active alveoli, strength of the respiratory muscles, etc., which further depends on the vital capacity.

(b) Oxygen transport : From lungs, the amount of oxygen taken into the blood has to be transported to the working muscles. The transport of oxygen depends on the circulatory system to carry this quickly to the working muscles. The amount of oxygen absorbed into the blood depends on the speed of blood flow through the lungs and on the blood hemoglobin. Training cannot enhance the concentration of blood hemoglobin, which is about 14-15% in sports persons. The transportation of oxygenated blood depends on the capacity of the heart which can be improved through training. As a result, there will be an increase in aerobic capacity.

(c) Oxygen uptake : From the blood, the amount of oxygen absorbed and consumed by the working muscles is called oxygen uptake. The oxygen uptake in the muscle cell depends on the rate of diffusion *i.e.*, the speed of blood flow, temperature partial pressure of oxygen and of CO_2 in the blood. Up to some extent, through training, this speed and amount of oxygen consumption can be improved as these depend on the number, size and metabolic capacity of the mitochondria.

(d) Energy reserves : The aerobic capacity depends on the availability of energy to the muscle for the activity. So, the aerobic capacity depends upon the muscle glycogen and sugar level in the blood. Fatigue occurs if the muscle glycogen level decreases lower than certain level. The muscle glycogen and liver glycogen reserves are vital for long duration activities. Fats can also be used as energy fuels in extremely long duration activities.

2. Lactic acid tolerance : The ability to tolerate higher concentration of lactic acid can help in improving endurance performance and is a vital factor in determining anaerobic capacity. For activities that last for about 40 seconds or more, the lactic acid tolerance is important. Training can improve the capacity of lactic acid tolerance.

3. Movement economy : For significant endurance performance, the movements performed should be economical. With less energy expenditure a runner can run at a set speed for longer duration. In endurance sports a good technique can save energy. For examples, if the movements are correct, 20-30% of the energy can be saved in swimming. For economical movement, the good runners raise their center of gravity less high; as a result, their unnecessary movements are less.

4. Muscle composition : For endurance or aerobic activities the slow twitch fibers are best utilized. They generate small level of force for extensive periods of time, this makes them suited for endurance activities. Actually, in muscles of the leg, the elite marathoners have been reported to have greater than 90 percentages of slow twitch fibers. The proportions of the slow twitch fibers are genetically regulated.

Physiological Factors Determining Flexibility

The range of movement potential at joint depends upon several factors. There are few trainable factors whereas some factors are trainable up to certain extent. The flexibility is determined by various factors which are described below :

1. Muscle strength : To make the movement possible especially against gravity or external force, the muscle should have a bare minimum level of strength. In reality, for achieving the higher range of movement feeble muscle can become a limiting factor. Strength of muscle is extremely trainable, hence, it can improve the flexibility.

2. Joint structure : In human body, there are numerous different types of joints. A number of joints intrinsically have a larger range of motion in comparison to others. For instance, the ball and socket joint of the shoulder has the maximum range of motion in contrast to the knee joint.

3. Age and gender : The flexibility is determined by gender as well, as females are likely to be more flexible in comparison to males. With the advancement of age, the flexibility decreases, though, it is trainable. As strength and endurance are enhanced, it can be improved with the help of training.

4. Stretch ability of muscles : Stretch ability of muscles determines the flexibility up to certain extent. In limiting the range of movements the stretch ability of the muscles is a crucial factor. Muscles have to contract to perform the movement at a joint. The stretch ability of muscles is trainable up to a certain degree. They tend to get shorter if muscles are not regularly stretched, it finally leads to confine the range of movement possible at a joint.

5. Internal environment : The flexibility is influenced by the internal environment of the athlete. For instance, a body temperature and flexibility increase in a warm bath of 10 minutes but, it reduces in 10°C outside in a stay of 10 minutes.

6. Previous injury : Thickening or fibrosing on the affected spot may result in injuries to connective tissues and muscles. Since, fibrous tissues are less elastic, it can direct to limb shortening and eventually reduce flexibility.

7.2. EFFECTS OF EXERCISES ON CARDIO-VASCULAR SYSTEM

During and immediately after intense exercise, the cardiovascular system undergoes radical changes. Yet to the demands of a regular exercise routine, the cardiovascular system makes valuable and long-term adaptations. The cardiovascular system meets the increased requirements of the body in several ways during exercise. The cardiovascular system delivers fuel to the active tissues of the body, by rushing oxygen to active muscles and returns used blood to the lungs for re-oxygenation. The effect of exercise can be discussed in two ways i.e., immediate effects and long term effects of exercises.

Immediate Effects of Exercises

1. Heart rate increases : In healthy adults, resting heart rate ranges from 60-80 beats per minute. It may be as high as 100 beats per minute in sedentary middle aged individuals. It has been recorded that in elite endurance athletes, the heart rate is as low as 28 - 40 beats per minute. The heart rate increases in expectancy even before exercise begins, this is acknowledged as the anticipatory response which occurs through the releases of neurotransmitters called epinephrine and nor-epinephrine. Subsequent to the early anticipatory response, until the maximum heart rate is reached, heart rate increases in direct amount to intensity of the exercise. Maximum heart rate is calculated with the method of deducting age from the beats at the time of birth (220 – Age). The only direct method is to exercise at increasing intensities for determining maximum heart rate until a plateau in heart rate is found in spite of the increasing rate of work.

Even though with the onset of activity heart rate increases rapidly, as long as exercise intensity remains steady, heart rate will level off. Where the demands of the active tissues can be sufficiently met by the cardiovascular system, this state is known as steady-state heart rate. Yet, there is an exception to this as particularly in a hot climate, in long-drawn-out steady-state exercise, a steady-state heart rate will slowly increase. This observable fact is identified as cardiac drift and is considered to take place owing to increasing in body temperature.

2. Stroke volume increases : The amount of blood ejected per beat from left or right ventricle is called stroke volume and is measured in ml/beat. With exercise intensity there is proportionate increase in the stroke volume. At rest, stroke volume in untrained individuals ranges from 50-70 ml/beat rising up to 110-130 ml/beat in intense physical activity. Resting stroke volume ranges from 90-110 ml/beat rising to the extent of 150-220 ml/beat in elite athletes. With the onset of exercise, the stroke volume increases because the left ventricle fills up totally, stretching it more, producing a more forceful contraction with the elastic recoil, this phenomenon is known as the Frank Starling mechanism.

3. Cardiac output increases : The amount of blood pumped by the heart in one minute is known as cardiac output and is measured in liters/min. It is a product of stroke volume and heart rate. Cardiac output increases if either of heart rate or stroke volume increases. With the response of heart rate and stroke volume to activity, cardiac output increases proportionately with intensity of exercise as well. At resting condition, the cardiac output is about 5 liters/min whereas during intense exercise it may increase to 20-40 liters/min.

4. Blood flow increases : The vascular system is capable of redistributing blood to the tissues with the maximum instant demand for oxygen and away from areas that have less demand. During rest, skeletal muscles are supplied with 15-20% of the circulating blood. Through dynamic or vigorous exercises it increases up to 80-85% of cardiac output. Blood is carried away from major organs *viz.,* the kidneys, liver, stomach and intestines. To promote heat loss, it is then redirected to the skin.

5. Blood pressure increases : In a healthy individual, at rest, a typical systolic blood pressure and diastolic blood pressure range from 110-140 mm Hg and from 60-90 mm Hg. respectively. In highly trained athletes, during exercise systolic pressure *i.e.,* the systolic contraction of the heart increases to more than 200 mm Hg and levels as high as 250 mm Hg. Regardless of exercise intensity, diastolic pressure remains comparatively unchanged. In actual fact, increase in exercise intensity results in an increase of more than 15 mm Hg indicating coronary heart disease and is used as indicator for ceasing an exercise tolerance test.

Long Term Effects of Exercises

1. Heart size increases : The size of heart and strength of the cardiac muscles increases due to regular exercises as to the maximum extent the left ventricle adapts. The walls of the heart develop into stronger and thicker as shown in recent studies and the thickness of myocardial wall increases as well.

2. Resting heart rate decreases : The resting heart rate decreases due to regular exercises. After duration of 10 week training programme, the resting heart rate may reduce up to 10 beats per minute from the normal of 72 beats per minute. The heart becomes more efficient due to regular exercises. In highly conditioned athletes the resting heart rate decreases to 30 beats/minute.

3. Stroke volume increases at resting conditions : The stroke volume increases at resting conditions due to regular exercises. The stroke volume at rest remains up to 50-70 ml/beat in untrained individuals; in trained individuals it ranges from 70-90 ml/beat and in the elite endurance athletes it ranges from 90-110 ml/beat.

4. Cardiac output increases : The cardiac output tends to increase as a result of regular exercise. At resting conditions in untrained individuals the cardiac output can possibly be 14 to 20 liters/minute, in trained individuals 25 to 35 liter/minute and cardiac output can be as high as 40 liters/minute in elite athletes.

5. Blood flow increases : The body increases its number of capillaries to the requirement of supplying more oxygen during exercise to the muscles. The existing capillaries open wider as well. Further, the redistribution of blood becomes efficient and effectual. As a matter of fact, blood circulation in the body increases.

6. Blood pressure decreases : At resting condition the systolic and diastolic blood pressure decrease by up to 10 mm Hg as a result of regular exercises.

7. Blood volume increases : The blood volume increases due to the regular exercises. Actually, as the blood volume enhances, there is an increase in plasma volume. Additionally, during heavy exercise, in order to keep the muscle supplied with oxygen, the body produces a greater number of red blood cells.

8. Faster recovery rate : Regular exercises speed up the recovery rate. In comparison to a beginner heart rate of trained athletes becomes normal earlier. The recovery becomes fast as the rate of respiration becomes normal very quickly as well.

9. Risk of heart diseases reduces : Stress related hormones progressively get reduced from circulating in the blood due to regular exercises. This increases the blood vessel pathway, which consecutively reduces the risk for the increase of plaque that leads to coronary heart diseases. Therefore, the risk of heart diseases reduces due to exercises.

7.3. EFFECTS OF EXERCISE ON RESPIRATORY SYSTEM

The procedure of energy liberation from nutrients is called respiration. The respiration system is responsible for taking in oxygen and releasing carbon dioxide and water vapors. The main organ of the respiratory system initiates from the passage in the nose, windpipe (trachea) bronchi and finally the lungs and air sacs (alveoli). Predominantly, due to endurance training many parameters of respiratory system get affected which are discussed as under :

1. Lungs volume : The lung volume and capacities increase with endurance training. After endurance training, vital capacity is increased *i.e.,* maximal volume of air forcefully expired out subsequent to a maximal inspiration. The trained athlete may have vital capacity of 5-6 liters but vital capacity of untrained individual is of 3-4 liters.

2. Breathing Frequency (BF) : Breathing rate is the number of breaths per minute. Breathing frequency decreases after training. In resting condition, normal untrained individual's breathing frequency is about 12-20 breaths/minute. In trained athletes or individuals, it reduces down to 7-8 breaths/minute. Exercises reduce respiratory rate that reflects superior respiratory efficiency.

3. Maximum minute ventilation : The amount of air which is inspired or expired in one minute is called minute ventilation. Maximum minute ventilation gets increased subsequent to training. In untrained individual, maximum minute ventilation is about 100 liters/minute, while it is increased to more than 150-160 liters/minute in trained athlete. Maximum pulmonary ventilation rates become twice the rate of untrained individuals in excess of 240 liters/minute in case of highly trained endurance athletes as rowers.

4. Tidal volume : The amount of air inspired or expired per breath is called the tidal volume. Endurance training increases tidal volume. Tidal volumes are about 500 ml/breath in untrained individuals whereas in trained persons it gets increased to more than 600-700 ml/breath.

5. Ventilatory efficiency : The trained person gets the similar amount of oxygen (O_2) from less amount of air. Generally, 15 liters of air is requisite to obtain one liter of oxygen, however, trained individual gets the similar quantity of oxygen from 12 liters of air. Training or physical exercises especially endurance training increases the ventilator efficiency.

6. Pulmonary diffusion : The exchange of gases that takes place in small air sacs of lungs (alveoli) is called pulmonary diffusion. For diffusion, more alveoli become active at the time of maximal level of exercise. The alveoli size increases as well which gives more space to diffusion oxygen (O_2) and carbon dioxide (CO_2).

7.4. EFFECTS OF EXERCISE ON MUSCULAR SYSTEM

The muscles contribute of about half the weight of our body helping the body to move. In our body there are about 650 muscles producing a particular movement. Muscles with the help of bones help our body to move. The cardiac muscles help to pump the blood throughout our body. Numerous movement actions results due to several muscles working together in our body.

There are three most important muscle contractions *i.e.* :

1. Isotonic contraction
2. Isometric contraction
3. Isokinetic contraction

1. Isotonic or concentric or dynamic contraction is a type of muscle contraction in which while lifting a constant load the muscle shortens with different tension.

2. Isometric or eccentric or static contraction is muscle contraction in which there is no change in the length of the muscle though the tension is developed.

3. Isokinetic contraction is muscle contraction performed at an unvarying pace moreover in such a way that the muscle tension develops while shortening in maximal more than the complete range of joint motion.

Muscular system gets affected to a great extent by training principally by resistance or weight training. After resistance training several parameters of muscular system gets altered, few of them are described below :

Muscle Hypertrophy

Hypertrophy is an increase in width of individual muscular fiber. The size of muscle fibers is usually responsible for the gains in strength and muscular endurance.

The weight training causes the condition of hypertrophy of muscle; the following are the effects of muscles hypertrophy:

1. For our muscle growth total amount of proteins increases essentially.

2. The size of the muscle fibers increases as a result of resistant training.

3. Quantity of connective tissue increases.

4. Flow of blood in the muscle increases.

5. Muscular strength and endurance increases because of hypertrophy.

6. Capillary density per fiber also increases which cause more energy production.

Biochemical Changes in Muscles

Alterations in Aerobic Capacity

1. Amount of mitochondria increases consequently producing more muscular energy.

2. Breakdown of carbohydrates and fat increases.

3. Oxygen-binding compound called Myoglobin content found in muscle tissue increases.

4. Enzymes are protein composite speed up chemical reactions in the muscles hence, increasing the level of activity of concentration of enzymes.

5. Quantity of glycogen store increases consequently because of training which is vital for energy production in the muscles.

Alterations in Anaerobic Capacity

1. ATP + PC System Capacity increases in that way releasing more energy.

2. As a result of training glycolytic capacity increases as well.

Body Composition Changes

1. The body composition changes significantly whereas in case of majority of individual weight training produces little or no change in total body weight.

2. There can be noteworthy loss of relative and absolute body fat.

3. The muscle mass increases considerably.

4. Alteration in muscle and joint motion occurs.

5. Flexibility increases subsequent to training enhancing the performance and preventing serious muscular injury.

7.5. PHYSIOLOGICAL CHANGES DUE TO AGEING

Meaning of Ageing

The process of becoming older is called ageing. The accumulation of changes in a person over time is represented by ageing. In humans, ageing is referred to a multidimensional process of physical, psychological, and social alterations. A number of dimensions of ageing develop and expand over time, whereas others decline. For instance, knowledge of world events and wisdom may perhaps develop but reaction time possibly will slow with age. Research shows that even late in life, potential exists for physical, mental, and social growth and development. Ageing is a significant component of every human society reflecting the biological changes that take place, however, reflecting cultural and societal conventions as well. In other words, a normal change in body functions that occurs after sexual maturity and continues until death is referred to as ageing.

Physiological Changes due to Ageing

As our age increases, we undergo a number of physiological changes, which affect not only how we look, but also how we function and respond to daily living. Overall, the changes in the later life span described below involve a general slowing down of all organ systems due to a gradual decline in cellular activity. It should be noted that individuals experience these changes differently - for some, the level of decline may be rapid and dramatic; for others, the changes are much less significant. The effects of these changes also differ widely. While approximately 85% of older adults experience chronic conditions, only about 20% experience significant impairment in their ability to function. For those with disabilities, this process may occur more rapidly.

The Outward Signs of Ageing

The most common external signs of aging involve the skin, hair, and nails.

1. Skin : Over time, the skin loses underlying fat layers and oil glands, causing wrinkles and reduced elasticity. Other contributing factors are nutrition, exposure to the sun, heredity and hormones.

With these changes comes an increased sensitivity to cold (hypothermia), bruising and bedsores. The ability to perspire is lessened because sweat glands are shrinking, making the individual more susceptible to heat (hyperthermia). In addition, the skin develops "age spots" due to deposits of melanin pigment.

Individuals with mobility impairments for example have greater risk of skin related problems. Those who are paralyzed and have lost feeling to different parts of their body must increase their vigilance to avoid pressure sores. Lack of blood flow in the skin is always a concern and precursor to skin breakdown and decubitus ulcers. As individuals age, this problem becomes more serious.

2. Hair : The hair loses its pigmentation and turns gray. Thinning or hair loss is a part of the aging process too.

3. Nails : The nails become thicker due to reduced blood flow to the connective tissues.

The Inward Signs of Ageing

1. Changes in the cardiovascular system : For persons with disabilities, changes in the cardio-vascular system may appear earlier than in individuals without disabilities. Individuals who have decreased activity that is accompanied by weight gain are much more likely to experience cardiovascular problems than those who are able to remain active and mobile in their aging years. An example are persons with high level spinal cord injury who may not be able to feel the early warning signs of angina or other heart related pains.

Individuals with developmental disabilities such as down syndrome have been shown to be at higher risk for heart defects resulting in heart attacks at an earlier age. These effects are congenital in nature and interventions to overcome congenital heart defects are not generally available.

People who are aging experience significant overall change by reduced blood flow to the body, which typically becomes serious in the eighth decade. This results from a number of factors including :

(a) Normal atrophy of the heart muscle, especially in the left ventricle which pumps oxygenated blood out to the body.

(b) Calcification of the heart valves.

(c) Loss of elasticity in artery walls (arteriosclerosis or "hardening of the arteries").

(d) Intra-artery deposits (atherosclerosis).

The reduced blood flow results in less strength since :

(a) Less oxygen is being exchanged

(b) Reduced kidney and liver function

(c) Less cellular nourishment

As a consequence, the individual is more vulnerable to :

(a) Drug toxicity

(b) Has a slower rate of healing

(c) A lower response to stress

Other consequences of these cardiovascular changes are :

(a) Hypertension with an increased risk of stroke

(b) Heart attack

(c) Congestive heart failure

2. Changes in the respiratory system : Respiratory problems in people with disabilities are common. For individuals with spinal cord injury, as an example, the number one cause of death is pneumonia. This is especially true for individuals who have experienced high level injuries.

As with the cardiovascular system, there is also a reduction in the efficiency of the respiratory system in later life. The airways and lung tissue become less elastic with reduced cilia activity, resulting in decreased oxygen uptake and exchange.

The muscles of the rib cage also atrophy, further reducing the ability to :

(a) Breathe deeply

(b) Cough

(c) Expel carbon dioxide

These changes worsen if the individual smokes or lives in a polluted environment. The result of these changes can include lower stamina with shortness of breath and fatigue, which in turn may impair one's ability to perform activities of daily living. Lack of oxygen can also increase anxiety.

3. Changes in musculature : A generalized withering of all muscles is normal in later years accompanied by a replacement of some muscle tissue by fat deposits. This results in some loss of muscle tone and strength. Some specific implications are :

(a) Reduced ability to breathe deeply.

(b) Reduced gastrointestinal activity which can lead to constipation.

(c) Bladder incontinence, particularly in women.

Although everyone experiences these changes to some degree, regular physical exercise appears to temper the extent of these changes. However, if a person has some type of disability, their ability to exercise and remain active is limited. Tendencies to gain excessive weight and be inactive cause the person with a disability to have accelerated and significant problems in later years with their muscle mass. Muscles, bones and joints become strained over time, making it more difficult to handle the stress and weight of the person's body.

In addition, individuals who use manual wheelchairs or mobility aids are much more likely to experience pain in arms and shoulder. About half the individuals who use wheelchairs experience problems with the rotator cuff more significantly between the age of 50 and 60. This problem is caused by extensive use in the arms and shoulders for propelling the wheelchair as well as transfers. Another common problem associated with wheelchair use is Carpal Tunnel Syndrome.

4. Changes in the skeletal system : Beginning at around age 35 in both men and women, calcium is lost and bones become less dense. This can result in osteoporosis and a reduction of weight bearing capacity, leading to the possibility of spontaneous fracture. Thinning of the vertebrae also results in a reduction in height. In addition, the vertebrae calcify, resulting in postural changes and increasing rigidity, making bending difficult. The joints also undergo changes.

In fact, arthritis, the degenerative inflammation of the joints, is the most common chronic condition in the elderly. The two most common forms are :

(a) Osteoarthritis (a wearing away of the joint cartilage)

(b) Rheumatoid arthritis (a disease of the connective tissue)

These conditions can impair mobility and the performance of daily activities of living. For persons with disabilities, this condition may occur at an earlier age.

5. Changes in the nervous system : After age 25, everyone loses nerve cells. Gradually over time, this results in a reduced ability of nerve transmission, changing response time and coordination. The brain also shrinks in size, which does not significantly affect functioning except in the most extreme cases. These changes may also affect sleeping patterns somewhat by decreasing the length of total sleep time and REM sleep.

6. Changes in the gastrointestinal system : As we age, we experience a reduction in the production of hydrochloric acid, digestive enzymes, and saliva, as well as a reduction in the total number of taste buds. These changes can result in :

(a) Gastrointestinal distress

(b) Impaired swallowing

(c) Delayed emptying of the stomach

Perhaps more importantly, the breakdown and absorption of foods may also be impaired, sometimes resulting in vitamin deficiencies of B, C, and K vitamins or, in extreme cases, malnutrition. If left untreated, these deficiencies may result in :

1. capillary weakening
2. easy bruising
3. muscle cramping
4. reduced appetite
5. weakness
6. mental confusion and/or illness

For individuals with disabilities, this may be a significant problem because of their existing problems of lack of activity, reduced blood flow, and body weakness.

7. Changes in the endocrine system : The endocrine or metabolic system is responsible for changing food into energy. After age 25, everyone experiences approximately a 1% decrease per year in their metabolic rate. This overall slowing results in food being less well absorbed and utilized as well as a decrease in the overall metabolism of drugs. Consequences can include reduced stamina and reserves as well as greater susceptibility to drug toxicity.

8. Changes in sexuality : Overall, sexual activity is more related to past life patterns than to age. Sexual desire and performance may continue well into an individual's seventh, eighth and ninth decade although frequency may decrease.

Physiological changes in women include :

(a) atrophy of the ovarian

(b) vaginal

(c) uterine tissues with decreased production of vaginal fluids

In men :

(a) sperm production is decreased

(b) the prostate enlarges

(c) overall sensitivity declines

Both older men and women generally require more stimulation to become aroused and more time to reach orgasm.

7.6. SPORTS INJURIES : CLASSIFICATION, CAUSES AND PREVENTION

From soccer fields to softball diamonds and kabaddi courts, every day, millions of people in the world take part in games and sports activities. Participation in sports improves physical fitness, coordination and self-discipline, and gives individuals important opportunities to learn teamwork. Games and sports can result in injuries as well some are minor, some are serious and some results in lifelong medical troubles.

Young athletes of the same age can be different to a great extent in size and physical maturity. Some youngsters try to perform at levels for which they are not ready; they may be physically less mature than their peers. Therefore, coaches, physical educators and parents should try to group youngsters not according to chronological age particularly during contact sports but according to skill level and size. They should alter the sport/game to put up the requirements of children with varying skill levels to be more practical.

Young athletes taking part in games/sports/ physical activities are in bulk and they are not simply small adults. Their bones, muscles, tendons, and ligaments are still growing, which makes them more vulnerable to injury. Growth plates are weaker than the nearby ligaments and tendons in youngsters. In a young athlete/sports person a serious growth plate injury can occur what is often a bruise or sprain in an adult.

Classification of Sports Injuries

Injuries among athletes may be classified into two critical categories :

1. Acute Injuries, and
2. Overuse Injuries.

Both types include injuries to the soft tissues *i.e.,* muscles and ligaments along with bones.

1. Acute injuries : Acute injuries are caused by an unexpected shock. Common acute injuries among young sports athletes include sprains *i.e.,* an incomplete or absolute tear of a ligament, strains *i.e.,* a partial or complete tear of a muscle or tendon, contusions (bruises) and fractures.

2. Overuse injuries : Not all injuries are sourced by a single, sudden twist, fall or collision. A sequence of small injuries to undeveloped bodies can cause minor fractures, minimal muscle tears, or progressive bone deformities which are known as overuse injuries. Common overuse injuries occur in the heels, elbows and knees with tears in the tissue wherever tendons attach to the leg bone or the heel bone.

Common Sports Injuries

Some of the common sports injuries are :

1. Sprain
2. Strain
3. Dislocation
4. Fracture
5. Abrasion and
6. Contusion

Causes of Sports Injuries

A huge number of situations can upshot in a sports-related injury. Sports injuries are most usually caused by structural abnormalities; weakness in muscles, tendons, ligaments; poor training methods; and risky exercising environments. Most sports injuries are caused by one or more of the following factors:

1. Overuse : Repetitive movements or overuse may be the most serious cause of sports injuries. Runners, swimmers and tennis players are chiefly prone to overuse injuries, including tennis elbow, tendinitis, shoulder impingement and shin splints.

2. Stops and twists : A high number of knee and ankle injuries is seen in the sports that include quick stopping and twisting motions *i.e.,* basketball, gymnastics and soccer. When an athlete rolls his foot and stretches the surrounding ligaments ankle sprains occur. The stabilizing muscles and cushioning cartilage around the knee, shoulder and other joints are prone to tearing from an uncontrolled twist or a sudden stop.

3. Falls : In addition to the obvious breaks that can happen from a fall, wrist sprains are common. Any athlete can fall in the middle of an activity. To break the fall, the natural instinct is to put the hands down when falling. The wrists bear the weight, which can easily stretch or tear a ligament.

4. Improper equipment : Lower back or arm pain may follow if athletes use a weight or a racquet too heavy for the athletes. Ill-fitting helmets and shoes may also cause injuries. Shoes that do not provide enough support may cause an injury to a runner. The inflammation of arch's shock absorber called plantar fascists is common when shoes do not fit suitably or give appropriate support.

5. New or increased activity : Plantar fascists or lower back pain can initiate if starting a new activity or increasing the level of activity too quickly. A cramp is a common result if athlete has begun a new exercise or sport as previously unused muscles may be in use or may increase the work of other muscles.

6. Fatigue : Resting between activities is essential to preventing muscle pulls as tired muscles are a common cause of muscle pulls.

7. Poor warm-up : Warm up delivers blood and oxygen to the various muscles allowing them to work more efficiently. Improper warm up initiates muscle cramping and pulls which results from jumping into an activity without properly preparing the muscles for it.

8. Impact and contact : Hard impacts are one of the causes following injuries such as shin splints and plantar fascists as more harsh impact on athlete's feet, legs, hips and back are caused. Injuries caused by impact and contact are common in sports such as football and rugby and further risky sports such as motor racing, boxing and skiing. Frequently, to make contact with other athlete can cause an athlete to be off balance, which may cause them to coil or alter direction rapidly; this often causes damage to connective tissue. A joint can be displaced if the contact is powerful and direct.

9. Unilateral movements : Lower-back pain threats golfers and tennis players since these activities require certain movements by only one side of the body. This can result in weaker muscles on the less active side causing lower back pain.

10. Technique or posture : Spasms and pulls are often the product of something as easy as moving the head clumsily to see a ball or an opponent. After riding with racing handlebars cyclists may experience neck pain. The position one must take to use the handlebars and still see where you're going tightens the neck muscles and causes a spasm.

Prevention of Sports Injuries

Participation in almost all sporting activities is accompanied with the risk of injury. There has been increase in the number of injuries in correspondence with the increase in the number of athletes in both competitive and recreational sports. Sports injuries can have intense, extended permanent effects particularly those not cared properly for on those who participate in sports. Here are some of preventive aspects of sports injuries mentioned underneath:

1. Athletes' medical checkup : Prior to the start of the activity or seasonal practice a pre-participation physical and medical check-up should be done on all athletes, which must comprise :

(a) A meticulous medical history.

(b) Body measurement such as height, weight and blood pressure, etc. should be checked.

(c) Medical check on circulo-respiratory components, abdominal, pelvic check, etc.

(d) Few major lab tests should be done.

(e) Orthopedic examination comprising of body structure, posture, flexibility, fat percentage, strength and maturation should be collected.

The athlete is given some remedial exercises or is restrained from doing activity, if any problems is/are found. The athlete should not be permitted to partake until the paucity has been made up or corrected.

2. Proper warm-up : To lessen the probability of injury while participating in sports, the most important and significant way is the warm-up. To prepare the muscles for strenuous activity a warm-up session for at least last 5-10 minutes involving stretching and other exercises should be given. It is essential to initiate the warm-up gradually and progress to a pace more vigorous and energetic.

Warming up allows to prevent injury, muscles receives increased blood flow, the flexibility of the muscle increases and considerably dropping the threat of straining a muscle.

3. Proper cooling down : Cooling down is basically lowering down the pace of the work out by performing stretching exercises and deep breathing relaxation exercises. Cooling down exercises prevent the post exercise soreness and stiffness. Cooling down exercises make exchange of blood easier.

4. Apply the correct protective equipment : To avoid damage to athlete, protective equipment is important for a few sports. This is mainly significant when the sport or activity involves physical contact with other players. Protective equipment may include shin pads, boxing gloves or protective head gear. All these equipment are intended to prevent injury to exposed parts of the body. When playing any sports, wearing correct footwear is very important as correct shoes provide support to the foot and prevent injury. Protective head gear, like helmets protect the skull and the brain from damage.

5. Technique : A particular technique can minimize the risk of injury in majority of sports. The correct techniques related with the chosen sport are important to learn. By practicing good technique an athlete can to a great extent decrease the risk of sports-related injury to muscles, tendons and bones.

6. Do not over-reach ourselves : When we start on a new sport, initiate slowly and progressively to keep away from pulling or straining muscles which the body may not be used to. It is extremely important to know the physical limits when taking part in sports. It is particularly significant to build up the stamina and strength slowly to avoid injury. Eventually, it will be noticed that the fitness increased and can be able to undertake sports for longer periods of time.

7. Stay hydrated : When we are active and exercising, water is essential to keep the body going. It is especially important to keep the body hydrated if we are exercising in heat or in sunny weather, as dehydration can considerably decrease mental and physical fitness.

8. Psychosocial conditions : In preventing injuries the psychosocial aspects of the athlete must also be taken into considerations. The athlete may be afraid of re-injury, or those that may not have a "mind set" of competitive athlete. Communication between the coach and student also affects and athlete becomes critical. Any diversions could cause an injury hence the athlete not focused completely on the game should not be allowed to participate.

7.7. FIRST AID–AIMS AND OBJECTIVES

Introduction

Initially, in the year 1879, the term 'First Aid' was officially adopted by the St. John Ambulance Association for the first time in England. To avoid probable complications, First aid was introduced which is a combination of simple however fairly effectual and active measures. First Aid is the treatment given or provided to the injured or wounded person till apt medical aid is received. In other way, first aid is said to be the procedure of running the indispensable emergency treatment of the injury or illness to facilitate the sufferer till the appropriate medical services are provided.

Thus, first aid is the instantaneous treatment provided to the victim or patient of an accident or unexpected sickness prior to implementation of the regular medical assistance.

Basic Requirements of the First Aid

Certain basic requirements of the first aid are:

1. The first aid should be given quickly and without any fuss or panic. This means that the person who gives the first aid treatment should be skillful, resourceful, calm and controlled to give the treatment.

2. People should not be allowed to crowed around the patient.

3. A first aid box or kit should be kept handy which contains all the necessary equipments which are required.

4. An atmosphere of re-assurance must be created not only for the patient, but others around should also be assured of proper treatment.

5. If breathing must be saved from shock.

6. Clothes should be removed, if necessary.

7. Immediate arrangement should be made to take the patient to a hospital or doctor.

Aims of First Aid

The main aims of 'First Aid' is to safeguard life, aid recovery and prevent aggravation of the condition, for the duration of transport to hospital or to the casualty's home, until the doctor's services are obtained. The other important aims of first aid are as follows:

1. To keep the patient alive till the doctor can attend to him/her.

2. To relieve pain or distress of the pain.

3. It promotes recovery and also involves preventing the condition from worsening and in some cases might completing a treatment.

4. First aid needs to be immediate in severe accidents complicated by bleeding, shock and loss of consciousness.

Objectives of First Aid

1. To conserve and save life.
2. To avoid further injury and worsening of the condition.
3. To obtain circulation of the blood.
4. To ensure an adequate supply of oxygen.
5. To maintain normal body temperature.
6. To place the injured person under medical cover as early as possible.

Importance of First Aid

Basic first aid plays a crucial role. Everyone should have basic knowledge of first aid because:

1. It gives you the ability to respond to emergencies such as natural disasters, accidents, ingestion of hazardous substances and health related issues like heart attacks.

2. Its ability to clean and dress a wound so that infections are reduced, it can save the person's time, medicine and lots of pain.

3. It reduces the chance of permanent damage, for example, rapid flushing of the eyes with water after a chemical splash can prevent blindness.

4. It helps to prevent an injury from becoming more serious, for example, cleaning and bandaging a cut can help prevent further problems.

5. It minimizes the length and extent of the medical treatment.

The First Aider

A First Aider is an ordinary individual who have learnt a customary technique of application of first aid suitable to his/her skill. First aider must be able to monitor carefully and act speedily. He/she should be capable to call doctor on the spot or move the casualties to hospital. First aider's fundamental responsibility ends after the doctor takes charge but he/she may assist the doctors afterward. He/she should give first aid systematically while waiting for the doctor.

Until 1894, the term "First Aider" was not coined. It was proposed to designate any individual who has received a certificate from an authorized association that he/she is competent to provide "First Aid".

First Aid Box

It is a small and handy kit box containing the articles which is required by the First Aider whilst providing First Aid. The articles in the box are as follows:

1. Sterile gauze pieces.
2. Bandages of different size.

3. Adhesive plasters of different sizes.
4. Scissors, safety pins, needles, tweezers etc.
5. Disposable sterile gloves.
6. Pads of various sizes.
7. Splints.
8. Antiseptics.
9. Thermometer.
10. Silver sulfa diazine cream.
11. Drugs such as analgesics, antibiotic, packets of O.R.S., etc.

The entire first aid box must be available in every home, institutions, public places, gymnasium halls, swimming pools, play fields and factories for instant utilization.

7.8. MANAGEMENT OF INJURIES

Injuries are common in all the sports it may be during practice, training or competition. Although various equipments have been developed for preventing injuries in sports, complete prevention is not yet been succeeded. It is certain that appropriate steps taken during competition may reduce the chances of getting injuries.

It is observed that not only a single type of injuries occur in sports. The injuries that take place may be in muscles, bones, joints etc.

Likewise sports injuries may be divided into various types. They are:

1. Soft tissue injury   2. Bone injury
3. Joint injury

As the injuries occur, it is also very important to manage if any type of injuries occurs during activities. It is essential to know how to identify, give treatment and to get recovery for the normal functioning which we say it as an injury management. So in this chapter sports injuries and about its management will be discussed.

Soft Tissue Injury

The damage in the muscles, ligaments, tendons, or nerves of the body is known as soft tissue injury.

Some type of soft tissue injuries are as follows :

1. Abrasion   2. Contusion
3. Laceration   4. Incision
5. Sprain   6. Strain

Abrasion

Abrasion is a wound caused by superficial damage to the skin, no deeper than the epidermis. It is less severe than a laceration, and bleeding. Mild abrasions, also known as grazes or scrapes, do not scar or bleed, but deep abrasions may lead to the formation of scar tissue. A more traumatic abrasion that removes all layers of skin is called an avulsion.

Abrasion injuries most commonly occur when exposed skin comes into moving contact with a rough surface, causing a grinding or rubbing away of the upper layers of the epidermis.

Management :

1. The abrasion should be cleaned and debris should be removed.
2. A topical antibiotic (such as Neosporin or bacitracin) should be applied to prevent infection and to keep the wound moist.
3. Dressing the wound is optional but helps to keep the wound from drying out which interferes with healing.
4. In case the abrasion is painful, a topical analgesic (such as lidocaine or benzocaine) can be applied, but for large abrasions a systemic analgesic may be necessary. Avoid exposing abraded skin to the sun as permanent hyperpigmentation can develop.

Contusion

Contusion is the medical name for a bruise that refers to an area of skin discoloration (typically black and blue) occurs when blood vessels are damaged or broken after the skin takes a hard hit or bumps. Blood leaks out of the damaged blood vessels into the surrounding tissues. A contusion may be painful to the touch because the blood that has pooled under the skin put pressure on nearby nerve endings. Contusions or bruises are common injuries in sports with a risk of collision or impact.

Bruises are classified as:

1. **Subcutaneous :** A bruise beneath the skin
2. **Intramuscular :** A bruise within a muscle
3. **Periosteal :** A bruise to a bone

Management :

1. As soon as the injury happens, follow RICE, Rest, Ice, Compression, and Elevation for the first 24 to 48 hours. Remember not to keep ice on the injury for more than 15 to 20 minutes at a time. It is possible to get frostbite from an ice pack if it's left in place for too long.
2. After the first day or two, switch from ice to heat (still no longer than 20 minutes at a time). Continue to elevate the injury when convenient. Compression is probably not helpful at this point.

3. Acetaminophen or ibuprofens are good for the pain. Ibuprofen is a non-steroidal anti-inflammatory drug (NSAID). It may help with the inflammation more than acetaminophen, but either is acceptable.

Laceration

A laceration is a wound that occurs when skin, tissue, and/or muscle is torn or cut open. Lacerations may be deep or shallow, long or short, and wide or narrow. Most lacerations are the result of the skin hitting an object, or an object hitting the skin with force. Laceration repair is the act of cleaning, preparing and closing the wound.

Management :

1. As is the first step in most injuries to the skin, cleaning the wound is of utmost importance as to stave off infection and inflammation.
2. For mild lacerations, the use of a topical ointment, such as Neosporin, is recommended, as it the application of a basic bandage.
3. For deeper wounds, as in those that affect the tissue beneath the skin and experience heavier bleeding, attention from a medical professional should be required, as the wound will likely need to be closed with stitches, staples or even sutures.
4. Stitches to the skin surface can help to stop bleeding, protect underlying tissues and lessen scarring.

Incision

It is a cut especially by a scalpel or similar medical tool in the context of surgical operation.

Management :

1. While changing and removing the dressing of the wound, an aseptic, non-touch technique should be used.
2. The frequency of changing the dressing of the wound should be kept minimum to avoid disrupting healing tissue.
3. For cleaning of the wound sterile saline should be used up to 48 hours after surgery.
4. If the wound has been separated or been surgically opened to drain pus. Tap water can be used for cleaning after 48 hours.
5. Antiseptic agents are considered unnecessary for general wound cleansing but may be of value when irrigating an infected cavity wound.
6. Patient can take shower safely 48 hours after surgery.
7. The incision should be rested till the complete healing takes place and no additional force should be applied on site of the incision.

Sprain

A type of injury that involves damage to one or more ligaments in a joint, often caused by trauma to a joint (the space between bones), Twisting or forces overstretch the ligaments (such as hyperextension or hyper flexion) and can cause tears in the ligament tissue, which can be graded from mild to severe depending on the amount of damage. Sprains can occur in any joint but are most common in the ankle and wrist.

Management : The treatment of sprains depends on the extent of injury and the joint involved. Generally the acronym RICE is used in treating of sprain.

1. **Rest :** The sprain should be rested. No additional force should be applied on site of the sprain.
2. **Ice :** Ice should be applied immediately to the sprain to reduce swelling and pain. It can be applied for 10–15 minutes at a time (longer application of ice may cause damage instead of healing), 3-4 times a day.
3. **Compression :** Dressings, bandages, or ace-wraps should be used to immobilize the sprain and provide support. When wrapping the injury, more pressure should be applied at the far end of the injury and decrease in the direction of the heart; the reason for this is that it more easily causes unnecessary fluid to be flushed back up the blood stream in order to be recycled. Compression should not cut off the circulation of the limb.
4. **Elevation :** Sprained joint should be kept elevated as it will help in minimizing swelling.

Medications like non-steroidal anti-inflammatory drugs can be used for relieving pain.

The joint should be exercised again fairly soon, in milder cases from 1 to 3 days after injury. Special exercises are sometimes needed in order to regain strength and help reduce the risk of ongoing problems.

Strain

A strain involves stretching or tearing of muscle or tendon that connects muscles to bones. Strains often occur in the lower back and in the hamstring muscle in the back of the thigh.

For the convenience of treating the muscles strain it has been simplified into three grades, depending on the severity of muscle fiber damage:

1. Grade I strain : In this mild strain, only a few muscle fibers are stretched or torn. Although the injured muscle is tender and painful, it has normal strength.

2. Grade II strain : This is a moderate strain where greater number of injured fibers and more severe muscle pain and tenderness. There will also be a mild swelling, noticeable loss of strength and sometimes a bruise.

3. Grade III strain : In this the muscle gets torn causing a "pop" sensation at times as the muscle rips into two separate pieces or shears away from its tendon. It causes complete loss of muscle function, as well as considerable pain, swelling, tenderness and discoloration.

Management : For the management of strain also the rule of ice is being followed :

1. Rest the injured muscle (and take a temporary break from sports activities).
2. Ice the injured area to reduce swelling.
3. Compress the muscle with an elastic bandage.
4. Elevate the injured area.
5. For relieving of pain it is suggested to take acetaminophen (Tylenol and others) or a non-steroidal anti-inflammatory drug (NSAID), such as ibuprofen (Advil, Motrin and others).
6. In case Grade II or Grade III strain, it is suggested to get referred to an orthopedic specialist.

Bone Injuries

Bone injuries occur in the bone due to some impact or a minimal trauma injury as a result of certain medical conditions that weaken the bone such as osteoporosis, bone cancer or osteogenesis imperfecta, etc.

There are some types of bone injuries. They are :

1. Simple fracture
2. Compound fracture
3. Greenstick fracture
4. Comminuted fracture
5. Transverse fracture
6. Oblique fracture
7. Spiral fracture
8. Pathologic fracture
9. Impacted fracture
10. Stress fracture

Now, brief discussion of the above mention types of fractures is as below :

1. Simple fracture : It is also called closed fractures, in this type of fracture a bone breaks but the broken bones remain within the body and do not penetrate the skin.

2. Compound fracture : Also called open fractures, in this type of fracture the broken bones penetrate through the skin and expose the bone to the exterior environment.

3. Greenstick fracture : This type of fracture involves bending of bone and cracks, instead of breaking completely into separate pieces.

4. Comminuted fracture : It involves the breaking of a bone into several smaller pieces.

5. Transverse fracture : When the broken piece of bone is at a right angle to the bone's axis it is called transverse fracture.

6. Oblique fracture : When the breaking bones have a curved or sloped pattern it is called as oblique fracture.

7. Spiral fractures : Spiral fractures are the results of an extreme twisting force being exerted on a bone.

8. Pathologic fracture : It is caused by a disease that weakens the bones.

9. Impacted fracture : In this type of fracture the ends of the broken bones get driven into each other.

10. Stress fracture : A stress fracture is a small crack in a bone. These fractures are most often a result of overuse and are commonly seen with an increase in activity.

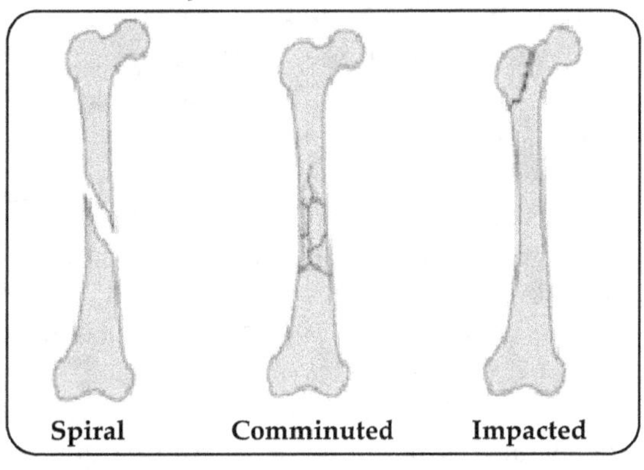

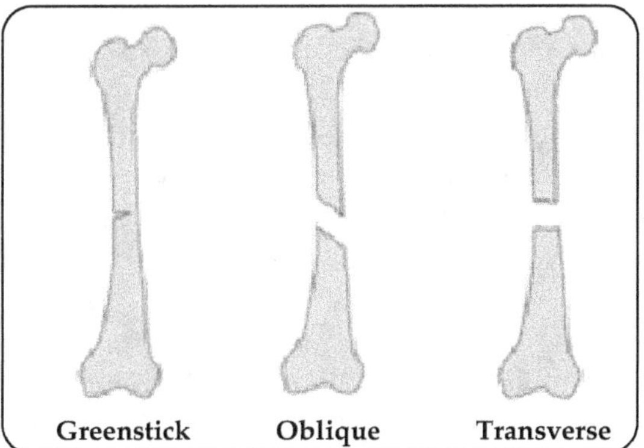

Types of Fracture

Management of Selected Bone Injuries

Management of the bone injuries will depend on the type of fracture, its severity, the individual's age and general health. The first priority in managing any fracture is to address the entire medical status of the patient. Medical personnel are trained not to allow a painful, deformed limb to distract them from potentially life-threatening injury elsewhere or shock. If an open fracture is accompanied by serious soft tissue injury, it may be necessary to control bleeding and the shock that can accompany loss of blood.

First aid is the appropriate initial treatment in emergency situations. It includes proper splinting, control of blood loss, and monitoring vital signs such as breathing and circulation.

Green Stick Fracture

A greenstick fracture involves bending of bone and cracks, instead of breaking completely into separate pieces. This type of broken bone most commonly occurs in children because their bones are softer and more flexible than are the bones of adults.

A common cause of a greenstick fracture is a fall, as falls can cause a bone to bend further than it is able too. Blunt trauma such as a blow can also cause such a fracture.

Management : Greenstick fractures management requires fracture reducing. This is done by:

1. Slightly pulling the bone apart and putting it into place to straighten it. To make sure that the fracture will heal correctly, it is needed to be immobilized.

2. Usually, casts are used or a removable splint for the convenience of the child. Since children's bones tend to heal faster than those of adults, the cast or the splint may be removed in a short span of three to four weeks.

3. Physical therapy is also directed to regain mobility and movement of the affected limb. If there are some instances that these measures do not take effect, surgery is advised to correct the fracture.

4. When surgery is done, post-operative traction may be used to straighten the hard fracture.

5. In order to reduce swelling on the affected site, anti-inflammatory drugs can be given.

6. Younger children may not able to express their feelings in the event greenstick fracture occurs or they can cry uncontrollably with the intensity of pain. That is why parents are advised to have their child seek consultation when they suspect that their child sustained a major fall.

Comminuted Fracture

A fracture in which the bone is broken into several pieces or is shattered, creating numerous fragments which is also called comminution, fragmented fracture.

This type of fracture may be caused due to severe fall, bullet injury, vehicular trauma or accident etc. In elderly people suffering from bone diseases such as osteogenesis, imperfecta or brittle bone disease and bone cancer the possibility of occurrence of this type of fracture is more as the bones are weak and can break even due to less stress.

Management : Managing of this type of fracture may be difficult because of the involvement of too many fragmented pieces. So for managing such type of fracture following principles need to be followed :

1. The shattered pieces are lined up in a procedure labeled as reduction.

2. Above and below the injured area fiberglass cast, plasters and splints are used to maintain the immobilization.

3. For managing of pain, ibuprofen can be used which is in similar effective to the combined acetaminophen and codeine.

4. In case if fragmented ends of the bones are forcefully jammed together by massive force, an invasive method termed as open reduction, involving surgical nails, screws, plates and wires, is used with the intention of preserving the original position of the splintered pieces.

5. If bone infection arises, meticulous antiseptic measures and prophylactic antibiotics are mandatory.

6. As this type of fracture takes more time to restore its normal condition, regular appointment with a doctor is recommended to guarantee the good condition of the bones and physical therapy may be needed for the patient to get rapid recovery.

Stress Fracture

A small crack that takes place in the bone due to overusing of the certain part of the body that commonly results due to increase in activity without proper recovery is said as stress fracture.

Management :

1. The initial management for a stress fracture is to elevate the extremity and rest while the bone heals itself.

2. Icing is recommended in the affected area for 24 to 48 hours and reducing the activity.

3. For relieving of pain, painkillers such as paracetamol or ibuprofen (an NSAID - non-steroidal anti-inflammatory drug) may be recommended.

4. The affected area should be immobilized.

5. When the swelling get decreased, seeing the skin creases, partial weight can be applied on the area.

6. In some cases, crutches or a walking stick may be necessary.

7. Avoidance in the activity that causes stress fracture is necessary until the pain is free.

8. During returning to the activity, activity should be done slowly as rushing back may injured again.

9. In case severe stress fractures that won't heal on their own may require surgery. Full recovery may require months or years.

Transverse Fracture

Type of fracture that involves breaking a part of bone in a spine and the part get extended from the main body of bone (knows as the vertebral body). Thoracic spine (the upper part and the middle part of the back) and lumbar spine (lower back) is the part where this type of injury mainly occurs.

Most of this type of injuries occurs as a result of a variety of accidents such as:

1. Falls.
2. Motor vehicle accidents.
3. Recreational activities.
4. Industrial, agricultural, and aviation accidents.
5. Gunshot wounds and direct blows to the back.
6. Parachuting incidents.

Management :

1. If the injury is not serious, then it is not necessary to have the hospital care.
2. Bed rest, medications for relieving pain, back bracing and avoidance in the activity is required until complete rehabilitation.
3. Operation may be required in case of severe cases like multiple fracture of spine.
4. After initial pain goes strengthening training under supervision is necessary, so that the bone attains its normal ability.
5. It is also important to have follow-up-care for prevention of further injury.

Oblique Fracture

When the breaking bone has a curved or sloped pattern, it is said to be oblique fracture. It mainly occurs when the bone gets trapped and another bone twists over it. This fracture is very rare and long bones are more prone to oblique fracture. Most of the oblique fractures develop at femur or humerus.

Management : The management options for an oblique fracture depend on the severity of the crack or break.

1. Anti-inflammatory medications and pain relievers may be required for handling pain.

2. Reduction may be required to perform, which is the process of resetting the bone.

3. Mobility may need to restrict for several weeks by placing the broken bone in a brace, sling or cast.

4. Sometimes surgery is required to insert nails, screws, wires or other devices to help the bones to heal.

5. It is very important to take care of the broken part of the bone even after recovery.

Impacted Fracture

It is a type of fracture in which the bone breaks into multiple fragments and gets driven into each other. It is caused mainly when someone falls from height with a great impact. The site of fracture mainly takes place in arms and legs.

Management :

1. As in the impacted fracture the bones get broken into fragments a sling or a splint may be required to keep the broken bones in place, so that it prevents the movement of the sharp ends of the broken bone, and further not drives into other bone fragments.

2. It often requires the use of plates, rods and screws to realign the bone.

3. Severe impacted fracture may require surgery.

4. After surgery for the period of time the affected area will likely require a cast or sling to allow bone fragments to reunite.

5. It is necessary to restrict movements while the treatment is going on.

6. It is required to severely limit mobility until it is fully healed.

7. It is important to take good care of the fractured part.

Joint Injuries

Joint injuries are the injuries that occur in the joint of the bones of the body like dislocation, which is a common joint injury.

Dislocation

A type of injury to a joint, where the bones in the joint gets forced out from its normal positions resulting with immobilization of joints. The sites for dislocations include the elbows, knees and hips, shoulder, elbows etc.

Dislocations mainly occurs in contact sports, such as football, hockey, and in sports that may involve falls, such as downhill skiing, gymnastics, volleyball and also during a motor vehicle accident.

Dislocation takes place in different location of the joints like:

1. Dislocation of shoulder joint
2. Dislocation of lower jaw
3. Dislocation of hip joint

1. Dislocation of shoulder joint : The shoulder joint is called a ball-and-socket joint as the rounded top of the bone in the upper arm (humerus) get fits into the socket. Shoulder is said to be dislocated when the top of the humerus moves out of the cup-shaped outer part of the shoulder blade leading to immobilization of joint. The chances of dislocation may be when the arm is pulled or twisted with extreme force in an outward, upward or backward direction and when sudden jerk or a fall on hard surface takes place.

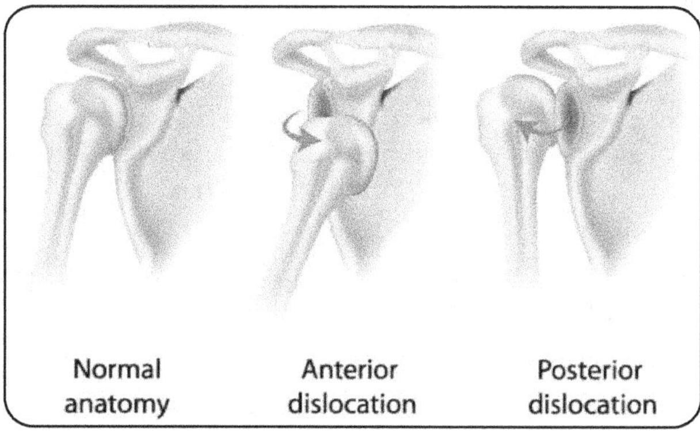

Shoulder Dislocation

2. Dislocation of lower jaw : An injury to the jaw joints that join the lower jawbone to the skull called the temporomandibular joints, and when the bones of these joints lie out from the skull it results in dislocation of the lower jaw.

The dislocation may be caused by forceful yawning or by an impact or force, such as being punched in the face or being in a car accident. Other activities that can lead to a dislocated jaw include laughing, vomiting, singing, eating, and even dental treatment.

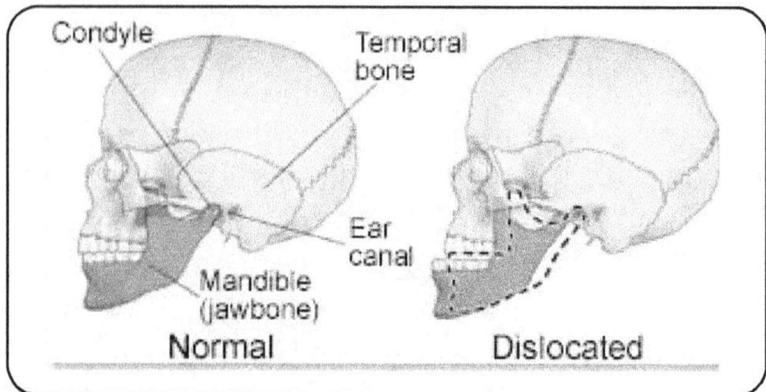

Dislocation of Jaw

3. Dislocation of hip joint : Dislocation of the hip is a common injury to the hip joint. Dislocation occurs when the ball-shaped head of the femur comes out of the cup-shaped acetabulum set in the pelvic. It may be caused due to motor vehicle collisions and falling from a significant height.

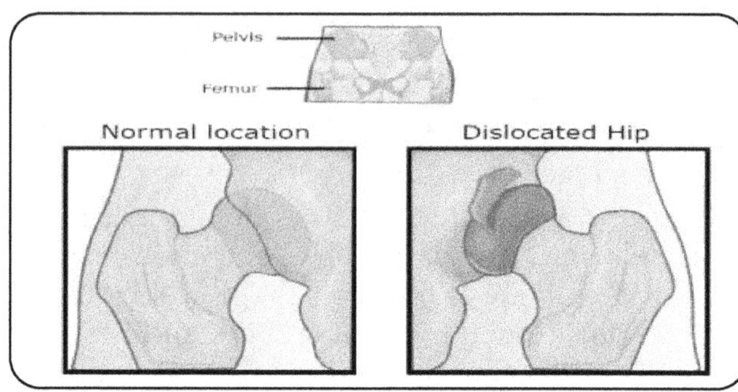

Dislocation of Hip Joint

Management of Dislocation

1. Apply cold packs around the dislocation area to relieve the pain.

2. Do not apply ice or cold packs directly to the skin as it may results damage to the skin.

3. Splint the injured area to keep it immobilized until professional dislocation treatment is given.

4. Monitor the dislocated area and ensure that it does not lose sensation, or exhibit a change in temperature or reduction in pulse as these signs could indicate an obstruction of blood flow or damage to the nerves leading down to the limb.

5. In case severe pain patient can be provided with ibuprofen or acetaminophen to get relief from the pain.

6. Offering food to the patient should be avoided as doctors usually prefer to work with a patient who has an empty stomach, particularly if surgery becomes necessary.

7. Keep the joint immobile and do not try to put the bones back into place on your own as it is the best to leave this part of the dislocation treatment to a professional who will handle the realignment correctly.

8. Once the doctor has placed the bones back into proper alignment, the joint need to be immobilized for a number of days or weeks to allow the joint time to heal. During that time, patients should rest the joint as much as possible and apply ice and heat to the area to reduce pain and swelling and use medication as per prescription.

EXERCISES

Multiple Choice Questions

1. As a result of strength training, the change in muscle tissue least likely to occur is :
   (a) Increased number of myosin filaments.
   (b) Increased size (diameter) of myosin filaments.
   (c) Increased number of myofibrils.
   (d) Increased sixe (diameter) of myofibrils.

2. A common adaptation to strength training is :
   (a) An increase in muscle fibre number.
   (b) A conversion of type 2A to 2X muscle fibres.
   (c) A greater increase in type 1 than type 2 fibre area.
   (d) An increase in the number of sarcomeres in parallel.

3. In regard to muscle architectural adaptations to strength and powedr training, it is true that :
   (a) Resistance training typically increases muscle fibre pennation angle (PA) due to fibre hypertrophy.
   (b) Sprint and explosive training may increase muscle fibre length (FL), which increases muscle contraction velocity.
   (c) An increase in FL can minimize or prevent the increase in PA resulting from fibre hypertrophy.
   (d) All options are true.

4. Which sport causes the most head injuries ?
   (a) Football   (b) Cycling
   (c) Swimming   (d) All of the above

5. Where is the largest (and often injred) tendon in the body ?
   (a) Neck   (b) Back
   (c) Ankle   (d) Shoulder

6. What's the exact cause of muscle cramps ?
   (a) Injury   (b) Dehydration
   (c) Vitamin deficiency (d) Unknown

7. A sprain is an injury to :
   (a) Muscle   (b) Tendon
   (c) Ligament   (d) Bursa

8. What causes the most emergency room visits ?
   (a) Cuts   (b) Broken bones
   (c) Sprains   (d) Bruises

9. What is R.I.C.E. treatment ?
   (a) Rest, Ice, Crutches, Elevation
   (b) Rest, Ice, Compression, Elevation
   (c) Rest, Ibuprofen, Crutches, Elevation
   (d) None of the above

10. What's the most common runner's injury ?
    (a) Shin splints   (b) Runner's knee
    (c) Achilles tendinitis (d) Plantar fasciitis

Very Short Answer Type Questions (Carrying 1 mark)

1. What is stroke volume ?
2. What do you mean by cardiac output ?
3. What do you mean by flexibility ?
4. State any one physiological factor determining flexibility.
5. What is ageing ?
6. What is understood by oxygen intake and uptake?
7. Explain in brief the fact on joint structure determining the flexibility.
8. Explain briefly regarding ageing.
9. Confer about the consequence of ageing on the size and strength of muscle.
10. Discuss the effect of age on bone density.
11. What is soft tissue injury ?
12. What do you mean by abrasion ?
13. What is sprain ?
14. In which year the term 'first aid' was first officially adopted ?
15. What is a first aid box ?
16. In which year the 'first aider' was termed ?
17. What is first aid?
18. Who is known as the 'first aider' ?

Short Answer Type Questions (Carrying 3 marks)

1. Discuss any three physiological factors determining strength.
2. Explain any three physiological factors determining speed.
3. Discuss any three physiological factors determining endurance.
4. Elaborate any three physiological factors determining flexibility.
5. Explain any three immediate effects of exercise on cardiovascular system.
6. Explain any three effects of exercise on respiratory system.
7. Elaborate any three effects of exercise on circulatory system.

8. Discuss any three physiological changes in human body due to ageing.
9. List the common sports injuries.
10. Name the types of soft tissues injuries.
11. What is green stick fracture ?
12. What do you mean by spiral fracture ?
13. What do you mean by comminuted fracture ?
14. What is dislocation of hip joint ?
15. Enlist the causes of sports injuries.
16. Describe the process of management for sprain.
17. List any five articles kept in the first aid box.
18. Explain the importance of the first aid.
19. Explain the two objectives of first aid.
20. Explain any three aims of the first aid.
21. Discuss the management procedure for contusion.
22. State the difference between acute and overuse injuries.
23. What do you mean by dislocation ?
24. What is mean by fracture ?
25. What is the management procedure for green stick fracture ?
26. What is bone injury and name any five bone injuries ?
27. Write notes on shoulder dislocation.

Long Answer Type Questions (Carrying 5 marks)

1. Elucidate the physiological factors determining strength.
2. Explain the physiological factors determining speed.
3. Discuss the physiological factors determining endurance.
4. Explain the physiological factors determining flexibility.
5. Elaborate any five immediate effects of exercise on cardiovascular system.
6. Discuss any five long term effects of exercise on cardiovascular system.
7. Discuss any five effects of exercise on respiratory system.
8. Discuss in detail any five effects of exercise on circulatory system.
9. In detail, discuss any five physiological changes due to ageing.
10. Discuss elaborately the impact of environment on athletes.
11. Discuss sports injuries along with classification and causes.
12. Write short notes on the following bone injuries:
    (a) Simple fracture   (b) Spiral fracture
    (c) Oblique fracture   (d) Comminuted fracture
13. Explain first aid in detail along with its aims and objectives.
14. Explain the basic requirements and importance of first aid.
15. Write short notes on the following soft tissue injuries:
    (a) Abrasion   (b) Contusion
    (c) Sprain   (d) Laceration
16. What is dislocation ? Describe the management process of dislocation.
17. What is impact fracture ? Write down its process of management.
18. What is stress fracture ? Write down its process of management.
19. Discuss oblique and transverse fracture along with their management.
20. What are joint injuries ? Discuss dislocation of shoulder, jaw and hip joint.

❑ ❑

8 BIOMECHANICS AND SPORTS

8.1. MEANING OF BIOMECHANICS

Biomechanics is the field in sport science that applies the laws of mechanics and physics to human

performance, in order to gain a greater understanding of performance in athletic events through modeling, simulation and measurement. It is also necessary to have a good understanding of the application of physics in sport, as physical principles such as motion, resistance, momentum and friction have their application in most sporting events. Biomechanics is a diverse interdisciplinary field, with branches in Zoology, Botany, Physical Anthropology, Orthopedics, Bio-engineering and Human Performance. The general role of biomechanics is to understand the mechanical cause - effect relationships that determine the motions of living organisms. In relation to sport, biomechanics contributes to the description, explanation, and prediction of the mechanical aspects of human exercise, sport and play. The word 'Biomechanics' is taken by the combination of two words 'Bio' and 'Mechanics'. 'Bio' is a Greek word meaning *life or living things* and 'Mechanics' refers to *the field of physics and the forces that act on bodies in motion.*

From historic times in physical education and sports, improving the performance had been the area of interest in individuals. In present scenario, the coaches, physical education teachers and trainers are more focused in assisting an individual to become skilled in moving efficiently. Pressure is on learning the basic motor skills in primary and high school as this gives a foundation for learning the complex sports skills. Best efforts are given by teachers as well as coaches in order to develop the performance of students in different competitive sports events. The improvement in the performance of students is only possible when the coaches/teachers have ample amount of knowledge on 'Biomechanics'. Currently, for improving the performance of sports persons, biomechanics is playing a very essential role.

Sports biomechanics is a quantitative study and analysis of professional athletes and sports activities in general. It can simply be described as the Physics of Sports. In this subfield of biomechanics, the laws of mechanics are applied in order to gain a greater understanding of athletic performance through mathematical modeling, computer simulation and measurement. Biomechanics is the study of the structure and function of biological systems by means of the methods of "mechanics." Mechanics is the branch of physics involving analysis of the actions of force. Within "mechanics", there are two sub-fields of study : statics, a study of systems that are in a state of constant motion either at rest (with no motion) or moving with a constant velocity; and dynamics, a study of systems in motion in which acceleration is present, which may involve kinematics (the study of the motion of bodies with respect to time, displacement, velocity, and speed of movement either in a straight line or in a rotary direction) and kinetics (the study of the forces associated with motion, including forces causing motion and forces resulting from motion).

Importance of Biomechanics

In sports, biomechanics, the laws of mechanics are applied to human movement in order to gain a greater understanding of athletic performance and to reduce sport injuries as well. It focuses on the application of the scientific principles of mechanical physics to understand movements of the action of human bodies.

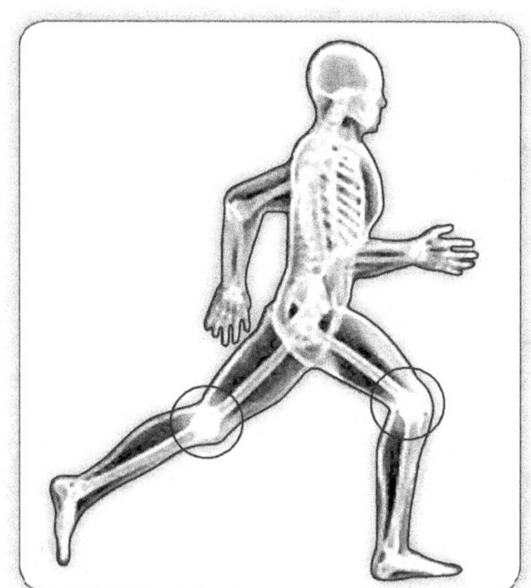

There are three groups of people who are interested in sport techniques *viz.*, physical educators, coaches and athletes. Since, each of these groups tends to view sport techniques in a somewhat different way, the importance of knowledge of biomechanics is to understand the movements of action of human bodies and sports. In biomechanics, how the different forces affect human motion and how the movement can be improved, is studied. The detailed description of importance of biomechanics is stated below :

1. **Improves understanding of human body :** The knowledge of biomechanics helps the teacher, coach and athlete to understand the complete human body and various internal and external forces that affect the movement of a human being through biomechanics. Both, the teacher or a student and coach or an athlete become capable enough to give proper training and teach scientifically about each and every muscle involved and is affected in a particular movement.

2. **Improves teaching and learning process :** In physical education, teachers and coaches explain the subject of biomechanics for improving teaching and learning process. In every sport, usually specific movements are involved, to be taught and the tutor explains the relevant techniques and skills. Here, biomechanics helps the teacher or the trainer to teach these techniques and skills systematically and it also helps the learner to understand all techniques easily and about their involvement in sports and physical activities.

3. **Helps in preventing injury :** If there is a sport going on, then there is a chance of injury. Biomechanics helps us to understand how to prevent the injury through the systematic knowledge and training. Biomechanics also helps in the process of rehabilitation of injuries and which exercises may help in the process of rehabilitation of injury. It also helps the coach or the trainer to identify the forces which may have caused an injury or its reoccurrence.

4. **Improves technique :** Biomechanics helps in improving proper technique of an athlete to correct or rectify the errors in order to improve the proper execution of a skill. It also helps to discover the new and more effective technique, for execution of correct skills to enhance the performance.

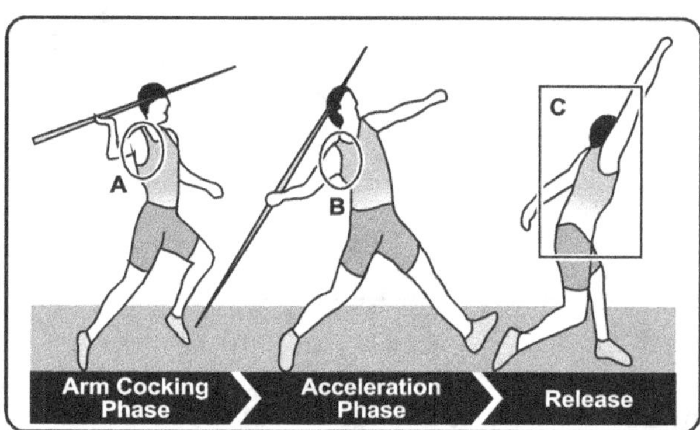

5. **Helps in enhancing the performance :** In scientific training, biomechanics helps in enhancing the performance by utilising mechanical principles to improve an athlete's technique. Biomechanics also helps the coach and the trainer to modify the technique used in sports competition. It also helps to develop such technique that helps to reduce the chances of injuries as well as changes the equipment to reduce injury.

6. **Helps in the improvement of training and equipment:** Biomechanics helps the coach and the trainer to perform proper mechanical analysis of the technical deficiencies of a sportsperson which can help the coach in identifying the type of training for the sportsperson to improve the performance of an athlete. It also helps in

improving designs for the equipments used in various sports. The equipment used in sports may have an effect on the performance either directly or indirectly. Bio-mechanics also helps in designing the sport clothes and equipments such as in skating, cycling and swimming costumes. Improvements in equipments would ultimately help in enhancing sport performance.

The Concept of Musculoskeletal System

The musculoskeletal system is the combination of muscular and skeletal systems which provides support to the body and allows multiple body movements. It is also called the Locomotors System of the human anatomy. It comprises of bones, muscles, tendons and ligaments of the body. The skeletal system's bones protect the body's internal organs and support the weight of the body. On the other hand, the muscular system's muscles contract and pull on the bones. These bones and muscles work altogether to facilitate smooth hand and leg movements.

The musculoskeletal system helps keep the body in shape, protects internal body organs and allows it to move. If this organ system is injured or not able to function properly, we will not be able to accomplish even daily tasks.

All the organ systems, including the vascular, nervous and integumentary systems, of the human body are inter-related. Thus, any disorder in any one of them affects the musculoskeletal system resulting in functional disorders or motion discrepancies. Malnutrition is the most common cause of musculoskeletal diseases worldwide.

Joints-Articulation of Bones

A joint, also known as articulation, is an interface between two bones. It is the place of connection between two bones, bones and cartilage or bones and teeth.

Joints can also be classified into three types based on their structure :

1. **Fibrous Joints :** A thick fibrous connective tissue binding articulating bones together making them immovable makes up a fibrous joint.

2. **Cartilaginous Joints :** A cartilage joining or binding two bones makes up a cartilaginous joint.

3. **Synovial Joints :** A synovial cavity or articular capsule present between two bones to join them, is supported and reinforced by surrounding ligaments, limiting movement to prevent injury makes up a synovial joint.

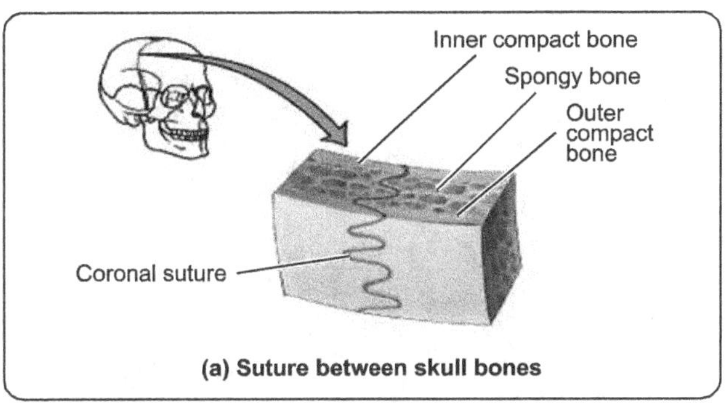

(a) Suture between skull bones

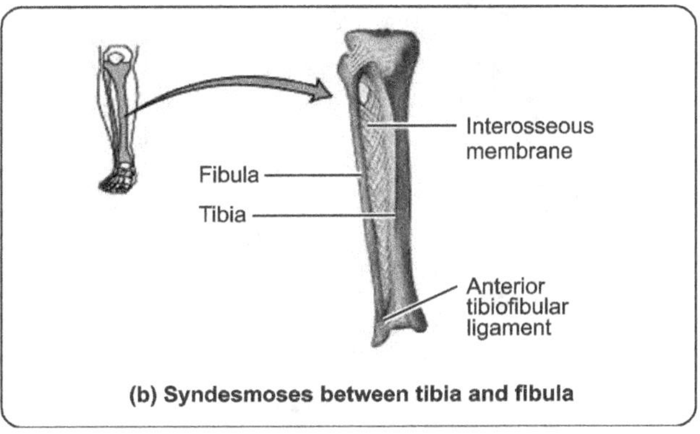

(b) Syndesmoses between tibia and fibula

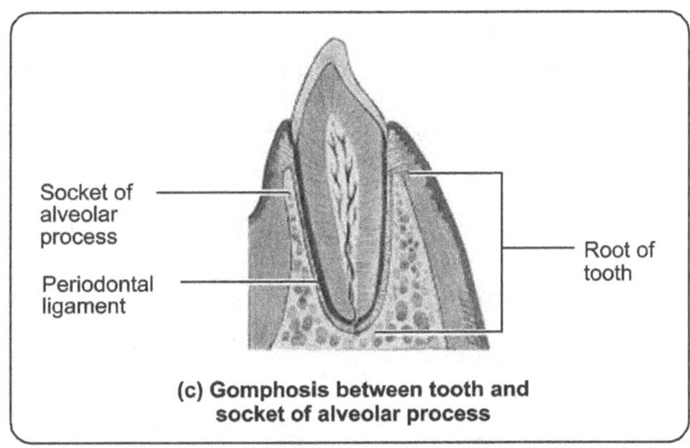

(c) Gomphosis between tooth and socket of alveolar process

Fibrous Joints

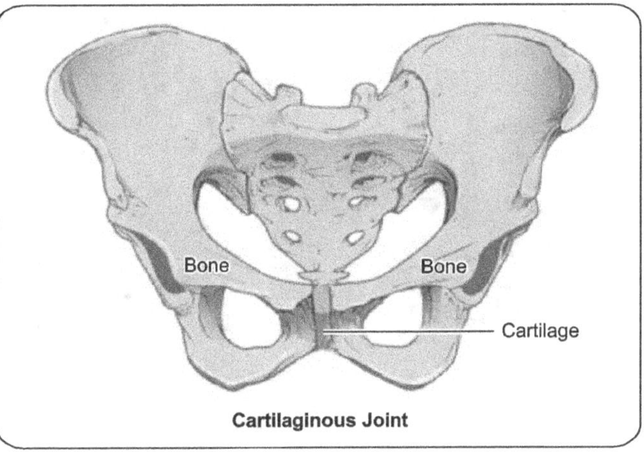

Cartilaginous Joint

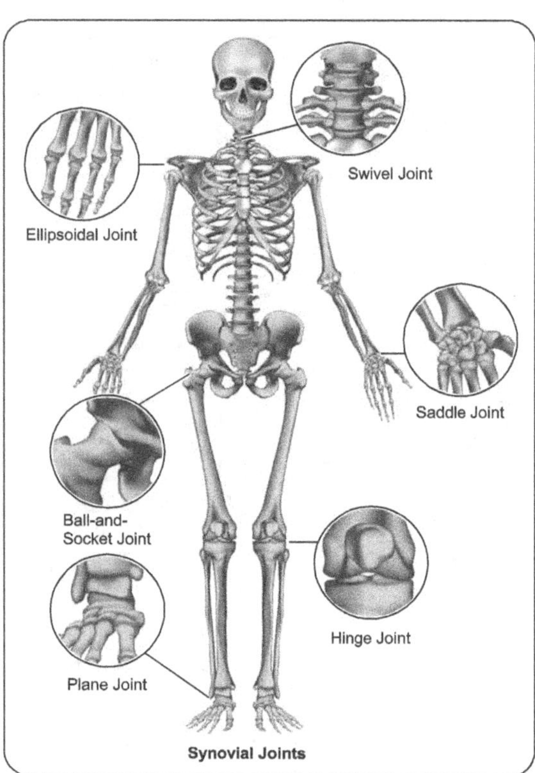

Joints can be classified into three types based on their functionality (degree of movement) :

1. **Synarthrosis :** Rigid, immovable joints are called Synarthrosis. The skull sutures, area between the teeth and the mandible and the area between the first pair of ribs and the sternum are the places where these joints are found.

2. **Amphiarthrosis :** The joints that allow little or slight movement are called Amphiarthrosis. The inter-vertebral disks of the spine and the pubic symphysis of the hips are the articulations that allow minimal movement.

3. **Diarthrosis :** The joints that allow complete or full movement are called Diarthrosis. These types of joints include many bone articulations in the upper and lower limbs. Elbow, shoulder, knee, wrist and ankle are the freely movable joints present in the human body.

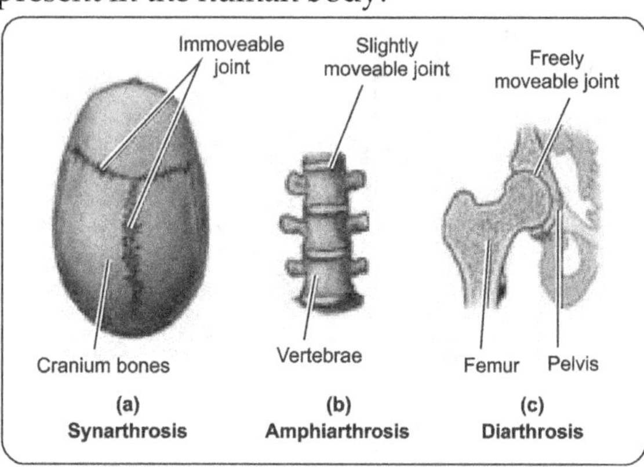

Major Muscles around the joints

Skeletal muscles are the major muscles involved in the movement. They are found around the joints safeguarding them and spread from one bone to another, passing at least one joint. They are connected to the bones by tendons :

1. **Major muscles in Neck :** Sternocleidomastoid and Trapezius.

2. **Major muscles in Shoulder :** Deltoid, Triceps, Biceps brachii, Teres major, Latissimus dorsi and Pectoralis major.

3. **Major muscles in Elbow :** Triceps, Biceps brachii and Brachio-radialis.

4. **Major muscles in Hips :** Gluteus Maximus, Psoas, Satorius, Quadriceps, Hamstrings, Adductor magnus and Gracilis.

5. **Major muscles in Knees :** Quadriceps, Hamstrings and Gastrocnemius.

8.2. NEWTON'S LAW OF MOTION AND ITS APPLICATION IN SPORTS

Everything that moves is governed by laws of motion formulated by Sir Issac Newton. These laws describe things move and make it possible to predict the motion of an object. There are three laws of motion which were formulated by Newton, and are as follows :

Newton's First Law (Law of Inertia) : *"A body at rest will remain in rest and a body in motion will remain in motion at the same speed and in the same direction unless acted on by same outside force".*

Example : In the field of sports and games, there are a great numbers of examples of Newton's first Law such as sprinting start, throwing the hammer and putting the shot put, javelin throw, etc.

Newton's Second Law (Law of Acceleration) : *"A change in velocity (acceleration) of an object is directly proportional to the force producing it and inversely proportional to its mass".*

Example : A sprinter's acceleration from the blocks is proportional to the force exerted against the blocks. The greater the force exerted, the greater will be the acceleration away from the blocks.

Newton's Third Law (Law of Reaction) : *"The law of action and reaction states that for every action there is an equal and opposite reaction".*

Example : (a) Swimming : A swimmer propels through the water because the water offers enough counterforce to oppose the action of her/his hands pushing, allowing her to move. An athlete can jump higher off a solid surface because it opposes his body with as much force as he/she is able to generate, in contrast to sand or other unstable surface.

(b) Basketball : A basketball exerts force on the ball and the ball strikes on the floor with a force and bounces up with an equal force from the floor.

8.3. AERODYNAMICS PRINCIPLES

Sports performance is a part of a multifaceted aspect depending on multiple factors. Analyzing performance is extremely difficult as the multiple factors, namely, psychology, physiology, biomechanics and technical advancement in equipment are all together involved assisting to reach to the final outcome.

Identifying the individual effects is indeed very complicated. But if we focus on the general point of view, aerodynamics properties are known to play a determinant role in more or less every sport, where the performance resulted because of the optimal motion of the multi-jointed mechanical system (athlete) and/or is solid system (equipment) in the air. Some basic principles of aerodynamic when applied can make the remarkable difference between creating winners and losers. From ball games such as soccer, basketball, volleyball, golf, tennis to athletics, cycling, skiing, motor sports and many more sports are the example where basic principles of aerodynamics function.

The way air move around things is known to be aerodynamics. Everything that moves in the course of air reacts to aerodynamics. Aerodynamics is associated with the flow of air around a projectile, which influences the speed and direction of the object.

Thus, aerodynamics in sport is essentially the pressure interaction between an athlete and/or his equipment (mechanic system) and the surrounding air. The athlete or the equipment can actually move in still or unsteady air.

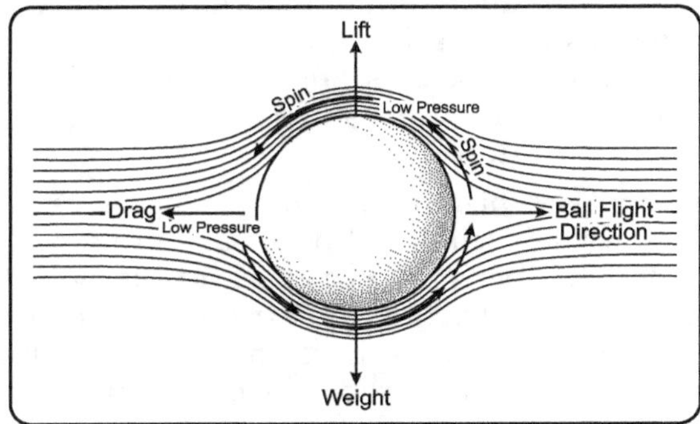

Principles of Aerodynamics

Every one of ball sports are governed by the mechanics related with aerodynamics. Aerodynamics plays a huge role in defining all of the sports. All of them observe curvature of the pathway of the ball even as in flight. The air flow around a ball thrown in the course of the air differs to a great extent depending on whether it has a smooth or a rough surface for instance, stitches on a cricket ball or dimples on a golf ball. Therefore, so as to comprehend the concept of aerodynamics we have to understand the principles or the operational components of an object when in air. There are basically four principles of aerodynamics which act upon an object to make it move up and down, and faster or slower. The principles discussed below are the ones which govern the moving object in air assisting the flight of it are weight, lift, drag and thrust.

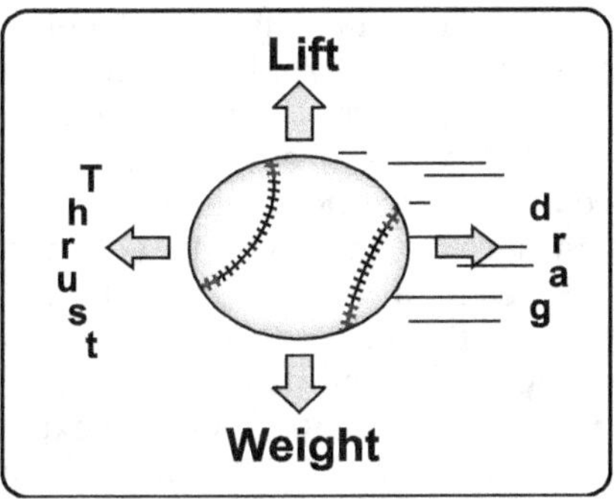

1. **Weight :** Weight is referred to be the force of gravity pulling the object down. Everything bears a weight on earth. This force comes from gravity pulling down on objects. To maintain the flight, the object needs something to push it in the opposite direction from gravity. The weight of an object controls the amount of push to be given. A lighter object needs lot less upward push than a heavier object.

2. **Lift :** Lift is the push that helps something move up. It is the force that helps to counter the object's weight. In other words, it is the force opposite to that of the weight. Every object in flight must have lift. High pressure below the object and low pressure above it generates a force that pulls up. For an object to move upward it must have more lift than weight.

3. **Drag :** The drag is the part or surface of the object providing resistance and slowing down the flight of the object. It is the force that tries to slow down something making it difficult for an object to move. Water causes more drag force than in air and that is the reason it is harder to walk or run through water than through air. The shape of the object is responsible for the amount of drag as majority of the round surfaces have less drag than flat ones. There will be more drag when more amount of air hits a surface as narrow surfaces generally have less drag than wider ones.

4. **Thrust :** Thrust is the forward force needed to travel for an object. It is the force opposite of drag as it is the push that moves something forward. For an object to keep moving forward, it must have more thrust than drag.

Hence, it can be understood that aerodynamics is principally concerned with the forces of weight, lift, drag and thrust which are caused by air passing over and around solid bodies.

8.4. FRICTION AND SPORTS

The Newton's Ist Law of Motion states that when the body is at rest, it will stay at rest and when a body is in motion, it will stay in motion at the same speed and in the same direction if no outside force acts upon it. Though the law is effectively accurate, however, when put into practice, it seems otherwise or differing. For instance, when a cricket or hockey ball is struck, it travels at a very high speed in the path of force on the ground. Likewise, a javelin, shot, discus or hammer when thrown, travels in the path of the force executed, although after traveling for a moment into air, it comes downwards and touches the ground. These aforementioned examples give you an idea that there are various invisible external forces which oppose the movement of the ball or hammer etc. as the force of gravitation acts on the body. From the above examples, we can say when two bodies in contact, move relative to each other, then there exists a force which has a tendency to oppose that movement which is called frictional force. The force of friction depends upon both surfaces in contact and the normal force.

Generally, there are two causes of friction : firstly the roughness or irregularities of surface and secondly, the strong atomic or molecular forces of attraction between the two surfaces at the points of actual contact.

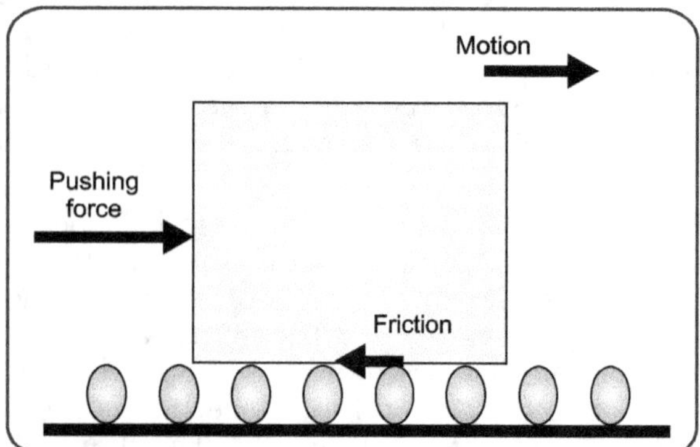

Characteristics of Friction

1. Friction is the force resisting the relative motion of solid surfaces, fluid layers, and material elements sliding against each other.

2. Friction is a force that is created whenever two surfaces move or try to move across each other.

3. Friction always opposes the motion or attempted motion of one surface across another surface.

4. Friction is also dependent on the amount of contact force pushing the two surfaces together (normal force).

There are in generally two different types of friction.

1. Static Friction
2. Dynamic Friction

Static Friction

Static Friction is when a force is applied to an object but it does not cause it to move. Example : Pushing on a wall. Static friction comes into play when a body is forced to move along a surface but movement does not start. The magnitude of static friction remains equal to the applied external force and the direction is always opposite to the direction of motion. The magnitude of static friction depends upon coefficient of static friction and N (net normal reaction of the body).

Dynamic Friction

Dynamic friction is the divergent force that comes into action when one body is in reality moving over the surface of one more body. Additionally, dynamic friction is of two types *i.e.,* sliding friction and rolling friction. These are explained as under :

1. Sliding friction : Sliding friction is the divergent force that comes into action as the body is in reality sliding over the surface of other body. For instance, ice-skating and in pole vault, planting the pole.

2. Rolling friction : Rolling friction occurs when an object rolls over another (something with wheels or circular like a ball). Example, riding a motorcycle. Rolling frictional force is a force that slows down the motion of a rolling object. Basically it is a combination of various types of frictional forces at the point of contact of wheel and ground or surface. When a hard object moves along a hard surface then static and molecular friction force retards its motion. When soft object moves over a hard surface then its distortion makes it to slow down.

Friction is typically named as a necessary evil, which is actually vital and necessary in games and sports as high performance in sports is not at all possible without friction. For instance, racers and jumpers make use of spikes and football players utilize studs to include proper friction while they run in a high-speed, running fast will not be possible without friction. To have friction, even gymnasts and weight lifters too use lime on their palms to perform on horizontal bar, uneven bars and roman rings and before holding the bar in jerk and snatch. In badminton, the players, before going to the wooden court, are usually seen rubbing their soles of shoes with lime. In sports field, there are a lot of examples depicting that friction is beneficial.

On the contrary, friction is disadvantageous in several of the sports and games, such as in case of the event of cycling, there must not be more friction between road and the tyres of cycle as more friction of the rider will be more wastage of energy. To reduce the force of friction in cycling, the tyres must be fully inflated. As in the case of roller-skating, for better performance there should be less friction. The requirement may differ or vary in different sports but up to certain extent, some force of friction is requisite in a variety of sports.

8.5. TYPES OF MOVEMENTS (FLEXION, EXTENSION, ABDUCTION AND ADDUCTION)

Performing various movements and actions help us to take part and perform all kinds of physical activities. Each and every movement is performed in one of three planes of movement *viz.*, sagittal, frontal or transverse/horizontal and of course around one of three axes *i.e.*, sagittal, frontal or vertical. Below mentioned are some of the major movements among several "types" of movement in and around the planes and axes.

1. Flexion
2. Extension
3. Abduction and
4. Adduction

Flexion

Flexion is done by bringing bones closer together which results in decrease of the angle in a joint *i.e.*, a bending movement. It can be expressed in other way as decreasing the angle between two bones is known as flexion which generally occurs in the sagittal plane.

The below given table shows the example of some of the joints where flexion can occur :

Flexion	
Joint	**Examples**
Elbow	Movement by bending the elbow which decreases its angle of the forearm to the shoulder.
Spine	Moving the chin downward towards the chest.
Hip	Movement of the femur forward or backward, *i.e.*, bringing knee into chest or towards the pelvis.
Knee	Moving the heel closer to the buttocks.
Shoulder	Raising the arms in front of the body in upward direction.

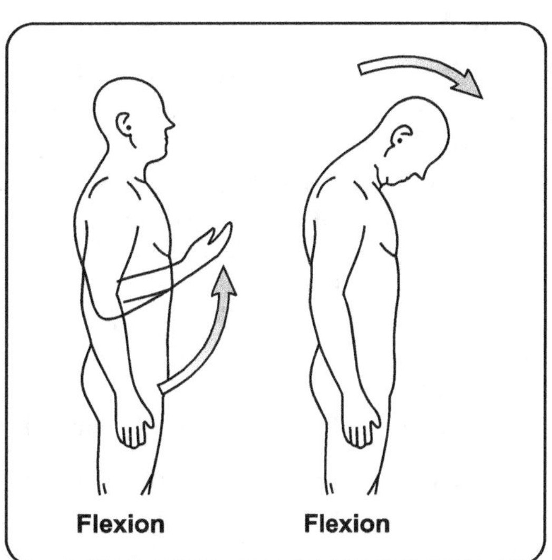

Extension

Extension leads to increase in the angle between two bones as the bones move apart further resulting in a straightening movement. This movement is opposite to that of flexion movement and occurs in the sagittal plane. The below given table shows the examples of the joints where extension occurs :

Extension	
Joint	**Examples**
Shoulder	Lowering the arms downwards from flexion and in the front of the body.
Elbow	It involves movement following flexion of the forearm away from the shoulder by straightening the elbow.
Spine	Moving the head backwards in the normal position which makes one look up straight.
Hip	Returning movement of the femur to the normal anatomical position from flexion.
Wrist	Movement of the hand in the direction of the back of forearm.

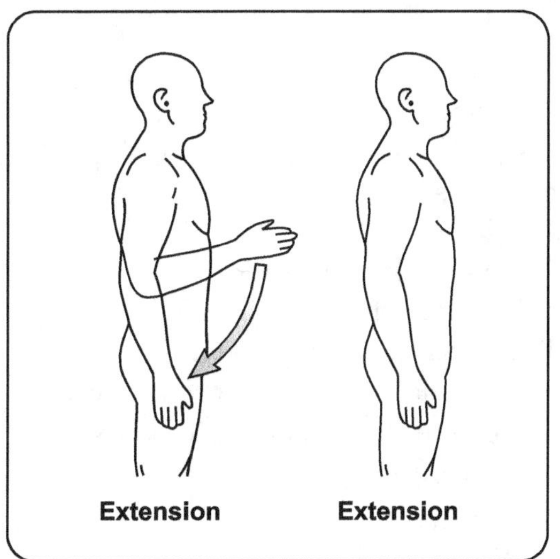

Abduction

Abduction occurs in the frontal plane. It is the lateral movement away from the midline of the trunk. For instance, lateral lift of arm is one of the examples of abduction. The below given table shows the examples of the joints where abduction occurs :

Abduction	
Joint	**Examples**
Wrist	Movement toward the lateral side of the forearm of the thumb side of the hand.
Shoulder	Lateral movement in upward direction of the humerus out to the side of the body.
Hip	In the frontal plane movement of the femur to the side away from the midline laterally.

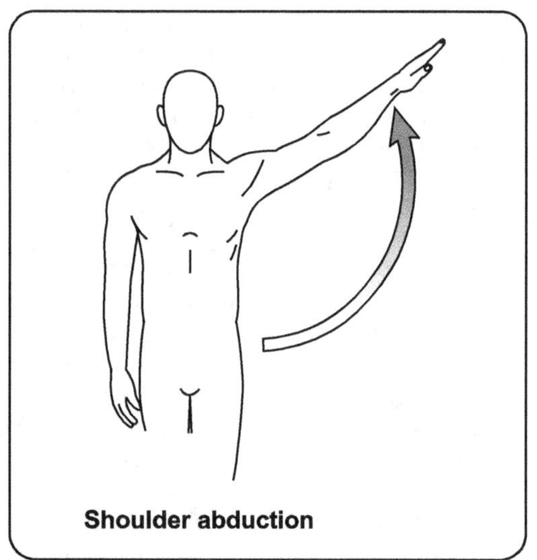

Shoulder abduction

Adduction

Adduction occurs in the frontal plane. It is the movement medially in the direction of midline of the trunk. Adduction is the return movement from abduction or it can be said as bringing the arm from abduction to normal position. The below given table shows the examples for each joint where adduction can be performed :

Adduction	
Joint	**Examples**
Wrist	Movement toward the medial side of the forearm of the little finger side of the hand.
Shoulder	In the frontal plane from abduction medially toward the body, the down-ward movement of the humerus.
Hip	In the frontal plane from adduction medially toward the midline, the movement of the femur. It is like putting the leg across the body.

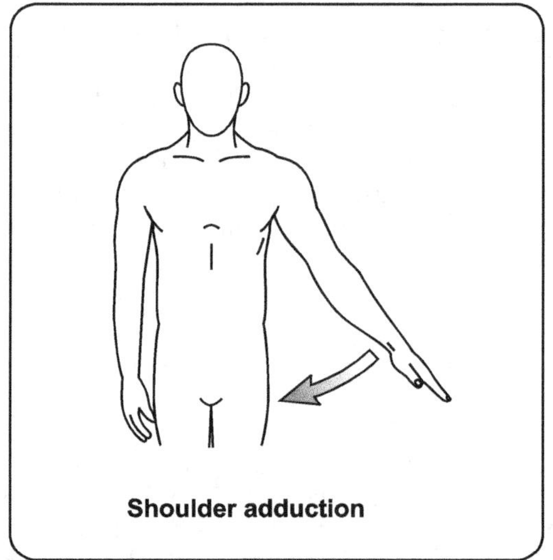

Shoulder adduction

EXERCISES

Multiple Choice Questions

1. Abduction and adduction take place about which axis ?
   (a) Oblique
   (b) Longitudinal or vertical
   (c) Frontal or mediolateral
   (d) Sagittal or anteroposterior

2. Anatomically, the term 'Superior' means :
   (a) Towards the midline of the body
   (b) Away from the trunk
   (c) Towards the head
   (d) Towards the feet

3. At touchdown in walking, the knee is normally :
   (a) Full extended   (b) Slightly flexed
   (c) Full flexed   (d) Slightly expended

4. Flexion and extension are :
   (a) Movements in the frontal plane about the sagittal axis.
   (b) Movements in the sagittal plane about the frontal axis.
   (c) Movements in the horizontal plane about the vertical axis.
   (d) None of the above

5. How do we define the phases into which we often break fundamental movements to simplify biomechanical analysis ?
   (a) Biomechanically distinct functions and easily identified boundaries.
   (b) Easily identified functions and clearly defined boundaries.
   (c) Anatomically distinct functions and easily identified boundaries.
   (d) Medically distinct functions and clearly defined boundaries.

6. In normal walking at a person's preferred speed, the ratio of the durations of the stance and swing phases is roughly :
   (a) 1　　　　　　　(b) 2-3
   (c) 2-1　　　　　　(d) 3-2

7. In plantar flexion of the foot about the ankle joint:
   (a) The foot moves upwards towards the front of the calf.
   (b) The foot moves upwards towards the rear of the calf.
   (c) The foot moves sideways.
   (d) None of the above

8. In the action phase of a countermovement vertical jump from a standing position, the leg joints :
   (a) Are synchronised, extending or plantar flexing together.
   (b) Are synchronised, flexing or dorsiflexing together.
   (c) Extend or plantar flex sequentially.
   (d) Flex or dorsiflex sequentially.

9. Internal and external rotation are movements in which anatomical plane ?
   (a) Sagittal　　　　(b) Frontal
   (c) Horizontal　　　(d) None of these

10. Movements that occur primarily in the sagittal plane are :
    (a) Adduction, lateral flexion, flexion, dorsi-flexion.
    (b) Flexion, extension, dorsiflexion, plantar flexion.
    (c) Flexion, extension, dorsiflexion, internal-external rotation.
    (d) Supination and pronation of the forearm.

Very Short Answer Type Questions (Carrying 1 mark)

1. What do you mean by biomechanics ?
2. What is linear aerodynamics ?
3. Enlist the four principles of aerodynamics.
4. What is friction ?
5. What is static friction ?
6. What is dynamic friction ?
7. Give any two example of extension movement.
8. What is lift ?
9. What is drag?
10. Name the two types of dynamic friction.
11. What do you understand by the term flexion ?
12. What is the difference between the movement of adduction and abduction ?

Short Answer Type Questions (Carrying 3 marks)

1. What is sports bio-mechanics ? and list the interdisciplinary branches of the subject.
2. Explain three principles of aerodynamics.
3. What do you mean by friction ? List the various types of friction.

Long Answer Type Questions (Carrying 5 marks)

1. Discuss the principles of aerodynamics.
2. Explain the role of friction in the field of games and sports with suitable examples.
3. Discuss elaborately about the movements of flexion, extension, adduction and abduction with suitable examples.

❏ ❏

9.1. PERSONALITY, ITS DIMENSIONS AND TYPES; ROLE OF SPORTS IN PERSONALITY DEVELOPMENT

Meaning of Personality

Generally, the word personality conveys the meaning of one's physical appearance, individual's habits, dressing sense, reputation, manners and other similar characteristics. We habitually find ourselves describing an individual by 'what an amazing personality he/she has' or 'he/she does not have an appealing personality'. This common notion of personality is very much unusual from the concept of psychologists. In psychological point of view, personality is all that a person is. It is the totality of one's behavior towards oneself and others as well. It includes everything about the person, his physical, emotional, social, mental and spiritual make-up. It is all that a person has about him.

The word personality has been derived from the Latin word *PERSONA*. In the beginning, the word *PERSONA* was used as the mask worn by the actors to change their appearance but later on it began to be used for the actors themselves. As a matter of fact, the term personality has been used to picturize the outward appearance or external behavior, etc. It is in this sense we have developed a wrong concept about the term personality. We cannot take personality as an equivalent word for outward appearance or behavior. It is a very explicit approach. We cannot ignore the inner aspect of one's personality. Personality includes the totality of one's behavior and hence both inner and outer behavior should be taken into consideration.

Definitions of Personality

According to **Allport,** *"Personality is a dynamic organization within the individual of those psychophysical systems that determine his unique adjustments to his environment."*

According to **Watson,** *"Personality is the sum of activities that can be discovered by actual observation over a long enough period of time to give reliable information".*

According to **Morton Prince,** *"Personality is the sum total of all the biological innate disposition impulses, tendencies, appetites and instincts of the individual and the dispositions and tendencies required by experience".*

According to **R. B. Cattell,** *"Personality is that which permits a prediction of what a person will do in a given situation".*

According to **Eysenck,** *"Personality is the more or less stable and enduring organization of a person's character, temperament, intellect, and physique, which determine his unique adjustment to the environment".*

According to **Carl Pearson,** *"Personality is the effect upon others of a living being's appearance and behavior so far as they are interpreted as distinctive signs of that being".*

According to **Munn,** *"Personality may be defined as the most characteristic integration of an individual's structures, modes of behavior, interests, attitudes, capacities, abilities, and aptitudes".*

According to **Guildford,** *"Personality is an individual's unique pattern of traits".*

According to **Morton Prince,** *"Personality is the sum total of all the biological innate dispositions, impulses, tendencies, aptitudes, and instincts of the individuals, and the dispositions and tendencies acquired by experiences".*

According to **S. Radhakrishnan,** *"Personality is the union of our acts and potentialities, a complex unity of body, mind and spirit. It is the symbol of human integrity, of a constant and unique form created in the midst of incessant flux".*

Dimensions of Personality

1. Physical dimension : The primary feature or dimension of human personality is the physical body structure or in short is the physique and all other dimensions are meek to it. For the development of this aspect of personality, heredity has a very significant role but proper environment is also needed for development of physical aspects of personality. Alone environment cannot take the credit of molding a personality as genetic support forms the base of personality development. It will be rightly expressed in a way that genetics gives the base of personality and environment supports in developing a beautiful structure of the individual.

The concept of expressing about how well a person looks like or how bad a person is looking, reflects the general idea attached to the physical dimension of personality in the society. It is a regular phrase we hear almost every now and then that 'first impression is the last impression'. Well, this first impression refers to individual's physical appearance about how one carries himself. The height, structure and muscular framework often regarded as physique has intense effect on every person, looking at the individuals. An individual tends to be more confident of himself when he possesses a well built physique. The way he carries himself has aesthetic value, is a source of admiration for others. It has been usually seen that individuals having frail, pale and malformed physique are not certain of themselves in comparison to individuals possessing tall, healthy and muscular built which contribute to effective appearance. Individuals having good and healthy physique are capable of mobilizing all their resources in order to lead enthusiastic and harmonious life. There is a positive relationship between good physique and health.

2. Mental and intellectual dimension : A well built individual, lacking in mental and intellectual abilities, is just similar to a statue without life. The human beings have been bestowed with higher mental and intellectual abilities. Human personality loses its significance without mind and intellect. Man is a psychophysical organism where the mind and body work jointly and one part is incompetent of successful survival without the other. Well-known psychologists, scientists, philosophers, and leaders are recognized for their mental and intellectual abilities. Individuals, who are intelligent and mentally vigilant, react swiftly to any sort of stimulation leading to understanding the things in an improved way. Mental and intellectual capabilities of an individual facilitate him in adjusting to circumstances and conditions of life in a more suitable way.

3. Social dimension : Naturally, by temperament man is a social being. He has learnt from the society in which he lives. He will not be able to survive for long if he is isolated completely from the society. Human beings have an innate tendency to get them noticed, and noticed favorably. Besides fulfillment of his biological needs and values, man fulfills emergent social values such as status, power, affection and goodwill. Psychological and sociological tendencies are closely related to each other. Each individual is psychologically born with precise innate attitudes, interests, tendencies, and capacities. He moulds and modifies his behavior, learns and acquires various manners, qualities and etiquette's, follows the rules, customs and traditions of the society in order to be an acceptable member of the society. The social interaction helps an individual to build up social attributes like tolerance, cooperation and fair play inculcating the spirit of service and sacrifice. Hence, it can be said that the spirit of an individual's development is the base of society's development. Sociability is a very imperative quality of human beings. It is an important aspect of personality, the way in which he interacts with other members of the society influencing their work and behavior and how he himself gets influenced by others. Social dimension is the summation of mixing of those traits which classify the typical reactions of one person towards other persons.

4. Emotional dimension : Emotion occupies a very high-flying place in our everyday life. Life without emotions is dull and unappealing. Our life is made worth living by emotions like love, affection, etc. Our life becomes exciting as well as boring, cheerful as well as miserable due to emotions. In all the stages of development and in life of each and every living organism, emotions play a very dominant role. Emotions differ from an individual to individual. A child learns to show different emotions by learning from experiences. As a result of emotions, every person responds to the situations differently. Our body involves many physical and physiological changes in every emotional experience as the energy mobilization in our body increases due to emotions. The outcome of emotions on our body may be positive or negative. According to **Ruch**, "Emotions play a vital part in our motivational pattern. Life without emotions would be, virtually, a life without motion." The kind of personal and social adjustment an individual will make not only as a child but also as an adult is determined. Supremacy of negative emotions is harmful for good personal and social adjustments and with interference of good emotional development, individual's adjustment in life increases. As we grow up, control over life, environment becomes progressively more difficult. To accept and adjust to unpleasant emotional experiences, we should learn to control emotions and develop emotional tolerance ability. A person with the ability to quickly control and shift an emotional reaction has fruitful and pleasant lifestyle.

Types of Personality

Personalities of individuals can be classified based on the universal factors that are found at the central part of each type. Consciously or involuntarily, everyone exhibits these personality traits which indicate the type of individuals we are. Human behavior is the complex issue to understand and often unpredictable in nature. By means of the development in the area of psychology which leads to in-depth understanding of the psyche of man, psychologists have come about with type A, B, C and D personalities. Individuals can be grouped under one of the types, may be based on the behavior and personality traits that they reveal. Yet, hardly ever does a personality type exclusively exhibit the traits of one type of personality. The personality types A, B, C, and D are explained in detail in the subsequent part :

1. Type 'A' personality : Individuals of this type are of an extremely independent, competitive, ambitious and optimistic in nature. They are self-driven and know the significance of positive thinking, motivation and goal setting. These individuals are impatient and have tendency towards rudeness and aggressiveness. Type A personality individuals are adventurous and risk takers and possess the ability of problem solving. These personality types are workaholics in nature, they are hardworking, sincere and dedicated towards work, and in fact these types of individuals have a low tolerance for incompetence. Individuals falling under this category suffer from hypertension, heart disease, stress, and societal seclusion.

2. Type 'B' personality : Type 'B' personalities are basically the literal contradictory of type 'A' personalities. Even in apparently stressful situations, they are almost not stressed out. They can be described as being happy-go-lucky, who are particularly undisturbed in any circumstances. They are by and large cheerful, light-hearted and fun to be around, usually entertaining to be with them. They love to relax and accept things as they approach. Individuals under this type are considered by their lack of urgency, as they do the work on their own pace. Type B personalities are less competitive, very tolerant, extremely patient, friendly, flexible, and adaptable in situations. They lead a complete social life, as they like interacting and forming strong emotional bonds.

3. Type 'C' personality : This personality type typically includes introverts and those concerned with facts. To find a fact they are interested in, they may perhaps spin heaven and hell upside down or inside-out. They are engrossed in finding out how things work precisely. Their thought processes are very systematic and logical. Due to this, they have a propensity to be natural problem solvers. They are extremely sensitive and thoughtful. These people tend to avoid social or human interaction. They are also over critical of the individuals around them. The type C personalities are of reserved in nature and alert as well.

4. Type 'D' personality : These individuals actually deem in apathy. They have a preference to join to the trampled ways and establish routines over the ambiguity of alteration. These are executors of the direct instructions and supporters of the used up deeds. When it comes to taking risk and responsibility they have the tendency to back out of the situations. With the assistance of professionals and guidance, all the way through total influence of self motivation or self-improvement, these individuals can rise above their negative qualities to some level. These individuals are afflicted by pessimism such as gloom, worry, irritability and barely self confident. They avoid sharing their negative emotions in order to avoid rejection. This causes them to suffer from massive stress which makes them prone to heart-related diseases.

Role of Sports in Personality Development

Sports and games play an important role in the development of human personality. They are no less important than food and fresh water. Research has shown that playing badminton, tennis, cricket or baseball is said to improve mathematical skills in children. It helps develop leadership qualities too and foster a sense of team spirit. A sport inculcates a sense of competition and helps an individual deal with success and failure with a positive spirit. Playing helps in the development of social skills. It teaches an individual to interact with people, communicate with them and collaborate as a team. It fosters collective thinking and harnesses an individual planning and delegation skills too.

The developed countries like England, Germany, France and USA have made games an essential part of education at the school level. It is interesting to note that there are many nurseries and training centres for games in these countries. They admit boys and girls for necessary training to become future athletes, gymnasts and sportsman. The value of games is now being increasingly recognized in India from personal, social, educational and national points of view. Games and sports are essential for the all round development of a personality. It is by playing games and sports that we can develop and maintain our health.

Participation in sports provides innate expression of individual's desires once the participation is made by individual's own wish. Such kind of participation leads to shaping of the personality and helping in unfolding the concealed talents and desires. Sports and games fulfil the essential requirements of individuals providing contentment, satisfaction, experience, providing sense of security and belonging, etc. Sports are also a source of recreation which creates a feeling of having active and gratifying personality, having keenness for life experiences making an individual perfectly happy, satisfied and balanced.

Physical appearance is one of the prime and perceptible aspects of individual's personality. Everyone is very much concerned of how they look, may it be a child or an adult, male or female. Sports are contributing to the growth and development of the physique. Personality of an individual improves when physique is robust and athletic in appearance. The way one carries himself has great impact on one's personality. Through sports and physical training, an individual develops appropriate neuro-muscular coordination for various movements. Today, majority of the youngsters are becoming more aware for workouts in gym for getting their biceps bulged, shoulders broad, chest expanded and trim waistline.

Participation in sports develops and helps in thinking critically, analyzing and interpreting new situations which improves the rational abilities of the participants and broadens their intellectual perspective. While participating in sports, may it be in competition or training session, individuals learn to control and normalize their emotions as well. Sports persons as part of the game, become skilled at taking up the success and failures, achievements and disappointments, they do not get unusually bothered by their emotions. Unutilized energy definitely has detrimental outcome on making up an individual's personality. Sports give a fascinating and demanding passage for such energy in addition to blowing out emotional storms formed within oneself.

Sports participation gives opportunities for communal exchanges, and forms the basis for harmonious interaction. Social recognition, status, respect and social acceptance are achieved as success

in such activities. Sports team consists of athletes belonging to diverse social, economical and cultural environment. Sports is the medium giving opportunities for interaction between athletes approaching from diverse regions, speaking various languages, belonging to dissimilar caste and religion, and therefore facilitate an individual to develop multifaceted personality. Sports is accountable for the growth of perfect character through the inculcation of qualities like dedication, respect for elders, moral values, sincerity, honesty, impartiality, punctuality, obedience of rules, etc. In sports, an individual learns to put in earnest efforts. May be in group or individually, which is a sign of optimistic development of an individual's personality. The sport situations providing various experiences and opportunities make important contribution in development of individual's personality. Tolerant attitude is developed as a result of participation in sports towards fellow teammates or as spectators. Joint efforts termed as the team spirit are the crucial features of any sports. For a team's success, cohesiveness is one of the chief rudiments. In order to attain the goal, an individual learns to adjust as a member of the team. A sports team is comprised of several members with varied roles they play on the field, however it is their combined effort and support for each other that ultimately produces the results. A member of the team learns to adjust within society and emotionally with other teammates may it be on or off the play field. All these are attributes of a healthy developed personality.

In sports and physical activities, competitive situations are natural. The athletic endeavour would be meaningless if not the goal to be achieved in clear. One of the primary principles of sports is to set realistic goals. Realistic goal setting helps an individual to systematize his way of living in diverse life situations in a healthier manner. For a thriving athletic endeavor, aggression to some amount is essential. Sports participation teaches an athlete to deal with and control his aggression and temper developing him into a balanced personality.

An athlete, moreover, learns to face failure whilst building efforts to win. He learns to prevail over and correct the mistakes and attempts yet again for success. To sports environment, negative approach is unfamiliar and an individual develops a positive point of view in the direction of life which creates a stable notion on his personality. Self confidence of the athlete contributes to successful sport performance as well. Athlete faces many problems, some on and some off the play field frequently creating several demanding situations. All the way through committed attempt and insight, an individual learns to resolve the problems and face the challenges of the life with complete confidence. Determination and perseverance are two significant qualities of an athletic performance. These qualities give steadiness to an individual and help in developing his personality.

Trait and Type (Sheldon and Jung Classification)

Sheldon Classification of Personality

Dr. William Sheldon (1898-1977) was an American psychologist predominantly active during the 1940s and eventually presented to the world the three major human personality traits which he named as Viscerotonia, Somatotonia, and Cerebrotonia. Sheldon believed that these personality traits had a direct relationship with each of three human body types (Endomorphy, Mesomorphy and Ectomorphy) also known as the Somatotypes.

About somatotypes, Sheldon reached to conclusion by carefully examining four thousand college going men by taking photographs of their carefully posed front, side and back view. Sheldon became convinced that there were three basic elements in assorted proportions which contributed to each individual's actual body type.

Sheldon believed that there was a relationship between these body type elements and the three layers *i.e.,* the endoderm, the mesoderm and the ectoderm of the human embryo. Hence as a result he named the three elements that he believed as contributing to every human physique as Endomorphy, Mesomorphy and Ectomorphy. In order to measure the three elements present in any individual's physique, Sheldon devised standardized measurement and numerical expression of the different degrees as well.

1. Endomorph : In this type, personality of athlete has rounded neck and well developed muscles. The distinguishing feature and characteristic of this kind of personality is increase in fatty tissues, physically quite 'round' and is fun-filled individuals. Endomorphs tend to possess :

(a) Wide hips and narrow shoulders, which make them rather pear-shaped.

(b) Quite a lot of fat spread across the body, including upper arms and thighs.

(c) They have quite slim ankles and wrists, which only serves to accentuate the other fatter parts.

Psychologically, the endomorph is :

(a) Sociable.

(b) Fun-loving.

(c) Food loving.

(d) Tolerant.

(e) Even-tempered.

(f) Good humored.

(g) Relaxed.

(h) With a love of comfort.

(i) And has a need for affection.

2. Mesomorph : The mesomorphs are designated between the endomorph (round) and the ectomorph (thin). The development of the bones and muscles are selective and controlled with a poor vital capacity in this kind of personality. Actually, mesomorphs have the "desirable" body and possess :

(a) Large head, broad shoulders and narrow waist (wedge-shaped).

(b) Muscular body, with strong forearms and thighs.

(c) Very little body fat.

They are generally considered as "well-proportioned". Psychologically, they are :

(a) Adventurous.

(b) Courageous.

(c) Indifferent to what others think or want.

(d) Assertive/bold.

(e) Zest for physical activity.

(f) Competitive.

(g) With a desire for power/dominance.

(h) And love to take risk/chance.

3. Ectomorph : The Ectomorph is a type absolutely opposite of the Endomorph. A typical skinny athlete falls under the category of ectomorph. This kind of personality possesses a light build with small joints and lean muscle along with long thin limbs with tough muscles. Gaining weight is very difficult for the ectomorphs as they have a fast metabolism which burns up calories very rapidly.

They tend to possess :

(a) Narrow shoulders and hips

(b) A thin and narrow face, with a high forehead

(c) A thin and narrow chest and abdomen

(d) Thin legs and arms

(e) Very little body fat

Psychologically they are :

(a) Self-conscious

(b) Private

(c) Introverted

(d) Inhibited

(e) Socially anxious

(f) Artistic

(g) Intense

(h) Emotionally restrained

(i) Thoughtful

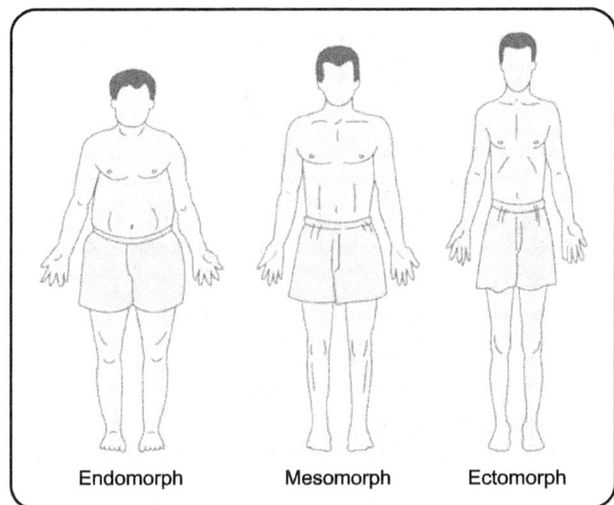

Jung Classification of Personality

Carl Jung was a well known Swiss psychologist who worked on founding of analytical psychology and his work on **psychological types**. Based on Carl G. Jung's typology, people can be classified using four mental functions named as sensing, intuition, thinking and feeling with the attitude (extraversion and introversion) which is discussed below :

1. **Extrovert :** Individuals under this category tend to be social and take special interest in social affairs and remain involved in wordily material activities and affairs. These individuals are more of a practical individual of action and take pleasure in mixing with others. Extroverts believe in increased acquaintances with others and take tremendous interest in sports and games thus making them dominant and sociable. These individuals are talkative, self-assured and deter-mined.

2. **Introvert :** An introvert does not easily mix with others. These individuals are more interested in the thought and feeling of their inner world rather than affairs and actions of the outer world. These individuals are usually shy, sensitive, nervous, easily hurt, withdrawn type with showing very little interest in worldly affairs. They prefer to have very little or no conversation and contact with others as possible.

3. **Ambivert :** In different situations, an individual may demonstrate both introvert and extrovert tendencies under this category. Therefore, the idea of permanently tagging an individual as one of the introvert or extrovert is not advisable for the psychologists as majority of the individuals are really ambiverts. Individuals of this category show signs of the introvert trait in some situations and those of the extrovert in other situation as well. For example, an individual may perhaps be an expensive writer and a good public speaker but prefer to work in solitude.

Big Five Theory

The most indispensable dimensions shaping the structure of human personality and inspiring the regularities in individual's thinking, feeling and behavior are said to be the Big Five personality traits. The five traits in the big five theory are dimensional where each of the traits describes a range between two extreme poles. In spite of the differences based on the age, gender or culture, every individual shares the same basic personality traits as well as differs on each of the traits also. The individualized big five traits of personality are:

1. Neuroticism (*vs.* Emotional Stability).

2. Extraversion (or Surgency).

3. Openness to Experience (also called Culture or Intellect).

4. Agreeableness (*vs.* Antagonism).

5. Conscientiousness.

The Big Five Dimensions

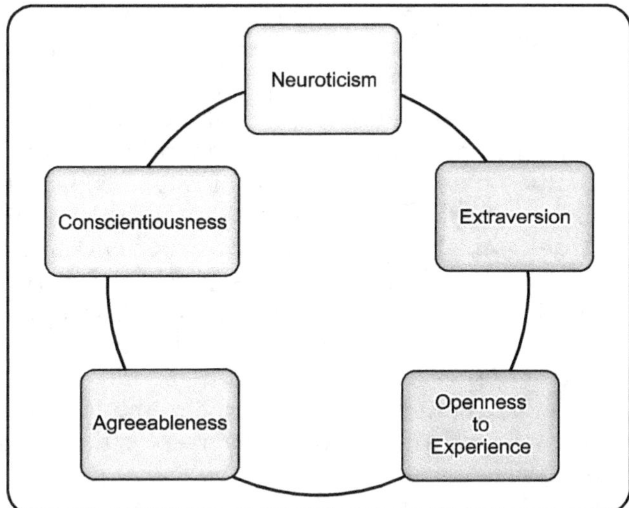

All of the Big Five traits are a combination of numerous different however closely related traits or characteristics. Hence, majority of the individuals who are honest and considerate would like to cooperate with others. Though, there are exceptions to this example as in the general population, the associations amongst these characteristics justifies combining them under the broader category of agreeableness. The term Five-Factor model is generally used to depict the hierarchy as specific facets are properly included in this model of Big Five traits :

1. **Neuroticism :** Like those individuals who fall under the category of Neuroticism projects certain peculiarities in their behaviour. Individuals whose scores are low in this category are emotionally stable and calm. They remain confident and experience hardly any negative emotions even under stressful situation. Whereas individuals who score high on Neuroticism are emotionally sensitive which makes them easily upset and experiencing negative emotions very frequently. Particular traits or characteristics under this category include sadness, anxiety, anger, self-consciousness, susceptibility to stress and an inclination to act hastily.

2. **Extraversion :** The individuals under this category with high scores on extraversion possess the qualities as they generally like to be around others, warm and talkative. They are found to be confident, lively and full of energy, joyful and positive and have a preference to stimulate the surrounding. Whereas in contrast to this kind are the individuals who are introvert, one who prefers to be alone or with few close friends only. These introverts are absolute opposite to the extroverts as they are reserved and serious, valuing their independence, rarely wanting to lead others and always preferring quiet environments.

3. **Openness to experience :** High scoring individuals of this category are generally curious, creative, having wide range of interests, effortlessly embracing unconventional ideas and values, sensitivity to aesthetic experiences and fantasy as well as capable of experiencing rich emotional life. Low scorer individuals in openness possess narrower set of interests and are further conservative in their outlook and actions. These individuals experience their emotions less intensely and are closed to new ideas, actions and values.

4. **Agreeableness :** The traits or characteristics of modesty and straightforwardness are related with agreeableness. Individuals with high scores on agreeable are cooperative, compassionate, selfless and have the capacity to trust good intentions of others. In contrast, disagreeable individuals, have the characteristics of rivalry, disbelief and a competitive attitude rather than being cooperative in life with others.

5. **Conscientiousness :** Individuals under this category possess the traits of achieving high standards and are self-disciplined, organized, purposeful and dutiful. Low scoring individuals under this category hardly ever plan ahead. They often prove to be careless, disorganized and aimless in life.

Though the Big Five are simply characterized by their extreme poles, but very few individuals are at the extremes as majority of the individuals revolve around the middle of the continuum. The Big Five have been connected to an extensive range of significant outcomes over the past years.

For instance, individuals with high Neuroticism have poor coping capabilities and are more probable to be diagnosed with psychiatric disorders. High extroversion scorers excel in sales and management positions. Open individuals make their prominence in creative professions. Individuals with poor agreeableness are linked with juvenile delinquency. Individuals with high conscientiousness are associated to healthy behaviors and longer life. These are the most important consequences of all the traits of the big five personality model.

In real life situations while evaluating based on the Big Five theory, it is very important to look at the full profile of an individual as an alternative of focusing only on individual traits. There is a wide range of real-life implications of the Big Five traits which helps to understand the basic structures of the individual's personality as it is not just an academic exercise however extremely appropriate for helping clinical psychologists, health care workers and teachers, etc., to adjust their strategies according to the needs and abilities of their clients.

9.2. MOTIVATION, ITS TYPES AND TECHNIQUES

Meaning

Birds gather bits and pieces to build nests in the corners of our houses. We remove them after knowing about it. But the bird yet again brings the pieces of leaves, twigs, straw, etc., and starts building its nest. What makes the bird work so hard ? From where and why did it learn to build the nest ? Likewise, we witness a boy persistently busy in learning how to cycle even after getting several cuts and bruises or student burning mid-night oil all through the examination days. What makes them to employ in one or the other kind of learning and carry on their attempts even after facing so many obstacles ?

These kinds of questions associated to 'learning' are at all times answered through a key word 'Motivation'. The bird building its nest, the boy learning how to cycle and the student studying hard is because of 'Motivation'. They learn for the reason that they are motivated to learn. They act this way because they are influenced to act to pursue their basic needs and accomplish the preferred goals. Interest is the fundamental feature in learning and motivation is associated to this aspect. As Crow and Crow said "Motivation is considered with the arousal of the interest in learning and, to the extent is basic to learning."

The word motivation is derived from a Latin word 'movere' meaning 'to change', 'to move'. When we say that one is motivated, it means that he is driven or moved by an inner urge or force to achieve the goal. We may refer motivation as a process through which an individual is inspired, stimulated, goaded or coaxed to act in a particular fashion or manner towards a particular direction. Motivation is concerned with the cultivation and spur of the learner's interest in the learning activities. It is the strength or a force which energizes an individual to act and to make continuous efforts to satisfy the indispensable motives.

Definitions

According to **Sage**, *"Motivation can be defined simply as the direction and intensity of one's effort."*

According to **Morgan and King**, *"Motivation refers to a state within a person or an animal that drives behavior towards some goal."*

According to **P.T. Young**, *"Motivation is the process of arousing action, sustaining the activity in progress, and regulating the pattern of activity."*

According to **Elizabeth Duffy**, *"Motivation is the direction and intensity of behavior."*

According to **Murray** *"Motivation is an internal factor that arouses, directs and integrates a person's behavior."*

Types of Motivation

Motivation is classified into two categories :

Intrinsic Motivation

This category of motivation is straightforwardly connected with the innate instincts, urges and desires of the individual. The individual who is intrinsically motivated performs any work as he finds concern in the activity. He is occupied in learning something as he drives gratification within the learning of that particular activity. The activity carries reward and the individual takes real interest in performing the activity owing to external motives and goals.

When a player tries to play football and the playing football itself gives him pleasure, we can say that he is intrinsically motivated. In this case, the source of pleasure lies within the activities. He plays the football for its own sake. Such type of motivation has real values in the learning task as it creates spontaneous attention and interest and sustains it throughout.

Extrinsic Motivation

In this kind of motivation, the basis of contentment does not stretch out within the assignment or task. This kind of motivation has no purposeful interaction to the job. The individual for obtaining desired goals or for receiving some external reward does or learns something and not for its own sake. Functioning for a better position or reputation, learning an ability to earn the living, getting praise and blame, rewards and punishment etc. fall in this category.

Techniques of Motivation

1. Innovative program : By the time the children reach primary school age, numerous basic skills, fundamental to sports improvement, get already developed. They are physically energetic and willing to take on play and sports. Both interest and opportunity to participate can be increased to further motivate the children through innovative program planning. Innovative training schedule facilitate in maintaining their interest and sustaining the improvement even as dealing with grown-up athletes.

2. Equipment : In the present state of affairs, equipment provided to an athlete assumes grand implication. Most recent gadgets, well maintained and striking equipment, not only have visual appeal but also set off the push for people to take part in the activity. In contrast, obsolete, exhausted and poorly maintained equipment can turn off the enthusiasm of even an energized athlete.

3. Teacher as a motivator : A highly skilled coach or teacher who has himself participated in the sports, capable of demonstrating and explaining the skill more precisely, and who can plan the subsequent competition sensibly is a big plus point in motivating the athletes. Methods and materials in teaching far exceed his influence as a person. The personality and preparation of a coach or teacher has massive effect upon the athletes, since they attempt to copy the teacher, take up his attitude and sense his moods.

4. Freedom to beginners : A greater level of freedom should be allowable in order to motivate beginners in their early attempts. They enjoy the experience more when given freedom and on their own, they will knock upon minute adjustments which fit more to their personal physical personality. The major aspect at this stage is supervision. The correction adds to motivation, if inconsiderate criticism is avoided and if correction is done with genuine intention to help.

5. Length of practice : The length of practice must be designed very cautiously for motivating young athletes to any activity. As the major reason at this phase is to persuade them for voluntary and informal practice for arousing their interest, formal practice should be comparatively short and lead-up games at the early stages should be involved. In the present day, education of extremely skilled athletes is owing to their boundless hours of voluntary and informal practice.

6. Diversity and uniqueness in activity : In sports, repeated practices can turn out to be extremely uninteresting. It is essential to frequently modify the practice plan and setting so as to break the boredom and sustain the motivational levels, this method has been known as Hawthorne Effect. Providing diversity and uniqueness in activity give an opportunity to young athletes to attempt new assignments. Doing this, they will have more fun and will put on awareness of their abilities as well to handle dissimilar situations. These perceived competences do optimistically influence their motivational level.

7. Assigning well defined roles : The perception of self competence enhances when athletes are assigned well defined role. Focusing on his own role helps him to concentrate on the activity or skill leading to gain mastery over the skill which ultimately develops a sense of responsibility in him and boosts his self-confidence. The higher will be the level of motivation, the more the athlete feels that his actions are self-determined and gives a sense of personal competency.

8. Environmental factors : The sport environment provided to the athletes, certainly, has a very vital role in motivating them. A well ventilated, equipped and decorated gymnasium or swimming pool can draw even a reluctant individual. Likewise, well maintained grounds and fields inspire an athlete to carry out his exercises. In extremely competitive sports set-up, a highly motivating atmosphere is a necessity, as we gain knowledge of and benefit from learning if the surroundings foster such learning.

9. Goal setting : Achieving performance goals is a symbol of competency that affects motivation positively, hence it is essential to set realistic goals based on individual's own abilities. The level of motivation gets adversely affected when goals are set up too high or too low. The goal should be realistic, precise and within reach but should at the same time be a difficult one. Goal settings have been acknowledged as an influential motivational technique as it mobilizes an athlete's hard work and extends his determination.

10. Reinforcement : Reinforcement is a vital motivational means. It refers to some kind of occurrence that increases or decreases the possibility of a similar reaction taking place in the future. Positive reinforcements enlighten the athlete at what time he is doing something accurate and support the continuance of the activity in the precise direction. Negative reinforcement is in general, of slight importance since it simply indicates that the actions are inaccurate devoid of providing information with respect to the accurate reaction or behavior. It has been established that positive reinforcement has to a large extent, more motivational value than negative reinforcement.

11. Praise, appreciation and criticism : Whether it is verbal or through gestures, praise can be powerful. It helps athletes to struggle continuously for further enhancement, it provides positive feedback. In motivating the athletes a simple pat on the back or a genuine and timely word of appreciation like "good job" can do wonders. Simultaneously, an excess of praise, especially if it is not actually deserved has unfavorable effects. The athletes can be motivated by criticism as well if it is focused on major errors and also if it is clear that modification may improve his performance. However, motivational level may be adversely affected if each and every minor error is criticized. We ought to consider the age, sex and other peculiar conditions related to an athlete for effectual use of praise and criticism.

12. Feedback : Appropriate feedback also has massive effect on motivation. Athletes getting feedback have a tendency to practice the task with better attentiveness. This may be owing to the reality that the feedback gives the athlete a benchmark of progress, or lack of it. Thus, the feedback is a critical feature influencing the motivation of an athlete.

13. Social pressure : It is currently a well-known reality that presence of others has influence on performance and motivational level. Planned sport and physical activity is carried out in the presence of others such as spectators, team-mates, coaches, officials or competitors. Through competitions in diverse social settings, social exposure to the athletes increases their level of motivation.

14. Grading : On the basis of their performance levels classifying athletes helps in motivating them to progress in their performance as well. For instance, on the basis of their performance level, as teams are graded the low graded members of team put in their finest effort for their upgradation. In the same way, the top graded members of team put in their best to sustain their position.

15. Role of media : In motivating athletes, media plays an important role as well. News coverage of their performance and of training session gives them the feeling of pride, prestige and recognition. Such reporting heightens their self confidence and competency and in addition motivates other young athletes to follow their achievement.

9.3. SELF-ESTEEM AND BODY IMAGE

Self-Esteem

Self-esteem is about the worth of ourselves; it is how we identify our worth to the humankind and how important we consider we are to others. Self-esteem affects nearly all components of our lives, be it our faith in others, our relations or our work. Self-esteem can be positive or low-esteem.

Positive Self-Esteem

Positive self-esteem provides us the potency and flexibility that help us to acquire charge of our lives and to grow up from our mistakes with no fright of negative response.

Signs of positive self-esteem :

1. Consciousness of personal strengths
2. Confidence
3. Self-direction
4. Optimism
5. Openness
6. An ability to learn from mistakes
7. Problem solving ability
8. A self-sufficient and supportive approach
9. Trustworthy
10. Assertive
11. Excellent wisdom of personal limitations
12. Excellent personal care

Low Self-Esteem

Low self-esteem is a state that prevents individuals from realizing their absolute capability. Individual with low self-esteem experiences feeling of worthlessness, incompetent and ineffectualness. In reality, individual with low self-esteem experiences disappointing concern about him or herself.

Signs of low self-esteem :

1. Pessimistic
2. Perfectionist
3. Distrusting others
4. Blaming actions
5. Fright of taking risks
6. Unlovable
7. Poor decision making capability
8. Fright of being ridiculed

Steps to improve low self-esteem

Low self-esteem is habitually build up over a life span, and letting go off inbuilt mind-set and behaviors is not a simple job, it possibly takes time, hard work and has need of proficient psychotherapy. However, at hand are a few easy positive thinking techniques to help out improving self-esteem. These are known as affirmations.

To prevent negative self-talk becomes easy by using affirmations resulting in raising self-esteem in a positive manner. Affirmations are hopeful communications which we can provide ourselves each day until they turn out to be part of our thoughts and values. When individual is relaxed, affirmations work in a most excellent manner. Individuals who are frequently upset start giving negative self-messages, they contradict negative messages with positive ones. Begin each day by looking in the mirror and giving yourself a positive message. The following affirmations can help to work towards a positive self-image :

1. I respect myself and others.
2. I am lovable and likable.
3. I am confident.
4. I care about myself.
5. I accept myself just as I am.
6. I look great.
7. Life is good, and I like being a part of it.

Body Image

Body image depicts the manner we think about our own bodies and the manner we imagine other people perceive about us. "Body image involves our perception, imagination, emotions, and physical sensations of and about our bodies. It's not static, but ever-changing, sensitive to changes in mood, environment, and physical experience. It is not based on fact. It is psychological in nature, and much more influenced by self-esteem than by actual physical attractiveness as judged by others. It is not inborn, but learned. This learning occurs in the family and among peers, but these only reinforce what is learned and expected culturally" (Lightstone, 1991).

Generally, Body image includes :

1. Visually how we perceive our bodies.
2. How we feel about our physical appearance, how we think and talk to ourselves about our bodies.
3. Our sense of how other people view our bodies.
4. Kinesthetic perception of our bodies.
5. Our level of connectedness to our bodies.

Types of Body Image

1. Positive body image : Positive body image is moreover known as healthy body image. The individuals having positive or healthy body image feel good about their bodies and accept the way they look. For such individuals the appearance does not matter. For, possessing a positive or healthy body image is viewing and thinking about the way an individual physically feels. To see as individuals really are also means having a healthy body image. In terms of the body image, one feels comfortable and confident.

2. Negative body image : Negative body image is known as unhealthy body image as well. Being discontented with the way you look means having negative body image. It is by and large related with the wish for changing the body shape, size, height or weight etc. When an individual feels that his body's features do not go with social or media standards, this type of body image gets developed. These individuals are generally dissatisfied with their body image. Negative body image can have a detrimental effect on one's mental and physical health. Negative body image typically leads to anxiety, low self-esteem and depression. They may go through a variety of troubles such as over exercising or over eating, anorexia and bulimia, etc. They stop being with the other people socially and discontinue doing healthy activities.

Factors Influencing Body Image

1. **Puberty and development :** At the commencement of puberty, the body goes through a lot of changes and in this phase, a number of individuals struggle with their body image. The difficulty is, not everybody grows or develops at the similar time or in the similar way. These changes, collectively with wanting to feel accepted socially allure us to compare ourselves with others.

2. **Media images :** We are constantly exposed to imagery from popular media such as movies, TV, web and magazines. This leads people to form ideas about a certain kind of 'ideal look' that they see as normal and desirable. Comparing yourself with these images may leave you feeling disappointed or not good enough.

3. **Family and school :** Sometimes our body images get influenced by our family life. A number of parents or coaches might be excessively paying attention on looking a definite way or "making weight" for a sports team. Family members might struggle with their own body image or disapprove of their kids' appearance. This influences an individual's self-esteem, particularly if they're sensitive to others peoples' remarks.

4. **Other influences :**

   (a) Ideals that we develop about physical appearance
   (b) The frequency with which we compare ourselves to others
   (c) Exposure to images of idealized versus normal bodies
   (d) The experience of physical activity
   (e) The experience of abuse, including sexual, physical, and emotional abuse
   (f) The experience of prejudice and discrimination based on race, ethnicity, religion, ability, sexual orientation or gender identity
   (g) Sensory experiences, including pleasure, pain and illness

Guidelines for Maintaining a Healthy Body Image

Maintaining a healthy body image is a challenge. Altering the appearance of the body doesn't take place suddenly and at once. It is a time taking process, requiring patience and a positive attitude to see oneself in a healthier manner.

1. Exercise : Exercise is the vital means to maintain a healthy body image. Exercising for at least 30 minutes a day builds up self-confidence and self-esteem, help in cutting the body fat, decreases the stress level and improves sleep.

2. Confidence : Confidence is an extremely essential element of maintaining a healthy body image. No matter what body type one may have, value yourself. The media portraying a "perfect figure" may be unachievable for countless people.

3. Proper nutrition : Consumption of healthy foods facilitates to maintain the weight, prevent diseases, and heightens the self-confidence.

4. Positive and optimistic attitude : Positive and optimistic attitude can help out individuals to develop body image and self-esteem. Involvement in physical activities increases positive attitude as well which eventually improves body image.

5. Spot your appearance practically : It is a well acknowledged reality that human beings are imperfect. Identify the entire aspects of your appearance which you can change realistically and which you can't change for improving body image. It is better to accept them such as height and structure.

6. Prevent intrinsic negative comments : Stop the negative comments immediately coming from the core of your heart in order to improve the body image. Humans are multifaceted and steadily varying. It is better to focus on the uniqueness and interesting elements of ourselves as a replacement for the negative comments.

7. Compliments on good things done : Do a few good things everyday to improve self esteem and body image so as to give compliments to yourself. This action will provide massive satisfaction. If such things are done regularly in life, there will be a change about how one feels about oneself.

8. Expert's advice : A therapist's advice may be useful as well. Become skilled to spotlight on the strengths plus develop a better thinking. Contact a therapist or a guidance counselor for assistance, in case you have negative body image. Then our conditions can be enhanced.

9.4. EXERCISE ADHERENCE, REASONS TO EXERCISE

The word adherence means attachment or commitment to a person, cause or belief. It also means the quality or process of sticking fast to an object or surface. The word reason means the power of the mind to think, understand and form judgements logically. Another version of reason is a cause, explanation or justification for an action or event. In short, adherence is to commit oneself to an action and the reason is to give justification for that action. Exercise adherence refers to maintaining an exercise schedule for a prolonged period of time following the initial adoption phase. Those having strong exercise adherence continue participating in physical activity despite pressures to withdraw. Reasons to exercise include logical reasons for exercising. We will further understand exercise adherence by examining the barriers in exercise adherence.

Barriers in Exercise Adherence

Reasons for not to adhere to an exercise program may be lack of time, less money, lack of interest, lack of social support or laziness.

Time : Not able to find time for exercise due to work related commitments, family commitments or other extra-curricular commitments acts as a barrier for exercise adherence. If one is not relaxed or feels hurried when working out, then one is less likely to enjoy the workout and so, will be less likely to adhere to one's program in the future.

Money : Many people like to do physical exercise in a Gym or Club due to the good facilities. While choosing a place to exercise, the facilities should be affordable. Membership in a Gym or Club may be costly. In such case, lack of money may act as a barrier for exercise adherence.

Energy : Lack of energy is often cited as an excuse for not adhering to exercise. There may be days when one doesn't feel like exercising because of tiredness or lack of energy resulting from a hectic work schedule.

Climate : Climate will affect exercise adherence. Often extreme weather condition prevents one from exercising. This is especially relevant to outdoor exercises such as running, cycling or outdoor team sports.

Social Influences : Family members or friends, group norms or cohesion in an exercise class, may act as a barrier in exercise adherence. For example, if a son feels that his mother is convinced that track is the safest form of exercise for him, this belief will influence the subjective norm of the son, who may be apt to run instead of playing baseball, football or another team sport. Alternatively, an individual who lives in a house full of other sedentary people may have a hard time initiating and sustaining an exercise regimen if the following is taking place : (1) subtle teasing ("Look at you wanting to be Mr. Universe"), (2) complaints about the time spent exercising.

Personality : Lack of confidence that one has the ability or the competency to complete a certain action acts as barrier in exercise adherence. When one's self-efficacy is low, the likelihood of valued outcomes also decreases. Inability to recognize and regulate emotional arousal can prevent one from staying focused on one's goals and that in turn prevents exercise adherence.

Physical Discomfort : While exercising, physical discomfort like sore muscles may act as a barrier in exercise adherence. The thought that exercise results in physical discomfort and injury may prevent an individual from continuing exercise schedule.

Reasons to Exercise

Some scientific studies show hugely positive effects, others show hugely negative effects, and some don't permit any conclusions at all. Most people agree that the best way to keep one's body and mind in top shape is to be physically active. Broadly, the reasons to exercise can be improved physiological health/physical fitness, enhanced physical appearance, improved psychological/emotional health and improved social relations. Following are the points that fall under the broad heading mentioned above :

To Builds aerobic power : Aerobic capacity is body's ability to work at maximum capacity by getting oxygen from the air to body's tissues. Ordinarily, people lose about 1 percent a year of their aerobic power. Building aerobic power is one of the most important reasons to exercise.

To Reduces blood pressure : Exercise helps reduce your blood pressure. Strengthening of heart muscle and widening of arteries helps blood flow through more freely and that helps to keep blood pressure normal.

To Lower Type 2 diabetes risk : By engaging in regular physical exercise, one improves one's body's ability to metabolize glucose, the key to lower Type 2 diabetes risk.

To make skin look better : Aerobic exercise revs up blood flow to the skin, delivering oxygen and nutrients that improve skin health.

To maintain immune functioning : Even short-term exercise programs can reverse some of the harmful effects of aging on this sensitive, complex, and crucial regulatory system which controls so much of everyday health.

To reduces body fat : A regular program of aerobic exercise can bring BMI (Body Mass Index) down to normal levels. The more one exercises, the more he/she is able to work off body fat because muscles "burn off" more calories, effectively speeding up metabolism.

To keeps bones strong : Normal age-related change is the loss of bone mineral strength. Exercise is the key to maintaining your bones' health. Resistance training is helpful in bone strength.

To improve breathing : Exercise can improve breathing by strengthening the muscles that help your lungs open up to bring in oxygen and compress to push out carbon dioxide.

To boost energy : Once exercise is made a part of daily routines, these workout bouts will actually seem less tiresome because it will make one feel more mentally and physically capable of carrying them out. Because the body is functioning more efficiently, there will be more oxygen to fuel body's cells.

To reduces the risk of arthritis : Flexibility training through yoga or other ways to increase the range of movement of joints will lower risk of injury through muscle tears or torn ligaments, and in the process, protect joints from damage caused by overuse.

To prevent cognitive decline : Exercise boosts the chemicals in the brain that support and prevent degeneration of the hippocampus, an important part of the brain for memory and learning.

To look better : People, who exercise, burn more calories and look more toned than those who don't. Exercise can help to have an attractive healthy physique.

To reduce stress : One of the mental benefits of exercise is stress relief. Exercise also increases concentrations of norepinephrine, a chemical that can moderate the brain's response to stress.

To boost happy chemicals : Exercise releases endorphins, which create feelings of happiness and euphoria. Studies have shown that exercise can even alleviate symptoms among the clinically depressed.

Social Benefits : As emotional health and self-esteem improves. One is more likely to reach out to others due to increased self-confidence. Participating in a sport or aerobics class will introduce one to new people that share a common interest and develop new friendships and support network.

9.5. PSYCHOLOGICAL BENEFITS OF EXERCISE

The studies continue to enlarge supporting chief healthiness benefits of regular physical activity and exercise together with a reduced risk of cardio-vascular disease, hypertension, and stroke as well as fortification against cancers and osteoporosis. Though, there is a growing body of knowledge as well that substantiates that physical activity improves psychological well-being as well.

The following are common psychological benefits gained through exercise.

1. Betterment of mood : The body feels more relaxed and calm when exercising and can lift the mood and improves the emotions. Balance the emotions by finding out some of the reasons and the best exercises to lift the mood. The chemicals released by the brain when you exercise, like endorphins, adrenaline, serotonin and dopamine work altogether to make you feel good. Additionally, a sense of accomplishment and the deeper relaxation of muscles are possible after exercising you easing tension and strain because of the workout.

2. Improved ability to cope with stress : An amazingly precious tool for stress reduction is exercising, particularly intense and long term exercise. Exercises leave us feeling peaceful, energized and positive. Exercises help in a great way to deal with daily troubles. It can be extremely helpful in reducing physical symptoms and risk and improves sleep. Exercises are powerful coping tool which decreases the short and long term stress.

3. Increase in self-esteem : Regular exercise boosts the energy levels, oxygen capacity, muscle tone and general fitness consequently increasing self-esteem. Just the success of creating an exercise plan and sticking to it allows one to take pleasure in a sense of achievement. Getting a move on is good for the body and mind.

(a) Improves the overall cognitive function : Benefits of exercise spin around other psychological factors improving IQ and overall cognitive function. Research studies shows that regular cardiovascular activity help improving the short term memory which supports and helps us with non verbal reasoning and mathematics tasks.

4. Enhanced body image : Exercise can help people with body image issues. Exercise is related with better contentment with appearance and professed vigor. We all are very concerned about our looks and spend lots of time thinking about the ways of getting an efficient and beautiful body. The exercises make positive changes to the body and consequently improve the body image.

5. High level of energy : Start off with just a few minutes of exercise a day and gradually increasing the workout which may make us feel more energized. Exercise helps to improve the confidence in us and eliminate the mental fatigue.

6. Reduced depression related symptoms : For the treatment of disorders related to depression, countless researches revealed that aerobic exercise along with counseling is more effectual than only counseling. Additionally, regular exercisers have lesser risk of depression compared to those individuals who are physically inactive. The "feel-good" chemicals treating anxiety have a positive impact on symptoms of depression as well.

7. Reduced level of anxiety : Exercise leads to notably reduced level of anxiety and less depressive symptoms. To take care of anxiety exercise has been prescribed since generations. The "feel-good" chemicals called endorphins along with other neurotransmitters like serotonin and dopamine are released when performing intense exercises which lessen the effects of anxiety.

9.6. STRATEGIES FOR ENHANCING ADHERENCE TO EXERCISE

Getting started and continuing an exercise programme can be a challenging, yet rewarding undertaking. There is no clear 'best strategy' for increasing exercise adherence, rather following interventions should be considered a tool box of strategies that could be used in order to find a successful formula for different groups or individuals for the purpose of adhering to exercise.

1. Work out with friends : It helps to have a companion, social support and encouragement. It's more difficult to skip a workout when someone else is counting on you being there. When working out with a partner, try to choose someone with a similar fitness level. As a beginner, one may work too hard if one exercises with an experienced partner.

2. Choose an activity you like : Start by identifying activities that you enjoy. One is more likely to stick to a program if it is fun and convenient. Activity of one's choice will pull one to continue practicing it.

3. Learning new activity : The new challenge will prompt one to come back and learn the activity being presented as a challenge.

4. Begin easy and slowly increase effort : Slowly increasing the load of performing the activity reduces the chances of sore muscles or injury. Aim for small but regular improvements.

5. Cross-training : Performing same thing everyday may be boring; try different activities. This type of training will keep one from becoming bored of exercise.

6. Goal Setting : Goals should be self-set, flexible, and time based. Setting realistic short-term goal will motivate one to do a task and note one's progress towards the goal. Documenting and monitoring goals related to physiological changes and physical activity behaviour motivates an individual to continue exercise.

7. Keep a record of progress : This act will help in noting one's improvement. It will also act as a progress chart, showing where one has reached and how much one has to progress. Seeing one's improvement motivates one's work towards one's goals.

8. Convenience : Some people find it more convenient to exercise at home. Others may find they have fewer distractions at an exercise facility. If one chooses to exercise at a gym, it is better to pick one that is nearby, since one may be less likely to exercise at a club that is further away.

9. Establish a routine : Fix a time for exercise. As one sticks to routine, exercise will become a habit. Schedule exercise before scheduling other meetings or activities. Get committed to the exercise program.

10. Combine family-time with exercise : Evening walk, yoga with family will help develop bond with family members and also result in increase in exercise adherence. As relationships develop, the need to maintain the relationship is often associated with the continuance of that physical activity which is responsible for the development.

11. Reinforcement and Incentives : Provide rewards for attendance and participation. Rewarding onesel for being rewarded by a group leader, on reaching an activity-related goal, will assist in exercise adherence.

12. Social Support : Taking part in physical activity as part of a group program and interactions with a health professional can increase exercise adherence as one will have a network of people working towards a common goal.

13. Provide cues for exercises : Place posters and quotes to motivate while performing an exercise.

14. Understanding that being fit helps in fulfilling responsibilities/expectations : Understanding that making time for oneself is important for fulfilling responsibilities. Quality of life is directly related to capacity to care for others. One can't take care of others if one is not well.

15. Dealing with the feeling of not working out : If one feels like not working out, one should agree with oneself to have a very short, light workout. Quite often, after getting ready and warming up, one will find enough motivation to push through a full workout.

16. Engage in utilitarian activities : Perform a variety of exercises and activities. Engage in utilitarian activities such as walking to the store, walking the dog, or catching up on yard work.

9.7. MEANING, CONCEPT AND TYPES OF AGGRESSIONS IN SPORTS

Concept

The word aggression is derived from a Latin word *"aggressio"* which means to attack. The word was first used in 1611 so as to reveal the sense of a motiveless attack. In 1912, as in English translation of Sigmund Freud's writing the psychological sense of "hostile or destructive behaviour" first came into prominence. The "aggressive drive" was theorized by Alfred Adler in 1908. From 1930 onwards, the child raising experts started using the word aggression in place of anger.

In humans, frustration caused due to blocked goals which may result in aggression later. It may take place moreover as in revenge or with no provocation. Aggression is an obvious behaviour which is harmful or destructive at times, social interaction with the intent of inflicting injury or other unpleasantness upon another individual.

Psychologically the term aggression is often used to refer "hostile or destructive behaviour" which depicts the act of initiating hostilities *i.e.,* the practice or habit of initiating attacks. Let us understand the **nature** of aggression which is pretty difficult as several facts are connected to it.

1. At the time of aggression, the attack is initiated with the intention of injuring or harming the other individual causing aggression to be deliberate and intentional. In soccer match, an unintentional collision between two opponents to have possession over the ball is not aggression, whereas forcefully pulling, pushing or abusing the opponent despite of the fact that he may get physically hurt, comes within the definition of aggression.

2. As the behavior of aggression gets stimulated a sequence of behaviour such as gesturing, abusing, pushing the opponent, etc., becomes prominent moving towards the goal of harming another individual in some or the other way.

3. The majority of the aggressive behaviour is frequently directed against the individual (living target) thus, instigating certain behaviour like hitting or striking another individual with a limb, a stick or any handy implement.

4. Aggression includes any form of behaviour directing towards the target of harming or injuring another individual who tends to avoid such a behaviour by guarding against the act in some or the other way.

5. There must be a logical probability that the aggression will be successful and that the target may be harmed, hence, excluding the behaviour where the individuals cannot be harmed, for instance in a situation where the aggressor and victim are separated by teammates.

Aggression is a part of sports domain for long. Russell (1993) stated that leaving apart war, possibly sports is the only setting where acts of interpersonal aggression enthusiastically applauded by large segments of society. Contemporarily, violence in sport is perceived as a major social problem both on and off the field. The aggressive behavior causing the physical, verbal, or gestural stimulus by one individual upon another constitutes aggression in sport. It has critically become a behaviour reflecting the act with intent to injure other individuals. In attempting towards the defining sport aggression, athletes, coaches or spectators physically hitting another individual and verbal abusing each other, is some of the wide ranging acts explaining aggression. According to Bredemeier (1983), sport aggressiveness behaviour means "the intentional initiation of violent and or injurious behaviour." The word 'violent' is used to explain physical, verbal, or non-verbal offence whereas the term 'injurious behaviours' signifies any harmful intentions or actions. Thus to conclude, an accidental situation or injury inflicted on another athlete because of the inferior skills will not be considered as part of aggression. Conversely, a premeditated foul even though not resulting in any harm or injury may be considered as sport aggression. Undeniably, in several sports like wrestling or boxing or other combative sports, aggressive behaviour is required to certain extent. Aggression is an important feature of attaining success performance as according to many coaches and athletes.

Definitions

According to **Aldermen**, aggression is *"the intentional response a person makes to inflict pain or harm on another person"*.

According to **Baron**, *"Aggression is any form of behaviour directed towards the goal of harming or injuring another living being who is motivated to avoid such treatment"*.

According to **Oxford Dictionary of Sports**, *"It is a form of overt behaviour intended to harm a living person either physically or psychologically. It includes physical attack and verbal abuse"*.

Forms of Aggression

There are a variety of forms of aggression which includes:

1. Physical	2. Mental
3. Verbal	4. Emotional

Time and again when we think of aggression it is purely in physical forms for instance as hitting or pushing. The psychological or mental aggression is also very destructive. Threatening or orally expressing the anger to another person is examples of verbal, mental and emotional aggression.

Purposes of Aggression

There are different purposes which are served by expressing aggression:

1. To accomplish a goal.
2. Try to win against others.
3. To emphasize supremacy.
4. As a response to fear.
5. To express control.
6. As a reaction to pain.
7. To frighten or threaten.
8. To convey annoyance or resentment.

Types of Aggressions in Sports

The two basic types of aggression indentified over the past years are :

1. Hostile aggression and
2. Instrumental aggression

1. **Hostile aggression :** The first type of aggression in sports is hostile aggression. The main target for individuals expressing hostile aggression is causing injury to another individual deliberately. The main aim is to make the individual suffer because of the aggression expressed resulting into attainment of pain and suffering as reinforcement. This type of aggression is constantly accompanied by anger as the element of the aggression. This type of aggression is frequently referred to as violence as the primary attempt is to cause injury and suffering. The result of the competition is not to win or lose but to harm the opponent. A good example of hostile aggression is a bowler in cricket throwing a bouncer to deliberately shake up the concentration of a batsman. Some cricketers have intentionally done this with the strong intent towards causing injury to the other player. Another instance may be that a hockey player uses his stick purposefully to hit the shin of his opponent so as to revenge for what the opponent was doing to him. This aggressive behavior was aiming at injuring the opponent and causing pain and suffering.

2. **Instrumental aggression :** The second type of aggression is instrumental aggression. In this type

of aggression, the individuals engaged have the intention to harm another individual however the chief aim is to receive, earn or realize some external rewards like money, triumph, status or prestige. The individuals expressing the aggressiveness hold the primary purpose in obtaining those external rewards only. When a boxer lands a solid blow to an opponent's head, injury or harm is inflicted. However, such an action is usually an example of instrumental aggression: the boxer's primary goal is to win the bout and he can do that by inflicting harm on his opponent. In the example the aggression expressed somehow plays an instrumental role in winning the bout as the primary aim.

It must be stressed upon that neither type of aggression is good enough. The individual expressing the anger is accountable of deliberately causing harm with the intention to injure another individual. At all levels of competition, particularly in the professional level, extreme aggressiveness must be discouraged, as young athletes have tendencies to follow the experienced and senior athletes.

There is a third category of behavior that is time and again confused with aggression known as assertiveness or assertive behavior. In general, when a coach instructs or encourages their athletes to be more aggressive, by this they mean that the coaches want their athlete to become more assertive. Coaches want their athletes to state themselves in an assertive way so as to make their presence felt. To achieve one's purpose, the use of justifiable physical or verbal force with no intent to harm the opponent is assertiveness. Even if by chance when trying to be assertive if the opponent gets harmed or injured is not necessarily aggression. As long as the game is played with the spirit of the rules and regulations and with no intention to harm assertiveness prevails. Any physical injury that may occur by means of assertive behavior is accidental and an unintentional by-product. For instance, a race car driver injures or kills the fellow competitor by running into the slowed down or stuck car coming out of turn is not an aggressive behavior as there was no intent to cause harm to anyone. In rugby, the players usually in process of snatching the ball from one another have to struggle physically by getting over one another is not an aggressive behavior as there is no intent to harm one another but to get the possession of the ball so as to score a goal and win the match is the ultimate aim.

EXERCISES

Multiple Choice Questions

1. Which of the following is a law of learning ?
   (a) law of readiness (b) Law of exercise
   (c) Law of readiness (d) All of the above

2. Mental development includes :
   (a) External and internal organs
   (b) Reasoning and thinking
   (c) Ethical and moral
   (d) Emotional maturity

3. Through which of the following methods, desirable channels are provided for the release of emotional energy ?
   (a) Inhibition   (b) Sublimation
   (c) Catharsis   (d) Repression

4. The rate of progress in learning slows down and reaches a limit beyond which further improvement seems impossible. It is known as :
   (a) Plateau   (b) Loss of interest
   (c) Boredom   (d) Difficult stage

5. The therapy of psychoanalysis was developed by:
   (a) Skinner   (b) Sigmund Freud
   (c) Plato   (d) Darwin

6. Sports performance is the bi-product of :
   (a) Skill   (b) Conditional ability
   (c) Total personality   (d) Tractical ability

7. The first metamorphosis falls between the ages of :
   (a) 7-10 years   (b) 3-5 years
   (c) 11-14 years   (d) 2-4 years

8. Which is the most effective method for encouraging self-learning ?
   (a) Demonstration method
   (b) Lecture method
   (c) Observation method
   (d) Task method

9. Which one is the simplest form of cognition ?
   (a) Conception   (b) Perception
   (c) Sensation   (d) Affection

10. The functional division of spinal cord are :
   (a) Somatic-motor   (b) Somatic-sensory
   (c) Visceral-motor (d) None of these

Very Short Answer Type Questions (Carrying 1 mark)

1. Define the term personality.
2. Name the Sheldon's body types.
3. List the Jung's classification of personality.
4. Name the personality traits of Big Five Theory.
5. What are the types of aggression ?
6. Define motivation.
7. What is meant by intrinsic motivation ?
8. What is extrinsic motivation ?
9. What do you signify by body image ?
10. What do you denote by self-esteem ?
11. What is meant by positive body image ?
12. What is negative body image ?
13. Briefly state any one dimension of personality.
14. What do you understand by mental dimension of personality ?
15. Briefly state emotional dimension of personality.
16. Who are known as the mesomorphs ?
17. What do you understand by ambiverts ?
18. What is agreeableness ?
19. Elucidate about any two techniques of motivation.
20. Briefly discuss intrinsic and extrinsic motivation.
21. Explain any two techniques of motivation.
22. What is body image and self-esteem ?
23. What do you understand by positive body image and negative body image ?
24. List ant two psychological benefit of exercise.
25. What is aggression according to Oxford Dictionary of Sports ?

Short Answer Type Questions (Carrying 3 Marks)

1. Clarify any three techniques of motivation for higher achievement in sports.
2. Explain any three techniques of anxiety management.
3. Elaborate the dimensions of personality.
4. Discuss the types of personality.
5. Define motivation and discuss its types.
6. What is body image ? Discuss its types in brief.
7. List the factors influencing body image.
8. Discuss two psychological benefit of exercise.

Long Answer Type Questions (Carrying 5 Marks)

1. Explain in detail, personality, its types and its dimensions.
2. Discuss elaborately the role of sports in personality development.
3. Discuss and define personality in details along with the Jung's classification of personality.
4. Discuss elaborately the Sheldon classification of personality.
5. Discuss the Big Five Theory of personality.
6. Define motivation. Explain any five techniques of motivation.
7. Explain body image and its types in detail.
8. Explain the factors influencing body image in detail.
9. Discuss in details the guidelines to improve the body image.
10. Discuss elaborately the psychological benefit of exercise.
11. Write the meaning and concept of aggression along with its definition.
12. Discuss in details about the types, purposes and forms of aggression with suitable examples.

❑ ❑

TRAINING IN SPORTS

Since ancient times the word 'Training' has been an element of human being, language. It depicts the procedure of training for some task. The term sports training is generally used, which denotes the approach of preparing sports persons to hit the highest point level of performance. In present days, sports training is a very vital subject that affects the entire human race which takes up physical activity or sports either for competition at diverse levels or for health and fitness. Thus, sports training is the physical, methodological, intellectual, mental and ethical training of an athlete by help of physical exercises.

So it can denote that sports training is thereby a largely technical and systematic process of training the sports persons, for achieving the utmost level of performance. Sports training consists of all those learning influences and processes that are intended to improve sports performance. According to Hardayal Singh, sports training is a pedagogical process, based on scientific principles, aiming at preparing sports for higher performance in sports competitions.

10.1. STRENGTH

Strength is possibly the essential motor ability in sports because it is a direct result of muscle contractions. Strength is a conditional capability which depends mainly on the energy liberation process in the muscles. Strength and training of strength, thus, possess high value for achieving excellent performance in each and every sport. For good posture, general health and for prevention of injuries, the role of strength training if habitually ignored may prove harmful in the long run.

Definition

According to **Hardayal Singh (1991)**, *"Strength is the ability to overcome resistance or to act against resistance. He claimed that strength must not be considered as a result of muscular contraction only. It is, actually, a result of contraction of voluntary muscle caused stimulus of the neuro-muscular system."*

Types of Strength

In sports activities, strength constantly appears in various combinations with the endurance and speed abilities. The strength required by a sprinter to go off from the blocks is dissimilar to the strength required by a weight lifter to raise a 200 kg barbell. So experts have classified strength into three types which is mentioned as under:

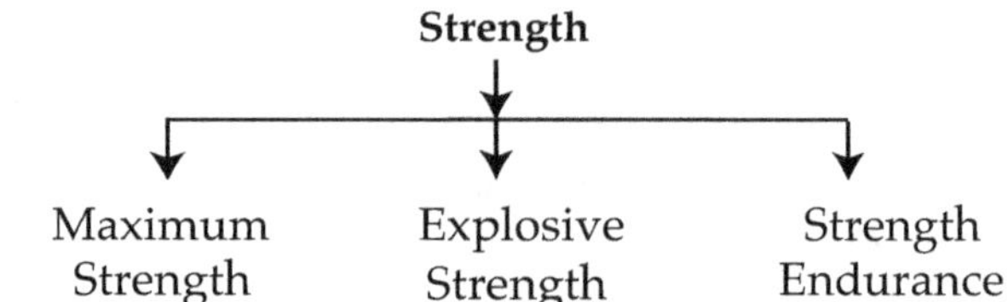

Maximum Strength

In a single muscular contraction it is the ability of muscle to contract over resistance of utmost intensity of stimulus. The most excellent examples are weight lifting and throwing events in track and field.

Explosive Strength

It can be stated as the ability to prevail over resistance by means of high speed. It combines strength and speed abilities and based on the nature of the blend of strength and speed, the explosive strength can be sub-divided further into start strength, power and speed strength. In the starting point of the movement, the ability to build up maximal muscle force is the start strength, for instance starting a sprint, weight lifting etc. Speed strength is the ability to prevail over lesser resistance by high speed like team games and lower weight categories of combative sports.

Strength Endurance

Similar to explosive strength, it is a result of two motor abilities as well. Under conditions of fatigue, it is the ability to work against resistance. Depending on the actuality whether the movement is static or dynamic, strength endurance can be there in form of static or dynamic strength. The strength endurance can be divided further into proper strength endurance and strength endurance depending on the kind of the blend of strength and endurance. Under conditions of fatigue, strength endurance is the ability to perform against high resistance as in case of combat sports, long duration events requiring strength. Strength Endurance is required for activities in which low resistance's are to be handled as in swimming, road cycling, etc.

Methods of Improving Strength

1. Isometric exercise : Since, there are no direct movements, for this reason they are not visible. In these, work is performed, however, it is not seen directly. In these exercises, a set of muscles carry out tension against the other group of muscles where muscles do not alter their length. They remain stable even though muscle does not entirely stay constant. For instance, pushing a wall, the force is generated in our muscles but it does not move from its place, therefore we consider that work is not done. As work is supposed to be done while the point of application of a force moves, *i.e.,*

> Work performed = Force × Distance moved in the course of force

Outgoing of energy is a common observable fact when these exercises are done. If these exercises are performed on a regular basis, muscles will be altered in terms of mass and shape. These exercises are used for the development and improvement of strength. The strength enhanced by means of isometric exercises is generally not of much significance in sports. These exercises can be performed anywhere as no equipment is requisite and need less time. These exercises are important for treatment purposes as individuals having injury can do these exercises. Children and untrained persons should not perform isometric exercises. The use of these exercises has to be limited one even though isometric exercises improve strength.

2. Isotonic exercises : Isotonic exercises tone up the muscles. Movements can be seen directly and work is done in isotonic exercises. By isotonic exercises, length of the muscle can be improved and muscles develop into flexible. In the field of sports, these exercises are of numerous values. Exercises with medicine ball, calisthenics exercises, and weight training exercises, running and jumping on the spot are the most appropriate examples of isotonic exercises. These exercises can be performed by means of or with no equipment.

3. Isokinetic exercises : These exercises were developed in the year 1968 by Perrine. Isokinetic exercises are done on particularly designed machinery. These exercises engage a definite kind of muscle contraction which is generally not pertinent in sports and games apart from water-sports like swimming and rowing. In isokinetic exercises, throughout the full range of movement contraction of muscle applies maximal force but, in isotonic exercises, contraction of muscle applies maximal forces at a particular position of its range of movement, only. The speed of contraction can be adjusted according to the individual's capacity. While performing isokinetic exercise on machine, the individual should keep in his mind that throughout the range of movement, force is to be applied. The isokinetic exercises can be used efficiently for the development of strength by fixing the number of repetition and by reducing or increasing the speed. Explosive strength and strength endurance by the help of these exercises can also be enhanced.

10.2. ENDURANCE

Endurance is an imperative ability used in games and sports. Endurance is the result of the entire physical and mental organs and systems. To recover rapidly from training and competition load, it is essential to develop the capacity of endurance. Endurance activities facilitate the sportsmen to defend against the exhaustion. It is the ability to continue prolonged work out or resist fatigue for longer duration. The aim of endurance training is to increase the energy production system to fulfill the demands of the event.

Definitions

According to **Harre (1986),** *"Endurance is the ability to resist fatigue."*

According to **Hardayal Singh (1991),** *"Endurance is the ability to do sports movements with the desired quality and speed, under the conditions of fatigue."*

Types of Endurance

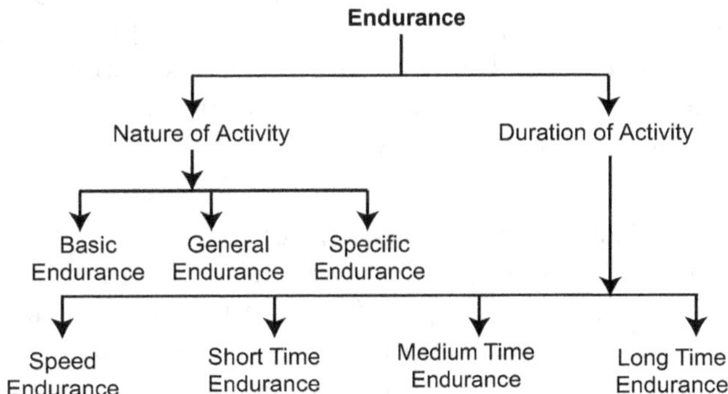

Experts in this field classify the endurance on the basis of two criteria *i.e.*, on nature of activity and duration of activity.

I. According to Nature of Activity

1. Basic endurance : The foundation for all types of endurance is basic endurance. It is the ability to carry out movement at reasonable pace for duration more than 30 minutes involving large amount of muscles, *e.g.*, jogging, walking and swimming. The time can be considerably less for sedentary and untrained persons.

2. General endurance : General Endurance helps a sportsman to perform different types of exercises without getting excessively fatigued. In general endurance exercises, the energy liberation depends on a combination of aerobic and anaerobic metabolism therefore, it can be done with high or low intensity. It is the ability to execute sports movements of general nature in conditions of exhaustion. It is developed all the way through general exercises and is not precise to one sport.

3. Specific endurance : The Specific Endurance can be basically equated with basic endurance in endurance sports, in which movements are executed at slower speed, however, for lengthy duration, namely in cross country and marathon etc. The ability to carry out movements of a particular sport in conditions of fatigue is specific endurance. The specific endurance may basically be determined by aerobic or anaerobic metabolism or by combination of both depending on the nature of sport.

II. According to Duration of Activity

1. Speed endurance : Speed Endurance is the capability to defend against fatigue in activities enduring up to 45 seconds, *e.g.*, 400 m sprint. This capability is extremely reliant on the power and glycolytic mechanism capacity of energy production.

2. Short time endurance : Short Time Endurance capability is desirable for cyclic activities enduring as of about 45 seconds to 2 minutes, for instance in 800 m race. In endurance activities of short time, the energy is created by a combination of oxidation and glycolysis. To a considerable amount, short time endurance depends on speed and strength endurance.

3. Medium time endurance : Medium Time Endurance is requisite for cyclic activities enduring from 2-11 minutes, *e.g.*, 1500 m and 3000 m run. It depends on strength endurance and speed endurance as well, however to a limited extent.

4. Long time endurance : The long time endurance is required for cyclic activities with duration more than 11 minutes, as in races of 5000 meters and 10000 meters.

Methods for Development of Endurance

To develop endurance, the subsequent methods are implemented :

Continuous Training

One of the most excellent methods for improving endurance is continuous training. In this method of training an activity is carried out with no break for an extensive period with low intensity. The suitable example of continuous method is cross-country race. The rate of heart beat remains in between 140-160 beats per minute in this method and the overall time length of the activity should not be less than 30 minutes. According to endurance ability of the sports person, the time of activity can be increased.

Advantages of continuous training :

1. Glycogen in muscles and liver increases.

2. The number and size of mitochondria increases.

3. The efficiency of heart and lungs increases as well.

4. Under the condition of fatigue it makes the individual strong-minded and improves the determination and self confidence.

5. Intensity can be increased for better outcome.

Interval Training

The German coach, Tonney, expresses, "When an athlete runs at the speed of 80%, his pulse rate will be 150 to 180. In the rest, the pulse rate should come down 120 to 140. This is the best recovery time for speed endurance." Bikila, the prominent athletic coach of Finland, designed this training method in 1920. In the method he stressed the significance of tempo connecting work and rest, and called it Terrace Training. He, instead of running 10 to 20 miles every day, used to run 400 m race 10 to 20 times on a daily basis. Jetopack also used the similar prototype to run 60 times 400 m every day. Later, this training method was coined and known as the interval training method. Through endurance training it is a training of heart.

Actually, this training method is based upon "effort and recovery theory". After each speedy work-out in interval training, recovery period is given to the athlete. According to the competence of athlete recovery period can be adjusted. By reducing the recovery period, the load can be increased. For a

400 meter athlete, the subsequent example can be related for this training :

(a) 400 m race by 80% speed.

(b) Until the heart rate approximately falls down to 120 to 140 beats, walking or jogging till then.

(c) 400 m race by 180% speed.

According to the level of athlete, recovery period and workout and the repetitions can be adjusted as well.

Advantages of interval training :

1. In short duration more workouts can be performed.

2. Both respiratory and circulatory systems can be trained at the same time.

3. It helps an athlete achieve the peak performance in a short time.

4. The athletes' improvement can be measured without difficulty.

5. Coach can give suggestions regarding any fault during recovery phase to athlete.

Fartlek Training

Fartlek training was developed in the year 1937 by Gosta Holmer. The Fartlek' is a Swedish word which means 'speed play' and is a method used for developing endurance. This method of training combines continuous training with interval training and emphasizes equally on the aerobic and anaerobic systems. The speed of the athlete is not predetermined in this method; according to the natural terrain viz., rivers, hills, forests, muddy roads, and grassy grounds, the speed can be changed. The heart rate ranges from 140 to 180 per minute. The period of training lasts a bare minimum of 45 minutes and depends upon the ability of athlete, can differ from aerobic walking to anaerobic sprinting. This training method can include any type of exercise, however, it is generally related with running. This training is done to improve performance and lessen the chances of injury, hence proper warm up should be done at the beginning and appropriate cooling down at the end of the training. A pattern of the Fartlek training schedule is as follows :

1. Warm up by jogging for 5 to 10 minutes followed by free hand exercises for diverse parts of the body for about 4 to 6 minutes.

2. Run at speedy stable speed over a distance of 800 m to 1200 m.

3. Fast walking for 5 minutes.

4. Perform easy running, separated by 40 to 50 meter sprint, repeating until symptoms of fatigue become visible.

5. Slow jogging for about 3 to 5 minutes.

6. Run up the hill at full speed over a distance of 80 to 100 meters. Run down the hill at a jogging speed subsequent to every repetition.

7. Walk for 5 minutes.

8. Run at quick speed for about one minute.

9. Jog about 1 to 1.5 km for cooling down.

10. Finish with free hand and stretching exercises.

Advantages of fartlek training :

1. Fartlek training allows adding an endless variety of intervals to the aerobic workouts, which helps to keep one stimulated.

2. Fartleks let runners to enhance the aerobic and anaerobic training systems equally.

3. Implementing Fartleks on a regular basis keeps the body physically powerful as much as necessary to uphold the technicalities of racing.

4. For people, Fartleks are a grand alternative because the fat burning part makes it an extremely efficient exercise.

5. Fartleks can be particularly modified and personalized to fit the requirements of diverse types of athletes and games.

10.3. SPEED

Speed ability is extremely movement specific. It is the ability to perform motor actions in minimum possible time under certain situations. Speed is a conditional ability as well, similar to strength and endurance, but to a considerable point speed depends on the nervous system unlike the two conditional abilities *i.e.,* strength and endurance. Consequently, speed is more complex in nature and is somewhat less trainable when compared to strength and endurance. The restrictive aspect in the development of speed becomes ability of the nervous system which can be influenced merely to a limited amount.

Definitions

1. **Theiss** and **Schnable** define, *"It is the performance prerequisite to do motor actions under given conditions (movement task, external factors, individual prerequisites) in minimum of time".*

2. **Barrow** and **McGee** define, *"Speed as the capacity of an individual to perform successive movements of the same pattern at a fast rate."*

3. **A.K. Uppal** defines, *"Speed is used in sports for such muscle reactions (motor movements) that are characterized by maximally quick alternation of contraction and relaxation of muscles."*

Types of Speed

Speed can be classified into following five types :

1. **Reaction ability :** In sports, signals/stimulus can be of diverse form *e.g.,* visual, tactile, auditory. It is the ability to respond or react efficiently and promptly to a signal. The reaction ability can be further differentiated into simple and complex reaction ability depending on the degree of complexity of the reaction.

2. **Movement speed :** It is the ability to carry out a particular movement in least amount of time. Movement speed is of high bearing in cyclic sports. In cyclic sports, technique and tactical action is very strongly bound with movement speed. On the basis of the nature of the movement in different sports, the movement speed ability depends on diverse multifaceted factors. However, it normally depends a great deal on explosive strength and technique.

3. **Acceleration ability :** To a huge amount, acceleration ability depends on technique, movement frequency and explosive strength. From a slow moving position it is the ability to attain high pace of locomotion as of a stationary position. In sprint events, performances are determined to a great extent by acceleration ability. Acceleration ability is vital in all team games and racket sports where high running speeds are achieved over short distances.

4. **Locomotor ability :** Capability to sustain utmost speed of locomotion for highest probable duration or distance is called locomotor ability. Locomotor ability is imperative in only some sports or events *e.g.,* swimming, rowing etc. In these sports, speed endurance is of high importance since all events last for more than 40 seconds as because of this, locomotor ability is not of much of significance on the other hand. To a great extent locomotor ability depends on mobility of the nervous system which allows for high movement frequency. The locomotor ability has a very low training impact. It further depends on technique, explosive strength and capability to relax.

5. **Speed endurance :** It is the ability to carry out sports movements with high speed in the condition of fatigue, it is a grouping of speed and endurance abilities. In cyclic and non-cyclic sports it is of a diverse form. Instead of the rapid fatigue accumulation at some stage in the activity, the speed endurance in cyclic sports is requisite to carry on movements at high speed. The speed endurance in non-cyclic sports is necessary to do movements all over again repeatedly with utmost probable speed in conditions of fatigue *e.g.,* recurring sprints in football. Speed endurance significantly depends on technique, anaerobic capacity and psychic factors.

Methods to Develop Speed

In actuality, speed is the result of hereditary and ecological factors. Nothing can be altered concerning the genetic factor; every human being has white fibers (fast twitch fibers) and red fibers (slow twitch fibers). An individual will have more endurance or stamina if he has high proportion of slow twitch fibers, on the contrary movement of individual will be speedier as he has high percentages of fast twitch fibers. The proportion of these muscle fibers cannot be altered. Therefore, the genetic factor of an individual sets the limit of speed up to definite level. Actually, central nervous system, muscular strength, flexibility, concentration, motivation and will power may add to the speed of an individual. For the development of speed in sprinting events, the following methods are generally adopted :

Acceleration Runs

To develop speed, acceleration runs are generally adopted particularly in attaining utmost speed from motionless position. We should change over to acceleration runs when the technique of any event is learnt in the beginning. For instance, we should practice 100 meter sprint race at a slow speed, and stress on the method to begin and complete running action. We should practice that technique at a higher speed subsequent to learning the correct technique. We may change over to acceleration runs after practice of complete technique in appropriate amount.

An athlete is required to run a definite distance for acceleration run. He starts from the starting line and attempts to achieve the utmost speed as early as possible and finishes the specific distance at that pace. With adequate intervals between runs the accelerated runs are repeated for practice purpose. After the stationary position sprinters generally attain their utmost speed in 6 seconds that is 50 to 60 meters is required to initiate, pick up the pace and sustain utmost speed. Extremely good athletes can sustain their utmost speed for 20 meters only. According to the age, experience and competence of the athlete the quantity of acceleration runs can be predetermined which may vary from 6 to 12 runs. Proper warm-up should be done prior to acceleration runs and there should be appropriate interval subsequent to each acceleration run so that the next run can be started with no fatigue. Normally, he should get the 4 to 5 minutes of rest in the middle of the runs.

Pace Runs or Races

Running the complete distance of a race at a steady speed is called pace race. In pace races, usually, 800 meters and above races are included where the races are run with consistent speed. For instance, the best time is 1 minute 40 seconds for a runner of 800 meter race; as a result he should run primary 400 meter in 49 seconds and subsequently the 400 meter in 51 seconds. This method is called pace race or run.

Therefore, the middle and long distance races must be run keeping the pace in mind. The race will not be complete if at the beginning, pace of run is too fast. According to the distance of a race the energy should be distributed. Normally, beginner athletes do not run a race in this manner. This is the reason of getting exhausted subsequent to completing just about half distance of the race and lastly run off the race.

Thus, an athlete while training for pace run should run at utmost steady speed for a distance of 10 to 20 percent extra than the racing distance. An athlete should run slightly below maximum speed concerning the repetition runs. For the next repetition, the rest periods should be sufficient to turn out to be fresh. Pace races are useful in maintaining the pace for more or less 20 to 45 meter where the speed is maintained all through this distance. This stage of continuance of utmost speed varies from individual to individual as this depends upon their level of performance and age. Repetitions can be predetermined according to the standard of the athletes; young children can maintain the utmost speed for 15 to 20 meters, while trained athletes can maintain the speed for 40 meters.

10.4. FLEXIBILITY

Meaning and Definition

One of the important components of physical fitness is flexibility. Many individuals may suffer from functional problems or disorders created due to lack of flexibility. Flexibility is not clearly a coordinative ability or a conditional motor ability. Flexibility depends partially on the coordinative process of the central nervous system and to some extent on energy release process. In general practice, flexibility is regularly equated with elasticity, stretchability, mobility, suppleness, etc. however, as a precise term the meaning of flexibility means much more. In general flexibility is coined as the capability to perform movements with superior range or amplitude. In other way, through a maximum range of motion, flexibility is the capacity to move the body joints without excessive tension.

Types of Flexibility

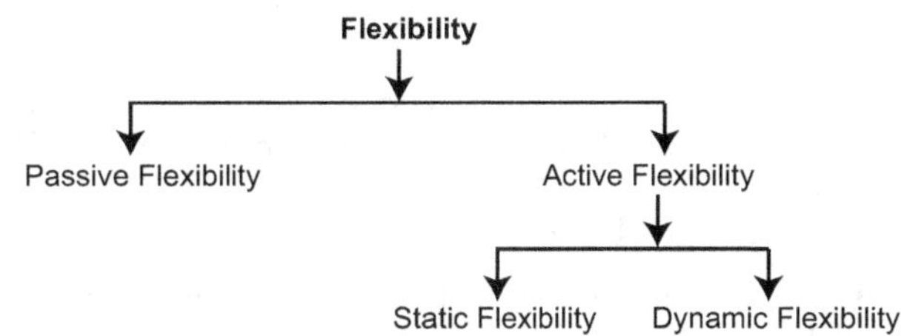

There are mainly two types of flexibility *i.e.,* Passive Flexibility and Active Flexibility.

Passive Flexibility

Passive flexibility is the base of active flexibility. Passive flexibility is the ability to do movements with greater amplitude by means of external assistance *e.g.,* with the help of a partner doing stretching exercises.

Active Flexibility

Active flexibility is the ability to perform movement with greater range, without external help *e.g.,* the sportsman himself stretches a joint with no external help. There are two types of active flexibility:

1. **Static flexibility :** While the sportsman is lying, standing or sitting, static flexibility is essential for movements done.

2. **Dynamic flexibility :** Dynamic flexibility is vital for performing movements when the sportsman is moving with superior amplitude.

For a general individual and for a sportsperson both types of flexibilities are essential. Stretching exercises assist in developing flexibility.

Methods to Improve Flexibility

Flexibility plays a significant role in training the athletes by means of increasing range of movement to permit technical development and helping in prevention of injury. Flexibility can be developed by practicing the stretching exercises. There are three methods of stretching exercises as experts have mentioned about in this field. These are Ballistic method, Slow Stretch and Hold Method and post isometric stretch.

Ballistic Method

The name ballistic method means stretching movement is done with a swing. Ballistic method means a joint is expanded steadily to its utmost range.

Note :

1. Ballistic method is perhaps the oldest method of doing stretching exercises.
2. In the recent years the effectiveness of this method has been repeatedly doubted because 'swing' movement leads to stretch reflex in the antagonist muscles, thereby hindering the optimum stretch of these muscles.
3. In ballistic method, there is a higher risk of injury because of high chances of over stretching the muscle.

Slow Stretch and Hold Method

By the given name of this method, we can comprehend the meaning of the slow stretch and hold method. It means before going back to the original position, the joint is gradually stretched to the maximum limit and is held there for a 3-8 seconds.

Note :

1. Slow stretch and hold method has been found to be very effective for improving passive flexibility which forms the basis of active flexibility.
2. For better effect the help of a partner should be taken in this method.

Post Isometric Stretch

In post isometric stretch, muscle is initially contracted for 6-7 seconds isometrically. The isometric contraction should be maximal involving muscular contraction not in favor of resistance in which the length of the muscle remains the same. Subsequent to this, the muscle is slowly stretched to its maximum, control is held in this spot for 8-10 seconds and repetitive for 4-5 times stretch muscle group.

Note :

1. It is based on the principle of proprioceptive neuro-muscular facilitation.
2. **Proprioceptive Neuromuscular Facilitation (PNF)** is a form of stretching in which a muscle is alternating stretched passively and contracted. The technique targets nerve receptors of a muscle to extend its length. This stretching procedure was designed for physiotherapist and occupational therapist in the 1940s and 1950s to treat the patients of paralysis. It is usually a combination of passive stretching and isometric contraction. The PNF positions encourage flexibility and coordination in the limbs. It helps to have quick gains in range of motion and specially used by athletes to improve performance. PNF is an advanced form of flexibility training that involves both stretching and contraction of the muscle group being targeted.

Additional Information for Improving Flexibility

1. In order to prevent decreases of muscle strength, flexibility exercises should be sensibly united with strength exercises. Exercises which engage stretching and strengthening at the similar time like dips on the parallel bar are the most excellent to make use of. Improvements of flexibility along with the continuation of strength of the muscle group being stretched are ensured by performing post isometric exercises.

2. Additional pressure on flexibility should be given in the period before puberty as the most excellent age for the improvement of flexibility.

3. During adolescence, if there is a gap in stretching exercises flexibility tends to deteriote.

4. Each muscle group must be stretched numerous times for good quality effect. At least 10-15 repetitions for each muscle group have been recommended by numerous experts. In ballistic method, number of repetitions is more.

5. The aim of flexibility training should be at optimal flexibility and not maximum flexibility as excessive flexibility means a reduced amount of joint stability and consequently higher chances of injury.

6. Fatigue negatively affects the stretchability of the muscles. It is perfect to do stretching exercises instantaneously after the warm up.

7. For stretching exercises, appropriate and systematic warm up is necessary as the muscle stretchability increases and also chances of muscle injury reduce.

8. For quicker improvement of flexibility, exercise can be done on a daily basis or twice a day. In daily routine of sportsman, stretching exercises should be incorporated and should be done on a regular basis and autonomously.

9. Stretching exercises should be accompanied by cognizant attempt to calm down the antagonist muscles.

10. Flexibility should be enhanced methodically. To initiate with passive stretching exercises should be slowly used to be replaced by active and dynamic flexibility exercises. The exercises should be rich in deviation, in that way enabling the sportsman to do the movement with greater amplitude in diverse conditions.

10.5. COORDINATIVE ABILITIES

Abilities of an individual which assist him to do a variety of interconnected activities correctly and competently are called Co-ordinative abilities. In the times of yore, five motor abilities were documented as machinery of physical fitness *viz.*, endurance, speed, strength, flexibility and agility. However, at present the term agility has been slowly replaced by the term co-ordinative abilities. Individual's accurateness, tempo, flow and steadiness depend on the coordinative abilities and it helps to constantly perform a series of movements easily and perfectly and may engage the muscular contraction, joint movements and senses. These abilities are very important in sports and games and are necessary for qualitative movements.

Typically, coordinative abilities are directly associated to the beautiful and stylish movements of our body. If we perform accurate movements, coordinative abilities can be improved. Whilst playing any games and sports we must keep away from inaccurate movements.

Definition

Zimmerman et. al, defines *"Coordinative abilities are understood as relatively stabilized and generalized patterns of motor control and regulation processes. These enable the sportsman to do a group of movements with better quality and effect."*

Types of Coordinative Abilities

Blume has recommended the subsequent seven co-ordinative abilities, which influence performance in games and sports. The significance of these co-ordinative abilities differs from sport to sport:

1. Combinatory ability : This ability depends upon the functional capacity of kinesthetic and optic sense organs as it has particular significance to gymnastics, combative sports and team games. For successful performance of a sports movement, it is the ability of a sportsperson to analytically and meaningfully unite the movements of different body parts. Furthermore, this reflects the ability of an individual to efficiently unite meaningful parts of movements into a complete of a skill in the skill learning process.

2. Ability to differentiate : This ability depends upon the functional capacity of kinesthetic sense organs. This ability helps a sportsperson to attain high level of excellence of separate body movements in phases of a motor action. When intention is to gain mastery over the skill this ability is stressed for effectual application in competition.

3. Orientation ability : Orientation ability depends upon the functional capacity of optic sense organ, vestibular apparatus and kinesthetic receptors. It is the ability of a sportsperson to examine and alter the location of the body and its parts in space and instance in context to performance area (*viz.* gymnastic apparatus, boxing ring, play field, etc.) or a moving thing (like, opponent, partner, ball, etc.).

4. Ability of reaction : Reaction ability depends upon the functional capacity of optic, acoustic and tactical sense organs. It is the ability of a sportsperson to react quickly to a known stimulus and perform well-directed movement following a stimulus.

5. Ability of balance : It is the capability of a sportsperson to sustain balance of the body together in static and dynamic conditions. Each and every one form of body movements is affected by the balance ability, however, when movements are done in a small area it has a special importance. The functional capacity of vestibular apparatus is responsible for balance ability.

6. Rhythmic ability : It is the talent of the sportsperson to comprehend the rhythm of movement and to perform the movement with requisite rhythm. The functional capacity of acoustic, optic, and kinesthetic sense organs are responsible for Rhythm ability.

7. Ability to adapt : According to predictable changes in circumstances, it is the capability of a sportsperson to result in an effectual alteration in the movement. Functional ability of sense organs like optic and auditory sense is responsible for coordinative ability.

Through general/specific exercises, such type of ability can be improved. Each and every sport requires the co-ordination of hands, feet and eyes. In sport scenario, it is principally reliant on the regulation process of central nervous system and motor control. The motor control and regulation process functions in a specific manner for each of the coordinative ability.

10.6. CIRCUIT TRAINING AND HIGH ALTITUDE TRAINING; INTRODUCTION AND ITS IMPACT

Circuit Training

In the year 1953, R.E. Morgan and G.T. Adamson, University of Leeds, England developed the circuit training method. Almost all of the training factors are involved in this type of conditioning. Circuit training is planned to develop the motor components, *i.e.,* cardiovascular endurance, muscular endurance, speed, agility, neuromuscular coordination, strength, power and flexibility.

Circuit training is one of the types of training in which an athlete performs a series of selected activities or exercises in a sequence or in a circuit. These circuits or stations to perform exercises in a sequence can be set up inside gymnasiums or outdoor on fields and courts. Generally, there are six to ten stations in a circuit where the athlete performs a specific exercise at each station and goes to the next station. The stations are spread all through the area remarked for the circuit training. The athlete must pass through the circuit as fast as possible making an attempt to increase the amount of work done at each station or to improve by lessening the total time it takes to complete or both. For cardiovascular conditioning, the distance between stations should be greater as the athlete have to run from one station to the next.

Planning of Circuit Training

Circuit training is a brilliant method to improve strength, stamina and mobility at the same time. The circuit training set-up can make use of a set of 6 to 10 strength exercises which can be performed one exercise after another. Every exercise at each station is performed for a prescribed time period or for a specified number of repetitions before moving on to the next station for next exercise. The exercises in each circuit are separated by short timed rest intervals and each circuit is separated by a longer period of rest. Depending on training level, *i.e.,* beginner, intermediate, or advanced athlete, or period of training (preparation or competition) or to fulfill the training objective the total number of circuits performed for the duration of a training session may differ from two to six sets or rounds.

Identify the probable exercises that can be performed with the accessible equipment. Chalk out on paper 3 to 4 circuits of 6 to 10 exercises. Try to make sure that in each circuit no two consecutive exercises are performed for the same muscle group, for instance, avoid press ups followed by pull ups.

Important points should be kept in mind when planning a circuit:

1. Use simple exercises that work large muscle groups.
2. Use a correct order of the exercises (no doubling up).
3. Ensure different muscle groups are exercised in turn.

4. Encourage simple exercise (less injury risk).
5. Set time or work intervals appropriate for developmental age and fitness.
6. Be sure that time of rest intervals includes rest time between each circuit.
7. Give active rest stations particularly for the younger age groups.
8. Keep the circuit simple until players gain more experience.
9. Give clear instructions regarding the organization of the players.
10. Consider the fitness level and game style requirements of the players.
11. Clearly state the direction of the circuit.
12. Ensure players breath out as they perform the power phase, and breath in as they relax back to the start position.
13. During the cool-down include flexibility exercises.

In order to work on each body part, a circuit should be set up like: total-body, upper-body, lower-body, core & trunk etc. Given below are the examples of exercises that can be used in a session of circuit training:

1. **Total-body :** Treadmills, burpees, skipping, squat thrusts.
2. **Upper-body :** Press ups, bench dips, pull ups, medicine ball chest pass, bench lift, inclined press up.
3. **Lower-body :** Squat jumps, compass jumps, astride jumps, hopping shuttles, bench squat, step ups and shuttle runs.
4. **Core and trunk :** Lower abdominals (sit ups), upper abdominals (stomach crunch), back extension chest raise.

Example sessions :

1. **Six exercises :** Treadmills, press ups, squat jumps, sit ups, squat thrusts and bench dips.
2. **Eight exercises :** Treadmills, press ups, squat thrusts, bench dips, squat jumps, sit ups, shuttle runs and back extension chest raise.

Note :
1. It is vital to do warm up with easy jogging and dynamic stretching exercises before stating the circuit and as a cool down an easy jog with static stretching after the session should be performed.
2. Approximately 20 to 30 seconds work on each exercise with a recovery of 30 seconds in between each exercise.

3. An athlete should perform 3 to 5 sets of circuit with a recovery of 3 minutes between each set.

4. The duration is based on time *i.e.*, 30 seconds or set to half the number of repetitions of the exercise the athlete completes in 60 seconds with 100% effort. If training is based on the number of repetitions in that case regular testing *i.e.*, in every 4 week should be carried out to decide the maximum number of repetitions to be completed in 60 seconds for each exercise.

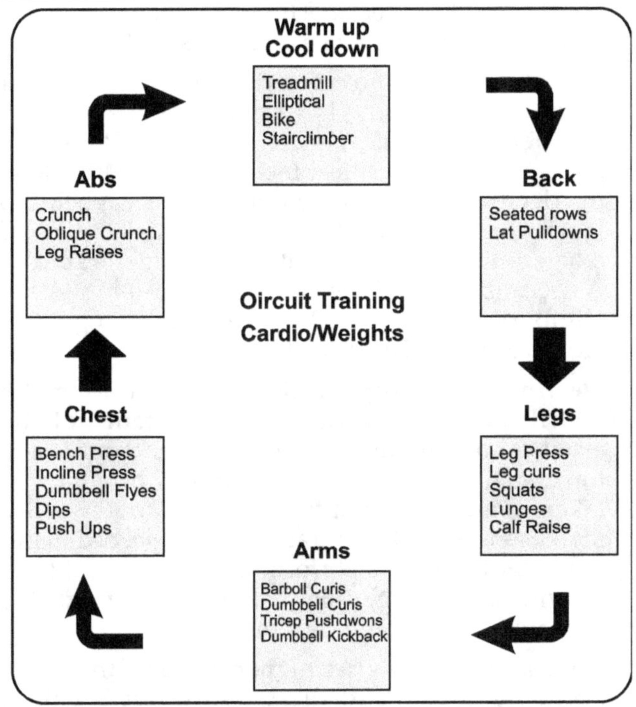

Importance of Circuit Training

Circuit training is a convenient way to exercise. It maximizes the total exercise volume in terms of number of sets, repetitions and amount of weight completed in a period of time. The time spent exercising is condensed as exercises are completed in a row. Cardiovascular training is not required separately.

Circuit training is a form of interval training which helps to increase the ability of burning calories when at rest. The athlete's heart rate goes up very high then returns to lower rate, yet in an elevated, state and then goes up very high yet again. During circuit training, the heart rate at no point returns to its resting rate. Overall, circuit and interval training helps to increase the amount of oxygen consumption of an athlete after exercise, and thus, increases the number of calories that an athlete burns all through the day.

Circuit training is a multipurpose training method that allows large number of athletes taking part in the same exercise session and requires less time than other method. The circuit weight training is an excellent method to improve the body composition, muscle strength and cardiovascular functions and to maintain functional capacity during aging. Resistance circuit training may be included in treating the patients with several diseases so as to improve their quality of life.

Mentioned below are the other importance of circuit training:

1. The total fitness is emphasized by combining the number of different components of training.

2. It provides an exciting training environment for the athlete in which the time and level are established to encourage the athlete so that they continue improving.

3. At a moderately low expense it can accommodate large groups of athletes.

4. It helps to develop strength and endurance.

5. It helps to develop the bone mineral density values.

6. For majority of the sports it is the most appropriate form of training.

7. Exercises are easy to complete which makes each athlete feel a sense of achievement within them.

8. The athlete's enthusiasm remains maintained as there are wide range of exercises to select from.

9. In this kind of training, progression in all activities is guaranteed.

High Altitude Training

High altitude training at actual or replicated altitude is enough to lessen the partial pressure of oxygen. (PO_2) considerably below that at sea level, increasing the oxygen-carrying capacity of the blood hence enhancing the sea-level aerobic perfor-mance. Though individual responses may vary extensively and other effects can be harmful as well. A live high - train lower training plan is presently more favoured, as the training can then be close to sea-level intensity. Even though some research has recommended that altitude training may possibly improve sea-level endurance performance.

The higher the altitude more rigorous will be the effects— the ability to perform physical work gets effected at altitudes of over 5000 feet.

A rise in altitude has numerous practical consequences on the athletes. It lowers the wind-resistance because of the reduction in the density of the air. The maximum oxygen transport gets restricted thus reducing the oxygen present in the air for breathing, consequently lowering the atmospheric temperature. The force of gravity also decreases in small amount. Athletes undergo physiological adjustment of body while remaining at high altitude for certain durations, *viz.*, increase in hemoglobin and red blood cells counts, restoration of normal fluid levels, reductions in tissue bicarbonate levels which leads to progressive improvement in endurance performance.

Wind resistance is responsible for a considerable fraction of energy expenditure in all events which produces quick movement of man or objects in air such as running, throwing and cycling etc. It was during these 1968 Olympic Games in Mexico City with elevation 2,240 meters (7,349 ft) that endurance events saw significant below-record finishing while anaerobic events like sprinting events broke all types of records. This type of result was expected as the altitude might affect the performances of those elite, world-class athletes. Because of these kinds of result researchers got inspired to investigate altitude training and the training principles were developed aiming to avoid underperformance.

Altitude Acclimatization

When one stays longer at high altitude the performance improves, but the performance is not above or equal to that level which is obtained at the sea level. Hence, the improved performance achieved during the stay at higher altitude is brought through acclimatization.

Acclimatization refers to particular physiological adjustments which considerably improve performance which are attained through constant exposure to altitude. For un-acclimatized individual, additional oxygen is essential at 5488 meter (18000 feet) above the sea level.

It varies from individual to individual, as some will never acclimatize and will suffer from altitude or mountain sickness. The symptoms of altitude sickness are vomiting, nausea, headache, fever, rapid pulse, loss of appetite, congestion of lungs and pulmonary edema. Mountain sickness can be treated by giving oxygen or taking the patient to lower altitude or both.

The barometric pressure decreases as the weight of the atmosphere becomes less when we rise above sea level. The major reason for decrease in performance at altitude is a product of the lowered oxygen partial pressure (PO_2) resulting in hypoxia *i.e.*, lack of sufficient oxygen. Depending upon the altitude and period of stay the hypoxia stimulates the acclimatization mechanism.

Importance of High Altitude Training

The importance of high altitude training are given below :

1. **Total barometric pressure decreases :** As we progress towards higher altitude, the total barometric pressure decreases as the weight of atmosphere decreases. At high altitude the force of gravity is lesser in comparison to that at the sea level thus the energy required to raise the body while performing the pole vault and high jump would decrease. Though the consequence on physical performance is rather small.

2. **Partial pressure of oxygen decreases :** The partial pressure of oxygen (PO_2) decreases because of the decreased barometric pressure. Physiologically, the most critical factor of high altitude is the decreased PO_2 as the individual's capacity to work depends principally upon his ability of oxygen intake and utilization of oxygen rapidly. As because of this reason the pilots and mountain climbers are required to take in oxygen at altitudes above 20,000 feet.

3. **Decline in density of air :** The decline in the density of the air reduces the resistance of the airways so as to the flow of air into and out of the lungs. This allows greater volumes of air to be taken in at the time of work without noteworthy increase in ventilation rate. The reduced density of the air favors the performances like sprint type activities, jumping, pole vaulting, throwing, etc., in which air resistance is a major factor.

4. **Cool and dry air :** At higher altitude the air is normally cooler and drier. Work out becomes pleasant at the cooler temperature and assists performances involving prolonged physical exertion. Dehydration may result because of the water loss from the respiratory tract increases due to the dry air. Athletes experience dryness of throat as a result of the dry air.

5. **Sunburn and snow blindness :** Sunburns and snow blindness at high altitude is a common experience for skiers and mountaineers. At high altitude, solar radiation is much more intense and the skin tends to be dryer at high altitudes along with the winds which generally blow harder at height. The burning of skin is also related to the decrease in density of the air at high altitude.

6. **Pulmonary ventilation :** At higher altitudes pulmonary ventilation increases both during rest and exercise. At higher altitudes, the air is less dense thus, the increase in ventilation is a compensatory mechanism which brings the equal number of oxygen molecules into the lungs same as the individual would take at sea level. The increased ventilation is same as hyperventilation

at the sea level where the CO_2 in the alveoli gets reduced hence causing more CO_2 to diffuse from the blood thus increasing the blood pH.

7. **Hemoglobin concentration in the blood enlarges :** The acclimatization increases the number of red blood cells which causes rapid production of the cells by the bone marrow. By and large due to the decrease in plasma volume the hemoglobin concentration gets increased. To assist acclimatization of individuals to high altitudes there are formation of many new cells which takes several weeks, though it is a slow process.

8. **Diffusion capacity of the lungs enhances :** During exercises at sea level or at high altitude the normal diffusing capacity for oxygen all the way through the pulmonary membrane increases. This increase results due to an enlarged pulmonary capillary blood volume, which expands the capillaries and increases the surface in the course of which oxygen can diffuse into the blood and add to lung volume, which most probably expands the surface area of the alveolar membrane.

9. **Vascularity of the tissues increases :** The hemoglobin molecules come into closer contact with the active tissue cells providing supply of oxygen to each cell yet with a fairly lower oxygen supply.

This increases the number of capillaries along with an improved distribution of blood to the areas *viz.*, muscles, heart, brain, and other organs which generally need large amounts of oxygen, where gaseous exchange occurs and is needed for optimal performance. As a result of vasodilatation there is a slight increase in arterial blood pressure along with a drop in total peripheral resistance. This enhances overall distribution of blood to the tissues which is brought about by the opening of new capillaries in the small blood vessels.

10. **Myoglobin content of the muscles increases :** The oxygen carrying pigment in the muscles called as myoglobin increases because of staying at high altitude, thus, favoring acclimatization.

11. **Efficiency in making use of the available oxygen and adjust to the low partial pressure of oxygen :** Individuals residing at the high altitude have a greater number of cellular oxidative enzyme systems in comparison to those who reside at sea level. The naturally acclimatized individuals at high altitudes can stay alive for quite a few hours without needing much of oxygen. The acclimatization attained by staying several weeks at high altitude will be lost within a period of about two weeks, after the individual returns to sea level.

EXERCISES

Multiple Choice Questions

1. Isometric exercise is the one in which muscle length is :
   - (a) Constant
   - (b) Shortened
   - (c) Lengthens
   - (d) None of these

2. 'Cyber' machine is based on the principle of :
   - (a) Isometric contraction
   - (b) Isotonic contraction
   - (c) Isokinetic contraction
   - (d) None of the above

3. Isokinetic method of training was introduced by :
   - (a) G. D. Sondhi
   - (b) J. Perrine
   - (c) Aristotle
   - (d) Hippocrates

4. Pushing against the stationary wall is an example of :
   - (a) Eccentric exercise
   - (b) Isometric exercise
   - (c) Isotonic exercise
   - (d) Isokinetic exercise

5. 'Super compensation' means :
   - (a) Fatigue
   - (b) Second wind
   - (c) Adaptation to load
   - (d) Oxygen debt

6. 'Stadiometer' is used to measure :
   - (a) Strength
   - (b) Weight
   - (c) Height
   - (d) Stadium area

7. 'Fertile Training' is used best to develop :
   - (a) Flexibility
   - (b) Strength
   - (c) Endurance
   - (d) Stadium area

8. Adaptation to training load at high altitudes is known as :
   - (a) Thermoregulation
   - (b) Super compensation
   - (c) Acclimatisation
   - (d) None of the above

9. Aerobic fitness is best achieved through :
   - (a) Swimming
   - (b) Circuit training
   - (c) Short sprints
   - (d) Long distance running

10. Progression method can equally be used in teaching the activities except :
    - (a) Hammer throws
    - (b) Mass physical training
    - (c) Dance
    - (d) Pole vault

Very Short Answer Type Questions (Carrying 1 mark)

1. What do you understand by the word 'training'?
2. What is sports training ?
3. Define strength.
4. What are isometric exercises ?
5. What are isotonic exercises ?
6. What are isokinetic exercises ?
7. What is meant by dynamic strength ?
8. What is meant by static strength ?
9. Define endurance.
10. Define speed.
11. What do you understand by fartlek training ?
12. What do you understand by continuous training method ?
13. What do you understand by interval training method ?
14. Define flexibility.
15. Describe explosive strength.
16. Describe maximum strength.
17. Describe strength endurance.
18. Describe passive flexibility.
19. Describe active flexibility.
20. What is continuous method of training ?
21. What is interval training ?
22. What is general and specific endurance ?
23. Define speed endurance.
24. What do you understand by short term endurance ?
25. What is acceleration ability ?
26. What is locomotor ability ?
27. What is speed endurance ?
28. What is dynamic flexibility ?
29. What are coordinative abilities ?
30. What is coupling ability ?
31. What is orientation ability ?
32. Describe balance ability.
33. In which year circuit training was established?
34. Who developed circuit training?
35. Which Olympic Games result got affected due to high altitude?
36. Discuss any one method to develop speed.
37. Elucidate any two methods to improve flexibility.
38. Explain pace runs as a means to develop speed.

Short Answer Type Questions (Carrying 3 marks)

1. Explain the types of Strength.
2. Explain in briefly any two methods of improving strength.
3. Briefly discuss the types of endurance according to the nature of activity.
4. Discuss types of endurance according to the nature of activity in brief.
5. Discuss the fartlek training method as a means of developing endurance in brief.
6. Elucidate the methods of improving speed.
7. What do you understand by flexibility ? Briefly discuss the various types of flexibility.
8. Define flexibility and give explanation on the methods to improve flexibility.
9. Discuss briefly any three types of coordinative abilities.
10. Enlist any five impacts of high altitude training.
11. What do you understand by dynamic strength and static strength ?
12. Define maximum and explosive strength ?
13. Brief about basic endurance and general endurance.
14. What do you understand by short term and long term endurance ?
15. In brief, state continuous training method.
16. Discuss reaction ability.
17. Discuss state acceleration and locomotor ability.
18. Explain pace runs as a mean to develop speed.
19. What do you understand by active and passive flexibility ?
20. Discuss about balance and rhythm ability.
21. Explain adaptation ability and differentiation ability.
22. What do you understand by circuit training ?
23. What is altitude acclimatization ?

Long Answer Type Questions (Carrying 5 marks)

1. Define strength and discuss in detail the methods of improving strength.
2. Define endurance and discuss in detail any two methods of improving endurance.
3. Define speed and in detail discuss the types of speed.
4. What do you understand by speed ? Explain the methods of improving speed.
5. What is flexibility ? Give in detail the methods of improving flexibility.
6. What is a coordinative ability ? State any four types of coordinative abilities.
7. Discuss in detail the coordinative abilities.
8. Write in details about planning circuit training and also discuss about the impact of circuit training.
9. Elaborately discuss about high altitude training and discuss in details about impacts of high altitude training.

PHYSICAL EDUCATION PRACTICAL

BASKETBALL

1.1. INTRODUCTION AND HISTORY

Basketball is played by 2 teams of 5 players each. The aim of each team is to score in the opponents' basket and to prevent the other team from scoring. The game is controlled by the officials, table officials and a com-missioner, if present. The basket that is attacked by a team is the opponents' basket and the basket which is defended by a team is their own basket. The team that has scored the greater number of points at the end of playing time shall be the winner.

World History

The game of Basketball was firstly invented by Dr. James Naismith of USA in December, 1891 at Spring Field College, United States of America. In the very beginning, the game was very interesting; 40 to 50 players used to be in one team. The game used to be played in Gymnasium. A pair of baskets was nailed on the walls facing each other. One had to climb up to get the ball out whenever a goal was scored. After that Dr. Smith framed certain rules of the game.

Indian History

Approximately 85 years ago in India, the game of Basketball was introduced by Y.M.C.A. College, Madras. Since then, Basketball has become popular in every part of India. The Indian Basketball Federation was formed in 1950.

1.2. GOVERNING BODIES

FIBA

FIBA, the International Basketball Federation/Fédération International de Basketball, is the world governing body for basketball, founded in 1932. FIBA brings together 214 National Basketball Federations from all over the world. FIBA organises and oversees international competitions. FIBA establishes the official basketball rules as well as the regulations that govern the relationships between the different members of the basketball communities.

BFI

The Basketball Federation of India (BFI), which came into being in 1950, is the governing and controlling body of basketball in India, responsible for the development and promotion of the sport at all levels. BFI oversees all the national level basketball operations in India.

Main Tips at a Glance		
1.	Number of teams	= 2
2.	Number of court players in a team	= 5
3.	Number of substitutes in a team	= 7
4.	Total players	= 12
	Dimensions of the court	
5.	Length of the court	= 28 m
6.	Breadth of the court	= 15 m
7.	Area of the court	= 4700 m^2
8.	Diameter of centre circle	= 3.60 m

Dimensions of the lines

9.	Width of the lines	=	0.5 cm
10.	Centre line shall extend	=	15 cm beyond each side line
11.	Furthest edge of free-throw line from the	=	5.80 m inner edge of the endline
12.	Free-throw line shall be	=	3.60 m long

Dimensions of Backboard

13.	Height of lower edge of board from the floor	=	2.90 m
14.	Thickness of the backboard	=	3 cm
15.	Backboard shall be	=	80 m horizontally
16.	Backboard shall be	=	1.05 m vertically
17.	Width of all the board lines	=	5 cm

Ball

18.	Circumference of the ball	=	75 to 78 cm
19.	Weight	=	600- 650 gm
20.	Air pressure at ball	=	7.5-8.5 pounds

Dimensions of Ring

21.	The rings have a diameter	=	450 mm-457 mm
22.	Metal diameter will be	=	16 mm-20 mm
23.	The top edge of the ring is at a height from the playing floor	=	3,050 m
24.	Duration of basketball game	=	4 durations of 10 minutes each
25.	Interval between two durations		{10-2-10-10-10-2-10}
26.	Officials		5 (1 = referee, 1 = umpire, 1 = scorer, 1 = timekeeper, 1 = 24 second operator)

1.3. FUNDAMENTAL SKILLS, GENERAL RULES AND TERMINOLOGY

Fundamental Skills of Basketball

1. Handling the ball
2. Passing
   (a) Chest or push pass
   (b) Baseball pass
   (c) Underhand pass
   (d) Overhead pass
   (e) Two handed bounce pass
   (f) Hook pass
   (g) Flip pass
   (h) Tip or volley pass
   (i) Back pass
3. Pivoting
4. Dribbling
   (a) High dribble
   (b) Low dribble
5. Shooting
   (a) Two hand shot
   (b) Lay up shot
   (c) Hook shot
   (d) Jump shot
6. Rebounding

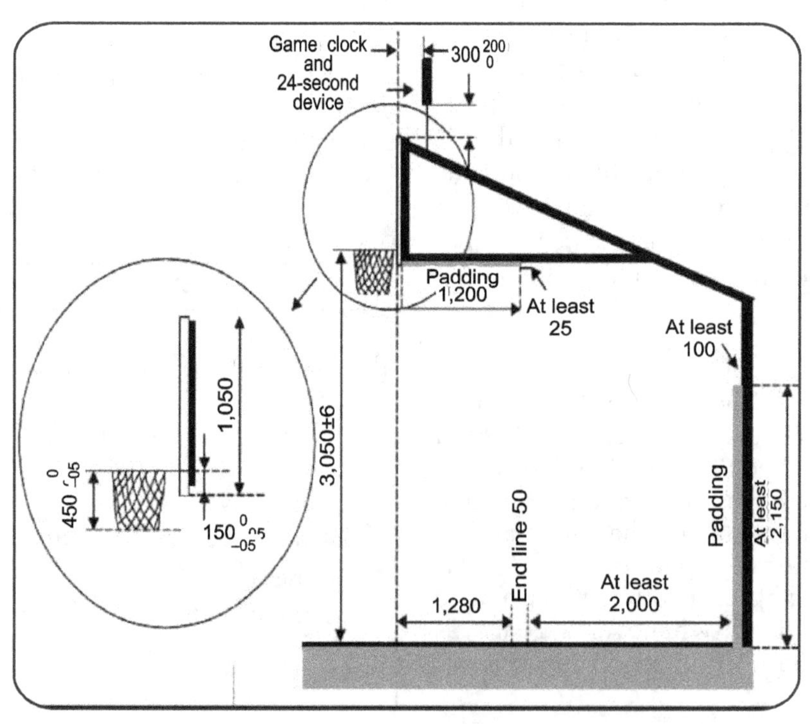

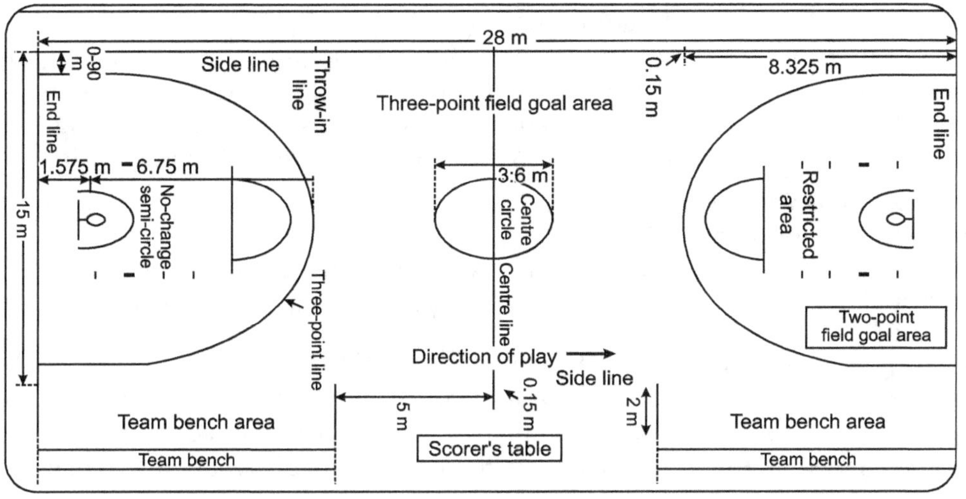

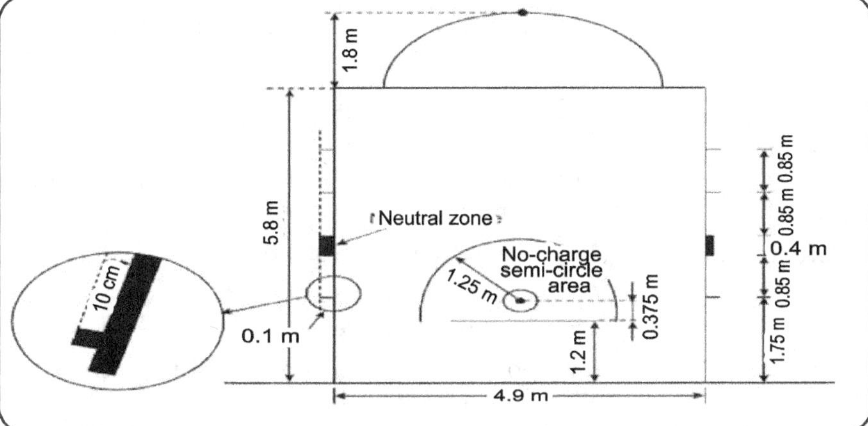

7. Defence
8. Dodge
   (a) To dodge with singles
   (b) By speed
   (c) By escape
9. Free throw
10. Offensive strategy
    (a) Faking
    (b) Screening
    (c) Triangular attack
    (d) Zonal attack
11. Defensive attack
    (a) Blocking
    (b) Tackling
    (c) Zonal defence
    (d) Guarding
    (e) Man to man defence

The brief description of some of fundamental skills mentioned below :

Dribbling

A dribble is the move-ment of a live ball caused by a player in control of that ball who throws, taps, rolls the ball on the floor or deliberately throws it against the back-board. It is of two kinds :

1. High dribbling : The objective in high dribbling is to advance the ball more quickly. It is always meant for advancing the ball; here bounce is comparatively higher up to waist level.

2. Low dribbling : It is used when the offensive in the ball is being guarded closely. Low dribble is controlled dribble. The ball is protected while putting the body between ball and the defensive player.

Pivoting

It is a very important skill because it helps basketball player to attack or defend himself and his position.

A pivot takes place when a player who is holding the ball steps once or more than once in any direction with the same foot, while the other foot called the pivot foot is being kept at its point of contact with the floor.

Shooting

In order to score points in basketball, you need to shoot the ball into the hoop. This requires the ability to properly hold and throw the ball into the air toward the basket while avoiding defenders. There are the kinds of shooting :

1. **Jump shot :** A jump shot or jumper is an attempt to score a basket by jumping, usually straight up, and in mid-jump, propelling the ball in an arc into the basket.

2. **Lay-up shot :** A shot in which a player reaches the ring by taking one and a half step.

3. **Dunk shot :** A shot is called the Dunk shot when a player jumps high enough to get the ball up and over the ring to press it forcefully into the ring.

Catching

Catching the ball is just an action that requires your hands placing a grip on the ball. The sole purpose is to receive the ball from another player.

Passing

Passing means the movement of the ball from one player to another. Passing is the best way to keep possession of the basketball and is a faster way of moving the ball up the court than dribbling. A good pass is smoothly handled and not forced. It is usually 12-18 feet (the longer ones can be easily intercepted) and is made with control.

1. Chest pass : This technique is used when there is no defender standing in the way between the passer and his intended receiver. The ball is gripped with both hands by placing the fingertips on both sides of the ball; the thumbs should nearly meet behind the ball.

2. Bounce pass : In bounce pass, the holding of the ball, body positions and passing action is approximately the same as in two hand chest pass.

(a) One-handed bounce pass : One handed bounce pass is used when the bounce pass is difficult for defender to steal. The change of direction is hard for the defender to judge.

(b) Two-handed bounce pass : The bounce pass is used to avoid a defender who is trying to block or intercept the ball.

3. Overhead pass : This technique is often used to break a defensive trap. The idea is for the passer to get the ball to a receiver who is tall and who is standing close to the basket.

4. Baseball passing : In this type of pass, the ball should be taken just behind the head on right or left direction with a support of the upper portion of palm and fingers. One foot should be kept in front of the other and the ball should be thrown with a swing with fingers. This pass is usually applied for long passes.

Ball Handling

Ball is held with both hands firmly. The fingers should spread evenly on the ball. The angle of thumb is to be at 400 facing angularly to each other. Relax the shoulders and elbows close to the body.

Jumping

Jumping is another skill that can define how good a basketball player is. Jumping is involved in offense during the jump ball in the beginning, while taking shots and sometimes while trying to catch a pass.

Rebounding

It means successfully gaining possession of the ball after a missed field goal or free throw. Power forwards and canters do most of the rebounding for their team as they should be two tallest players in the team.

Blocking

When a player attempts to screen and block the opponent in restricting the move towards scoring.

General Rules of Basketball

Although there are rules variations between men, and women's basketball and between the various levels of play, there are basic rules that govern play at any level.

1. Only five players can play in each team at one time.

2. Any number of substitutions may be made during any dead ball.

3. Substitution must wait by the scorer's table until called into the call by an official.

4. Any player may request a time out.

5. A goal is scored when the ball passes through the basket from the above.

6. Two points are scored for a goal from the court other than from the three point's area.

7. Each successful free throw awarded for fouls score one points.

8. If the players put the ball into the basket of the opponent, a goal is scored.

9. A goal is stopped when an official indicates a handball.

10. The ball is put into the play at the beginning of the game by a jump ball into a centre circle by two opposing teams.

11. A players is out of bounds when he touches the floor on or outside of the boundaries lines.

12. The ball is out of bounds when it touches the person or thing that is on or outside the boundary of or the supports or back of the backboards.

13. A team is awarded a throw-in at the place where opposing team causes the ball out-of- bounds.

14. An offensive player may not remain in the free throw lane (the area between the endline, free throw line, and free throw lane lines) for more than 3 seconds during play.

Equipment Needed to Conduct the Basketball Match

The following equipment will be required:

1. Backstop units, consisting of :
   - (a) Backboards
   - (b) Baskets comprising (pressure release) rings and nets.
   - (c) Backboard support structures including padding.
2. Basketballs
3. Game clock
4. Scoreboard
5. Shot clock
6. Stopwatch or suitable (visible) device (not the game clock) for timing time-outs.
7. 2 separate, distinctly different and loud signals, one each for the
   - (a) Shot clock operator,
   - (b) Scorer/timer
8. Score sheet
9. Player foul markers
10. Team foul markers
11. Alternating possession arrow
12. Playing floor
13. Playing court
14. Adequate lighting

Terminology Related to Basketball

1. **Blocking out :** When a player positions him set or herself under the backboard in such a way that it prevents the opposition from achieving good rebounding position.
2. **Cut :** Quick offensive maneuver by a player in order to get in position to receive a pass.
3. **Dodging :** Pretending to move or throw the ball in one direction but actually moving or throwing the ball in a different direction.
4. **Double foul :** Two opposite players commit fouls against each other at the same time.
5. **Dribble :** Continuously bouncing the ball onto the floor without touching the ball with both hands at the same time, allowing the ball to stop its continuous movement, or losing control.
6. **Fake (Feint) :** Use of deceptive move to pull the opposing player out of position.
7. **Fast break :** Moving quickly into defensive position before the defensive team has an opportunity to set up.

8. **Free throw :** A penalty shot awarded to a player where the opposition has committed a foul.
9. **Held ball :** A situation in which opposing players both hold the ball, neither of them can get possession; this is resolved by the referee by throwing the ball in the air between them.
10. **Jump ball :** Method of putting the ball into play that involves tossing the ball up into the air between two opposing players in the centre circle.
11. **Multiple foul :** A foul on an opponent by two or more players at the same time.
12. **Outlet pass :** Direct pass from a rebound that starts a fast break.
13. **Rebound :** Term used for the action of the ball as it bounces off the backboard or ring.
14. **Screen :** Offensive player gets in position between a defender and a teammate in order to give the defender an uncosted shot at the basket.
15. **Set shot :** An unhindered shot taken from a well balanced position is called a set shot.
16. **Technical foul :** A non-contact foul by a player, team or coach for unsportsman like behaviour or failure to follow the rules and regulation.
17. **Throw in :** Putting the ball into play from out of bounds.
18. **Travelling :** Player in possession of the ball moves illegally in any direction.

Main Fouls

1. **Personal foul :** A personal foul is that foul when a player involves contact, blocks and catches, an opponent.
2. **Intentional foul :** It is a personal foul which is committed intentionally by a player.
3. **Double foul :** A double foul is that when two opponents commit foul against each other almost at the same time.
4. **Multiple foul :** A foul on an opponent by two or more players at the same time.
5. **Technical foul :** A non-contact foul by a player, team or coach for unsportsman like behaviour or failure to follow the rules and regulation.
6. **Five foul :** If a player commits five fouls either personal or technical, he or she shall be turned out for whole match.

Main Rules to Understand

1. **Three seconds rules :** A player shall not remain in the opponents' restricted area for more than

three consecutive seconds while his team is in control of a live ball in the frontcourt and the game clock is running.

2. **Five seconds rules :** According to the new rules, when a closely guarded player, who is holding the ball, does not pass, shoot, roll or dribble the ball within five seconds, it shall be considered a violation with a side line throw for the opponents.

3. **Eight second rules :** After the attacking team gains possession of the ball in their own half, they have eight seconds to move the ball into the opposition's half otherwise they will lose the possession.

4. **Twenty four seconds rules :** A team shall attempt a shot within 30 seconds after taking control of the live ball.

5. **Travel rules :** Travelling or progressing while holding the ball, moving either with one or both the feet, shall be considered out of bounds.

1.4. SPORTS AWARDS, TOURNAMENTS AND VENUES AND SPORTS PERSONALITIES

Sports Awards

Arjuna Awardees	
Name	**Year**
Sarbjit Singh	1961
Khushi Ram	1967
Gurdial Singh	1968
Hav. Hari Dutt	1969
Gulam Abbas Moontasir	1970
Man Mohan Singh	1971
S. K. Kataria	1973
Anil Kumar Punj	1974
Hunuman Singh	1975
T. Vijayaragavan	1977/78
Om Prakash	1979/80
Ajmer Singh	1982
Suman Sharma	1983
Radhey Shyam	1991
Sajjan Singh Cheema	1999
Parminder Singh	2001
Satya (Sports)	2003
Ms. Geetu Anna Jose	2014

Dronacharya Awardees	
Name	**Year**
Aparna Ghosh	2002
Ram kumar	2003

Tournaments And Venues

International Tournaments

Men's tournaments

1. Basketball at Olympics
2. FIBA World Championship
3. Euro Basket
4. FIBA American Championship
5. FIBA Asia Championship
6. FIBA Africa Championship

Women's tournaments

1. Women Basketball at Olympics
2. FIBA World Championship
3. Euro Basket
4. FIBA American Championship
5. FIBA Asia Championship
6. FIBA Africa Championship

National Tournaments

1. Federation Cup
2. Senior National Championship
3. Junior National Championship
4. Youth National Championship
5. Sub-Junior National Championship
6. All India Ramu Memorial Trophy
7. C. Munni Swami Cup
8. B.C. Gupta Trophy

Sports Personalities

Indian Personalities	
Hunuman Singh	Radhey Shyam
T. Vijayaragavan	Sajjan Singh Cheema
Om Prakash	Parminder Singh
Ajmer Singh	Satya (Sports)
Suman Sharma	Ms. Geetu Anna Jose
International Personalities	
Michael Jeffrey Jordan	Wilton Norman Chamberlain
Earvin Johnson Jr.	Shaquille Rashaun O'Neal
Kareem Abdul-Jabba	Patrick Aloysius Ewing
Larry Joe Bird	Karl Anthony Malone
Hakeem Abdul Olajuwon	David Maurice Robinson

GENERAL QUESTIONS AND ANSWERS

Q. 1. What are the dimensions of the basketball court ?

Ans. Length 28 m, Breadth 15 m.

Q. 2. What is the area of the basketball court ?

Ans. 4700 m².

Q. 3. What is the radius of the centre circle ?

Ans. 1.80 m.

Q. 4. What is the width of the lines of the basketball court ?

Ans. 0.5 cm.

Q. 5. What is the height of the lower edge of board from the floor ?

Ans. 2.90 m.

Q. 6. What is the thickness of the backboard ?

Ans. 3 cm.

Q. 7. What is the circumference of the ball ?

Ans. 75 to 78 cm.

Q. 8. What is the weight of the ball ?

Ans. 600-650 gm.

Q. 9. What is the air pressure of the ball ?

Ans. 7.5-8.5 pounds.

Q. 10. What is the height of the top edge of the ring from the floor ?

Ans. 3,050 mm.

Q. 11. What is the duration of basketball game ?

Ans. 10 M -2 M (Rest)-10 M-10M (Rest)-10 M-2 M (Rest)-10M.

Q. 12. How many players are there in the basketball teams ?

Ans. 12 (5 players+ 7 substitutes).

Q. 13. What is the number of court players in a team ?

Ans. 5.

Q. 14. How many time-outs can be taken in a match ?

Ans. Two time-outs to each team in first half and 3 times-outs to each team in second half.

Q. 15. What is the duration of a time-out ?

Ans. One minute.

Q. 16. How many kinds of foul are there in basketball game ?

Ans. There are five kind of fouls in basketball game. These are :

(I) Personal Foul (II) Technical Foul (III) Double Foul (IV) Multiple Foul (V) Intentional Foul.

Q. 17. If a player commits 5 fouls in first half, can he play in second half ?

Ans. After committing 5 fouls, the players cannot play in the same match.

Q. 18. What is the method of giving points ?

Ans. A basket beyond 3 points line = 3 points.

A basket from inside the 3 points line=2 points.

A basket by free throw = 1 point.

Q. 19. What is the full form of FIBA ?

Ans. Federation International de Basketball.

Q. 20. What is the full form of BFI ?

Ans. Basketball Federation of India.

Q. 21. Give 5 fundamental skills of basketball ?

Ans. (I) Handling the ball (II) Passing (III) Shooting (IV) Dribbling (V) Pivoting.

Q. 22. What are the 5 major fouls in basketball ?

Ans. (I) Personal Foul   (II) Intentional Foul (III) Double Foul (IV) Multiple Foul (V) Technical Foul.

Q. 23. What do you mean by "three seconds rules"?

Ans. A player shall not remain in the opponents' restricted area for more than three consecutive seconds while his team is in control of a live ball in the frontcourt and the game clock is running.

Q. 24. What do you mean by "five seconds rules" ?

Ans. When a closely guarded player, who is holding the ball, does not pass, shoot, roll or dribble the ball within five seconds, it shall be considered a violation with a side line throw for the opponents.

Q. 25. What do you mean by "twenty four seconds rules" ?

Ans. A team shall attempts a shot within 24 seconds after taking control of the live ball.

Q. 26. Give 5 major international tournaments of basketball conduct under the controlled of FIBA.

Ans. (I) Basketball at Olympics (II) FIBAWorld Championship (III) Euro Basket.

(IV) FIBA American Championship (V) FIBA Asia Championship.

Q. 27. Give 5 major national tournaments of basketball conducted under the control of FBI.

Ans. (I) Federation cup (II) Senior national championship (III) Junior national championship (IV) Youth national championship (V) Sub junior national championship.

Q. 28. What are the different types of passing in basketball ?

Ans. Push pass, bounce pass, baseball pass, hook pass, one handed side pass, and underhand pass.

Q. 29. Who invented the basketball for the first time?

Ans. It was firstly invented by Dr. James Naismith of USA in December, 1891 at Spring Field College.

Q. 30. What is pivoting ?

Ans. It is a very important skill because it helps basketball player to attack or defend himself and his position; a pivot takes place when a player who is holding the ball steps once or more than once in any direction with the same foot, while the other foot called the pivot foot is being kept at its point of contact with the floor.

□□

2.1. INTRODUCTION AND HISTORY

Football which is now commonly known as soccer is one of the most popular game in the world, as well as most spectacular sport. The games is played by two opposing teams, with eleven members each team including the goal keeper. It is played in a rectangular field of specific measurements, each team aiming to score a goal into the opponents goal mouth. The game is primarily played with feet and only the goalkeepers are allowed to touch and handle the ball with hands. The game is of ninety minutes with forty five minutes each half and the team that scores more goals within awarded time is declared as winner.

World History

Football is one of the most important games in the world. It has a vivid and interesting history in the world of sports. The evidence of the game is being alluded that Chinese used to play football in 2nd and 3rd century B.C. by the name of "Tsu chu" which means kicking the ball. Moreover it was also played popularly by Greeks and Romans. The growth of modern football started in England. F.I.F.A. the governing body of football was established in 1904 with its headquarter in Zurich (Switzerland). The first F.I.F.A. world cup was started in the year 1930.

Indian History

Football in India was introduced by British soldiers in mid- nineteenth century and was spread in some parts of the country by forming regimental teams. Durand cup which is India's oldest tournament held (incidentally the third oldest in the world) was founded in 1888. AIFF the governing body of football in India was established in 1937. India participated in Olympics in 1948 and 1956. The year 1951-1962 was considered as golden era of Indian football as India won gold in 1951 and 1962 Asian Games. India qualified for 1950 F.I.F.A. World Cup but failed to participate due to fiscal problem. In 1956 Olympics, India was the first country from Asia to enter the semifinal of football. This achievement was considered as an apex position of Indian football.

2.2. GOVERNING BODY

Fédération Internationale de Football Association (FIFA)

The Fédération Internationale de Football Association (FIFA) is the international governing body of association football, futsal and beach soccer. FIFA is responsible for the organization of Football's major international tournaments, notably the World Cup which commenced in 1930 and the Women's World Cup which commenced in 1991. FIFA was founded in 1904, with its headquarter in Zurich (Switzerland).

All India Football Federation (AIFF)

The All India Football Federation (AIFF) is the organization which manages the game of association football in India. It administers the running of the India national football team and also controls the I League, India's premier domestic club competition, in addition to various other competitions and teams. The AIFF was founded in 1937, gained FIFA affiliation in the year 1948 and A.F.C. affiliation in the year 1954. Currently it has its office at Dwarka, New Delhi.

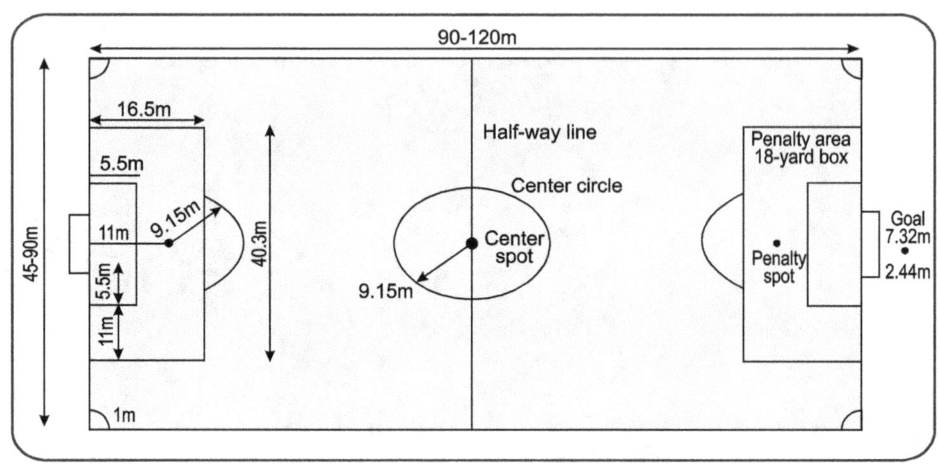

Football Field

2.3. SPECIFICATION, FUNDAMENTAL SKILLS, TERMINOLOGY, GENERAL RULES AND EQUIPMENTS

Football Fields Specification

Shape of the playfield	:	Rectangular
Dimensions of play field		
Length (touch line)	:	Maximum120m
		Minimum 90m
Width (goal line)	:	Maximum 90m
		Minimum 45m
Dimensions of play field in international matches		
Length (touch line)	:	Maximum 110m
		Minimum 100m
Width (goal line)	:	Maximum 75m
		Minimum 64m
Height of goal post	:	2.44m
Width between two goal posts	:	7.32m
Height of corner flag	:	Not less than 1.50m
Radius of corner arc	:	1m
Radius of Centre circle	:	9.15m
Distance from penalty mark to Centre of goal line	:	11m
Distance from corner flag to optional mark	:	9.15m
Shape of the ball	:	Spherical
Circumference of the ball	:	27" to 28" (inches)
Weight of the ball	:	410g to 450g (14 to 16 ounce)
Pressure in the ball should be	:	0.6 to 1.1 atmospheres at sea level
Width of the lines should be	:	12cm (5inch)
Duration of match	:	90 minutes
Duration of half time (interval)	:	Not exceeds 15 minutes
No of officials' for match	:	4 (1 referee, 2 assistant referees, 1 table official)
No of players in each team	:	11 + 7 (extra) = 18 players (as per law book 11 + 12 extra = 23)
Players that can be substituted are	:	3 players
Minimum players required to start the game	:	7 members in each team

Football Field Markings

1. Touch line : Touch Line (length of the field) which is also known as side line is a line as the side of the football field. If the ball goes out of the touch line, the game will be restarted with throw-in.

2. Goal line : Goal Line (width of the field) which is also known as end line, at the end of the pitch. If the ball goes out of the goal line touching the attacker then, the game will restart with goal kick and if the ball goes out touching the defender at the last moment before it crosses the goal line the game will restart with the corner kick.

3. Half way line : Half way line or a center line is the line through the middle of the football field that divides the field into two equal halves.

4. Centre circle : It is a circle that is made in the center of the football field, at the Centre line with radius of 9.15m from the center mark that bounds the opponents from interfering the start of the game at the time of kick off.

5. Centre mark : Centre Mark or the Centre spot is a mark or a spot in the center of the football field, at the middle of the center circle, where the ball is placed during kick-off.

6. Penalty box : Penalty Box, also called a Penalty Area is 16.5 m × 40.32 m area, at each end of the playing field. The foul committed against attacking player inside that area is punishable with the penalty kick.

7. Penalty mark : It is a mark or a spot inside the penalty area at a distance of 11m from the center of the goal line.

8. Penalty arc : Penalty Arc is the semi-circle on the top of the penalty box with its radius of 9.15 m from penalty mark, where no player is allowed to be inside it, during penalty kick, except the penalty kicker and opponent's goalkeeper.

9. Goal box : It is a small area of 5.5m × 18.32m within the penalty box, where goal kick is taken from area anywhere within a goal box.

10. Corner arc : A semi-circle area with radius of 1m, at each corner of the playing pitch is called Corner Arc. It is the area of the arc where the ball is to be placed during the corner kick.

11. Technical area : It is the area of box drawn 1m away from the touch line in front of each team dug out, where only one person at a time is allowed to instruct from.

Fundamentals Skills of Football

Kicking

1. Kicking with inside of the foot
2. Kicking with inside of the instep
3. Kicking with full instep
4. Kicking with outside of instep
5. Kicking with outside of the foot

Receiving

1. Receiving the ball with the inside of the foot
2. Receiving the ball with the full instep (stop volley)
3. Receiving the ball with the outside of the instep
4. Receiving with the sole of the foot
5. Receiving with the heel
6. Receiving with the thigh
7. Receiving with the chest

Heading

1. Heading forward from a stationary position
2. Heading ball with side of the forehead
3. Heading from standing jump off both feet
4. Heading ball after a slight run and from a jump off one foot
5. Heading sideways from stationary position
6. Heading ball from diving header

Dribbling

1. Dribbling with inside of the instep
2. Dribbling with full instep
3. Dribbling with the outside of instep

Tackling

1. Sliding tackle
2. Interception tackling
3. Sideways tackling

Passing

1. Short pass
2. Long pass
3. Through pass

Short description of some of the above mentioned fundamental skills :

Kicking

1. Kicking with inside of the foot : It is a technique of kicking that involves the part of the foot bordered by the base of the big toe, the heel bone and the inner ankle.

2. Kicking with inside of the instep : It is a kicking technique that involves the inner surface of the foot stretching from the base of big toe to the inner part of the ankle or more precisely the part of inner ankle.

3. Kicking with full instep : Technique of kicking that involves the part of foot extending from the base of the toes to the curve of ankle, in other words, the part which is covered by the laced part of the foot.

4. Kicking with outside of instep : Kicking that involves, the part of the foot extending from the outer edge of the full instep to the outer edge of the foot bordered by the base of small toe and stretches almost up to the outside of the ankle.

Receiving

1. Receiving with the thigh : Receiving with the thigh involves, receiving the ball by resting on the standing leg which is bent at knee, while the other leg rising from the hip with the knee bent leading the thigh to be at angle of 50° to 60° to that of the shin, thigh blocking the ball.

2. Receiving with the chest : Technique which involves controlling the aerial ball by contacting the ball with the chest and allowing the ball to fall perpendicularly in front of him to attain a ball possession.

Heading

Heading ball from diving header : A way of heading by which the player heads the ball finding that the only way to reach the ball is to fling himself in a dive to head it from off both feet or sometimes off one foot.

Tackling

Interception tackling : The way of tackling by making a jump ahead of the attacker from behind to head or kick the ball away or take possession of it.

Football Cards

The cards that are used in football are of size same as playing cards, which the referee holds up to indicate serious fouls or any unsporting behavior of the players. The cards that are used in football are of two colors *i.e.,* Yellow and Red cards.

Yellow Card

A player is cautioned and shown the yellow card if he/she commits any of the seven offences given below :

1. Unsporting behavior.

2. Dissent by words or action.

3. Persistent infringements of the laws of the game.

4. Delaying the restart of the play.

5. Failure to respect the required distance when play is restarted with a corner kick, free kick or throw-in.

6. Entering or re-entering the field of play without the referee's permission.

7. Deliberately leaving the field of play without the referee's permission.

A substitute or substituted player is cautioned if he/she commits any of the following three offences-

1. Unsporting behavior

2. Dissent by word or action

3. Delaying the re-start of play

A player who receives two yellow cards is given red card and ejected.

Red Card

A player substitute or substituted player is sent off if he commits any of the seven offences given below:

1. Serious foul play.

2. Violent conduct.

3. Spitting at an opponent or any other person.

4. Denying the opposing team a goal or an obvious goal scoring opportunity by deliberately handling the ball (this does not apply to a goalkeeper within his own penalty area).

5. Denying an obvious goal scoring opportunity to an opponent moving towards the player's goal by offences punishable by a free kick or a penalty kick.

6. Using offensive, insulting or abusive language and/or gesture.

7. Receiving a second caution in the same match.

Player shown a "red card" and sent off may not be replaced during that game (*i.e.,* his team must play a player short for the rest of the game).

A player substitute or substituted player who has been sent off must leave the vicinity of the field of play and the technical area.

Terminology Related to Football

Kick off, goal kick, direct free kick, indirect free kick, corner kick, set play, throw-in, penalty kick, hand ball, passing, dribbling, heading, receiving, shooting, foul, defender, midfielder, striker etc.

Short description of the mentioned terms are given below :

1. Kick off : The method of starting a game or restarting it after each goal, a player passes the ball forward to a teammate from the center spot. The ball must move into the opponent's half of the field.

2. Goal kick : Kick made from inside the goal area away from the goal. A goal kick is awarded to the defending team when a ball crosses the goal line that was last touched by a player of the attacking team.

3. Direct free kick : A free kick that is taken from any of the areas outside the penalty box and can be kicked directly or indirectly to score a goal.

4. Indirect free kick : A free kick which cannot be scored directly and can score only if the ball touches the other player.

5. Corner kick : A method of putting the ball into play after it has crossed the end line and was last touched by a member of the defending team. A kick is to be started from within corner arc.

6. Set play : It is a planned strategy that a team uses when a game is to be restarted with a free kick, penalty kick, corner kick, goal kick and throw-in.

7. Throw-in : It is a method of restarting play after the ball has traveled outside the touchline. The ball must be held with two hands and released directly over the head while both feet are touching the ground.

8. Penalty kick : A kick that is taken from a penalty mark in case a foul committed by a defending player towards attacker inside the penalty box. A penalty kick is awarded to attacking team.

9. Hand ball : This term means deliberate handling of a ball by a player other than the goal-keeper in the Penalty Area. This is considered as a deliberate action by the player and is penalized normally if there is movement of the hand towards the ball.

10. Passing : When a player kicks the ball to his teammate to keep the ball in possession and away from an opponent or to give the ball to a player who is in a better position to score.

11. Dribbling : Skill of advancing and controlling the ball close to the feet while playing.

12. Heading : The way of controlling, clearance or scoring the goal with the head.

13. Receiving : The way of controlling the coming ball with the feet, head, chest, thigh etc.

14. Shooting : When a player kicks the ball towards opponent's net in an attempt to score a goal.

15. Foul : The violation of the rules. In response to a foul, a referee calls for a direct free kick, an indirect free kick or penalty kick in case a foul is committed within penalty box.

16. Defender : A player who functions primarily in the defensive third of the field and whose major role is to repel attacks on the goal by the opposing team.

17. Mid fielder : Player who functions primarily in the central (neutral) third of the field and whose principal job is to link the defense and the attack through ball control and passing.

18. Strikers : Players who function primarily in an attacking third of an opponent, to score a goal.

Latest General Rules of Football

1. Goal keeper can move on the goal line at the time of penalty kick; earlier the goal keeper was not allowed to do so until the execution of penalty kick.

2. Now the golden goal rule is not applied, instead of it, extra time of two halves (15 minutes-15 minutes) is given to the teams to decide the winner if the match remains draw in normal time of 45 minutes - 45 minutes and if the match still remains draw in extra time the penalty shoot takes place.

New Amendments in the Rules of Football

1. Where head covers are worn, they must—

   (a) Be black or of the same main colour as the jersey (provided that the players of the same team wear the same colour).

   (b) Be in keeping with the professional appearance of the players equipments.

   (c) Not be attached to the jersey.

   (d) Not pose any danger to the player wearing it or any other player (*e.g.,* opening/closing mechanism around neck).

   (e) Not have any parts extending out from the surface (protruding elements).

2. Now there can be 23 players instead of 18 players, out of these, 12 players are called substitute players *i.e.,* 11 players and 12 substitutes. Where as only 3 players can be substituted from 12 substitute players.

Necessary Equipment's

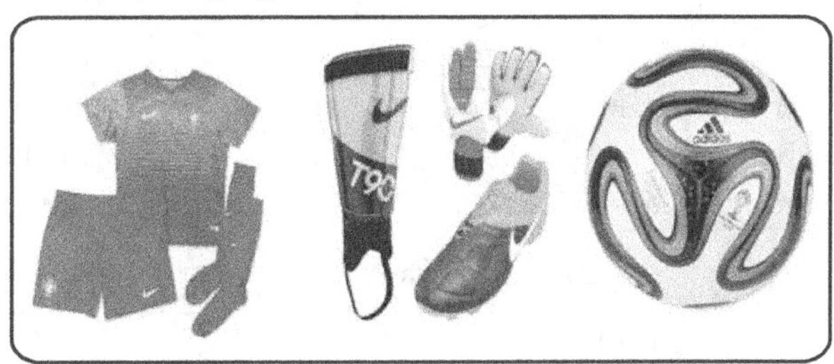

1. Football cleats/football shoes
2. Stockings/ football socks
3. Shin guard
4. Jersey
5. Shorts
6. Goalie apparel (jersey, shorts and pants)
7. Goal keeper gloves
8. Football
9. Supporters & cups
10. Head gear

2.4. SPORTS AWARDS, TOURNAMENTS AND VENUES AND SPORTS PERSONALITIES

Sports Awards

Arjuna Awardees	
Name	**Year**
P. K. Banerjee	1961
Tulsidas Balaram	1962
Chuni Goswami	1963
Jarnail Singh	1964
ArunLal Ghosh	1965
Yusuf Khan	1966
Peter Thangaraj	1967
Inder Singh	1969
Syed Naeemuddin	1970
C. P. Singh	1971
Magan Singh	1973
Gurdev Singh Gill	1978-79
Prasun Banerjee	1979-80
Mohammed Habib	1980-81
Sudhir Karmakar	1981
Shanti Mullick	1983
S. Bhattacharjee	1989
Brahmanand Sankhwalkar	1997
Baichung Bhutia	1998
I. M. Vijayan	2002
Deepak Kumar Mandal	2003
Deepak Kumar Mondal	2010
Sunil Chettri	2011
Padmashri Awardees	
Gostha Paul	1962
Sailen Manna	1971
Chuni Goshwami	1983
P.K. Banarjee	1990
Baichung Bhutia	2008
Dronacharya Awardee	
Sayed Nayeemuddin	1990

Tournaments and Venues
International Football Tournaments

1. Soccer Champions League
2. UEFA Cup
3. UEFA European League
4. F.I.F.A. World Cup
5. European Championship
6. European Championships Women
7. CONCACAF Champions League
8. Dubai Cup
9. Confederations Cup
10. Copa America
11. AFC Champions League

National Football Tournaments

1. Indian Super League
2. I-League
3. I-League 2nd Division
4. Calcutta Football League
5. Youth League
6. Federation Cup
7. Durand Cup
8. Santosh Trophy
9. Indian Super Cup

National Venues

1. Salt Lake Stadium, Kolkata (West Bengal)
2. Jawaharlal Nehru Stadium, Kochi (Kerala)
3. Gurunanak Stadium, Ludhiana (Punjab)
4. Indira Gandhi Stadium, Guwahati (Assam)
5. Kanchenjunga Stadium, Siliguri, (West Bengal)

International Venues

1. Old Trafford, Manchester (England)
2. San Sairo, Milan (Italy)
3. Olyampiastadion, Berlin (Germany)
4. EstadioAzteea, Mexico City (Mexico)
5. Millennium Stadium, Cardiff (Wales).

Sports Personalities

Indian Personalities	
Baichung Bhutia	I.M. Vijayan
Sunil Chhetri	Subrata Pal
Jibon Singh	Jeje Lalpekhlum
Peter Thangaraj	Giurmangi Singh
Gostha Pal	Renedy Singh

International Personalities	
1.	Lionel Messi (Argentina and Barcelona)
2.	Cristiano Ronaldo (Portugal and Real Madrid)
3.	Luiz Suarez (Uruguay and Barcelona)
4.	Andres Iniesta (Spain and Barcelona)
5.	Yaya Toure (Ivory Coast andManchester City)
6.	Gareth Bale (Wales and Real Madrid)
7.	Phillip Lahm (Germany and Bayern Munich)
8.	Arjen Robben (Netherland and Bayern Munich)
9.	Robin Van Persie (Netherland and Manchester United)
10.	Zlatan Ibrahimovic (Sweden and Paris saint German)

GENERAL QUESTIONS AND ANSWERS

Q. 1. What is the dimension of football field in international matches ?

Ans. Length: 100-110 m, Width: 64-75m.

Q. 2. What is the height of the goal post ?

Ans. 2.44 m.

Q. 3. What is the width between the two goal posts in the goal line ?

Ans. 7.32 m.

Q. 4. What should be the height of corner flag ?

Ans. It should not be less than 1.50 m.

Q. 5. What is the circumference of the ball ?

Ans. 27 to 28 inches.

Q. 6. What should be the weight of the ball ?

Ans. 410 gm to 450 gm (14 to 16 ounces).

Q. 7. What should be the pressure in the ball ?

Ans. 0.6 to 1.1 atmosphere pressure.

Q. 8. What should be the width of the lines of markings in football field ?

Ans. 12 cm (5 inches).

Q. 9. In which year was the governing body of football F.I.F.A established ?

Ans. 1904.

Q. 10. What is the full form of F.I.F.A ?

Ans. Federation International De Football Association.

Q. 11. When was the first F.I.F.A. world cup started?

Ans. 1930.

Q. 12. When was A.I.F.F. established ?

Ans. 1937.

Q. 13. What is the full form of A.I.F.F ?

Ans. All India Football Federation.

Q. 14. Where is the Headquarter of F.I.F.A ?

Ans. Zurich, Switzerland.

Q. 15. Where is the office of A.I.F.F ?

Ans. Dwarka, New Delhi.

Q. 16. In which year did A.I.F.F. get its affiliation from F.I.F.A ?

Ans. 1948.

Q. 17. What is the shape of football field ?

Ans. Rectangular.

Q. 18. What should be the duration of Half Time Interval ?

Ans. It should not exceed 15 minutes.

Q. 19. What should be the minimum number of players in each team to start the game ?

Ans. 7 players.

Q. 20. Who is the one and only Dronacharya Awardee in football till date ?

Ans. Sayed Nayeemuddin.

❐❐

3.1. INTRODUCTION AND HISTORY

Kabaddi is a popular team sport, which needs skill and power, and conflates the characteristics of wrestling and rugby. The objective of the game is for a single player on offence, referred to as a "raider", to run into the opposing team's half of a court, tag out as many of their defenders as possible, and return to their own half of the court, all without being tackled by the defenders, and in a single breath. It is popular in South Asia and other surrounding Asian countries. The game is known by numerous names in different parts of South Asia.

History and Game

Earlier times it was used not only as an entertaining game but also was used to build physical strength and stamina needed to deal with the day to day work. They used it as a self-defensive tool. A hint about the existence of the game far behind from the pre historic time can be seen nowhere else but in great Hindu mythology Mahabharata, where Abhimanyu's Chkrabyuha Trap and his defense against that was itself self-explanatory. There are also accounts of Gautama Buddha having played the game recreationally.

In the year 1918, kabaddi was given national game status. All rules and regulations were also formulated in the same year but officially implemented after 1923 but it took quite a long time (1938) to be introduced into Indian Olympics. After being demonstrated again at the 1982 Asian Games in Delhi, Kabaddi was added to the Asian Games' programme beginning in 1990.

3.2. GOVERNING BODIES

All India Kabaddi Federation (AIKF)

To increase the popularity of kabaddi as a sport in India, All India Kabaddi Federation (AIKF), was founded in 1950. Since, its establishment, the AIKF has been working towards improving the standards of the game. For this purpose, it conducts National level kabaddi championships regularly since 1952, as per the rules and regulations. The first men's national tournament was organized in Madras (Chennai) and the first women's national tournament was held in Calcutta (Kolkata).

The Asian Amateur Kabaddi Federation (AAKF)

The Asian Amateur Kabaddi Federation (AAKF) was formed in the year 1978. The 1st Asian Kabaddi Championship was held in the year 1980 and included as a demonstration game in the 9th Asian Games, New Delhi in the year 1982. The game was included as a regular sports discipline in the 11th Beijing Asian Games.

Amateur Kabaddi Federation of India (AKFI)

The Amateur Kabaddi Federation of India (AKFI) is the central institution to administrate and promote Kabaddi in India. It was established in 1973. Mr Janardhan Singh Gehlot is the current AKFI President. He is also the president of the Asian Amateur Kabaddi Federation (AAKF) and the International Kabaddi Federation (IKF).

3.3. SPECIFICATION, BASIC RULES, FUNDAMENTAL SKILLS AND TERMINOLOGY

The Court

The court measures 13 meter length and 10 meter wide. A mid line is drawn in the court, splitting into two halves. The depth of the court is 1 foot in which sand is filled by removing mud.

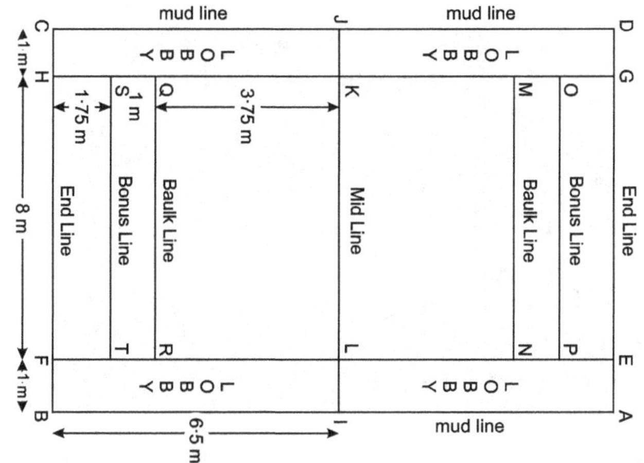

Marking of Lines

In the 13 × 10 meter playground, the outer lines, known as Boundary lines, are marked with coloured sands. Playing areas are marked with one meter space from each side of the 10 meters boundary line.

To separate the territory of each team, a middle line is drawn in such a fashion that it divides the whole court in to two equal 6.5 × 8 metre sections. The position of baulk lines can clearly be seen from the above picture. They are positioned at a distance of 3.75 meters on the either side of the middle line. On the either side of the middle line, bonus lines are drawn which are present at a distance of 1 metre from it.

Rules

1. It is a seven a side game where one player from one side chants "*kabaddi…kabaddi..kabaddi..*" and enter's the opposition's half and tries to touch at least one player of the opposition so, that he can go back to his own half safely.

2. On the other hand, all of the seven players try to stop that opposition player to go back to his half safely by trying to grab him and keep him under their control till he loses his breath.

3. If a player touches the opposition player and returns to his half safely then not only the player whom he has touched is out but he can make a player alive from his own side who had been out before him, just in case.

Fundamental Skills

Raiding

After winning the toss, the team takes turn and sends players, often known as raiders into opponent team's sections. The sole aim of the raider is to tag the members of the opposite team and run back into his team side. Each player he touches on the opponent's side gives his team one point. The team with the maximum score at the end is declared as winner.

1. Kabaddi – If a match end in a tie, then two 5 minutes durations are given.
2. If the tie still exists after (20 + 20 + 5 + 5) 50 minutes of play, then the team that
3. Scored first will be declared the winner.

Raid Mechanisms

The attacking style is known as raid mechanism. One difficult thing in kabaddi is that the raider will be one, while the defender will be many. So, the raider must have skilled tactics to tag the opponents and come back safely towards the middle line. The whole game of kabaddi can be changed in couple of minutes with the help of few good raiders. Therefore. it is utmost necessary to understand the raiding mechanism very carefully. The raiding depends upon number of factors. Some of the important ones are:

1. Entry
2. Cant
3. Footwork
4. Settling path of attack
5. Tactics
6. Retreat

Cant

The most unique feature of kabaddi is its cant. Beginners often find themselves in difficult position in doing this. The rule says you have to chant the word "kabaddi" as soon as you enter the defending zone and should continue till you come back to your side by crossing the middle line. If the player fails in this at any moment during his raid, he will be out of the match. So, indirectly the duration of cant can be used as an Imeasurement tool of kabaddi.

Entry

A raider can use right, left, or central zone for his entry into the court. However; his entry depends upon the following factors very strongly:

1. The position of the raider at the time of his act as team's defense system.
2. The direction of attacking side
3. His moving direction

Footwork

The movement of the foot of the raider during his raid is most important. The footwork however depends upon the following factors:

1. Position of the body
2. Stance of the raider
3. Speed with which he moves
4. Agility
5. Style of movement

Necessary Skills

A man needs skills to have mastery upon techniques. Some touches that are legal in kabaddi are :

1. Foot touch
2. Toe touch
3. Thrust
4. Squat leg
5. Kicks
6. Touching of hand through upper limbs

Defense

You should not tag yourself by the raider. Doing such will fetch a point to the raider's team. To avoid yourself from being tagged, you should run as far as possible from the raider, till he becomes breathless of saying "Kabaddi". If he tags you, wait till the raider becomes breathless and as soon as the raider stops saying kabaddi, grab him with your team mates before he touches the middle line. You cannot pull the cloths or hairs of the raider. Rather you can grab him only at his limb or torso.

3.4. SPORTS AWARDS AND TOURNAMENTS

Tournaments

International

1. Asian Games
2. World Cup
3. SAFGames

Domestic

1. Pro Kabaddi League
2. National Games

Awards

Padma Shri		
Year of Award	Name of Recipient	State
2014	Ms. Sunil Dabas	Haryana
2019	Mr. Ajay Thakur	Himachal Pradesh

Dhyanchand Award Winners of Kabaddi		
Year of Award	Name of Recipient	State
2007	Mr. Shamsher Singh	Haryana

Dronacharya Award Winners of Kabaddi		
Year of Award	Name of Recipient	State
2002	Mr. Ejjapureddi Prasad Rao	Andhra Pradesh
2005	Mr. Balwan Singh	Services
2012	Ms. Sunil Dabas	Haryana

Arjun Award Winners of Kabaddi		
Year of Award	Name of Recipient	State
2001	Mr. B.C. Ramesh	Karnataka
2002	Mr. Ram Mehar Singh	SSCB
2003	Mr. Sanjeev Kumar	Indian Railway
2004	Mr. Sunder Singh	Delhi
2005	Mr. Ramesh Kumar	Haryana
2006	Mr. Navneet Gautam	Rajasthan
2009	Mr. Pankaj Navnath Shirsat	Maharashtra
2010	Mr. Dinesh Kumar	Delhi

2011	Mr. Rakesh Kumar	Indian Railway
2011	Ms. Tejeswini Bai V	Indian Railway
2012	Mr. Anoop Kumar	Delhi
2014	Ms. Mamtha Poojari	Indian Railway

2015	Mr. Manjeet Chhillar	Indian Railway
2015	Mr. Abhilasha Shashikant Mahatre	Indian Railway
2017	Mr. Jasvir Singh	ONGC

GENERAL QUESTIONS AND ANSWERS

Q. 1. How Many Players are there in a team ?

Ans. A team consist of 12 players including 5 substitutes.

Q. 2. What is the measurement of Court ?

Ans. The court measures 13 meter length and 10 meter wide.

Q. 3. What is Cant ?

Ans. The continuous clear sounding recitation of the approved word "kabbadi" within the course of one respiration is called cant.

Q. 4. How are players revived in the game?

Ans. A player or players can be revived in the same order as they were out when one or more opponents are out.

Q. 5. If both teams have equal points after the second half, will extra time be given to them?

Ans. Yes, if a match end in a tie, then two 5 minutes durations are given.

Q. 6. How many Players can be substituted for injury?

Ans. Only five players can be substituted.

Q. 7. Can a player be caught by head only?

Ans. No, a player can be caught by trunk and limbs.

Q. 8. Name some necessary skills for raider.

Ans. Some necessary skills for raider are foot touch, toe touch, thrust, squat leg, kicks, touching of hand through upper limbs.

Q. 9. Why a raider must start his cant before entering the opponents's court?

Ans. Yes, a raider must start his cant before entering the opponents's court. If he fails to do so he will lose his chance to raid.

Q. 10. How many players are necessary to start the game?

Ans. A team cannot start a game with less than five players.

Q. 11. In how many ways a raider can choose his entry in the court?

Ans. Raider can use right, left and central zone for his entry in the court.

Q. 12. Which line divides the whole court in to two equal section?

Ans. Middle line.

Q. 13. What is the measurement of middle line?

Ans. 6.5×8 metre.

Q. 14. Name some Arjun Awardees.

Ans. Mr. Abhilasha Shashikant Mahatre, Mr. Jasvir Singh, Mr. Manjeet Chhillar.

Q. 15. Name some persons related to kabbadi who won Dronacharya Award.

Ans. Ms. Sunil Dabas, Mr. Balwan Singh, Mr. Ejjapureddi Prasad Rao.

❑❑

KHO-KHO

4

4.1. INTRODUCTION AND HISTORY

Kho-Kho is a popular Indian team game. It is played by twelve players as team but only 9 players of the team enter the field who try to avoid being touched by members of the opposing team. One team becomes the chasers and the other is the runners. The chaser pursues the runners; to make them out, the chasers tag and touches the runners. A standard match consists of two innings with each team chasing and defending. Each inning consists of chasing and running for 9 minutes each. The team that takes the shortest time to tag the entire opponents will be the winner.

History and the Game

The beginning of Kho-Kho is hard to sketch, however numerous historians consider, that it is a modified variety of 'Run Chase', which involves chasing and touching a person. The game was originated in Poona (Maharashtra). The recognition and growth of this game has been linked with the advancement of Akharas and Vyayamshalas in Maharastra. The modern form of this game is provided by Hanuman Vyayam Pracharak Mandal, Baroda. In the beginning of the 20th century the rules of the game were framed. To frame its rules, a Committee was formed in 1914, at Gymkhana, Poona. In 1924, the first rules on Kho-Kho were published from Gymkhana, Baroda. In 1959-60, in Vijayawada (Andhra Pradesh), the first national Kho-Kho championship was organized.

4.2. GOVERNING BODIES

Kho-Kho Federation of India (KKFI)

KKFI is the administrative and controlling body of India which was formed in the year 1960.

Main Tips At a Glance			
Shape of the play field	= Rectangular	**Square (sitting area)**	
Dimensions of the court		Number of square in each lane	= 8
Length of the playfield for men	= 29 m	Dimension of square	= 30 cm × 30 cm
Breadth of the playfield for men	= 16 m	**Measurement of post**	
Length of the playfield for women & junior	= 27 m	Height of the post	= 1.20 m (120cm)
Breadth of the playfield for women & junior	= 16 m	Circumference of the post	= 30 cm to 40 cm
Total area including lobby	= 33 m × 21 m	Distance between the posts	= 23.50 m
Free zone	= 2.75 m × 16 m	**Playing time or duration of play**	
Centre lane	= 23.50 m × 30 cm	For men and women per innings	= 9 minutes
Cross lane	= 16 m × 30 cm	Interval	= 5 minutes
Distance between last line And 1st cross line	= 2.50 m	Total innings	= 4 (2 innings for each team)
		Players	
Each court divided by the Centre line	= 7.85 m	Total number of players in a team	= 12
		Court players	= 9
		Substitute players	= 3
Lobby	= 2 m	**Officials**	= 5
		(a) Umpires- 2 (b) Timekeeper-1 (c) Scorekeeper-1 (d) Referee-1	

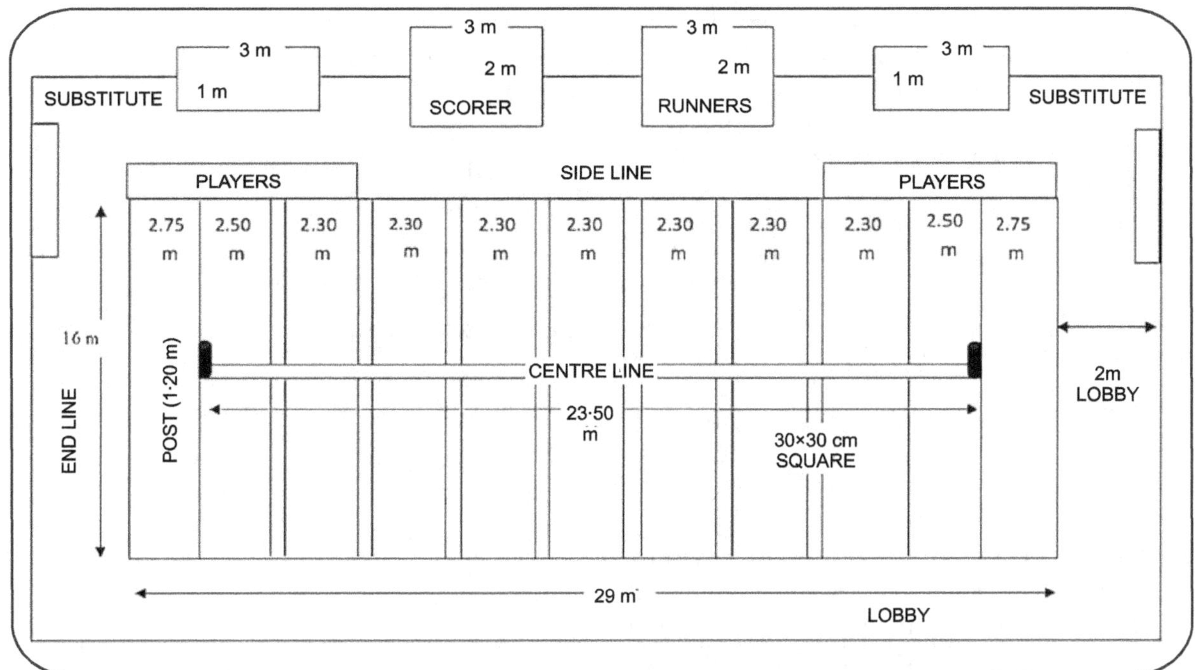

Asian Kho-Kho Federation (AKKF)

AKKF was established in the year 1987 during 3rd SAF Games, held at Kolkata, India. The member countries were India, Bangladesh, Pakistan, Sri Lanka, Nepal and Maldives.

4.3. SPECIFICATION, BASIC RULES, FUNDAMENTAL SKILLS AND TERMINOLOGY

Kho-Kho Field Marking

1. Posts : Two strong wooden posts, smooth all over 120 to 125 cm above and perpendicular to the ground are known as posts. The posts shall not taper and the top of the posts shall be free from any sharp edges.

2. Central lane : Central lane is a rectangle in between two posts measuring 30 cms × length of the court which divides the court into two equal halves and forms squares at the intersection of cross lanes.

3. Cross lane : Each of the rectangles measuring 30 cm × width of the court that intersects the central lane at right angle is known as cross lane.

4. Square : The area 30 cm × 30 cm formed by the intersection of the central lane and the cross lane is known as a square.

5. Free zone : The remaining portion of the field on either end of the court is known as free zone.

6. Lobby : The area surrounding the field is known as lobby.

Basic Rules of The Game

1. The play ground (Field) should be rectangular in shaped.

2. Referee shall call both the captains for the spin of the coin (Toss).

3. The winner captain tells the referee whether he/she has opted to be 'chaser' or 'runner'.

4. The scorer will record which team is runner and chaser in the score sheet.

5. Crossing/touching of central lane by any part of the body except note is an offence. It shall be treated as Foul.

Attacker Rules

1. If a Kho is to be given, it shall be given from behind a Chaser. It shall be given in a sufficiently loud tone so that the Defenders and the officials can hear. The Chaser shall not get up without getting a Kho.

2. After giving a Kho, an Attacker shall chase to be so and shall sit down immediately in the Square of the Chaser to whom he has given a Kho.

3. After getting a Kho, Chaser will immediately be an Attacker and shall go to the half that he/she is facing and shall go in the direction which he/she has taken by going the Cross Lane or turning his/her shoulder towards any of the Posts.

4. An Attacker shall take the direction according to one of the actions, whichever he/she has performed first.

5. An Attacker shall take the direction to which he turns his/her Shoulder Line. When Attacker, while going in a particular direction, turns his/her shoulder line through more than a right angle to the direction which he/she has already taken, it shall be a Foul.

6. Once, an Attacker has taken a direction, he/she shall go in that direction till he reaches the Free Zone unless he gives a Kho before that. An Attacker shall not go to the other half of the court unless he/she turns around the Post through the Free Zone.

7. If an Attacker leaves the Free Zone, he/she shall go in the direction of the other Free Zone, remaining on that half of the Court where he/she was, when he/she left the Free Zone.

8. The rules about taking the direction and receding shall not be applicable in the Free Zone.

9. The chaser shall sit in a manner which shall not obstruct the Defenders. If a defender becomes out by such an obstruction, he/she shall not be declared out.

Runner Rules

1. The runner must be careful while running so that he should not touch any part of the body of a chaser. If so done, he will get a warning and the double faults shall rule him out.

2. A runner should not touch the boundary line otherwise players shall be 'ruled out'.

3. The runner should enter the field with a batches of three players each according to the order of entries

4. The runner batches should enter the field before the 'Kho'.

Latest Rules

1. Now, the length and breadth of kho-kho court is 29 m × 16 m.

2. Pole to pole distance is 23.50 m.

3. Each team plays for 9 minutes instead of 7 × 1/2 minutes.

4. If three runners are made out, consecutively by an active chaser, he cannot touch the forth runner; he will have to kho to any sitting chaser.

5. Sitting chaser is not allowed to create any obstruction in the way of runners. If any runner is touched by an active chaser due to such obstruction, the runner will not be considered out.

6. A toss of coin should decide the right to choose chasing or defending.

7. When the turn starts, a chaser should not leave the square without getting a 'kho'.

8. Once, all the runners are out before time, they send their runners again in the same order.

9. A 'Kho' by a chaser should be given from behind a sitting chaser loudly.

10. After giving Kho, an active chaser should sit immediately on the vacated square.

Equipment Needed to Conduct the Match

The equipments used in Kho-Kho are as follows:

1. Posts
2. Strings
3. Measuring tape (metallic)
4. Lime powder
5. Wire nails
6. Two watches
7. Score sheets and stationery to write results etc.

Penalties

1. For a minor offence, such as talking to opponents, spectators or officials, shouting, etc., a verbal warning will be given by the Referee. In case of repetition of the offence, warning will be given by showing a yellow card.

2. For a serious offence, Referee may disqualify the concerned players and others from rest of the match by showing a red card.

Fundamental Skills of Kho-Kho

1. Chasing Skills
   (a) Giving Kho   (b) Tapping
   (c) Diving   (d) Taking Direction
   (e) Turning Round the Pole
   (f) Fake Kho   (g) Sudden Change
   (h) Trapping   (i) Late Kho

2. Running Skills
   (a) Position on the Court
   (b) Running
   (c) Avoiding Trapping
   (d) Positioning near the Post
   (e) Dodging
   (i) Front Dodge
   (ii) Back Dodge
   (iii) Round the post dodge

The brief explanation of some of the fundamental skills is given below :

Chasing Skills

1. Giving kho : To chase a defender by saying the word "Kho" when touching the sitting chaser.

2. Pole turning : To turn the pole in continuation of attack.

3. Covering on cross lane : To cover the defender on cross lane.

4. Pole drive : Taking support of pole and touching the defender.

5. Taking direction : Simultaneously taking the direction with his/her first step out of the cross lane after receiving the kho from the active chaser.

6. Tapping : Touching an active runner by extending an arm.

7. Trapping : Active chaser tries to bring two or three runners to one side or towards the post.

8. Diving : A chaser pounces on an active runner to touch the runners spontaneously.

Terminology Related to Kho-Kho

1. Chasers : The players who chase the opponents with a view to put out them and at the same time score points are known as chasers.

2. Attacker : A player who pursues the players of the opposite side *i.e.,* defenders with a view to tag and touch them is known as an attacker.

3. Runners : The players of the side other than the Chasers are known as runners.

4. Defenders : The runners who are inside the field for their turn of defence are known as defenders.

5. Active chaser : Player who persuades the runners to put them out.

6. Advance kho : Running ahead of defender and dropping Kho.

7. Deceptive kho : Kho to deceive defender by different body movement.

4.4. SPORTS PERSONALITIES, TOURNAMENTS AND SPORTS AWARDS

Sports Personalities

1. N. C. Sarolkar
2. Usha Vasant Nagarkar
3. Shreerang J. Inamadar
4. SR. Dharwadkar
5. Km. Sushma Sarolkar
6. Shri. M. Takalkar
7. Km. Veena Narayan Parab
8. Shri S. Prakash
9. Km. S. B. Kulkarni
10. Ms. Shoba Narayan

Important Tournaments

1. Federation Cup
2. Nehru Gold Cup
3. National Kho-Kho Championship
4. Inter University Championship
5. Senior National Championship
6. Asian Championship
7. Junior National Kho-Kho Championship

Sports Awards

Arjuna Awardees	
Name	**Year**
Shri Sudhir B. Parab	1970
Km. Achala Suberao Devra	1971
Km. B. H. Parikh	1973
Km. N. C. Sarolkar	1974
Km. Usha Vasant Nagarkar	1975
Shreerang J. Inamadar	1975
S. R. Dharwadkar	1976
Km. Sushma Sarolkar	1981
Shri. M. Takalkar	1981
Km. Veena Narayan Parab	1983
Shri S. Prakash	1984
Km. S. B. Kulkarni	1985
Ms. Shoba Narayan	1998
Dronacharya Awardee	
Phadke Gopal Purushottam	2000

GENERAL QUESTIONS AND ANSWERS

Q. 1. What are the dimensions of Kho-Kho field ?

Ans. 29 m × 16 m.

Q. 2. What is the length and breadth of women and junior Kho-Kho field ?

Ans. 27 m × 16 m.

Q. 3. What is the full form of KKFI ?

Ans. Kho-Kho Federation of India.

Q. 4. What is the full form of AKKF ?

Ans. Asian Kho-Kho Federation.

Q. 5. When was the Kho-Kho Federation of India formed ?

Ans. 1960.

Q. 6. What is the height of the pole ?

Ans. 1.20 m.

Q. 7. What is the circumference of the poles ?

Ans. 30 to 40 cm.

Q. 8. What is the dimension of the square ?

Ans. 30 cm × 30 cm.

Q. 9. What is the total area of playfield including lobby ?

Ans. 33 m × 21 m.

Q. 10. What is the dimension of free zone ?

Ans. 2.25 m × 16 m.

Q. 11. How many squares are there in the field ?

Ans. 8.

Q. 12. What is the duration of the Kho-Kho match for men and women ?

Ans. 9 minutes × 2 innings each team.

Q. 13. How many innings are there in the Kho-Kho match ?

Ans. 4 (2 innings for each team).

Q. 14. How many officials are required to conduct a Kho-Kho match ?

Ans. 1. Umpires-2 2. Timekeeper-1 3. Scorekeeper-1 4. Referee-1.

Q. 15. How many cards are there in the Kho-Kho ?

Ans. 2 (yellow card and red card).

Q. 16. Mention the five basic equipments needed to conduct the match.

Ans. Posts, Strings, Measuring tape (metallic), Lime powder, Wire nails.

Q. 17. What is diving ?

Ans. If a chaser, pounces on an active runner to touch the runners spontaneously.

Q. 18. Mention five fundamental skills used in Kho-Kho.

Ans. 1. Dodging 2. Diving 3. Trapping 4. Running and 5. Tapping.

Q. 19. Give three important tournaments of the game Kho-Kho ?

Ans. Federation Cup, Nehru Gold Cup and National Kho-Kho Championship.

Q. 20. What is deceptive Kho ?

Ans. Deceptive Kho is to deceive defender by different body movement.

Q. 21. Mention five Arjun awardees of the game Kho-Kho ?

Ans. Shri M. Takalkar, Veena Narayan Parab, S. Prakash, S. B. Kulkarni and Shoba Narayan

Q. 22. Is the player considered out, if his feet are outside the court ?

Ans. Yes, he/she will be considered out.

Q. 23. What do you understand by the term "tapping" ?

Ans. If a chaser tries to touch an active runner by extending his or her arm.

Q. 24. How many court players are there in Kho-Kho field ?

Ans. 9.

Q. 25. Who are called chasers ?

Ans. The players who chase the opponents with a view to put out them and at the same time score points are known as chasers.

❏❏

5.1. INTRODUCTION AND HISTORY

Volleyball is a team sport in which two teams of six players each are separated by a net. Each team tries to score points by grounding a ball on the other team's court under organized rules. A player on one of the teams begins a 'rally' by serving the ball (tossing or releasing it and then hitting it with a hand or arm), from behind the back boundary line of the court, over the net, and into the receiving team's court. The receiving team must not let the ball be grounded within their court. The team may touch the ball up to 3 times but individual players may not touch the ball twice consecutively. The rally continues, with each team allowed as many as three consecutive touches, until either, a team makes a kill, grounding the ball on the opponent's court and winning the rally or a team commits a fault and loses the rally. The team that wins the rally is awarded a point, and serves the ball to start the next rally.

World History

Volleyball has come a long way from the dusty old YMCA gymnasium of Holyoke, Massachusetts, USA, where the visionary, William G. Morgan, a physical education director, invented the sport back in 1895 called Mintonette. After an observer, Alfred Halstead, noticed the volleying nature of the game at its first exhibition match in 1896, played at the International YMCA Training School, the game quickly became known as volleyball. Volleyball is now one of the big five international sports, and the FIVB, with its 220 affiliated national federations, is the largest international sporting federation in the world.

Indian History

The Y.M.C.A. College of Physical Education in Madras (now Chennai) first began training its students in the sport, which eventually spread to other parts of the country. Initially, the game was managed by Indian Olympic Association and the Interstate Volleyball Championship was conducted every 2 years, between the years 1936 and 1950. At the time, the Championship was organized for male players only. In the year 1951, the Volleyball Federation of India was established and since then the national team has participated in several international championships like Asian Championship, Commonwealth Games, and Asian Games etc. After Indian independence, the first Indian National Championship was organized in 1952 at Chennai. The game was thereupon organized for both men and women. The Indian Volleyball team won Gold medal in 1955, at the Invitation Asian Meet held at Japan.

5.2. GOVERNING BODY

Fédération Internationale de Volleyball (FIVB)

The Federation Internationale de Volleyball (International Federation of Volleyball), commonly known by the acronym FIVB, is the international governing body for the sports of indoor, beach and grass volleyball with activities involving worldwide planning and organization of volleyball events, sometimes in conjunction with other international governing bodies such as the IOC. It was founded in the year 1947, with it's headquarter located at Lausanne, Switzerland.

Volleyball Federation of India (VFI)

The Volleyball Federation of India, commonly known by the acronym VFI is the governing body of volleyball in India. It organizes various competitions of volleyball in the country. It was formed in 1951.

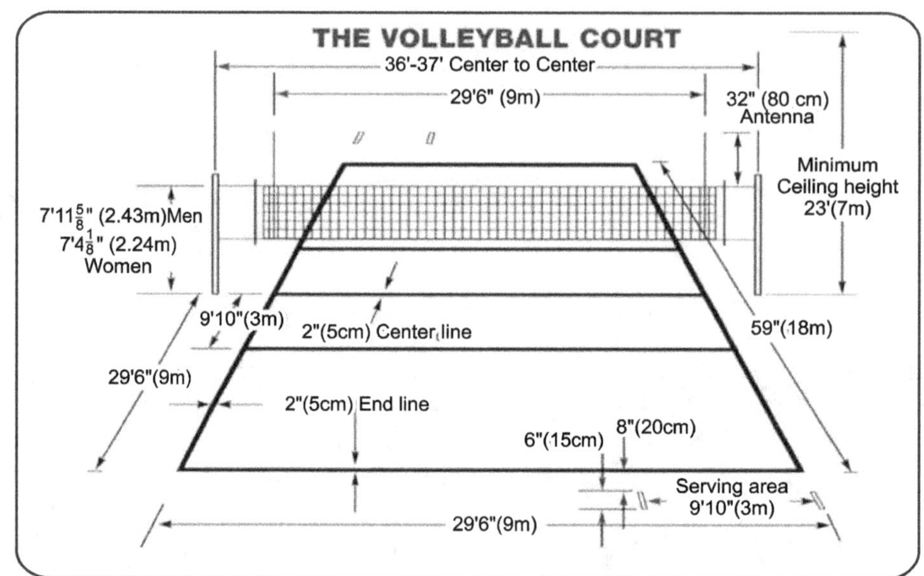

5.3. SPECIFICATION, FUNDAMENTAL SKILLS, TERMINOLOGY AND GENERAL RULES

Volleyball Court Markings

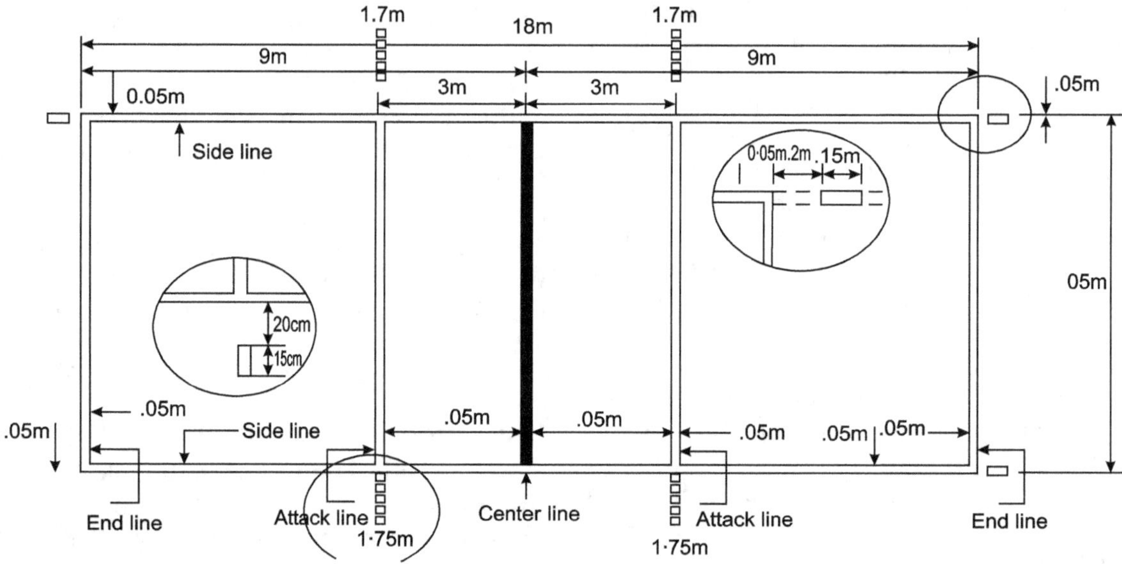

1. **Center line :** It is a line below the net and between the posts that divides the court into two equal halves.
2. **Front zone :** It is the area from center line to the attacking line from where the attackers spike the ball.
3. **Attacking line :** It is a line between the center line and the end line which is of 3 m from the center line and 6m from the end line, that divides 9 × 9 m court into front and back zones.
4. **Back zone :** It is the area from attacking line to the end line or 6 × 9 m area.
5. **Service zone :** It is the area outside the end line from where the player serves the ball.
6. **End line :** It is a line of 9 m at the end of the court that connects both the side lines of the court.
7. **Side line :** It is a line of 18 m at both the sides of the court which with its connection with end lines seems the complete volleyball court.

Volleyball Specifications

Dimensions of volleyball court	:	18 m × 9 m
Width of the lines	:	5 cm
Dimensions of the net	:	9.50 m × 1 m
Horizontal band at the top of the net	:	7 cm wide
Horizontal band at the bottom of the net	:	5 cm wide
Height of the net from the ground for men	:	2.4 3m
Height of the net from the ground for women	:	2.24 m
Circumference of the ball	:	65 to 67 cm
Weight of the ball	:	260 to 280 gm
Length of antenna	:	1.80 m
Distance of the pole from the side line	:	1 m
Number of players in volley ball	:	6
Number of substitutes	:	6
No of officials	:	7 (1 referee, 1 umpire, 1 scorer and 2 to 4 lines men)
Size of net mesh	:	10 cm
Distance from Centre line to attacking line	:	3 m
Distance from attacking line to end line	:	6 m

Fundamental Skills of Volleyball

Service

A player stands behind the end line and serves the ball, in an attempt to drive it into the opponent's court. With objective to make it land inside the court, it is also desirable to set the ball's direction, speed and acceleration so that it becomes difficult for the receiver to handle it properly. A serve is called an "ace" when the ball lands directly onto the court or travels outside the court after being touched by an opponent.

1. **Underhand service :** A serve in which the player strikes the ball below the waist instead of tossing it up and striking it with an overhand throwing motion. Underhand serves are considered very easy to receive and are rarely employed in high level competitions.

2. **Tennis service :** A form of service that involves tossing the ball above head and striking the ball with forward swing of the arm. This may be topspin or backspin.

3. **Top spin :** An overhand serve where the player tosses the ball high and hits it with a wrist span, giving it topspin which causes it to drop faster than it would otherwise and helps maintain a straight flight path.

4. **Back spin :** An overhand serve where the player tosses the ball high and hits it with a wrist span at the bottom of the ball, giving it backspin.

5. **Side arm service :** A service similar to the under hand serve, but in sidearm service, the ball is hit by the wrist part from the side of the body swinging the hand sidewards.

6. **Floating service :** An overhand serve where the ball is hit with no spin so that its path becomes unpredictable in its flight pattern.

7. **Jump serve :** An overhand serve where the ball is first tossed high in the air, then the player makes a timed approach and jumps to make contact with the ball, hitting it with much pace and topspin.

Pass

The pass is the attempt by a team to properly handle the opponent's serve, or any form of attack and making it reach the position where the setter is standing quickly and precisely.

1. **Under hand pass :** The pass where the ball touches the inside part of the joined forearms or platform, at waist line.

2. **Upper hand pass :** The pass that involves passing the ball with the tips of the fingers in front of forehead.

Set

The set is usually the second contact that a team makes with the ball with goal to put the ball in the air in such a way that it can be driven by an attack into the opponent's court.

Attack or Spike or Smashing

The attack, also known as the spike, or smashing is usually the third contact a team makes with the ball. The object of attacking is to handle the ball so that it lands on the opponent's court and cannot be defended.

1. **Back court (or back row)/pipe attack :** An attack performed by a back row player where the player jumps from behind the 3 meter line before

making contact with the ball, but may land in front of the 3 meter line after contacting.

2. **Line and cross-court shot :** It refers to hitting the straight trajectory parallel ball, which is towards the side line, so that it crosses through the court in an angle. A cross-court shot with a very pronounced angle, resulting in the ball landing near the 3 meter line, is called a cut shot.

3. **Quick hit/"One" :** An attack where the approach and jump begin before the setter contacts the ball. The set (called a "quick set") is placed only slightly above the net and the ball is struck by the hitter almost immediately after leaving the setter's hands.

4. **Double quick hit :** A variation of quick hit where two hitters, one in front and one behind the setter or both in front of the setter, jump to perform a quick hit at the same time. It can be used to deceive opposite blockers and free a fourth hitter attacking from backcourt, may be without block at all.

Block

Blocking refers to the actions taken by players standing at the net to stop or alter an opponent's attack.

1. **Roof block :** A spectacular offensive block that redirects the power and speed of the attack straight down to the attacker's floor.

2. **Soft block :** The block which aims to control and deflect the hard driven ball up so that it slows down and becomes easier to be defended.

Terminology Related to Volleyball

Diving, boosting, booster, blocking, antenna, libero, ace, attack, rally, cut shot, double contact, dump, joust, kill, rotation, six back, six up, spike, cobra etc.

Brief description of the above mentioned terms :

1. Diving : A way of receiving by which the player receive the ball finding that the only way to reach the ball is to fling himself in a dive to receive it from off both feet or sometimes off one foot.

2. Boosting : Lifting the ball up in the air for the spiker to spike the ball.

3. Booster : A player within a team who lifts the ball for the spiker is called booster.

4. Blocking : A player attempting to check the smash close to the net by taking jump and raising the hands to block the ball.

5. Antenna : A rod fixed vertically above the side line in the net, which is 1.80 m allowing the ball to pass opponents court between it.

6. Libero : A special player of a team, for the defensive purpose, whose dress is different from others.

7. Ace : A serve which lands in the receiving team's court without being touched by the receiving team, or one that is touched by only one member of the receiving team, and is not passed legally back over the net.

8. Attack : Usually the third of a team's three contacts, an attack is any attempt by the offense to score a point against the defense (this does not include free balls or overpasses).

9. Rally : It is the exchange of hits between the teams; the teams that wins rally gets the service as well as points.

10. Cut/cut shot : Attack with an extreme angle (nearly parallel to the net).

11. Double contact/double : A fault in which a player contacts the ball with two body parts consecutively.

12. Dump : A surprise attack usually executed by a front row setter to catch the defense off guard; many times executed with the left hand, sometimes with the right, aimed at the donut or area 4 on the court.

13. Joust : When the ball is falling directly on top of the net, two opposing players jump and push against the ball, trying to push it onto the other's side.

14. Kill : Successful, legal, point scoring play. It can be from a spike attack, tip or dump.

15. Rotation : It is a process of changing the positions of the players within a court in clockwise direction after getting a chance to serve.

16. Six back : Defensive system where the player in 'six' (the middle position in the backcourt) plays deep in the court covering attacks through the seam in the block, attacks over top of the block, and attacks that go high off the block. With certain blocking schemes the player in 'six' might also be responsible for deep line roll shots.

17. Six up : Defensive system where the player in 'six' (the middle position in the backcourt) plays up behind the block with the responsibility of defending against a tip attack.

18. Spike : When an offensive player attacks the ball with a one arm motion done over the head, attempting to get a kill.

19. Cobra : With the fingers extended straight and stiff, the ball is poked with the fingertips.

Latest General Rules of Volleyball

The latest general rules of volleyball that are being implemented are listed below :

1. The breadth of service area is 9m instead of 3m.
2. The attacking line has been extended up to 1.75m outside on both sides in dotted marking.
3. Uniform shirts may be numbered from "0" through "99".
4. Timeout Length has been changed from 60 seconds to 75 seconds. A timeout may be less than 75 seconds if both teams are ready to play.
5. It is not required that the libero's shorts be identical to teammates.
6. The terminology for "scorekeeper" has been changed to "scorer".

New Amendments in the Rules of Volleyball

1. **Warm up protocol :** (a) For junior competition, when one team has exclusive use of the court, the other team must either be at its team bench or out of the playing area.

(c) A player interferes with the opponent's play by (amongst, others) making actions which hinder an opponents legitimate attempt to play the ball.

3. **Net contact rules :**

(a) Contact with the net by a player is not a fault, unless it interferes with the play.

(b) Players may touch the posts, ropes, or any other object outside the antennae, including the net itself, provided that it does not interfere with play.

(c) When the ball is driven into the net and causes it to touch an opponent, no fault is committed.

The following are defined as interference which results in a net violation.

1. A player interferes with the opponent's play by (amongst others) : touching the top band of the net or the top 80 cm of the antenna during his/her action of playing the ball.
2. Taking support from the net simultaneously with playing the ball.
3. Creating an advantage over the opponent.
4. Making actions which hinder an opponent's legitimate attempt to play the ball.

<table>
<tr><td colspan="4" align="center">Free zone</td><td colspan="4" align="center">Free zone</td></tr>
<tr><td></td><td align="center">Side line</td><td></td><td></td><td></td><td align="center">Side line</td><td></td><td></td></tr>
<tr><td rowspan="3">Free zone</td><td rowspan="3">End line/baseline</td><td align="center">5</td><td align="center">4</td><td align="center">2</td><td align="center">1</td><td rowspan="3">End line baseline</td><td rowspan="3">Free zone</td></tr>
<tr><td align="center">6   Attack line</td><td align="center">3   Centerline</td><td align="center">3   Attack line</td><td align="center">6</td></tr>
<tr><td align="center">1</td><td align="center">2</td><td align="center">4</td><td align="center">5</td></tr>
<tr><td></td><td></td><td align="center">Side line</td><td></td><td></td><td align="center">Side line</td><td></td><td></td></tr>
<tr><td colspan="4" align="center">Free zone</td><td colspan="4" align="center">Free zone</td></tr>
</table>

(b) Warmings up with balls at the team bench or in the spectator walkways is not permitted.

2. **Centerline rules :** Any other part of the body may contact the opponent's court provided it does not interfere with the opponent's play.

The following are centerline faults :

(a) A player interferes with the opponent's play while penetrating into the opponent's space under the net.

(b) A player's, foot (feet) penetrates completely into the opponents court.

Players Position and Rotation

Playing volleyball is incomplete without knowing the positioning and rotation in the game :

Positioning

In volleyball, the numbering is done anti-clockwise. At the moment the ball is hit by the server, each team must be within its own court (except server) in two rows of the three players. The three players along the net are front row players occupying positions 4 (left), 3 (center) and 2 (right). The other three are back row players and occupy positons 5 (left), 6 (center) and 1 (right).

Rotation

The rotation in volleyball is done in clockwise direction. When the receiving team has gained the right to serve, its players must rotate one position clockwise *e.g.,* player in position 2 will rotates to position 1 to serve and player in 1 rotates to position 6.

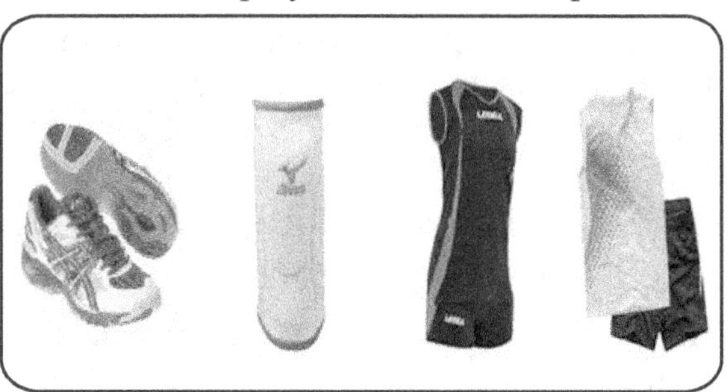

Necessary Equipment's

Below is the list of required equipments by the volleyball players to play comfortably :

1. Jersey
2. Shorts
3. Shoes
4. Kneepads
5. Socks
6. Sports bra (women)
7. Ankle braces (optional)

5.4. SPORTS AWARDS, TOURNAMENTS AND VENUES AND SPORTS PERSONALITIES

Sports Awards

Arjuna Awardees	
Name	**Year**
A. Palanisamy	1961
Nripjit Singh	1962
Balwant Singh "Ballu"	1972
G.M. Reddy	1973
M.S. Rao	1974
Sub. Insp. R. Singh, K.C.Elamma	1975
Jimmy George	1976
A. Ramana Rao	1977-78
Kutty Krishnan	1978-79
S.K. Mishra	1979-80
G.E. Sridharan	1982
R.K. Purohit	1983
Saley Joseph	1984

Cyril C. Valloor	1986
Abdul Basith	1989
Dalel Singh Ror	1990
K. Udaya Kumar	1991
Sukhpal Singh	1999
P.V. Ramana	2000
Amir Singh	2001
Ravikant Reddy	2002
K. J. Kapil Dev	2010
Mr. Sanjay Phogat	2011
Tom Joseph	2014

Dronacharya Awardees	
Name	**Year**
Shri A. Ramana Rao	1990
Shri M. Shyam Sunder Rao	1995
Mr. G. E. Sridharan	2007

Dhyan Chand Awardee	
Name	**Year**
Om Prakash	2003

Tournaments and Venues

International Tournaments

Olympic Games

World Championship

World Cup

World Grand Champions Cup

World League (Men)

World Grand Prix (Women)

Club World Championship

Men's U23 World Championship

Women's U23 World Championship

Men's U21 World Championship (Junior)

Women's U20 World Championship (Junior)

Boys' U19 World Championship (Youth)

Girls' U18 World Championship (Youth)

National Tournaments

Junior National VB Championship

Sub Junior National VB Championship

Senior National VB Championship

Youth National VB Championship

National Games

RD Sharma Memorial All India Tournament

Taya Ji Memorial All India VB Tournament

Angamaly All India Tournament

Paradise All India Volleyball Tournament

A.C. George Memorial All India Tournament

Sports Personalities

Indian Personalities	
Balwant Singh Sagwal	Abdul Basith
Jimmy George	K. Udayakumar
Cyril C. Valloor	Shyam Sunder Rao
Arikapudi Ramana Rao	V M Kuttikrishnan
Kuldip Vats	T. Gopal
Tom Joseph	Ramavtar Singh Jakhar
G. E. Sridharan	

International Personalities	
Name	**Country**
Bartosz Kurek	Poland
Pedro Hernandez	Mexico
Lukasz Zygadlo	Poland
Max Holt	USA
Matt Anderson	USA
Michal Winiarski	Poland
Seyed Mousavi	Iran
Cristian Savani	Italia
Tsvetan Sokolov	Bulgaria
Luca Vettori	Italia
Ivan Zaytsev	Italia
Jenia Grebennikov	France
Saeid Marouf	Iran
Luciano De Cecco	Argentina

GENERAL QUESTIONS AND ANSWERS

Q. 1. What is the dimension of volleyball court ?

Ans. 9 × 18 m.

Q. 2. What is the width of the lines of the volleyball court ?

Ans. 5 cm.

Q. 3. What is the size of the net mesh ?

Ans. 10 cm.

Q. 4. What is the height of the net from the ground for men ?

Ans. 2.43 m.

Q. 5. What is the height of the net from the ground for women ?

Ans. 2.24 m.

Q. 6. What is the circumference of the ball ?

Ans. 65 to 67 cm.

Q. 7. What is the weight of the ball ?

Ans. 260 to 280 gm.

Q. 8. What is the height of the antenna ?

Ans. 1.80 m.

Q. 9. What is the length of the service area ?

Ans. 9 m.

Q. 10. What is the distance between centerline and attacking line ?

Ans. 3 m.

Q. 11. What is the distance between attacking line and end line ?

Ans. 6 m.

Q. 12. Who was the founder of volleyball ?

Ans. William G. Morgan.

Q. 13. When was the governing body of volleyball FIVA formed ?

Ans. 1947.

Q. 14. When was the governing body of volleyball in India BFI formed ?

Ans. 1951.

Q. 15. What was the name of volleyball at its ancient time ?

Ans. Mintonette.

Q. 16. Where is the headquarter of FIVB located ?

Ans. Lausanne, Switzerland.

Q. 17. In which direction does the rotation in volleyball take place ?

Ans. Clockwise.

Q. 18. In which direction does the numbering of positions of players in volleyball take place ?

Ans. Anticlockwise.

Q. 19. Name any three Arjuna awardees in volleyball.

Ans. R.K. Purohit, Nripjit Singh and Saley Joseph.

Q. 20. Name the types of service in volleyball.

Ans. Under hand, tennis serve, floating serve, etc.

HANDBALL

6.1. INTRODUCTION AND HISTORY

Handball also known as team handball is a team sport in which two teams of seven players each (six outfield players and a goalkeeper) pass a ball to throw it into the goal of the other team. A standard match consists of two periods of 30 minutes, and the team that scores more goals wins.

World History

The game was originated at the end of the 19th century in Germany by German gymnast Konard Koch. The first international games were played under these rules for men in 1925 and for women in 1930. Men's handball was first played at the 1936 Summer Olympics in Berlin as outdoors, and the next time at the 1972 Summer Olympics in Munich as indoors, and has been an Olympics sport since. Women's team handball was added at the 1976 Summer Olympics.

Indian History

In the history of Handball it is presumed that Game Handball was brought to India arguably by Shri J.S. Chauhan of Haryana in 1970. He conducted two all India seminar on Handball at Rohtak in Haryana before the formation of Federation in year 1971-72. Amateur Handball Federation of India (AFHI) was formed in 1972 and got provisional affiliation with International Handball Federation.

6.2. GOVERNING BODIES

International Handball Federation (IHF)

IHD is the administrative and controlling body for international team handball.

Main Tips at a Glance	
Dimensions of the court	
Length of the handball ground	= 40 m
Width of the handball ground	= 20 m
Width of the goal lines between goal posts	= 8 cm
Length of 7-metre line	= 1 m
Length of 4-metre line	= 15 cm
Width of safety zone	
Side lines	= 1m
Behind the goal line	= 2m
Measurement of goal post	
Height of the goal post	= 2 m
Width of the goal post	= 3 m
Distance between the goal post	= 40m
There are two D's on the handball court:	
(a) Outer D's r = 9m	
(b) Inner D's r = 6m	
Width of the lines	
All the lines, except goal lines shall be	= 0.05m
The goal lines (between the goal-posts) shall be	= 0.08m
Ball size in terms of weight and circumference	
For men and male youth (over age 16)	= 425-475 g, 58-60cm
For women, female youth (over age 14) and male youth (age 12 to 16)	= 325-375 g, 54-56cm
For female youth (age 8 to 14) and male youth (age 8 to 12)	290-330g, 50-52cm
Playing time or duration of play	
For men and women (above 16 years)	= 2 halves of 30 minutes (Interval of half time break is 10 minutes)
For youth teams (age group of 12 to 16 years)	= 2 halves of 25 minutes (Interval of half time break is 10 minutes)

For junior teams (age group 8 to 12 years)	= 2 halves of 20 minutes (Interval of half time break is 10 minutes)
Players	
Total numbers of players in a team	= 12
Court players	= 12
Substitute players	= 7
Officials	= 7
(a) Referees- 2 (b) Timekeeper-1 (c) Scorekeeper-1	

Asian Handball Federation (AHF)

AHF is the administrative and controlling body for Asian team handball. It represents the national handball associations of Asia.

Handball Federation of India (HFI)

HFI is the administrative and controlling body for team handball in India.

6.3. SPECIFICATION, BASIC RULES, FUNDAMENTAL SKILLS AND TERMINOLOGY

Handball Court Marking

1. Short lines : The shorter ones are called goal lines (between the goalposts) or outer goal lines (on either side of the goal).

2. Centre line : The centre line connects the midpoints of the two sidelines.

3. Free throw line (9 metre line) : It is a broken line, drawn 3m outside the goal area line. This line should be parallel to the goal line.

4. 7-metre line or penalty line : It is a 1m long line directly in front of the goal. It is parallel to the goal line and 7m away from it (measured from the rear edge of the goal line to the front edge of the 7m line).

5. Goalkeeper's restraining line (4-Metre line) : It means that beyond this area only the goal keeper can go. It is a 15cm long line directly in front of the goal. It is parallel to the goal line and 4m away from it (measured from the rear edge of the goal line to the front edge of the 4m line).

6. Substitution line : The substitution line is the place from where the player is substitution takes place and the line for each team extends from the centre line to a point at a distance of 45m from the centre line.

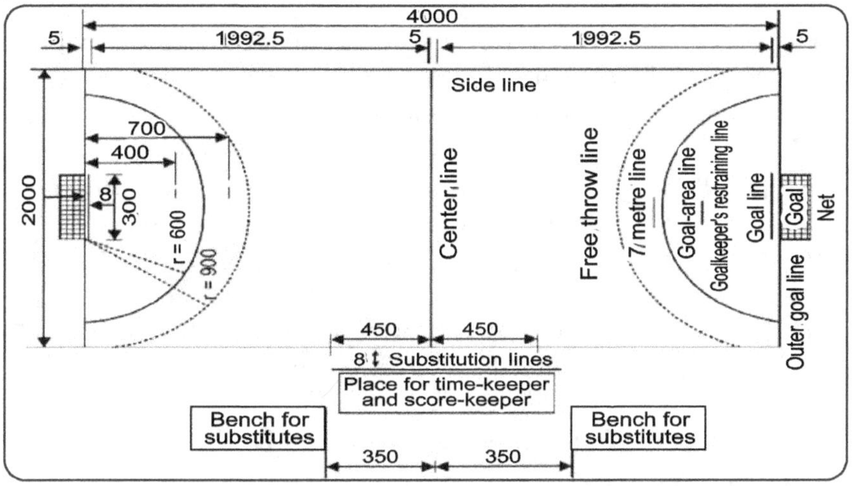

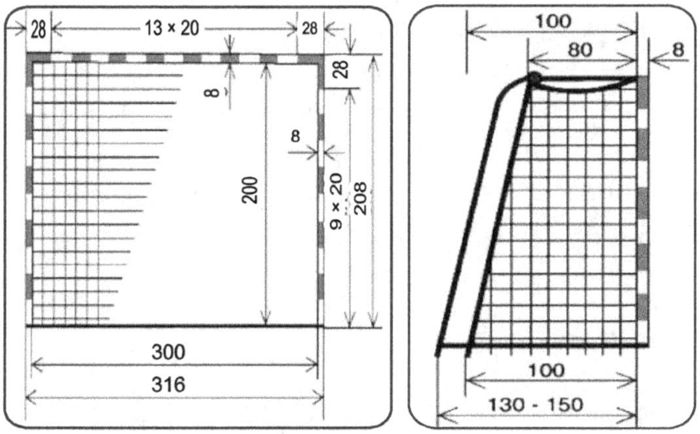

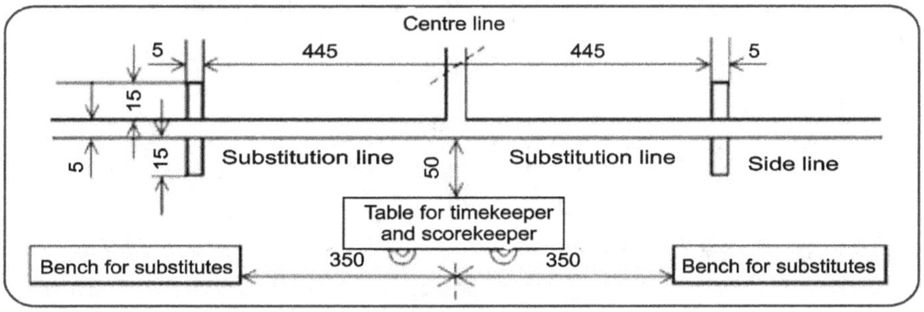

Basic Rules of the Game

1. The game begins by giving the pass to another player from the centre line.

2. A player may be changed at any time during the game.

3. Each team has the right to receive one 1-minute team time-out in each half of the regular playing time, but not in overtime.

4. In the case of an injury to a player, the game may be stopped at any time on the instructions of the referee and the injured player may be replaced by the other player.

5. In the game, running by holding the ball is not allowed.

6. If ball goes out of court during the game, the opposing team shall be given a throw from the same place.

7. A goal keeper shall not go out through the outer "D".

8. The team that scores maximum goals shall be considered the winner.

9. A referee may turn a player out of the game for two minutes after giving two warnings.

10. No other person except the goal keeper shall enter the goal area.

11. A goal scored from inside the "D" (*i.e.,* 6 m line) shall not be considered.

Throws used in the Game

1. Throw off 2. Throw in 3. Goal-keeper throw 4. Free throw 5. 7-meter throw 6. Referee throw 7. Corner throw

1. Throw-off : A throw off is used to start play at the beginning of each half or after a goal has been scored.

2. Throw-in : A throw-in is awarded when ball goes out of bounds on the sideline or when the ball is last touched by a defensive player (excluding the goaline) and goes out of bounds over the endline. The throw-in is taken from the spot where the ball crossed the sideline, or if it crossed the endline, from the nearest corner. The thrower must place one foot on the sideline to execute the throw. All opposing players must stay 3m away from the ball.

3. Free-throw : For a minor foul or violation, a free-throw is awarded to the opponent at the exact spot it took place. If the foul or violation occurs between the goal area line and the 9m line, the throw is taken from the nearest post outside the 9m line. The thrower must keep one foot in contact with the floor, then pass or shoot.

4. The goalkeeper-throw : The goalkeeper throws the ball back in bounds after he or an opposing player has knocked the ball over the backline

5. 7-metre throw/penalty throw : A penalty throw is a throw awarded when there is an infringement in any part of the court and spoils a clear chance of scoring.

6. Referee throw : A referee throw is awarded when the ball touches anything above the court after a simultaneous infringement of the rules after simultaneous possession of the ball.

7. Corner throw : A corner throw is awarded when a defender, other than the goalkeeper, has knocked the ball over the backline. The team on offense throws the ball back in bounds from a corner closest to where the ball went out of bounds.

Punishments

Fouls such as reaching around, holding, pushing, hitting, tripping and jumping into an opponent are to be punished progressively.

1. **Warnings (yellow card) :** The referee gives only one warning to a player for rule violations and a total of three to a team. Exceeding these limits results in 2-minute suspensions thereafter.

2. **Disqualification and exclusion (red card) :** A disqualification is the equivalent of three 2-minute suspensions. A disqualified player must leave court and bench, but the team can replace player after the 2-minute suspension expires.

Fundamentals Skills of Handball

1. Holding and catching the ball
2. Throw the ball
3. Pass the ball

   (a) Bounce pass (b) Hook pass

   (c) Chest pass (d) Overhead pass

   (e) Jump pass (f) Shoulder pass

   (g) Side arm pass

4. Dodge
5. Dribble

   (a) Low dribble and (b) High dribble

6. Shot

   (a) High jump shot and long jump shot.

   (b) Dive shot

   (c) Underhand shot

   (d) Reverse shot

The brief explanation of some of the fundamental skills is given below :

Shot

1. Jump shot : A shot attempted while leaping.

2. Dive shot : The player stretches the body out and directs the momentum towards the goal. The ball should be released at the last possible moment by taking a dive.

Pass the Ball

1. Hook pass : It is used when a player is in the air for a jump shot. The ball is simply released, while at the top of the jump, to his/her teammate, who is expected to penetrate towards the goal.

2. Chest pass : The chest pass is used frequently in handball. It is a short distance pass. This pass is the most accurate pass. Generally, it is given by both hands.

3. Bounce pass : In bounce pass, the ball should be thrown in such a way that it should bounce towards the teammate. It should bounce approximately three feet in front of the receiver.

Dribble

To move the ball by bouncing it on the floor.

Terminology Related To Handball

1. Fast–break : When the defence gains possession of the ball because of blocked shot, interception or rule violations the team is at that moment in a position to begin a fast break.

2. Double–dribble : A player may run three steps, dribble any number of times, pick the ball up and run three more steps. If the player dribbles again after the last sequence of steps, it is called double dribble.

3. Screen : It means the players of the serving team must not prevent their opponents from seeing the ball.

4. A line cut : When the ball crosses the goal line, opponent team player throws the ball inside the field without touching the goal line. If he touches the line then it is called a line cut.

5. Court player : Any player playing on the court except a goalkeeper, are known as a "court player."

6. Fake : When the ball strikes the hand or arm of a player, if the referee deems that a player has deliberately handled the ball, a direct free-kick will be awarded to the opposing team.

7. Running : If a player moves more than three steps while holding the ball in his hand, he is called for running.

8. Passive play : It is illegal to keep the ball in a team's possession without making a recognizable attempt to attack and to try to score. In other words, a team cannot stall (free-throw awarded to the other team).

9. Fault : A fault is illegally served ball.

6.4. TOURNAMENTS, VENUES AND SPORTS AWARDS

Important Tournaments And Venues

International Tournaments

1. World Championship
2. World Games
3. Men's Youth World Championship
4. Olympic Game
5. Super Globe
6. Asian Games
7. SAF Games

National Tournaments

1. Federation Cup
2. Inter-university Handball Championship
3. School National
4. National Championship

Sports Awards

Arjuna Awardees	
Name	**Year**
Manjit Singh	1978
Roshan Singh	1984
Surjeet Singh	1990
Malkit Singh	1994
R Lubhaya	1997

Sports Personalities

International Personalities	
Name	**Country**
Bertrand Gille	France
Ivano Bal	Croatia
Henning Fritz	Germany
Arpad terbi	Serbia and Montenegro
Nikola Karabatic	France
Thierry Omeyer	France
Slawomir Szmal	Poland
Filip J'cha	Czech Republic
Mikkel Hansen	Denmark
Daniel Narcisse	France
Domagoj Duvnja	Croatia
Indian Personalities	
Surjit Singh	Roshan Lal
R. Lubhaya	Manjit Singh
Malkit Singh	

GENERAL QUESTIONS AND ANSWERS

Q. 1. What are the dimensions of handball ground ?

Ans. 40 m × 20 m.

Q. 2. What is the width of the goal lines between goal posts ?

Ans. 8 cm.

Q. 3. What is the full form of IHF ?

Ans. International Handball Federation.

Q. 4. What is the full form of HFI ?

Ans. Handball Federation of India.

Q. 5. What is the width of safety zone ?

Ans. Sidelines- 1 m, behind the goal line – 2 m.

Q. 6. What is the height of the goal post ?

Ans. 2 m.

Q. 7. What is the width of the goal post ?

Ans. 3m.

Q. 8. What are the two D's on the handball court ?

Ans. Outer D's r = 9m, inner D's r = 6m.

Q. 9. What is the width of the lines except goal lines ?

Ans. 0.05 m.

Q. 9. What is the weight of the handball for men and women ?

Ans. 425-475 g and 325-375 g.

Q. 10. What is the circumference of the handball for men ?

Ans. 58-60 cm.

Q. 11. What is the circumference of the handball for women ?

Ans. 54-56 cm.

Q. 12. What is the duration of match for both men and women ?

Ans. 30-10-30 min.

Q. 13. What is the total number of players in teams?

Ans. 14.

Q. 14. How many officials are required in handball match ?

Ans. 4 (referees-2, time keeper-1, score keeper-1).

Q. 15. How many players are required to start the match of handball ?

Ans. At least 5 players.

Q. 16. When was the handball included in Olympics game ?

Ans. Berlin, 1936.

Q. 17. Mention the number of court players.

Ans. 6 court players and 1 goalkeeper.

Q. 18. What is free throw line (9m line) ?

Ans. It is a broken line, drawn 3 m outside the goal area line. This line should be parallel to the goal line.

Q. 19. What do you understand by the dive shot ?

Ans. The player stretches his body out and directs his momentum towards the goal. He should release the ball at the last possible moment by taking a dive.

Q. 20. What do you mean by corner throw ?

Ans. A corner throw is awarded when a defender, other than the goalkeeper, has knocked the ball over the backline. The team on offense throws the ball back in bounds from a corner closest to where the ball went out of bounds.

Q. 21. How many cards are there in the handball ?

Ans. 2 (yellow card and red card).

Q. 22. What is hook pass ?

Ans. It is used when a player is in the air for a jump shot. He simply releases the ball, while at the top of his jump, to his teammate, who is expected to penetrate towards the goal.

Q. 23. What is bounce pass ?

Ans. In bounce pass, the ball should be thrown in such a way that it should bounce towards the teammate. It should bounce approximately three feet in front of the receiver.

Q. 24. Mention five fundamental skills used in handball.

Ans. (a) Holding and catching the ball (b) Throw the ball (c) Pass the ball (d) Dodge and (e) Dribble.

Q. 25. When did handball born in India ?

Ans. 1970.

□ □

7.1. INTRODUCTION AND HISTORY

Field Hockey is an eleven-a-side game played on a pitch of 91.40m × 54.86m with a ball which has a 23cm circumference. Each player has a stick with a rounded head to play the ball with an objective to score goals by putting the ball in the opposing team's goal, for the duration of 60 minutes. Sticks are anywhere between 28 inches and 39 inches long and weigh between 340 g and 790 g. Protective equipment is worn in the form of full body armor, pads, gloves, kickers and a helmet by the goal keepers and shin guards and mouth guards for outfield players.

World History

The origins of the game can be traced back to the earliest civilizations of the world, but the modern game of field hockey was developed in the British Isles. The modern game was started in England in the mid 1800's and the first formal field hockey was formed in 1861. Many rules and concepts changed during the early years as the game spread throughout the British Empire. From these origins sprung not only the formidable field hockey nations of India, Pakistan and Australia but the development of the game in over 100 countries making field hockey the second largest team sport in the world, after soccer.

Indian History

Hockey became popular in India when the British Regiments played the game in India and introduced it to the British Indian Regiments, who quickly picked up the game. The first hockey club was formed in Calcutta (Kolkata) in 1885-86 followed by Bombay (Mumbai) and Punjab. The Bengal Hockey was the first Hockey Association in India founded in 1908. With the popularity of the game, associations were formed in different states like Maharashtra, Bihar, Orissa and Delhi. India participated for the first time In the Olympic Games, in 1928, held in Amsterdam. In the final match India defeated Holland by three goals to nil. India men's field hockey team is the most successful field hockey team in Olympics with 8 gold,1 silver and 2 bronze medals.

7.2. GOVERNING BODIES

International Hockey Federation (FIH)

The Federation Internationale de Hockey (English: International Hockey Federation), commonly known by the acronym FIH, is the international governing body of field hockey and indoor field hockey. FIH was founded on 7 January, 1924 in Paris by Paul Léautey, who became the first president, in response to field hockey's omission from the programme of the 1924 Summer Olympics. Its headquarter is located in Lausanne, Switzerland and FIH is responsible for field hockey's major international tournaments, notably the World Cup.

Hockey India

Hockey India is the governing body of field hockey in India. It was formed after Indian Hockey Federation was dismissed in 2008 by IOA. Hockey India launched its own logo in a grand ceremony on July 24, 2009, in India. It resembles Ashok Chakra of Indian flag. It is made up of field hockey sticks. In a significant way forward, Indian Hockey Federation (I.H.F) & Hockey India (H.I), on 25 July 2011, signed an agreement leading up to formation of a joint executive board which shall perform the function of the National Sports Federation for field hockey.

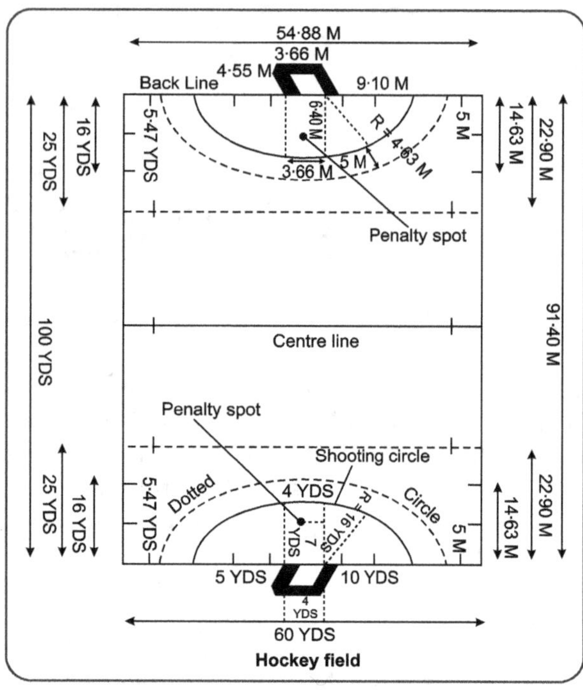

Hockey field

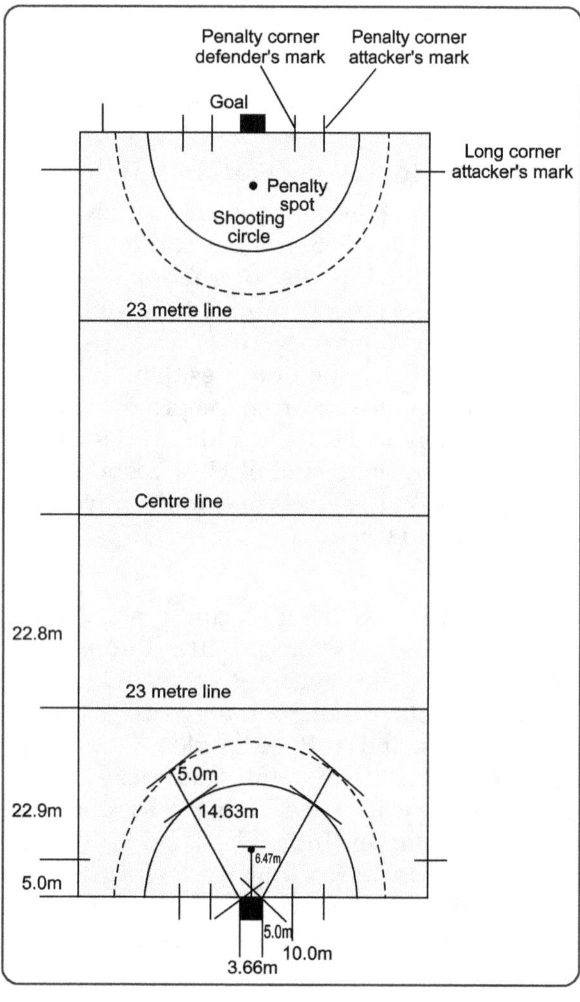

7.3. SPECIFICATION, GENERAL RULES, FUNDAMENTAL SKILLS AND TERMINOLOGY

Hockey Specification

No. of players	:	16 (11 and 5 substitutes)
Length of the field	:	90.40 m
Breadth of the field	:	55 m
Duration of the match	:	60 minutes
Half time interval	:	5 minutes
Weight of the ball	:	156 to163 gm
Circumference of the ball	:	224 to 235mm
Weight of the stick	:	737 gm/280 inches
Height of stick	:	40 inches
Width of the goal post	:	3.66m
Height of the goal post	:	2.14m
Height of the goal back board	:	460 mm
Radius of "D" or the circle from the center of the end line	:	14.63m
Distance of penalty spot from the back line	:	6.40m
No. of officials	:	5
Distance of dotted circle from goal	:	19.63m
Depth of the back board	:	1.20m
Width of the lines	:	75mm
Diameter of penalty spot	:	150mm
Size of the flag on flag post	:	300mm
Height of flag posts	:	1.20 to 1.50m
Cards used in hockey	:	three types (red, green, yellow)

Hockey Court Markings

1. Side line : The longer perimeter line (90.40 m).

2. Backline : The shorter perimeter line (55 m).

3. Goal-lines : The back-lines between the goal-posts.

4. 23-meter area : The area enclosed by and including the line across the field 22.90 meters from each back-line, the relevant part of the sidelines, and the back-line.

5. Penalty spot : Penalty spot is marked in front of the center of each goal in the center of each spot 6.40m from the inner edge of the goal-line.

6. Playing distance : The distance within which a player is capable of reaching the ball to play it.

7. Shooting circles : There are two shooting circles, one in front of each of the goals. The shooting circles are 14.63 m semi-circles and it is measured from the inside front corner of the goal-post to the outer edge of that line.

8. Dotted circle : There are two dotted circles one in front of each of the goals which is 19.63m measured from the inside front corner of the goal-post to the outer edge of that line.

9. Long corner mark : It is a mark at a distance of 5m from the corner flag, for the purpose of taking a long corner.

Latest General Rules of Hockey

1. The two minute green card will be penalized for using the stick above the shoulder.
2. The breaking at penalty corners. Regulation has effected a significant reduction in the number of breaks at tournaments, by both attackers and defenders. As a consequence, the requirement that a penalty stroke be awarded for defenders persistently crossing the back-line before permitted has been deleted.
3. The ability to take attacking free hits, awarded within 5 meters of the edge of the circle, from the point of the offence. The ball still has to travel at least 5 meters before it can be played into the circle, or alternatively has to be touched by another player of either team, other than the player taking the free hit. Having to take the ball back to the 5 meters dotted line slowed the play and was seen as a real disadvantage to the attacking team and the flow of the game.
4. The re-start after the ball has unintentionally been played over the back-line by a defender or deflected by a goalkeeper or player with goal-keeping privileges, and no goal is scored. Play will now be re-started with the ball on the 23 meters line and in line with where it crossed the back-line.
5. There is also a lifting of the ban on certain types of face masks, in particular those with metal grills, recognizing that the primary objective of wearing a face mask to defend a penalty corner should be safety. Nevertheless, players wearing face masks are not permitted to conduct themselves in a manner which is dangerous to other players by taking advantage of the protective equipment that they wear.

New Amendment in the Rules of Hockey

1. Now, the players cautioned with the green card will be suspended for 2 minutes.
2. The duration of the match is of 60 minutes.
3. Ball intentionally played over the back-line by a defender and no goal is scored. If it is clear that the action is intentional, umpires should not hesitate to award a penalty corner.
4. Obstruction, umpires should penalize shielding the ball with the stick more strictly. They should also look out for a tackling player who by pushing or leaning on an opponent causes them to lose possession of the ball.
5. Ball stationary at a free hit, umpires are sometimes not strict enough on requiring the ball to be stationary, although very briefly, for a free hit especially if it is taken using a self-pass.

Fundamental Skills of Hockey

Hitting, Push Pass, Dodging, Dribbling, Scooping, Lunging, Feinting, Flick, Reverse Flick, Tackling, Push etc.

Brief description of the above mentioned skills :

1. Hitting : Hitting involves, contacting the ball with a stick with hard firm forward swing, leading the ball to move fast.

2. Pass : It involves pushing the ball with the stick, for short and accurate pass.

3. Dodging : Dodge is used to gain space or time for either passing or dribbling by making the opponent go to the wrong way. It is to get away from close marking, a player may shift his weight and dodge to the left and draw his opponent to move in the same direction.

4. Dribbling : Dribbling is running with the ball while shifting it right and left and keeping it in perfect control so as to pass it at any time or change its direction to beat a player.

5. Scooping (Side line hit) : A "scoop" occurs when a stationary or slow moving ball is raised off the ground with a slow movement of the stick, after the head of the stick is placed slightly under the ball.

6. Lunging : Lunging is used to increase the reach, to play the ball which is out of reach. The player is required to hold the stick at the top of the stick by either hand. Holding the stick and the arm extending fully and body lunging forward on one leg, knees comfortably bent. It is used when the ball is out of the two-handed reach.

7. Feinting : When a player dribbles to mislead his opponent. Feinting with the ball is to draw the ball sideways to the left or right at an angle to the line of the dribble, just in front of the opponent to make the opponent sway to that side, beating an opponent with a body-swerve (to dodge) produced by a shift of weight.

8. Flick : It occurs when the ball is pushed and is consequently raised off the ground. It is used to pass the ball to a teammate or place the ball into the goal.

9. Reverse flick : It means to raise the ball with the reverse stick to give pass over the stick of an opponent towards the right side or to place the ball into the goal

10. Tackling : It is an attempt to take possession of the ball from an opponent's control or an action to stop an opponent from retaining the possession of the ball.

11. Push : A method of moving or passing the ball in which the stick is in contact with the ball and the ground as the player pushes the ball up the field.

Terminology Related to Hockey

Rolling substation, shoveling, 16 yard hit, hit in, Misconduct, Corner Push, Carried, Sudden death, Stroke, Reverse Hit, Bully, Pass Back, Back stick, Goalkeeper, Field Player with Goalkeeping Privileges, Attack (Attacker), Defence (Defender), Back-line, Goal-line, Side-line, 23-meters Area, Push, Flick, Scoop, Forehand, Tackle, Offence etc.

Short description of the above mentioned terms :

1. Rolling substitution : It is the continuous replacement of one player from another throughout the game, as long as each side has only 11 players on the field at once.

2. Shoveling : It is the simplest and the most basic shot. Its execution is simply to push in the desired direction, be the forehand, backhand or the spearing motion.

3. 16 yard hit : A 16 yard hit is a type of free hit, awarded for defense, when the ball goes wholly over the backline and the attacking team was the last to touch it in any way. It is taken in line with where the ball crossed the back-line, up to 14.63 m from the backline.

4. Hit in : This is a powerful stroke for long passes or to score goal. A player raises the stick at back and then hits the ball with the full swing of the stick whereas hands hold the stick from the top. When the ball goes out on the sideline, the opposite team gets a hit in.

5. Misconduct : Rough or dangerous play, time-wasting, deliberate breach of any rule or any other behavior, which in the umpire's opinion amounts to misconduct.

6. Corner push : It is a technique of attack within the hockey field, when the ball is pushed involving the Penalty Corners.

7. Carried : When a ball hits the leg (foot) while dribbling or tackling an opponent, it is considered as a foul (foot foul), opponents can intentionally hit the ball on the leg to free hit. One has to be careful while tackling an opponent.

8. Sudden death : If a hockey match is tied after the end of regulation time then an extra time of two 7.5 minute periods is played. During this period, the team which scores the first goal is declared winner. It means 'the game ends as soon as one team scores'.

9. Stroke : To pass the ball to the teammate at short or long distance or to score a goal with a powerful blow from a stick.

10. Reverse hit : It means to hit the ball towards the right side to run without changing the position of the ball or body with the reverse side of the stick.

11. Bully : It is a call used to start or restart play. The referee puts the ball between two opposing players. The players tap the flat sides of their sticks three times and then go for the ball.

12. Pass back : To restart the game, a player hits the ball from the center line to one of his teammates.

13. Back stick : It is an illegal shot in which the ball strikes the rounded face of the hockey stick.

14. Goalkeeper : One of the participants of each team on the field who wears full protective equipment comprising at least headgear, leg guards and kickers and who is also permitted to wear goalkeeping hand protectors and other protective equipment.

15. Field player with goalkeeping privileges : One of the participants on the field who does not wear full protective equipment but who has goalkeeping privileges, this player wears a different color shirt to their other team members as identification.

16. Attack (Attacker) : The team (player) which (who) is trying to score a goal.

17. Defense (Defender) : The team (player) which (who) is trying to prevent a goal from being scored.

18. Back-line : The shorter (55 meters) perimeter line.

19. Goal-line : The back-line between the goal-posts.

20. Side-line : The longer (91.40 meters) perimeter line.

21. 21-meters area : The area enclosed by and including the line across the field, 22.90 meters from each back-line, the relevant part of the side-lines, and the back-line.

22. Push : Moving the ball along the ground using a pushing movement of the stick after the stick has been placed close to the ball. When a push is made, both the ball and the head of the stick are in contact with the ground.

23. Flick : Pushing the ball so that it is raised off the ground.

24. Scoop : Raising the ball off the ground by placing the head of the stick under the ball and using a lifting movement.

25. Forehand : Playing a ball which is to the right of the player in a forwards direction.

26. Tackle : An action to stop an opponent from retaining possession of the ball.

27. Offence : An action contrary to the rules which may be penalized by an umpire.

Hockey Cards

Three cards are sanctioned at the time of offence in hockey :

1. **Green card :** Temporarily suspended for about 2 minutes.

2. **Yellow card :** Temporarily suspended for a minimum of 5 minutes of playing time and the players must remain in a designated place until permitted by the umpire who suspended them to resume play. The intended duration of a temporary suspension may be extended for misconduct by a player while suspended.

3. **Red card :** Permanently suspended from the current match and can not return. The players must leave the field and its surrounding area. A player is suspended when he violates some rule, time wasting, deliberate breaches or any other misconduct.

Necessary Equipment's

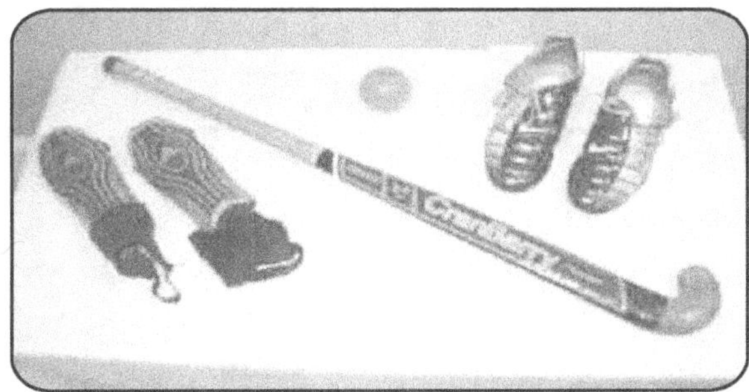

1. Field hockey stick
2. Shoes
3. Supporter
4. Shin guards
5. Mouth guard
6. Socks
7. Cold/Hot weather gear
8. Helmet (goalkeeper)

7.4. SPORTS AWARDS, TOURNAMENTS, VENUES AND SPORTS PERSONALITIES

Sports Awards

Arjuna Awardees	
Name	**Year**
Baljeet Singh Saini	2000
Tingonleima Chanu	2000
Gp. Capt. R. S. Bhola	2000
Balkishan Singh	2000
Jalaluddin Rizvi	2000
Madhu Yadav	2000
DilipTirkey	2002
Gagan Ajit Singh	2002
Mamta Kharab	2002
Devesh Chauhan	2003
Suraj Lata Devi	2003
Deepak Thakur	2004
Innocent Helen Mary	2004
Viren Rasquinha	2005
Jyoti Sunita Kullu	2006
Prabhjot Singh	2008
Surinder Kaur	2009
IgnaceTirkey	2009
Jasjeet Kaur Handa	2010
Rajpal Singh	2011
Sardar Singh	2012
Saba Anjum Karim	2013
Rani	2016
V.R. Raghunath	2016

Padmashree Awardees	
Name	**Year**
Balbir Singh	1957
K.D. Singh Babu	1958
Charanjit Singh	1964
Krishan Lal	1966
Prithipal Singh	1967
Shankar Laxman	1967
Leslie Cladius	1971
Vasudevan Baskaran	1981
Mohd. Shahid	1981
Eliza Nelson	1982
Jhaman Lal Sharma	1990
Selma D'Silva	1991
Ajit Pal Singh	1992

Pargat Singh	1998
Dhanraj Pillay	2001
Mukesh Kumar	2003
Dilip Tirkey	2004
Balbir Singh Kullar	2009
Ignace Tirkey	2010
Zafar Iqbal	2012

Rajiv Gandhi Khel Ratna Awardee	
Name	**Year**
Dhanraj Pillay	1999-2000

Dhyan Chand Awardees	
Name	**Year**
Ashok Diwan	2002
Charles Cornelius	2003
Dharam Singh Mann	2003
Hardyal Singh	2004
Rajinder Singh	2005
Nandy Singh	2006
Varinder Singh	2007
Mukhbain Singh	2008
Gundeep Kumar	2012
Syed Ali	2013

Tournaments

International Tournaments

1. Hockey World Cup
2. Women's Hockey World Cup
3. Hockey Junior World Cup
4. Women's Hockey Junior World Cup
5. Olympic Games
6. Hockey World League
7. Hockey Champions Trophy
8. Hockey Champions Challenge

National Tournaments

1. MCC Murugappa Gold Cup
2. Gurmeet Memorial Hockey Tournament
3. Indian Oil Surjit Hockey Tournament
4. Chhatrapati Shivaji Hockey Tournament
5. Aagha Khan Hockey Tournament
6. Bombay Gold Cup Hockey Tournament
7. Obaidullah Khan Gold Cup Hockey Tournament
8. Jawaharlal Nehru Hockey Tournament
9. Lal Bahadur Shastri Hockey Tournament
10. Liberals Hockey Tournament
11. Shri Shadilal Rajendralal Memorial Hockey Tournament
12. Indira Gold Cup Hockey Tournament
13. Beighton Cup Hockey Tournament
14. Senior National Hockey Tournament
15. Junior National Hockey Tournament
16. Sub-junior National Hockey Tournament

Venues

1. Aishbagh Stadium
2. Bangalore Hockey Stadium
3. Birsa Munda Hockey Stadium
4. CAFVD Sports Stadium
5. Dhyan Chand National Stadium
6. International Hockey Stadium
7. Kollam Stadium
8. Rajnandgaon Stadium
9. Kalinga Stadium
10. Mahindra Hockey Stadium
11. Mayor Radhakrishnan Stadium
12. PCMC Hockey Stadium
13. Surjit Hockey Stadium

Sports Personalities

International Personalities	
Name	**Country**
Brent Livermore	Australia
Eli Matheson	Australia
Pedro Ibarra	Argentina
Rodrigo Vila	Argentina
Andrew Eversden	England
Chris Seddon	England
Benedikt Sperling	Germany
Maik Gunther	Germany
Philip Sunkel	Germany
Andrew Eversden	Netherland
Jesse Mahieu	Netherland
MartijnDe Jager	Netherland
Adnan Maqsood	Pakistan
Rehan Butt	Pakistan
Shakeel Abbasi	Pakistan
Clive Terwin	South Africa
Clyde Abrahams	South Africa
Alfonso Pombo	Spain
Andreu Enrich	Spain

Indian Personalities			
Dhyan Chand	Leslie Claudius	Gagan Ajit Singh	Harjot Singh
Balbir Singh Sr.	Ajit Pal Singh	Rupinder Pal Singh	Kothajit Singh
Udham Singh	K. D. Singh Babu	Manpreet Singh	Sardara Singh
Mohammed Shahid	Dhanraj Pillay	Yuvraj Walmiki	Dharamvir Singh
		Mandeep Singh	V.R. Raghunath

GENERAL QUESTIONS AND ANSWERS

Q. 1. What is length of the hockey field ?
Ans. 90.40 m.

Q. 2. What is the breadth of the hockey field ?
Ans. 55 m.

Q. 3. What is the duration of the hockey match ?
Ans. 60 minutes (30 minutes × 2 halves).

Q. 4. What is the weight of the hockey ball ?
Ans. 156 to 163 gm.

Q. 5. What is the circumference of the hockey ball?
Ans. 224 to 235 mm.

Q. 6. What is the weight of the hockey stick ?
Ans. 737 gm.

Q. 7. What is the height of hockey stick ?
Ans. 40 inches.

Q. 8. What is the width of the goal post ?
Ans. 3.66m.

Q. 9. What is the height of the goal post ?
Ans. 2.14 m.

Q. 10. What is the height of the goal back board ?
Ans. 460 mm.

Q. 11. What is the radius of "D" or the circle from the center of the end line ?
Ans. 14.63m.

Q. 12. What is the distance of penalty spot from the Back Line ?
Ans. 6.40 m.

Q. 13. How much should be the total number of officials in hockey ?
Ans. 5 .

Q. 14. What is the distance of dotted circle from goal ?
Ans. 19.63 m.

Q. 15. What is the depth of the back board in goal ?
Ans. 1.20 m.

Q. 16. What is the width of the lines ?
Ans. 75 mm.

Q. 17. What is the diameter of penalty spot ?
Ans. 150 mm.

Q. 18. What is the size of the flag on flag post ?
Ans. 300 mm.

Q. 19. What is the height of flag posts ?
Ans. 1.20 to1.50 m.

Q. 20. How many types of cards are used in hockey ?
Ans. Three types (Red, Green, and Yellow).

8.1. INTRODUCTION AND HISTORY

Cricket is a team sport for two teams of eleven players each. A formal game of cricket can last anytime from an afternoon to several days. Although the game play and rules are very different, the basic concept of cricket is similar to that of baseball. Teams bat in successive *innings* and attempt to score *runs*, while the opposing team fields and attempts to bring an end to the batting team's innings. After each team has batted an equal number of innings (either one or two, depending on conditions chosen before the game) the team with the most runs wins.

History and the Game

No one knows when or where cricket began but there is a body of evidence, much of it circumstantial, that strongly suggests the game was devised during Saxon or Norman times by children living in the Weald. Cricket was brought to Indian sub-continent by the British. In the beginning the game was played amongst the Britishers. By the beginning of the 9th Century, the local population also started taking interest in the game particularly in the cities of Bombay, Calcutta and Madras. India played its first official test against England in 1932 and has played nearly since 1954 official tests against Australia, England, Pakistan, New Zealand and West Indies.

8.2. GOVERNING BODIES

The International Cricket Council

The International Cricket Council (ICC), which has its headquarters in Dubai, is the international governing body of cricket. It was founded as the Imperial Cricket Conference in 1909 by representatives from England, Australia and South Africa, renamed the International Cricket Conference in 1965, and took up its current name in 1989.

ICC

Board of Control of Cricket (BCCI)

BCCI was formed in 1928 by players of Delhi's Roshnara Club under the Tamil Nadu Societies Registration Act. It is comprised of state cricket associations. It is a full member of the International Cricket Council (ICC) with Test and One Day International (ODI) status.

8.3. SPECIFICATION, FUNDAMENTAL SKILLS, TERMINOLOGY, GENERAL RULES AND EQUIPMENTS

Specification

The field : A cricket field is a roughly, elliptical field of flat bounded by an obvious fence or other marker. There is no fixed size or shape for the field, although large deviations from a low eccentricity ellipse are discouraged.

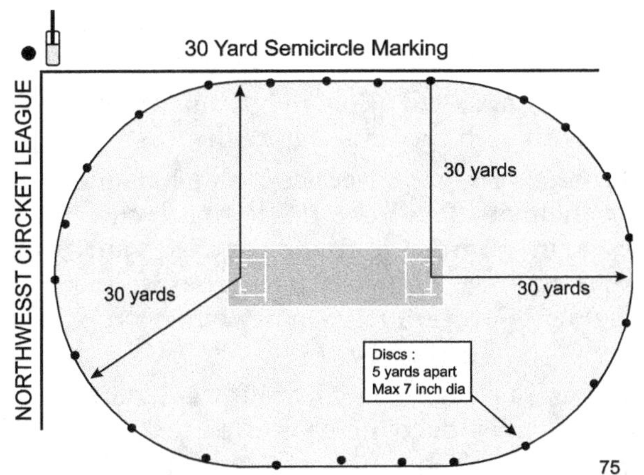

30 yards circle : A painted circle (or ellipse), centered in the middle of the pitch, of radius 30 yard marked on the field. The purpose of 30 yard circle is separating the infield from the outfield.

Pitch

The cricket pitch consists of the central strip of the cricket field between the wickets.

It is carefully prepared rectangle of closely mown and rolled grass over hard packed earth. It is marked with white lines called creases.

1. Bowling crease
2. Popping crease
3. Return crease

Dimensions

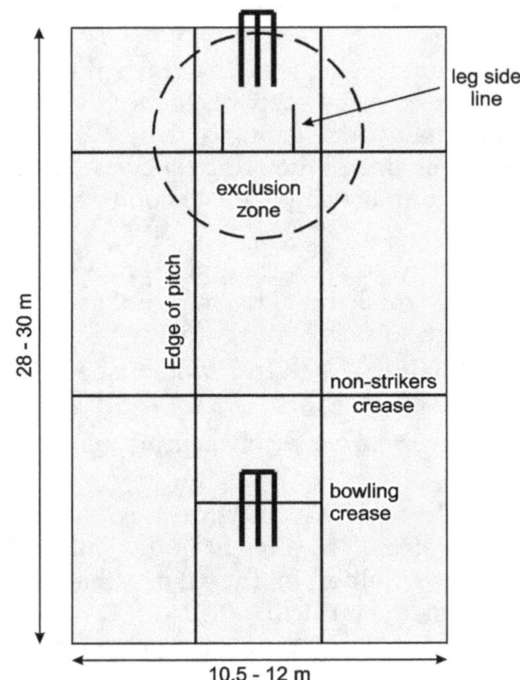

1. Cricket field area -100-160 yards.
2. Pitch area and distance between two sets of wicket -22 yards long and 10 feet wide.

3. Bowling crease -8 feet 8 inches.
4. Popping crease -6 feet.
5. Return crease -8 feet.

Rules of Cricket

1. Cricket is a game played between two teams made up of eleven players each. There is also a reserve player called a "twelfth man" who is used when a player gets injured during play.
2. The twelfth man is not allowed to bowl, bat, wicket keep or captain the team. His sole duty is to act as a substitute fielder.
3. The original player is free to return to the game as soon as they have recovered from their injury.
4. To apply the law and make sure the cricket rules are upheld throughout the game. There are two umpires in place during games. Umpires are responsible for making decisions and notifying the scorers of these decisions.
5. There is also a third umpire off the field who is in charge of video decisions.
6. This is where the call is too close for the on field umpires and they refer it to the third umpire who reviews a slow motion video to make a decision.

Equipment

Cricket Ball : Hard, cork and string ball, covered with leather.

Cricket ball's measurement

1. Circumference of ball - Between 22.4 - 22.9 cm.
2. Weight of ball- Between 156 - 163 grams.

Cricket Bat : Blade made of willow, flat on one side, humped on the other for strength, attached to a sturdy cane handle.

Cricket bat measurement

1. Maximum width of blade 10.8 cm
2. Maximum length of whole bat 96.5 cm

Wickets : The stumps and bails, together form a wicket at each end of the pitch. A complete wicket looks like shown in figure below.

Stumps : The stumps are three vertical posts which support two bails. They have spikes extending from their bottom end and are hammered into the ground in an evenly spaced row and positioned in such a way that they are just close enough together that a cricket ball cannot pass between them.

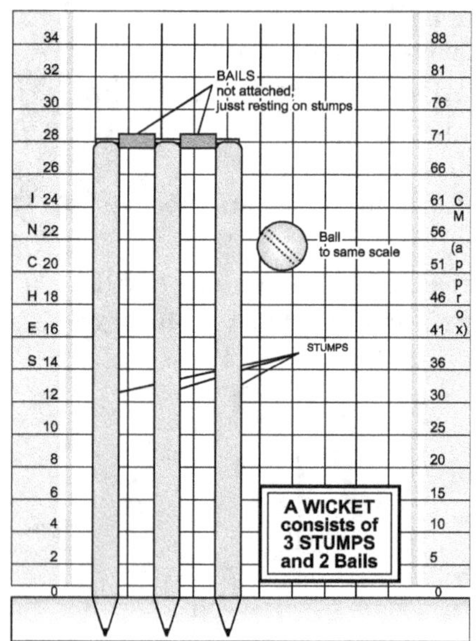

Bails : Two carved wooden crosspieces placed on stumps called stamps.

Sightscreen : It is a large screen positioned beyond the boundary so that it forms a backdrop behind the bowler, so that the striker can see the ball clearly. Sightscreens are white when a red ball is used, and black for a white ball.

Boundary : A rope demarcating the perimeter of the field known as the boundary.

The size of boundary varies with the play grounds but it should be 75 to 85 yards.

The umpire shall agree the boundary of the field of play with both captains, before the toss.

Protective Gear : Keeper's and batsman pads, gloves, helmets, Pad man, thigh guard, chest guard, elbow-arm guards, abdomen guard, jock strap, cricket hats, Box and fielder leg guard for batsmen and fielder to prevent from injury when struck by the ball.

Shoes : Leather, usually with spiked soles for grip on the grass or to increase force.

Clothing : Long pants, shirt (long or short sleeved depending on the weather) possibly a sleeveless or long-sleeved woollen pullover in cold weather. Add a hat or cap to keep the sun off. There are no regulations regarding identifying marks or numbers on clothing.

Terminology related to Cricket

1. **Duck :** If a batsman gets out without scoring any runs.

2. **A Ferret :** He is an *extremely* poor batsman (because he "goes in after the rabbits").

3. **A Golden Duck :** A batsman gets out while facing the first delivery of the innings.

4. **A Rabbit :** He is a player (almost invariably a bowler, but sometimes a wicket-keeper) who is a very poor batsman.

5. **A stance :** The way in which the batsman positions himself as he prepares to face the incoming bowler. Normally batsmen place their feet 6-8 inches apart, on either side of the popping crease, with their weight distributed evenly for a good balance and mobility.

6. **Danger Area :** A rectangular protected area of the pitch on which bowlers may not run in their follow through so as to avoid damage.

7. **Dead ball P:** A ball from which no runs can be scored or wickets taken.

The delivery of six consecutive balls by one bowler.

8. **Overthrow :** An overthrow is an extra run scored by a batsman as a result of the ball not being collected by a fielder in the centre, having been thrown in from the outfield.

FUNDAMENTAL SKILLS AND TECHNIQUES

Batting

Batting in cricket is probably the most popular of all skills. Firstly, it allows the player to score, and secondly he has the full attention of not only both teams, but also the spectators.

Some Shots in batting

1. Drive   2. Cut   3. Leg Glance

Fielding

In the sport of cricket fielding is the action of fielders in collecting the ball after it is hit by the batsman, to restrict the number of runs that the batsman scores and to get the batsman out by catching the ball in air or by running out the batsman.

Throwing

In cricket, throwing ball is an important aspect of fielding. Throwing is a fielding skill which is used to throw the ball quickly and with accuracy to the wicketkeeper, bowler or the stumps.

Wicket Keeping

In the sport of cricket the wicket-keeper is a player on the fielding side who is positioned behind the wicket or stumps being attentive of the batsman and be prepared to take a catch, stump the batsman out and run out a batsman when chance arises.

Footwork

Footwork is the most significant thing for a wicketkeeper. If our feet are right, all things moves with it. Poor wicket keepers have to dive a lot.

Catching the ball

For a wicket keeping catching the ball is the key point. Judge the position where the elevation of the ball begins to decrease, that would be the ideal place for a keeper to stand.

Diving

Diving often compensates for bad footwork so diving a lot should remind us to move our feet. However, diving becomes essential for the keeper when the ball is extremely out of his standing range.

Fundamental skills of bowling

In cricket bowling is the action of delivering the ball toward the wicket guarded by a batsman. Some skills are :

1. Inswing   2. Outswing

8.4. TOURNAMENTS AND AWARDS

Tournaments

International Tournaments

1. ICC Cricket World Cup
2. ICC Champions Trophy
3. ICC World cup T20

National Tournaments

1. Ranji Trophy   2. Duleep Trophy
3. Vijay Hazare trophy   4. Deodhar Trophy
5. Irani Trophy   6. IPL

Awards

Arjun Awards	
Year	**Name**
1994	Sachin Tendulkar
1995	Anil Kumble
1996	Javagal Srinath
1997	Ajay Jadeja
1997	Sourav Ganguly
1998	Rahul Dravid
1998	Nayan Mongia
2000	Venkatesh Prasad
2001	VVS Laxman
2002	Virender Sehwag
2003	Harbhajan Singh
2003	Mithali Raj
2005	Anju Jain
2006	Anjum Chopra
2009	Gautam Gambhir
2010	Jhulan Goswami
2011	Zaheer Khan
2012	Yuvraj Singh
2013	Virat Kohli
2014	R Ashwin
2015	Rohit Sharma

Dronacharya Award	
Year	**Name**
2004	Sunita Sharma
2016	Rajkumar Sharma
2018	Tarak Sinha
2019	Sanjay Bhardwaj

Rajiv Gandhi Khel Ratna Award	
Year	**Name**
1997–1998	Sachin Tendulkar
2007	Mahendra Singh Dhoni
2018	Virat Kohli

GENERAL QUESTIONS AND ANSWERS

Q. 1. Explain the Bowling crease term in cricket.

Ans. The white line marked at each end of the pitch through the wicket and ending at the return creases.

Q. 2. Explain the Popping crease term in cricket.

Ans. It is a line 4 feet in front of and parallel with either bowling crease that marks the forward limit of the batsman's ground.

Q. 3. Name the equipments wore by the batsman ?

Ans. Bat, Protective Gear like batsman pads, gloves, helmets, Pad man, thigh guard, shoes, clothing.

Q. 4. What is the purpose of the 30 yard circle in the game?

Ans. The purpose of the 30 yard circle in the game is to separate infield from outfield.

Q. 5. What is the measurement of Cricket field?

Ans. 100-160 yards.

Q. 6. Explain the role of a third umpire in a match.

Ans. The third umpire (or TV Umpire) is an off-field umpire in cricket matches who makes the final decision in questions referred to him by the two on-field umpires.

Q. 7. What is the measurement of cricket ball?

Ans. Circumference of ball is between 22.4-22.9 cm and weight of ball is between 156-163 grams.

Q. 8. What is the measurement of cricket bat?

Ans. Maximum width of blade is 10.8 cm and maximum length of whole bat 96.5 cm.

Q. 9. What do you mean by duck?

Ans. When a batsman gets out without scoring then the term duck is used.

Q. 10. Give the measurement of wickets?

Ans. Maximum and minimum diameter is 3.81 cm – 3.49 cm height /tall measurement is 71.1 cm overall width of each wicket is 22.8 cm size of bails.

Q. 11. Name some shots in batting.

Ans. 1. Drive 2. Cut 3. Leg Glance

Q. 12. What is rabbit in Cricket?

Ans. A rabbit or bunny is a cricketer who has been chosen as a specialist wicketkeeper or bowler and has been allocated the No. 11 batting position as he cannot bat.

Q. 13. What do you mean by bail?

Ans. Two carved wooden crosspieces placed on stumps called bail.

Q. 14. Name any three national tournament.

Ans. 1. Irani Trophy 2. Duleep Trophy 3. Ranji Trophy.

Q. 15. Name some Arjun Awardees.

Ans. Jhulan Goswami, Zaheer Khan, Yuvraj Singh, Virat Kohli, Rohit Sharma, R Ashwin.

❐❐

9.1. INTRODUCTION AND HISTORY

Bocce is played with 8 large bowling balls called Bocce balls and one smaller target ball or pallino. Bocce is played between two players or two teams of up to four players in a team. The object of the game is to roll the bocce balls closer to the pallino than the opponent. The placement of the pallino is determined at the beginning of each frame by one team throwing it between the center line of the court and the far boundary line. Each team then takes alternating turns to throw their balls toward the pallino in hopes of either: placing their ball closest, moving the pallino closer to their ball, or moving the opponent's ball away from the pallino.

History

Bocce sometimes anglicized as bocci is a ball sport belonging to the boules family, closely related to British bowls and French pétanque, with a common ancestry from ancient games played in the Roman Empire. Developed into its present form in Italy (where it is called bocce, the plural of the Italian word boccia which means 'bowl' in the sport sense), it is played around Europe and also in overseas areas that have received Italian migrants, including Australia, North America, and South America (where it is known as bochas, or bolas criollas ('Criollo balls') in Venezuela, bocha in Brazil). Bocce was initially played among the Italian migrants but has slowly

become more popular with their descendants and the wider community. The game is governed by Fédération Internationale de Boules (abbreviated FIB) is part of the "Confédération Mondiale des Sports de Boules" which is the highest international authority of bocce sports acknowledged by the International Olympic Committee.

9.2. BOCCE: SPECIFICATION, TERMINOLGY, EQUIPMENTS AND GENERAL RULES

Shape of the court	:	Rectangle
Width of the court	:	4 meters
Length of the court	:	26.5 meters
Diameter of bocce ball	:	107 mm (4.2")
Weight of bocce balls	:	920 grams
Diameter of pallino	:	0 mm (1.6")
Height of the score board	:	4
Diameter of score board	:	12" minimum
Length of the measuring tape	:	12' to 25'
Raised barrier around the edge of the rectangle	:	20 cm

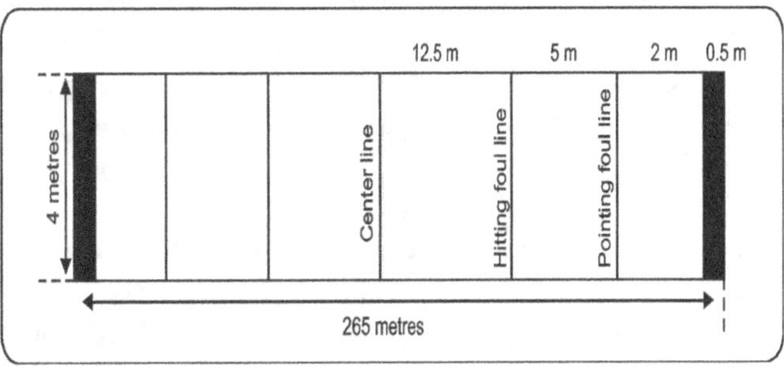

Bocce Court Surface

Bocce is played on a variety of surfaces such as carpet, crushed stone, dirt, oyster shells, clay, and most recently synthetic carpets and poured liquid creating a smooth, extremely fast surface.

Equipments

The equipments that are required for playing or conducting bocce are given below:

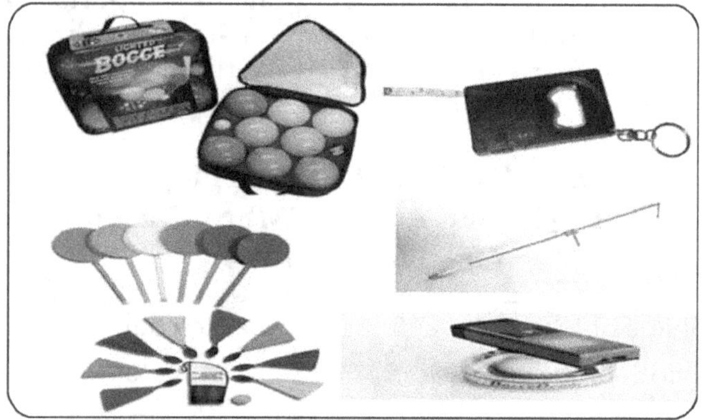

1. Bocce Balls	2. Pallino
3. Scoreboard	4. Bocce Cup Measurer
5. Measuring Tape	6. Measuring Rod
7. Referee Paddle	8. Referee Flags
9. Court Brush	10. Court Scraper

Terminology

1. **Advantage :** The team throwing the pallino is said to have "pallino advantage" because they get to place the pallino where they want it on the court and have a clear shot to place the first bocce ball.

2. **Backboards :** The shorter court walls at each end of the court sometimes called endboards or backwalls.

3. **Banking :** Throwing the bocce ball such that it hits and bounces off the sideboards towards the pallino.

4. **Court bocce :** A sport played on a standard court consisting of a rectangular playing area defined by a backboard at each end and two sideboards with a level and smooth playing surface.

5. **Dead ball :** A dead ball is a bocce ball removed from play during a frame for reasons defined in the game rules.

6. **Kiss :** A term that describes the condition where the bocce ball is touching the pallino, sometimes it is called Baci.

7. **Pallino :** A small ball used as a target ball for throwing the bocce balls, sometimes it is referred to as "object ball", "jack", "pill", "cue ball", "bullet", or "pallina".

8. **Penalty :** Action taken against a team or player for violating game rules.

9. **Sideboards :** The longer court walls parallel to the direction of throwing.

10. **Social bocce :** Social bocce is basically a group of people getting together and forming temporary teams for the day to play the game but not in a scheduled league or tournament play.

11. **Score board :** Numbers 1 through 12 arranged similar to a clock face with an arrow pointing to the score for the red or green team. The scoreboard can be a single set of numbers with a red and green arrow or a set of numbers for each colour.

12. **Bocce cup measurer :** A small cup like device that fits over the pallino with a rotatable locking tape measure centered on top of the cup.

13. **Measuring tape :** Standard retractable and locking measuring tape. Some special types come with attached calipers.

14. **Measuring rod :** Telescoping pocket rod used to measure short distances and have some special types which come up with attached calipers.

15. **Referee paddle :** Round paddle coloured red on one side and green on the other side.

16. **Referee flags :** A red flag and a green flag.

17. **Court brass :** A court brush with long handles used to drag the court to smooth it out.

18. **Court scrapper :** A wide blade, smooth on one edge and serrated on the other edge with a long handle. It is used to loosen high spots, move material around, and smooth the court. (Check with a tennis court equipment supplier.)

General Rules and Regulations

For playing of bocce it requires a set of 8 balls, four for each team, with different colours and a target ball called a "jack" or "pallino". Games can be played one-on-one (singles), pairs (doubles), triples, or foursomes.

1. **Foul lines :**

(a) Foul lines should be clearly marked both on the court surface and the side boards.

(b) There should only be one line for pointing and shooting and the recommendation is 13′ from the back wall.

(c) Players may step on but not have their foot completely over the foul line before releasing the pallino or the bocce ball.

2. Starting the game :

(a) Game begins with a flip of a coin between the Captains of each team. The winner of the coin flip will determine the end from which game will start and also has control of the pallino. The winning team chooses the colour of balls they wants to use (applies when "house" balls are used). Coin flip winner throws the pallino.

(b) Toss is valid if the pallino passes center line and does not touch the back wall on opposite end.

(c) If the player fails to place the pallino in valid area, the opposing team will put the pallino in play.

(d) If both players fail, the pallino returns to the original team for an additional attempt. Alternating process continues until pallino is in valid position.

(e) The team that originally tossed the pallino, will play the first ball.

3. The game:

(a) The first ball may be rolled by any member of the team that originally threw the pallino. Winners of coin toss or previous frame.

(b) If the bocce ball hits the backboard, without touching or hitting the pallino, or another bocce ball, considered as a dead ball and removed from or hitting court.

(c) The same team must throw again and continue rolling until a valid point is established.

(d) Once the point is established, the opposing team must point or shoot until they make a new (closer) point.

(e) Players may use side boards at any time.

(f) Balls can be measured at any time and, in case of doubt, an official referee or Tournament official should be called. In the event a tie is determined, the last team to roll a ball must roll again until the tie is broken.

(g) If after all balls are played there is still a tie, no points are awarded and play resumes with the team last scoring tossing the pallino from the opposite end of the court.

(h) In the event a ball/balls are moved during a measurement by an official, the balls are returned to approximate positions and official will still make the call. If however, a member of a team currently playing measures and moves a ball, the point is awarded to the opposing team. In any case, the decision of a referee or official is final.

(i) One team member can cross the centerline to measure balls. Other players need to remain at their respective end of the court.

4. Scoring :

(a) Only one team scores in a frame (unless there is a tie)

(b) Games are usually played to 12 points

(c) Final games are usually played to 15 points (USBF recommended)

> **Note :** Tournament Directors can decide any variation to game points but should do so prior to the start of the event.

9.3. TOURNAMENTS

1. World Bocce Championships.
2. Special Olympics.
3. Bocce Championship Trophy.
4. Australian Bocce Championship.
5. Canadian Bocce Championship.

GENERAL QUESTIONS AND ANSWERS

Q.1. What is pallino?

Ans. A small ball used as a target ball for throwing the bocce balls.

Q.2. What is the governing body of bocce game?

Ans. The game is governed by Fédération Internationale de Boules (abbreviated FIB).

Q.3. What is the length and width of the bocce court?

Ans. Length of the court is 26.5 meters and width is 4 meters.

Q.4. What is the weight and diameter of the bocce balls?

Ans. Weight is 920 gms and diameter is 107 mm(4.2") of the bocce balls.

Q.5. What kind of court surfaces are used in the game of bocce?

Ans. Bocce is played on a variety of surfaces such as carpet, crushed stone, dirt, oyster shells, clay, and most recently synthetic carpets and poured liquid creating a smooth, extremely fast surface.

Q.6. List the equipments used in the game of bocce.

Ans.
1. Bocce Balls
2. Pallino
3. Scoreboard
4. Bocce Cup Measurer
5. Measuring Tape
6. Measuring Rod
7. Referee Paddle
8. Referee Flags
9. Court Brush
10. Court Scraper

Q.7. What are the other names used for the 'Backboards'?

Ans. Sometimes they are called as endboards or backwalls.

Q.8. What do you understand by the term Kiss?

Ans. A term that describes the condition where the bocce ball is touching the pallino, sometimes called Baci.

Q.9. What is social bocce?

Ans. Social Bocce is basically a group of people getting together and forming temporary teams for the day to play the game but not in a scheduled league or tournament play.

Q.10. What is court scrapper?

Ans. A wide blade, smooth on one edge and serrated on the other edge with a long handle. It is used to loosen high spots, move material around, and smooth the court.

Q.11. What are the events of the Bocce game played?

Ans. Games can be played one-on-one (singles), pairs (doubles), triples, or foursomes.

Q.12. How many balls are required to play the game Bocce?

Ans. For playing of bocce it requires a set of 8 balls, four for each team, with different colours and a target ball called a "jack" or "pallino".

Q.13. How does a Bocce game begin?

Ans. Game begins with a flip of a coin between the Captains of each team.

Q.14. What is the scoring system used in the Bocce game?

Ans.
1. Only one team scores in a frame (unless there is a tie).
2. Games are usually played to 12 points.
3. Final games are usually played to 15 points (USBF recommended).

Q.15. What is dead ball?

Ans. If the rolled ball hit the backboard without touching the pallino, it is a dead ball and removed from the court.

Q.16. Where are the Foul lines marked on the court?

Ans. Foul lines should be clearly marked both on court surface and side boards. There should only be one line for pointing and shooting and the recommendation is 13' from the back wall.

Q.17. What is banking?

Ans. Throwing the bocce ball such that it hits and bounces off the sideboards towards the pallino.

Q.18. What is Referee paddle?

Ans. Round paddle coloured red on one side and green on the other side.

Q.19. What happens in case of a Tie in the game?

Ans. If after all balls are played there is still a tie, no points are awarded and play resumes with the Team last scoring tossing the pallino from the opposite end of the court.

Q.20. Name the major Bocce tournaments.

Ans.
1. World bocce championships
2. Special Olympics
3. Bocce championship trophy
4. Australian bocce championship
5. Canadian bocce championship

UNIFIED BASKETBALL
(Differently-abled Children)

10.1. INTRODUCTION

Unified Sports gained popularity since 1989 and in recent times it has been included as the Special Olympics International program. It is considered to be the fastest growing programme bringing individuals together. Unified Sports is a sports program or event which brings all the special individuals in one platform with and without the intellectual disabilities. Unified sports develop the feeling of friendship and understanding among individuals and are based on the principle of playing and training together. Unified sports are a vital part of Special Olympic in which teams are made as per the individuals' ability and age as well. Unified sports are established to be the highly effectual in developing social inclusion and mutual relationship between teams.

For the individuals with or without intellectual disabili-ties, unified sports basketball is considered to be the favourite sports in which the players can participate according to their abilities and in different ages.

10.2. GOVERNING BODIES

Special Olympics are international governing bodies of unified basketball competitions. The Special Olympics form the rules and regulation of the unified basketball competition and the rules is made based on the Federation International de Basketball.

Special Olympics Bharat is a National Sports Federation who aims to promote the unified sports in the country to transform the lives of children and adults having intellectual disability.

10.3. UNIFIED BASKETBALL : SPECIFICATION, EVENTS, RULES, EQUIPMENTS AND TERMINOLOGY

Specification

1. **Basketball :**
   Circumference : 29.5 inches to 30.7 inches (male 12 years and above).
   28.5 inches to 29 inches (female under 12 years of age and above).
   27 inches to 28.6 inches (male & female under 12 years of age and below).

> **Weight of the ball :** 567 to 650 grams (20 oz to 23 oz for male 12 years and above).
>
> 510 to 567 grams (18 to 20 oz for female under 12 years of age and above).
>
> 397 to 453 grams (14 oz to 16 oz for male & female under 12 years of age and below).
>
> **2. Basket :**
>
> **Basket ring :** 3.05 meters above the floor.
>
> **Shorter basket :** 2.44 meters above the floor (junior division competition).

10.4. OFFICIAL EVENTS

The following is a list of official events in Unified Basketball.

1. Speed Dribble
2. Individual Skills Competition
3. Team Skills Competition
4. Team Competition (5-on-5)
5. Half-Court Competition (3-on-3)
6. Unified Sports Team Competition (5-on-5)
7. Unified Sports Half-Court Competition (3-on-3)

10.5. RULES OF UNIFIED BASKETBALL

Speed Dribble Rules

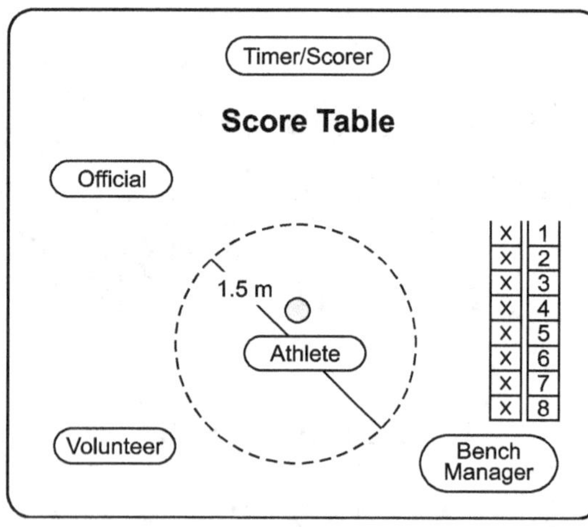

Speed Dribble

Equipments

Measuring tape, floor tape or chalk, one basketball, stopwatch, whistle, etc., is required for this event.

Set-up

Mark a circle with a 1.5 meter diameter.

Rules

1. The objective of this event is to dribble the ball in a given time.

2. Athletes are allowed to used single hand while dribble the ball.

3. As per the rules athlete can either be in standing position or sitting in a wheelchair or another type of chair with same dimensions in a competition.

4. After the whistle, athlete can only starts and stops the dribbling.

5. Time of sixty seconds will be given for dribbling the ball.

6. While dribbling, athlete must stay in the designated circle.

Scoring

1. One point will be counted to athletes in each successful dribble within sixty seconds.

2. When the ball goes thrice time out of the circle than the scorer will stop counting and the event ends.

Individual Skills Competition Rules

There are 2 two levels of Individual Skills Competition which are as follows :

Level 1

It comprises of three events, they are given below:

1. **Target pass :**

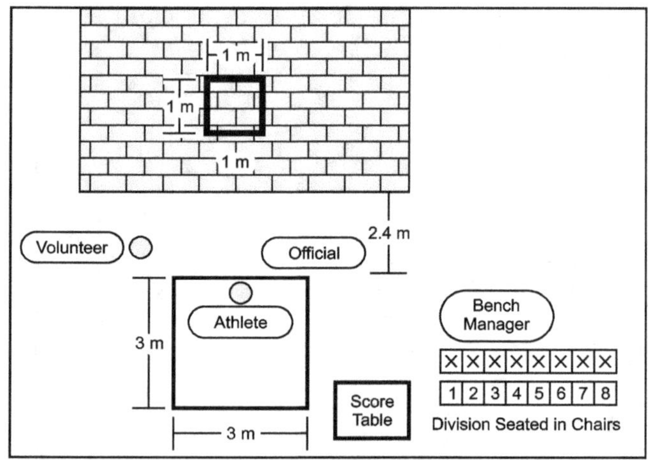

Target Pass Measurement

(a) **Purpose :** To measure a passing skill of basketball.

(b) **Equipments :**

(i) Two basketballs (women's and junior division),

(ii) Measuring tape,

(iii) Flat wall and

(iv) Chalk or floor tape.

(c) **Description :** A square shaped area of 1 meter is marked by using tape on a wall. From the floor, the bottom line of square is marked at 1 meter. Another square is marked at 3 meter on the floor 2.4 meter away from the wall. The athlete must stand inside the 3 meter squared box ensuring that the wheel axle of a wheelchair is not passing over the line. The athlete gets five passes.

(d) **Scoring :** Different points are awarded on hitting the wall. When athletes hit the wall inside the square three points are awarded. Two points are awarded for hitting the lines of the squares whereas one point is awarded for hitting at any parts at the side of the squared box on the wall. One point is awarded for catching the rebounded ball directly from air or even after one or more bounces from the 3 meter squared box. The athletes are awarded zero points if the ball bounces prior to hitting the wall. The final score will be calculated considering the sum of the total athlete's score in the five passes.

2. **Ten (10) meter dribble :**

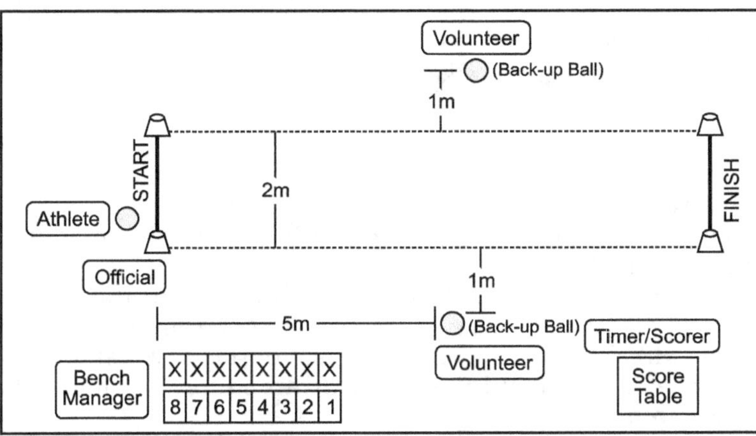

10 meters Dribble Measurement

(a) **Purpose :** To measure an athlete's speed and skill in dribbling a basketball.

(b) **Description :** The athlete will start from the starting line, standing behind it and in between the cones. The athlete will start only after the officials signal. The athlete will starts dribbling the ball with one hand upto the distance of 10 meter from the starting line. For the permissible dribbling of wheelchair athlete have to alternate taking two pushes followed by two dribbles. The athlete must finish by crossing between the two cones marked finish line picking up the basketball to cease the dribbling. The clock continues to tick during recovering the ball if the athlete loses control over the ball. In order to continue the event, the athlete gets the chance to pick up the nearest back-up basketball or the

same ball which went out if in case the ball goes outside the 2 meter lane.

(c) **Scoring :** The athlete's best score of the two trials will be considered as a final point. In case of a tie, the actual timing scored by an athlete will be used to differentiate place.

3. **Spot shot :**

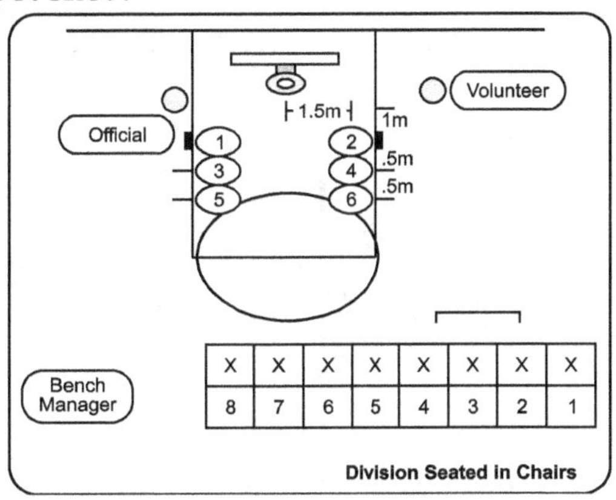

Spot Shot Field Measurement

Conversion Chart	
Seconds	Points
0–2	30
2·1–3	28
3·1–4	26
4·1–5	24
5·1–6	22
6·1–7	20
7·1–8	18
8·1–9	16
9·1–10	14
10·1–11	12
12·1–14	10
14·1–16	08
16·1–18	06
18·1–20	04
20·1–22	02
22·1 andover	01

(a) **Purpose :** To measure an athlete's shooting skill in basketball.

(b) **Equipments :**

(i) Two basketballs (for women's and junior divisions),

(ii) Floor tape or chalk,

(iii) Measuring tape,

(iv) Regulation goal with backboard (3.05 meter)

(c) **Description:** Six spots are required to mark on the floor. All the measurement must start from a spot on the floor (under the front of the rim). The athletes have to attempts to score goals from all the six spots. The attempts are taken at spots 2, 4 and 6, and then at spots 1, 3 and 5. The spots are marked as follows :

The distance between spot 1 and 2 is 1.5 meter (to the left) and 1 meter out (right plus), spot 3 and 4 is 1.5 meter to the left and right plus 1.5 meter out and spot 5 and 6 is 1.5 meter to the left and right plus 2 meter out.

(d) Scoring : The athletes who score in every field goal made at spots 1 and 2 then two points will be awarded, spots 3 and 4 (three points) and spots 5 and 6 (four points).

Level 2

There are three events in Level 2 Individual Skills Competition :

1. **12 meters dribble :**

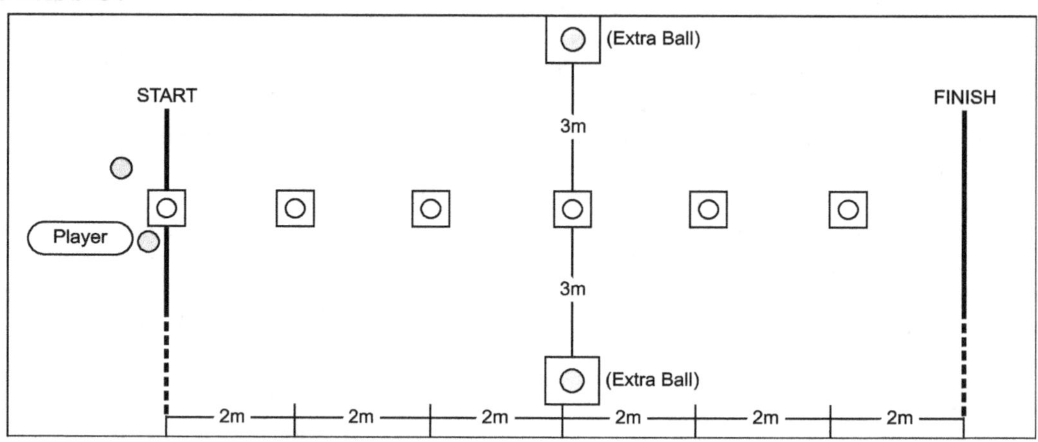

12 Meter Dribble Field Measurement

(a) Purpose : To measure an athlete's dribbling speed and skill of basketball.

(b) Equipments :
  (i)   A goal
  (ii) Floor tape and
  (iii) Two basketballs (one extra ball for back up)

(c) Description : An athlete initiate with dribbling the ball and passing alternately to the right and left of the six obstacles placed in a line on a 12-meter course and 2 meters apart.
From the first obstacle marked with the cones, the athlete can start either from right or to the left side. Athletes must pass all obstacles alternately until the last obstacle is passed when the athlete is instructed to dribble around the cone and reach back the initial position by passing each obstacle (cone) to the right and left alternately. Until the end this process is repeated and points are awarded for crossing each and every obstacle. For one trial, sixty seconds are given.

(d) Scoring : One point shall be awarded to the athletes for every midpoint crosses. Only a legal dribble is allowed and controlling of the ball in order to get credit for the midpoint of the cones is must for successfully passed. Number of cone midpoints that a players passes in sixty seconds.

2. **Perimeter shooting :**

Field Measurement of Perimeter Shooting

(a) **Purpose :** To measure an athlete's skill in shooting a basketball.

(b) **Equipments :** A goal, floor tape and two basket-balls.

(c) **Description :** A player is instructed to stands anywhere within the free throw circle.

The player shall start dribbling toward the goal and attempts to score a field goal according to player's choice outside the 2.75 meter arc. This attempt must be taken anywhere outside the 2.75 meter arc marked off by a dotted line.

The player then rebounds the basketball (made or missed shot) and dribbles anywhere outside the arc before attempting another field goal.

The player shall try to make as many field goals in one one-minute trial. Sixty seconds time will be given for one trial.

(d) **Scoring :** Two points shall be given for each field goal made within the one-minute trial.

3. **Catch and pass :**

in standing position by holding the basketball to start the activity. The ball will feed by the official from behind the Cone C.

(c) **Description :** On "Go" signal, the athlete pass the ball to the feeder and moved quickly to either of the cone marked A or B. The feeder must pass the ball to the athlete subsequent to reaching the end line. At the time of catching the ball the athlete have to place at least one foot over the lines. From behind the end line, the player must pass the ball to the feeder after catching it. Either of the feet or both should remain in contact with the ground at the time of passing the ball back to feeder from behind the end line. The athlete move to the opposite cone speedily after the ball is passed to receive the next pass. Athletes with lowered ability may use a bounce pass. The time given for one trial is 60 seconds.

(d) **Scoring :** One point will be awarded for each good pass made to the feeder and for each good catch made by the athlete. The athletes must have the ball under control or no point can be scored.

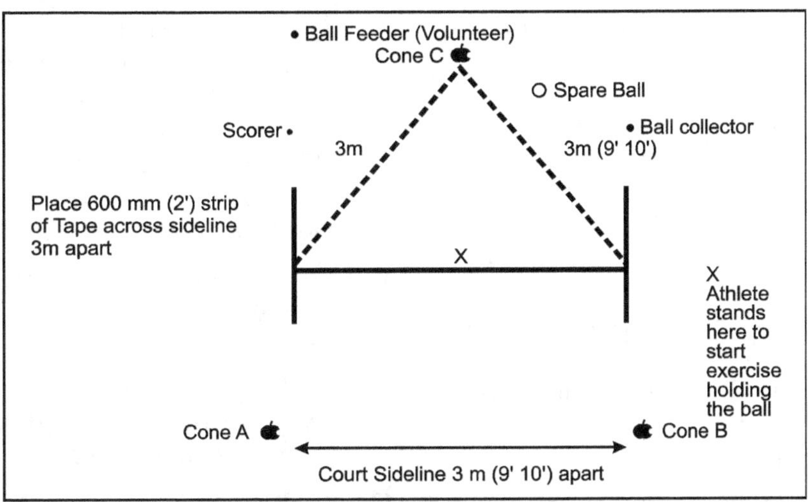

Field Measurement of Catch and Pass

(a) **Purpose :** To measure an athlete's passing and catching skill in basketball.

(b) **Equipments :**
  (i) 3 Cones,
  (ii) 2 Basketballs,
  (iii) Floor Tape, Whistle,
  (iv) Score Bench and
  (v) Clock.

Two strips of tape 600 millimeter (2 ft) long are laid across the court sideline three meters apart (9 ft 10 in) at cones A & B. Cone C is laid out three meter from each end of the sideline forming a triangle. In the middle of Cones A and B, small cross made of tape is laid where an athlete remain

Team Skills Basketball

Equipments

1. Two basketballs,
2. Metric tape measure,
3. Floor tape or chalk,
4. Score sheets and
5. Scoreboard.

Set-up

Around the floor the five spots shall be made, like 2–1–2 zone defence and the players must be 4 meters apart from each other. 2 meters spot must be marked (6 ft 6 3/4 in) from a spot under the front of the goal's ring. Every team must submit a roster prior to the start of the game. Teams should wear numbered uniforms or shirts.

Rules

1. The director of the event shall decide the number of the match for the competition. Once at a time only one team is allowed in one round. A member must consist of five members in a teams and both the teams must stand opposite to the ends of the playing court.

2. The match consists of two halves having five rounds each and all players will be given one chance to each position during the half.

3. First five-member of the team *i.e.,* each player must attempt to catch the basketball and then attempt to throw the ball to the player standing at the next position accurately.

4. The player in position 1 throws the ball to the player at position 2. The player at position 2 throws the ball to the player at position 3. This sequential throwing rotation continues until the ball reaches the player at position 5.

5. Each player must pass the ball in numerical sequence in any manner. Only one bounce is allowed.

6. When the passes ball reaches the player in position 5, athletes must attempt to convert a field goal in one attempt.

7. Following the completion of the round by the first team, the second team will conduct their initial round.

8. Players shall rotate in numerical sequence to the next position after each round.

9. Time of five minutes shall be allowed in between the halftime.

Scoring

The team who complete correct pass will awarded 1 point, 1 point for each successful catch, and two points for each successful field goal and one point for complete successful round of passing, catching and made field goal as a bonus. Total of 55 maximum points can be achieved by a single team number of points that can be accumulated by a single team during one half. The final team score is determined by adding the scores from each of the 10 rounds. The team with the highest score is the winner. If the teams are tied at the end of regulation play, additional rounds are conducted. The first team to score more points in a round than its opponent is the winner.

Team Competition (5-on-5)

1. A team shall consist of five players.

2. The composition of a team, including substitutes, may not exceed 10 players.

3. Point of emphasis: It is a violation for a player to double dribble.

4. All players must wear basketball attire with identifying numbers and flat rubber sole athletic shoes.

5. Team uniform shirts and shorts must be identical in trim colour and style.

6. Undershirts, if worn, must match the colour of the body of the uniform (not the trim) and must be identical in colour. Undershirts may be worn by some or all of the players, and may be short sleeve or tank top.

7. Length of game may be adjusted at the discretion of the competition manager and 24 second or 30 second shot clock shall apply at the discretion of the competition management team.

8. A player may take two steps beyond what is permitted by NGB rules. However, if the player scores, is deemed to have "traveled" or escapes the defense as a result of these additional steps, an advantage has been gained. A violation is called immediately.

9. The free throw shooter shall release the ball within 10 seconds from the time it is placed at the shooter's disposal by one of the officials.

10. During frontcourt throw-in, ball can be thrown directly into backcourt.

11. Five second closely guarded count only in the front court.

12. Two free throws awarded beginning with the seventh team foul in each half.

Half-court Competition : 3-on-3 Competition

The Game

The game starts with a flip of a coin for possession. All jump balls will be administered by alternate possession. The game last for 20 minutes duration and each field goal will get two points, unless attempted from the three-point field goal area. Running clock may be applied until the end minute of play. The clock will remain stop during the dead ball situations (*e.g.,* fouls, violations, field goals, and timeouts). Team who score twenty points first will declare as the winner of the game.

If tie occur in the match then it will again start with a flip of a coin for possession. Three minutes is given for the tie situation to decide the winner.

The Goal

Half-court may be used for Special Olympics basketball competition. It is a way of increasing the maximum numbers of teams and help to assist the athletes with lower ability.

Playing Area

An half court with proper marking of end line, two sidelines and the half-court line may be used.

Equipments

Each team must wear a proper uniform and have numbering at the front and back of the shirt as per NGB specifications.

Team and Players

A team may consist of five players, which shall include three starters and two substitutes.

Fouls and Penalties

There are no individual or team foul limits in 3-on-3 half-court competition.

An offensive player, including the shooter, may allow staying in the free throw lane for three seconds if not penalty shall be given as loss of possession.

A player making a throw-in shall have five seconds to release the ball. The penalty for taking more than five seconds shall be loss of possession.

Unified Sports Team Competition (5-on-5)

To start the match, minimum of five players are required. After the start of the match and during the matches, the following ratio of players must be follow *i.e.*, 3 players and 2 partners, 2 players and 2 partners, 2 players and 1 partner, 1 athlete and 1 partner. Team who fail to follow the above ratio shall be forfeit. FIBA rules allow a team to continue to play with a line up with as few as 2 players before a game is forfeited. All the teams are required to own a coach who will responsible for the line up and to manage the team during the competition.

Unified Sports Half-court Competition (3-on-3)

Half-court basketball is a unified game base on three-on-three. Each team must consist of three players in the beginning of the game and may reduce below three once the game is started due to player injury or illness. The ratio of the game is one athlete and one partner. A team may not drop below a minimum of two athletes or will have to forfeit the game.

10.6. TERMINOLOGIES RELATED TO UNIFIED BASKETBALL

1. **Speed dribble :** Dribble is done within the time of sixty seconds, with a one hand only while dribbling athlete must stay in the designated circle.

2. **Target pass :** In unified basketball, target pass refers to the athlete's ability of passing skill accurately to the partner or opponent.

3. **Spot shot :** In unified basketball, the term spot shot refers to the athlete's ability of shooting skill from one spot.

4. **Perimeter shooting :** It helps to measure the athlete's skill in shooting a basketball.

5. **Catch and pass :** Catch and pass is the terms which measure an athlete's passing and catching skill in a basketball.

10.7. IMPORTANT TOURNAMENTS

International Tournament

Summer Olympic Games.

National Tournament

National Special Olympics Bharat Championship.

GENERAL QUESTIONS AND ANSWERS

Q. 1. What is Unified Sports and from when it is popular ?

Ans. Unified Sports is a sports program or event which brings all the special individuals in a one platform with and without the intellectual disabilities. It gained popularity since 1989.

Q. 2. Name the international and national governing bodies of Unified Basketball.

Ans. Special Olympics and Special Olympics Bharat.

Q. 3. What is the circumference of the basketball used in unified sports for under 12 years of age and below ?

Ans. 27 inches to 28.6 (for male & female both).

Q. 4. What is the weight of the basketball for female under12 years of age and above ?

Ans. 510 to 567 grams (18 to 20 oz for female)

Q. 5. At what height the basket ring is placed from floor ?

Ans. 3.05 meters above the floor.

Q. 6. Name any three official events in Unified basketball.

Ans. Speed dribble, individual skills competition and team skills competition.

Q. 7. State any three rules of speed dribbling in Unified Basketball.

Ans. 1. After the whistle, athlete can only start and stop the dribbling.

 2. Sixty seconds time will be given for dribbling the ball.

 3. While dribbling athlete must stay in the designated circle.

Q. 8. What are the events in individual skills competition- Level 1 ?

Ans. Target Pass, 10 Meter Dribble and Spot Shot.

Q. 9. What is the purpose of the 10 Meter Dribble event in Level 1 in individual skills competition ?

Ans. To measure an athlete's speed and skill in dribbling a basketball.

Q. 10. What is the scoring pattern in 12 meter dribble ?

Ans. One point shall be awarded to the athletes for crossing the every midpoint. Only a legal dribble is allowed and controlling of the ball in order to get credit for the midpoint of the cones is must for successfully passed. Number of cone midpoints that a player passes in sixty seconds.

Q.11. What is the time given for one trial in perimeter shooting ?

Ans. Sixty seconds time is given for one trial.

Q.12. What are the equipments required for the event of catch and pass ?

Ans. 3 cones, 2 basketballs, floor tape, whistle, score bench and clock.

Q.13. Mention any two rules for team skills basketball.

Ans. 1. Players shall rotate in numerical sequence to the next position after each round. 2. Five minutes time shall be allowed in between the halftime.

Q.14. What will be composition of team in Team competition (5-on-5) ?

Ans. The composition of a team, including substitutes, may not exceed 10 players. The team shall consist of five players.

Q.15. What is the duration of half court competition- 3-on-3 played for ?

Ans. 20 minutes.

Q.16. What do you understand by the term 'sport shot' ?

Ans. In unified basketball the term spot shot refer to the athlete's ability of shooting skill from one spot.

Q.17. What is perimeter shooting?

Ans. It helps to measure the athlete's skill in shooting a basketball.

❏❏

www.ingramcontent.com/pod-product-compliance
Lightning Source LLC
Chambersburg PA
CBHW060112120726
48003CB00009B/2608